THE STATE AND THE POOR
IN THE 1980s

THE STATE AND THE POOR IN THE 1980s

EDITED BY MANUEL CARBALLO AND MARY JO BANE

Contributors

MARY JO BANE
DAVID BLUMENTHAL
WALTER BROADNAX
DAVID CALKINS
MANUEL CARBALLO
DAVID ELLWOOD

SUSAN ESTRICH
JOSE GOMEZ-IBANEZ
HELEN LADD
HERMAN LEONARD
ROSEMARY SALOMONE
JOHN YINGER

With a Foreword by Samuel H. Beer

 Auburn House Publishing Company
Boston, Massachusetts

Sponsored by the Institute of Politics
John F. Kennedy School of Government, Harvard University

Library of Congress Cataloging in Publication Data

Main entry under title:

The State and the poor in the 1980s.

"Sponsored by the Institute of Politics, John F. Kennedy School of
Government, Harvard University."
 Includes index.
 1. Economic assistance, Domestic—Massachusetts—
Addresses, essays, lectures. I. Carballo, Manuel,
1941–   . II. Bane, Mary Jo. III. John Fitzgerald
Kennedy School of Government. Institute of Politics.
HC107. M43P6375 1983   362.5'8'09744   83–11883
ISBN 0–86569–064–2

Printed in the United States of America.

FOREWORD: A NEW LOOK AT POVERTY

by Samuel H. Beer

Concern for the poor has fallen off since the 1960s when John Kennedy and Lyndon Johnson launched their War on Poverty and made state and local government in Massachusetts, as elsewhere, the main instruments of the new programs. Yet today the need for study and for action is as great as it was then—or even greater.

In the early sixties faith in the economy and in government was high. We had only recently realized how rich we were. Our newly discovered affluence assured us that we had the means to fight poverty and challenged us to do it. Government had led us out of the Great Depression and through the war with Hitler, and in the postwar years it had presided over the longest boom in the history of capitalism.

Moreover, the heightened pace and widened scope of the scientific revolution were providing the public sector with new capacities for action. Physicists invented nuclear weapons, transforming defense and foreign policy, and in the late 1950s supplied the intellectual launching pad for the space program that led to the moonshot of 1969. Advances in medicine made possible the development of the National Institutes of Health and a great expansion of federal programs in public health, even under the cautious Eisenhower. In the greatest novelty of all, the social sciences of economics, psychology, sociology, and political science seemed to achieve in their "behavioral revolution" the capacity for the specific social control necessary to make them the foundation for effective government action. Social engineering based on policy analysis gained new prestige. In the 1960s federal programs drew heavily for conception and implementation upon "professional specialisms" in the fields of health, housing, crime, education, the environment, and—not least—poverty.

Since then the performance of the economy has taken the bloom off rosy expectations of easy material progress. Periods of slow growth have been bracketed by stubborn recessions. A sense of straitened resources has dampened enthusiasm for social spending. The confusion of economists trying to explain what has happened and how to remedy it has been matched by doubts among other social scientists that government programs can control outcomes. Vietnam and Watergate have clouded the promise of federal leadership. Revolt at the local level against the burdens of government has spread upward, culminating in the election of Ronald Reagan, who in 1980 "brought Proposition 13 to Washington." To sum up in the recent words of a Brookings scholar, "The benefit-and-government-expanding public philosophy of the 1960s [has been] challenged and, in some respects, routed by a cost-and-government-containing spirit." Given that mood, as he continues, "little is said about the needs of the poor and the disadvantaged."[1]

Perhaps the anti-poverty effort is an idea whose time has passed, but it would be neither decent nor prudent to let a general mood of austerity and skepticism dictate an answer to that question. Centering their inquiry on the experience of a single state, Massachusetts, the authors of this book have fashioned a precise, balanced, and authoritative reply which has national relevance. Let us now consider the reasons for their focus on a single state, and then conclude with a brief overview of the method and outcome of their work.

The poor can be found in every state, and countless books have been written analyzing the nature of poverty as a national problem and recommending federal action to prevent and to alleviate it. The authors of this book recognize the fact of federal leadership and in some ways ask for its extension. The role of the states, however, is crucial in coping with this national problem. Historically, the activities of government dealing with poverty have been functions of state and local governments. Despite the new directions imposed by the federal initiatives of the 1960s, the states have retained wide constitutional authority and have exercised major influence in the relevant fields of policy. The new federalism of the Reagan Administration has further enlarged these responsibilities by its reduction of federal control and financial assistance. If we are to assess progress and recommend further steps, therefore, we must examine the performance and the potential of government at the state level.

[1]Lawrence D. Brown, *Politics and Health Care Organization: HMOs as Federal Policy* (Washington, D.C.: The Brookings Institution, 1983), pp. 3 and 5.

Yet states differ; that is why they exist as separate entities. They differ in the demographics of poverty, in their traditional approaches to the problem, and in their capacity and willingness to take action. This diversity limits the usefulness of general discussions of the role of the states. Recognizing these facts, the present book focusses on the experience of a particular state, bringing out as fully as possible the realities of its experience and the potentialities of its future.

At the same time, there are many similarities. The states resemble one another in the responsibilities they have assumed and in their powers for meeting them. All in some degree confront the same nationwide conditions, such as the ups and downs of the business cycle, the extension and retraction of federal control, or the rise and fall of tax revolts among voters generally. So, although there is no such thing as "the" typical state or "the" ideal model of a state anti-poverty program, the states can and do learn from one another. Accordingly, the authors make a point of showing how far their findings and recommendations with regard to Massachusetts can be generalized to other states. The introductions to the three main parts of the book also give special emphasis to this comparative national perspective.

In taking this new look at the old problem of poverty, these authors are making an affirmative response to the current mood of skepticism of government action in general and of anti-poverty programs in particular. Yet, in a fundamental sense, they share that mood—and their response carries greater conviction for that reason. Their approach represents a third phase in the development of policy analysis. During the first phase in the mid-sixties, hope sometimes did outstrip technique, laying open the programs spawned by policy analysis to a second phase of severe criticism at the hands of policy analysis itself. The present authors belong to a generation brought up on this criticism, and they have expertly absorbed its lessons. More skilled in technique, more specialized in training, and better equipped with data, they make a stronger case for government action than the poverty warriors of earlier days.

A comparison will illustrate the advance. Some thirteen years ago, another faculty study group of the Institute of Politics brought out a book entitled *The State and the Poor*. Its subject was the same as that of the present volume and its chapter outline was virtually identical. The initiative came from faculty, and the authors were professors in the Boston area. A major contrast between the two books is the abundance of new data sources utilized in the present volume. For example, the *Annual Housing Survey*, which provides much of the detailed information on the

Boston metropolitan area used in the chapter on housing, has
been available only since 1975. Another notable addition, also
dating from the mid-seventies, is the *Survey of Income and
Education*, which is based on personal interviews throughout the
country and embraces large enough numbers to yield reliable
data for a single state. Simply opening the two books at random
reveals the technical improvement: Tables abound in the recent
product. As a rule, when findings are reported or recommendations offered, empirical tests are drawn on for support. Statements are made not in a flat affirmative or negative but with
indications of the degree of reliability that the evidence supports.

Although academic in training and technique, the present
authors have not lost touch with that other great source of good
sense about public affairs—viz., practical experience. Nearly all
have seen government service in fields related to their academic
interests. In the way they assess evidence and foresee results, the
reader will detect the influence of not only the findings of
research but also the voice of experience. Necessarily the 1970
study relied much more heavily upon this latter source. The
present authors have strengthened the argument for an anti-
poverty effort by a shift of emphasis from expert opinion to
expert research, but without giving up the value of the mix in
method.

What they say may surprise some readers familiar with only the
criticism of earlier anti-poverty programs. While the discipline of
evaluation has dealt harshly with some of those initiatives, revealing inadequacies in design and bad side-effects in outcomes, the
rigorous standards of this volume vindicate not a few success
stories. For example, community health centers, once criticized as
expensive and ineffective, have been shown to be a cost-effective
means of providing health care for the poor. They not only
reduce illness and infant mortality but also lessen the utilization of
certain expensive and unnecessary services. The supplemental
food program for women and children (WIC) has lowered the
number of neo-natal deaths and low-birth-weight infants, and
during the 1970s the level of infant mortality in Massachusetts fell
sharply, especially among blacks. The ability of health maintenance organizations (prepaid medical care) to provide services to
Medicaid beneficiaries at reduced cost is "well-established." In
the 1970s housing quality for poor households improved. Experimentation with state programs showed that subsidies to low-
income residents (Chapter 707) are "much more cost-effective"
than public housing or subsidies to developers in alleviating the

primary problem facing poor households today—namely, high rent burdens. In the field of regional economic development, the city of Lowell, which was cited as a severely depressed area in the 1970 book, now appears as "a nationally publicized success story." In Massachusetts, as throughout the country, the situation of the elderly, one of the most afflicted groups some years ago, has "improved dramatically," thanks to social security and supplemental security income. These same programs have also helped move the disabled out of poverty.

The success stories sustain a reasoned faith that government can help. By contrast they emphasize the near intractability of some poverty problems. To cite the most striking example: the "feminization of poverty." As Mary Jo Bane points out, the lone mother with her dependent children is increasingly the typical figure; about half the poor now live in such families. Should these women be encouraged to turn over the care of their children to others and join the regular labor force? If the goal is to see that they become self-supporting, what scheme of cash assistance will be the most effective incentive? On the other hand, if they are expected to occupy themselves at home, how can they be protected against becoming indefinitely dependent on welfare? Generally accepted answers to these mixed questions of fact and value are yet to be found.

In the 1980s in Massachusetts, as in most other parts of the country, the problems of poverty present an ever more acute challenge to state government. One reason, as we have just seen, is the size and complexity of the problems. Another is financial. The depressed condition of the economy has reduced revenues and added to social spending. Like many other states Massachusetts is caught in a bind between the revolt against local taxation (Proposition 2½ in this state) and the new federalism's onslaught against federal spending. At the same time that state resources are being drawn on for more local aid, they are also being drained by the reduction of federal assistance.

And there is a long-run financial problem. During the 1960s spending by state governments from their own resources grew at an even faster rate than federal spending. Massachusetts was no exception. From 1963 to 1973, usually under Republican governors and Democratic legislatures, state spending rose from $759 million to $2.75 billion. Governor Francis Sargent's budget recommendations for fiscal 1975 sounded the alarm. His figures showed that spending growth regularly outstripped revenue growth, mainly because of the automatic and semi-automatic increases, largely in social programs, to which the state had committed itself.

Since that time—and again parallels can be found elsewhere— cost containment has continued to be an urgent concern of state government. Poverty-related programs comprise a large part of total state spending. The Anti-Poverty Budget prepared for fiscal year 1983 by the Massachusetts Senate Ways and Means Committee calculated the amount as 49 percent of the whole budget. If this burden on the taxpayer is to be controlled, there must be some such overview of the total cost in comparison with other fields of state activity. One may also hope that an anti-poverty budget will show how coordination can contain costs, as when, for instance, expenditures directed toward the relief of poverty can be directed to supportive services that will enable some of the poor to become self-supporting. On the other hand, at a time when politicians and administrators are trying to find programs to cut, it is imperative that the more vulnerable members of society not be made to bear an excessive burden simply by oversight. An anti-poverty budget informed by research and experience and reflecting community standards of decency will serve both the interests of the taxpayer and of the poor.

From this background of growing needs and harsher constraints the present study emerged. The initiative came from the legislature when Chester Atkins, chairman of the state Senate Ways and Means Committee, asked members of the Kennedy School faculty whether the 1970 study might be brought up to date and made relevant to circumstances of the 1980s. Manuel Carballo, Lecturer in Public Policy, responded by recruiting a team of scholars with the appropriate expertise. Individual research, coordinated by group meetings, moved the manuscript through to completion early in 1983. As in 1969–1970 the Institute of Politics sponsored the study in accord with its mandate of "encouraging more constructive relationships between academic resources and practitioners in politics and government." The responsibility for what is said in this book, of course, rests with its authors, not with the Kennedy School of Harvard University.

The authors wish to repeat the invitation of 1970. They hope that what they have written will prove useful to legislators and governors; to candidates, office holders, and members of the interested public; to writers of editorials, speeches, and position-papers; and to civil servants, task forces, and pressure groups. Their work is strictly nonpartisan, and they would happily exchange recognition for influence.

CONTENTS

ABOUT THE EDITORS

Manuel Carballo began his career in public service with the New Jersey Department of Community Affairs. Starting as a special assistant to the Deputy Commissioner, he was soon named to the position of Acting Chief for the Bureau of Relocation and Acting Director of OEO Legal Services. He also served a brief term as staff to the Governor's Committee on Poverty and the Law before becoming Assistant Counsel to the Governor of New Jersey. Later he was Secretary of Wisconsin's $1.5 billion Department of Health and Social Services and Deputy Transportation Commissioner for the State of New Jersey.

At Harvard Professor Carballo directed the university's program in Public Policy and Corporate Management, taught courses in public management, and chaired a faculty group that studied "the state and the poor." He took time from his teaching to serve as Deputy Assistant Secretary at the federal Department of Health and Human Services.

In January of 1983 Manuel Carballo was appointed Secretary of the Massachusetts Executive Office of Human Services by Governor Michael S. Dukakis. In this position he oversees the administration of fourteen state agencies that serve the elderly, the disabled, criminal offenders, families under stress, children, and the poor, with a budget of over $3 billion dollars.

Mary Jo Bane is Associate Professor of Public Policy and Vice Chair of the Public Policy Program at Harvard University's John F. Kennedy School of Government. She is also Chair of the Advisory Board for the Panel Study of Income Dynamics, centered at the Institute for Social Research, University of Michigan.

Professor Bane is currently interested in the dynamics of poverty and welfare, state government and the poor, patterns of public spending for social welfare services, and family and household change in the United States. She has also written extensively on family policy, day care, the condition of children in Massachusetts, and equal opportunity in higher education. She authored *Here to Stay: American Families in the Twentieth Century*, which is widely cited in the debate on the state of the family, and was co-author of *The Nation's Families*, which describes trends that signal dramatic societal changes in household composition, family structure, and women's working patterns.

ABOUT THE CONTRIBUTORS

David Blumenthal is Executive Director of the Center for Health Policy and Management and Lecturer in Public Policy at the John F. Kennedy School of Government, Harvard University. He is on the staff of Massachusetts General Hospital and is a consultant to the general director of the hospital. He has pursued research on the politics and management of federal policy toward health care technologies, ownership as an influence on the behavior of health care facilities, university-industry relationships in the life sciences, and health policy toward the poor.

Walter D. Broadnax is Lecturer in Public Policy and Management at the John F. Kennedy School of Government, Harvard University. He previously served as Principal Deputy Assistant Secretary for Planning and Evaluation at the U.S. Department of Health and Human Services, Commissioner of Social Services for the State of Kansas, and Professor of Public Administration at the Federal Executive Institute. He has written and lectured widely in the fields of public policy and public management.

David Calkins is Instructor in Medicine at Harvard Medical School and a member of the Division of Health Policy Research and Education, Harvard University. He previously served as Special Assistant to the Secretary, U.S. Department of Health and Human Services.

David T. Ellwood is Assistant Professor of Public Policy at the John F. Kennedy School of Government, Harvard University. He is a labor economist currently studying youth employment, the dynamics of poverty, the forces that move people in and out of poverty, the influence of right-to-work laws on union organizing, and specific social programs such as AFDC and Medicaid. He is a faculty research fellow at the National Bureau of Economic Research and a consultant at Urban Systems Research and Engineering.

Susan Estrich is Assistant Professor of Law at Harvard Law School. Her primary areas of teaching and research include criminal law, federalism, and labor law. She has worked as a special assistant to Senator Edward F. Kennedy, as Deputy Director of Issues and Platform Coordinator for the Kennedy for President Campaign, and as a law clerk to Justice John Paul Stevens, U.S. Supreme Court.

Jose A. Gomez-Ibanez is Associate Professor at the John F. Kennedy School of Government, Harvard University. Interested in urban transportation policy, he is the co-author of *Autos, Transit, and Cities* and is currently involved in a study of airline deregulation. From 1980–1981 he served as the senior staff economist for regulation, transportation, and the environment on the President's Council of Economic Advisors. He has been a consultant to numerous government agencies, including the U.S. Department of Transportation, the U.S. Office of Management and Budget, and the Ministry of Finance of the Republic of Singapore.

Helen F. Ladd is Associate Professor of City and Regional Planning at the John F. Kennedy School of Government, Harvard University. She is the co-editor of *Tax and Expenditure Limitations* and the author of many articles on the causes and consequences of Massachusetts' tax-limitation law, Proposition 2½; on property tax and school finance reform; and on the fiscal relationships among levels of government.

Herman B. Leonard is Associate Professor of Public Policy at the John F. Kennedy School of Government, Harvard University. His current research focuses on management of the public's finances. He has written numerous articles on the capacity of government at all levels to meet its current and future financial obligations, and on the appropriateness of alternative tax systems for doing so, and on their distributional impacts, particularly on the poor.

Rosemary Salomone is Associate Professor of Education Law and Finance at the Harvard Graduate School of Education. She is both a lawyer and former educational administrator who has written numerous articles on law, equity, and social policy. Her current research includes a book-length study on the political and legal context of educational equity, an analysis of recent litigation on religious liberty and freedom of educational choice, and a comparision of the dynamics of judicial and legislative decisionmaking.

John M. Yinger is Associate Professor of City and Regional Planning at the John F. Kennedy School of Government, Harvard University. He is a specialist in housing policy, local public finance, and urban economics. He has served as a senior staff economist with the President's Council of Economic Advisors and as a consultant on fair housing for the city of Boston and the U.S. Department of Housing and Urban Development. His current research includes studies on the effect of property taxes on housing values, an analysis of the market for real estate broker services, and projects concerning racial discrimination in housing.

INTRODUCTION

by Manuel Carballo

The faces of poverty are many and varied. At the most essential level we are talking about people: Weary young faces, and buoyant old ones. Children in patched, spotless dresses, and children covered with grime. Blacks, whites, native Americans. Speakers of "spanglish," Black English, broken English, and the King's English. All of these people are in the gallery of poverty's faces.

Some are poor because nature betrayed them at birth; others, because a textile plant moved to Taiwan. Some are poor because they were not taught; others because they did not study. Still others are poor because at times Protestants have despised Catholics, and Catholics have despised Protestants; because men have oppressed women; because whites have enslaved non-whites; and because the greedy have exploited the hewers of wood and drawers of water from times before history. Some are poor despite unending virtue, work, and toil; a few, because they revel in sloth, cunning, and artifice.

"Poverty" and the Poor

When the "war on poverty" began in the 1960s, there was a rich debate about the nature of the enemy. Was poverty a measure of wealth relative to others? If so, only strict equality of wealth would ever eliminate it, and the poor will indeed always be with us. Was poverty more of a cultural phenomenon, more of a "lifestyle" than a matter of wealth alone? If so, how do we account for the many luckless Horatio Alger's who are "poor" by more common usage? Or, more mordantly today, if poverty is simply the result of an out-of-the-mainstream "unAmerican" lifestyle, then we have to explain the growing number of other nations with higher per capita incomes.

Such a debate is ignored in this book in favor of a basic measure of physical survival—the OMB-Census Bureau standard. Grounded on a least-cost nutritious diet and on data indicating that people spend roughly one-third of their income on food, the poverty line is set at three times the estimated current cost of the least-cost diet. If you have less income than that amount, you are "poor," even though you may own a castle or a shack, or be seriously ill without health insurance or healthy with Medicaid. Obviously this is a flawed measure of poverty, but it is "official," is generally used, and allows comparisons over time. We will use it in this book, although the data often forces us to speak of the more vaguely defined "low-income" population.

It is also the measure that allows some analysts to claim that substantial progress has been made against poverty since 1960 (although the latest estimates show an increase in poverty since 1980 to 15 percent). Without question, great progress has been made in reducing the number of persons with incomes below the poverty standard. Still, 15 percent of our population having less income than that needed to eat a nutritious meal is over thirty million people—about the population of Canada. More profoundly, however, it shows the weakness of any one measure of poverty. Whatever the income statistics say, few of us who go to the public hospitals of our cities, the health clinics of Appalachia, or the *barrios* of the Southwest would say that poverty is not with us.

Another debate we avoid explicitly is the question of what causes poverty. We do so because our purpose in this book is to assist in formulating public policy for dealing with poverty—no matter how it came about. We build the discussion very much on the substantive research of ourselves and others, but seek to cast it here in terms of public policy and debate. The intent is to partially bridge the gap between theory and practice, and thereby improve both. None of which means that we do not operate within an implicit framework.

One implicit premise is that the causes of poverty are multiple: Different people are poor for different reasons. Some are poor because the economy is bad and will cease being poor when the economy recovers. Others are poor because they are single parents who have no choice but to, or indeed out of simple love want to, rear their own children rather than entrusting them to "strangers." Still others are poor because of limitations of age, health, mind, or body.

This variety of causes suggests that a variety of responses and remedies are needed. Some situations will require remedies from the several areas discussed in our chapters; others require merely sound nutrition at birth. For conceptual purposes, however, it may be useful to think of remedies in three categories: (1) activities that might prevent poverty; (2) those that ameliorate its condition while permanently or temporarily present; and (3) those that finance and direct preventive and ameliorative activities. As will become apparent, the categories are totally artificial because all these elements interact and overlap, just as do our chapters on jobs, housing, and transportation. But we must distinguish the parts before we can appreciate the whole. This complexity in defining who is poor and what should be done is compounded by a parallel complexity in deciding who should do what can be done.

The New Federalism

Federalism is this nation's attempt to deal with the general diversity of humankind. How well it can deal with the diversity of the poor in this country is partially explored in this book by looking at one state, Massachusetts. What can or should a state do about poverty? That is the central question addressed by this book.

In his State of the Union message for 1982, President Ronald Reagan called for a "new federalism," a phrase borrowed from President Nixon but an idea rooted in a historic vision of the role of state government as the pivot of American federalism. As originally presented, the core of the President's proposal was an "exchange" of fiscal and administrative responsibility for three major programs serving the poor. Medicaid, which provides health care for the poor, would be removed from state administration and partial state financing and would join Medicare, which provides health care for the elderly as a fully federally financed and administered program. In return, the states would assume full administrative and fiscal responsibility for Food Stamps (an idea since dropped) and Aid to Families with Dependent Children (AFDC), which is what most people think of when they say "welfare."

In addition, a number of special-purpose programs directed at certain categories of recipients or needs (such as alcohol and drug abuse) were to be consolidated into more fungible and flexible blocks of funds to be administered by the states for a broader range of related purposes. This shift from "categorical" to "block" grants, begun under Nixon, had already been further advanced by the Omnibus Budget Reconciliation Act of 1981. While continued federal funds for these block grants would be provided for a transitional period, these would eventually end and the state could choose either to continue the programs from its own tax base or end them.

As an exercise in conservatism the proposal had a number of peculiar features, such as almost off-handedly creating the groundwork for national health insurance by joining Medicaid and Medicare at the federal level. More profoundly, however, it chose to raise the flag of federalism on the battlefield of poverty. For conservatives this is a strange constitutional choice. Given traditional conservative "strict constructionist" attitudes about the "general welfare" clause, one could more easily see federal assumption of programs such as unemployment insurance or transportation plausibly tied to the express federal power to regulate interstate commerce and the economy than federal assumption of health care, an area more arguably reserved to the states and the people under the Tenth Amendment.

The proposal is best explained not in terms about federalism alone (nor indeed the budgetary and political realities of the moment) but in terms of conservative attitudes about poverty and the role and size of government. Conservatives from Hobbes to the present day have felt that the causes and cures of individual poverty are essentially not political or economic, but moral. Anyone willing to work hard can "make it." Therefore, those who have not made it must be unwilling to work and lazy. This theme has been behind every conservative solution to poverty from almshouses to "workfare."

If poverty is thus a moral turpitude of sorts, where in our federal system does the power lie to remedy it? First, outside government in family, church, and temple, in neighborhood and community. These are inherently local institutions. Second, within those parts of government that can be watched most closely and deal directly with moral laxity. In at least one state, the names of those receiving relief are posted on the courthouse door. By pushing concerns about poverty to the local level, Reagan moved to limit both the need for government intervention and to increase accountability for public action.

Unfortunately for this rationale, the Reagan proposal pushes programs not to the *local* level but to the *state* level. In doing so he returns to the New Deal's reliance on the states, abandoning the Great Society's truly radical departure in federalism—non-profit, non-public, community-based organizations accountable to and directly funded by the national government. Community Mental Health, Community Action, Community Development Corporations—a whole galaxy of federal progeny—arose outside the hierarchy of state and local government since 1964. These will now either disappear or become, like municipalities, creatures of the states.

Liberals view the restoration of state power with alarm, in part because they too have developed a renewed affinity for localism. But most fundamental is a factor unmentioned so far: race. The fundamental flaw of the Reagan proposal is that by keeping its focus on the Tenth Amendment, which reserves powers to the states and the people, it ignores the wrenching changes in federalism brought about by the Civil War and the Thirteenth, Fourteenth, and Fifteenth Amendments. Indeed, the delay of the Reagan Administration in endorsing the extension of the Voting Rights Act, changes in civil rights enforcement, and the differentially higher impact of budget cuts on programs benefiting minorities suggests a pattern.

The central missing element, by omission or commission, in the conservative view of poverty, drawn as it is from the intellectual roots of a then racially homogenous Great Britain, is its failure to grasp the basic relationship in multi-racial America between racism and poverty. While most of the poor are white, disproportionate numbers of the poor are black, Hispanic (that is, primarily mulatto or mestizo), and native American "people of color." Less concerned or sensitive to these issues, the New Deal warred on poverty through the states. Forged concurrently with the peak of the civil rights movement, the Great Society often bypassed the states.

Racism is by no means the sole or indeed perhaps even the primary cause of poverty among minorities. Neither is integration the sole or primary solution to it. But racism does have a lot to do with the concentration of minorities in municipalities whose tax base cannot carry quality public education; in neighborhoods that make minorities the disproportionate *victims* of crime; in jobs that are part-time, low-wage, and without the benefits of health insurance, pensions, or even social security.

It was the recognition of these facts—and their relationship to poverty—that shaped the Great Society. Head Start, for instance, virtually became an alternate public school system in segregationist Mississippi. These facts also underlie the continued liberal distrust of the states. (Even in historically liberal Massachusetts, a mayor of Boston has called the state's capital a racist city.) It would seem that if a "new federalism" is to succeed in dealing with poverty even as conservatives see it, it must contain at least a credible and visible federal regulatory role to keep the state and local political processes free of sclerosis of racist public actions. Some states, like Massachusetts, will try to do their share, as their own constitutions require, but the nation's Constitution puts that charge squarely and primarily in the federal arena.

The New Poverty

Almost twenty years after the "war on poverty," another link with poverty becomes apparent: sexism. And another is appearing on the horizon: our treatment of the elderly—most of whom are, not incidentally, women. As to the former, as the following chapters will show, a large number of the poor are in female-headed families, which are a growing percentage in Massachusetts. Is Massachusetts a bellwether or an anomaly in this regard?

As to the elderly, their number among the poor has declined dramatically, a true success of the past two decades. The engine of this success, however, has been Social Security. How this national program changes during the 1980s will dramatically affect the number of poor persons the states must deal with by themselves.

As the descriptions of these "newer" elements of poverty and the previous discussion indicate, the features of poverty are complex and the roles of different levels of government interdependent. The authors of this work have no single theory of poverty or its cures; each speaks with her or his own voice. A few of their conclusions should be considered here to set the stage for the book:

- *The causes and remedies for poverty are as different as the individuals and families who are poor.* For some, poverty can be banished by provision of transportation to a job; for others, extensive health services and support are needed; yet others need nothing more than being judged as individuals rather than as racial minorities or as women.

- *To be effective, public action at the state level must be complemented and supported by federal, local, and private actions.* No state can carry the burden alone. There are not sufficient resources, and in some cases, there is not the will. Moreover, no public agency can substitute fully for caring and concerned families, neighbors, and communities.

- *A state can play a major role in reducing poverty and, in some areas, a pivotal one.* Education, transportation, law enforcement, and local governance are primarily the domain of the states, and all can contribute to alleviating the poverty of some and eliminating it for others.

• *State efforts can be most effective if there is a strategy which embraces a comprehensive view of what needs to be done.* State action must be sensitive to changing human needs and diversity, as well as to shifting federal rules. Its programs must support one another, from day care to schools, from transportation to jobs, from income maintenance to income taxation.

We hope that others will study other states and come to their own conclusions.

Chapter 1

THE POOR IN MASSACHUSETTS

by Mary Jo Bane

As Massachusetts entered the new decade, the 1980 Census showed that about 550,000 (almost ten percent) of its citizens were poor. Although this is a lower rate of poverty than that found nationally, it is higher than Massachusetts had in 1969 and is much closer than the 1969 rate to the national average.[1] This is a disturbing trend, and poverty in Massachusetts is a disturbing phenomenon. The poor are a very mixed group, but in Massachusetts as in most states the majority are women and children, many of them in female-headed families. As this chapter will show, the poor often tend to be isolated, cut off from the labor market, and dependent to a large extent on transfer payments. The poor in contemporary Massachusetts include not only temporary hard-luck cases but also people caught for long periods of time in difficult, persistent situations. This chapter explores these phenomena, looking at the characteristics of the poor in Massachusetts, changes over the last decade, and the differences between Massachusetts and the nation as a whole.[2]

Who Are the Poor?

It is no longer true—if it ever was—that the poor are the same as the rest of us, but have less money. Some groups of people are far more likely to be poor than others. Historically, racial minorities, Southerners, residents of rural areas, and the elderly have had incomes below the poverty line more often than other groups. Female-headed families with children have been far more likely to be poor than husband-wife families. Single-person households,

1

Table 1-1 Poverty Rates in Massachusetts and the United States, 1969 and 1979, and Percentage Distribution of Poor Persons, 1979

| | Poverty Rates (%) | | | | % of Poor Persons | |
| | Mass. | | U.S. | | Mass. | U.S. |
	1969	1979	1969	1979	1979	1979
All persons	8.6%	9.8%	13.7%	12.5%	—	—
Elderly persons	18.8	9.6	27.3	14.7	11.9%	12.9%
Children	8.8	13.8	15.2	16.0	37.8	36.8
	Poverty Rates for Families				% of Poor Persons* (estimated)	
Families:						
male head with children	3.7%	5.1%	7.6%	7.5% ⎫	30.0%	33.5%
male heads no children	4.5	2.8	8.6	4.7 ⎭		
female head with children	37.3	45.3	43.3	40.5 ⎫	39.8	41.2
female heads no children	6.4	3.8	14.5	9.7 ⎭		
Single-person households:						
less than 65	26.2	21.2	29.5	23.5	21.5	17.1
more than 65	41.1	20.2	50.8	29.1	8.7	8.2
Race:						
White	8.0	8.6	10.9	9.4	82.0	62.9
Black	25.6	26.6	35.0	30.2	10.3	28.2
Spanish origin	22.4	16.0	23.5	23.8	9.3	12.4

SOURCES:
U.S. Bureau of the Census, 1980 Census of Population and Housing, Supplementary Report, *Provisional Estimates of Social, Economic and Housing Characteristics, States, and Selected SMSAs* (Washington, D.C.: U.S. Government Printing Office, 1982).
U.S. Bureau of the Census, 1970 Census of Population, Vol. 1, *Characteristics of the Population*, Part 1, United States Summary, and Part 23, Massachusetts (Washington D.C.: U.S. Government Printing Office, 1973).
U.S. Bureau of the Census, 1980 Census of Population and Housing, Supplementary Report, *Advance Estimates of Social, Economic and Housing Characteristics*, Part 23, Massachusetts (Washington D.C.: U.S. Government Printing Office, 1982).
* The published 1980 Census data did not report poverty rates of persons by family status and we did not have access to computer tapes. The percentage of the poor in female-headed families has been estimated here by assuming that male- and female-headed families had the same average family size.

especially of the elderly, also tend to be poor. That the poor have these characteristics is not surprising, since race, residence, and age are associated with earnings opportunities and capacity and since household composition affects both income-producing opportunities and needs.

Table 1-1 gives data on these group differences in poverty rates for Massachusetts and the nation as a whole in 1969 and 1979. Looking first at the data for 1979, the table shows some interesting facts about poverty in the state:

Age. Nationally both the young and the old are more likely to be poor than men and women age 25-64. Families with children, especially large families, are more likely to have incomes below the poverty line; thus poverty rates for children are higher than those for adults. The elderly, especially those living alone, are also more likely to be poor than other age groups.

Massachusetts follows the national pattern of above average poverty rates among children. Interestingly, however, poverty rates for the elderly are considerably below national rates and below the overall poverty rate for the state. Thus children make up a large proportion (38 percent) of the poor in Massachusetts—a larger proportion than in the nation as a whole, even though Massachusetts has a smaller than average proportion of children in the population as a whole. The elderly, in contrast, make up a smaller proportion of the poor in Massachusetts than of the population generally.

Family Status. The data on family status provide one explanation for the disproportionate presence of children among the poor. Female-headed families, especially those with children, are far more likely to be poor than other types of families. In Massachusetts in 1979, almost half of all female-headed families with children were poor. The poverty rate for this group was actually higher for Massachusetts than for the nation generally, even though the overall poverty rate in the state was less than two-thirds of the national rate.

Adults and children living in female-headed families thus accounted for about 40 percent of the poor in Massachusetts in 1979. Men and women living alone, many but by no means all of them elderly, made up another 30 percent of the poor. People living in husband-wife and other male-headed families, which included about 70 percent of the total population of Massachusetts, were only about 30 percent of the poor.

Race. Nationally and in Massachusetts, blacks and Hispanics are much more likely to be poor than non-Hispanic whites. Because of the very low proportions of minorities in Massachusetts, however, blacks make up only 10 percent and Hispanics another 10 percent of the poor. Nationally, blacks and Hispanics make up over a third of the poor.

Residence. The source from which Table 1–1 is drawn did not allow for calculation of poverty rates by place of residence. Other data suggest, however, that the poor are disproportionately (but by no means exclusively) residents of large cities. Massachusetts is a highly urbanized state, with about 78 percent of its population in urbanized areas. Its seven largest cities have higher poverty rates than the state as a whole, ranging from a poverty rate of 20.2 percent in Boston to 12.6 percent in Brockton. These seven large cities (Boston, Brockton, Fall River, Lowell, New Bedford, Springfield, and Worcester) in 1980 held 21 percent of the state's population but 38 percent of its poor.[3]

Massachusetts and the Nation

In both 1969 and 1979, as Table 1–1 shows, Massachusetts had a lower overall poverty rate than the nation as a whole. What accounts for its lower poverty rate? Data from 1975, collected through the Survey of Income and Education (SIE), can be used to identify some of the important determinants of state differences in poverty rates.[4]

State-to-state variations in poverty rates in 1975 can be explained quite well by a combination of economic and demographic characteristics and by the level of welfare payments. Massachusetts benefits from a relatively prosperous state economy and from relatively high welfare payments. The demographic structure of the state works both for and against a low poverty rate, as we shall see shortly. On the one hand the state has a relatively low proportion of minority residents, while on the other hand it has a large elderly population and large proportions of women and children in female-headed families.[5]

In general the economy of the state is relatively strong, generating a median income (and also a consumer price index) well above average. In 1975, median family income was $15,531 in Massachusetts and $14,094 in the nation. The states' population is relatively well educated, with 70 percent of the adults high school graduates in 1975, compared with 64 percent nationally. There are very low proportions of blacks and other minorities (3.3 percent black in 1975, compared with 11.5 nationally).[6]

In contrast, the age and family structure characteristics of the Massachusetts population work against low poverty rates and may be responsible for the increase in the poverty rate during 1969 to 1979. There is a higher than average proportion of elderly, although the elderly are much less likely to be poor than elderly generally. Massachusetts also has relatively high proportions of non-elderly "unrelated individuals"—men and women living alone—who also tend to have high poverty rates. Some of these are students or young people beginning work; others are disabled or deinstitutionalized adults trying to make their way in the community.

The proportion of households that are female-headed and the proportion of children in female-headed families are quite high (ranking fourteenth and seventeenth among the states in 1975). Divorce and separation rates and birth rates among unmarried women are relatively high. Another interesting measure is the proportion of household heads who are not working because of "family responsibilities"—a measure that reflects both the proportion of female heads with children in the population and the tendency of female heads to work. On this measure, which makes an important contribution to state-to-state differences in poverty rates, Massachusetts ranked second in the nation in 1975.

Massachusetts also ranked second in the nation in 1975 in its level of Aid to Families with Dependent Children (AFDC) payments. In general, high levels of AFDC payments are associated with low poverty rates, not only because welfare raises some families' incomes above the poverty line but also because high welfare levels reflect generally prosperous state economies.

Changes Over Time

Table 1–1 shows some of the changes in poverty rates in Massachusetts and the nation between 1969 and 1979. The overall poverty rate in Massachusetts went up over the decade, from 8.6 percent in 1969 to 9.8 percent in 1979. The national poverty rate went down somewhat, from 13.7 to 12.5 percent. Thus Massachusetts' poverty rate moved closer to that of the nation.

The trends differed by demographic groups. Poverty rates for the elderly, for male-headed families, and for unrelated individuals dropped over the decade even more dramatically in Massachusetts than in the nation as a whole. Poverty rates for families with children, however, were rising in Massachusetts at the same time that they were falling nationally. The increase was most dramatic for female-headed families with children, for whom the poverty rate went from 37.3 percent in 1969 to 45.3 percent in 1979. The Massachusetts poverty rate for female-headed families with children is now higher than the national rate.

The trends in Massachusetts thus seem to reflect national patterns in some ways and to differ from (or perhaps to be ahead of) national trends in other ways. The biggest declines in the poverty rates nationally took place during the high growth periods of the 1970s. Since then, poverty rates have fluctuated with the business cycle. Figure 1–1 shows the trends in national poverty rates from 1959–1981.

The patterns have been different for different demographic groups. Along with demographic changes per se, they have led to substantial changes nationally in the poverty populations. Almost certainly because of urbanization, general economic prosperity, and the movement of wives into the labor force, poverty rates among non-elderly husband-wife households have dropped dramatically.[7] Smaller families have contributed to this decline as

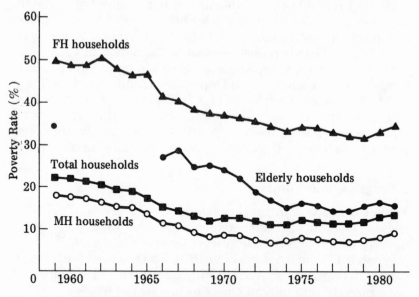

Figure 1-1   National Poverty Rates from 1959-1981 for Male-Headed, Female-Headed, and Elderly Households. *Source*: U.S. Bureau of the Census, Current Population Reports, Series P-60, No. 134, *Money Income and Poverty Status of Families and Persons in the United States: 1981* (Advance data from the March 1982 Current Population Survey) (Washington D.C.: U.S. Government Printing Office, 1982).

well, with many fewer very large families whose needs strain the income-producing capabilities of their adult members.

Husband-wife families thus make up a smaller proportion of the poor than they did previously. Poverty rates among the elderly have also declined dramatically, despite the increased tendency of the elderly to live alone. The increased economic well-being of the elderly is unquestionably attributable to social security (specifically, to increased coverage and higher benefit rates), with average benefits now comfortably above the poverty level.

In contrast, poverty rates among single-parent families have fallen proportionately less sharply, despite increased AFDC benefits and despite steadily incresing proportions of women in the labor force. These families seen unable, now as twenty years ago, to bring in sufficient income to get themselves above the poverty line. Over the same twenty-year period there has been a dramatic increase in the number of female-headed families. High and rising divorce and separation rates, high birth rates among young unmarried women, and a high proportion of single-parent families living independently rather than doubling up with parents or sending children to foster care have led to an increase of single-parent families from a national rate of 7.4 percent of all families with children in 1969 to 17.5 percent in 1980. With poverty rates declining sharply for other groups but remaining high for this one, female-headed families have come to make up a larger and larger proportion of the poverty population.

Trends in Massachusetts parallel the national data for childless husband-wife families and the elderly. During the decade of the 1970s, poverty rates for both male-headed and female-headed families with children in Massachusetts rose while they were falling nationally. The more rapid growth in the Massachusetts poverty rate for male-headed families may simply reflect the business cycle rather than an underlying trend. Although the poverty rate in Massachusetts had settled into a 4 to 5 percent range by the late 1960s, unemployment in the state was extremely low in 1969 and relatively higher in 1979, a change producing a somewhat exaggerated growth rate in unemployment over that census period.

The increase in the poverty rate for female-headed families with children is less easy to explain away—or indeed to explain at all. Changes in the minority percentage cannot account for the change in the poverty rate. Overall, the percentage of black went from 3.7 percent of the Massachusetts population in 1970 to 3.9 in

1980. Black female-headed families were 13.3 percent of such families in 1970 and 14.1 percent in 1980. As Chapter 10 on income security shows, single parents in Massachusetts have relatively low employment rates and are quite highly dependent on welfare income. It is possible that employment among single parents decreased over the decade or that unemployment increased, perhaps because single parents were younger and less well educated, and were thus less able to participate effectively in the labor market.

For whatever reason, however, it is clear that the composition of the poor changed quite dramatically over the decade in Massachusetts. In 1969 the Massachusetts poor included much larger proportions of elderly and husband-wife families than ten years later. The shift to a poverty population made up of a substantial proportion of women and children in single-parent families and of non-elderly adults living alone took place during this decade.

One way to look at the Massachusetts experience is to see the state as the leader of a general national trend. As a prosperous, well-educated urbanized state, Massachusetts had low poverty rates among husband-wife families and the elderly earlier than the nation as a whole. Like the nation, Massachusetts has experienced large and increasing numbers of female-headed families and persistently high poverty rates among those families. Thus the shift in the composition of the poor toward women and children has followed the same trend as that for the nation, but it has proceeded at a faster rate.

An interesting and disconcerting difference between Massachusetts and the nation is in the racial composition of the poor, especially poor female-headed families. Larger proportions of blacks than whites live in poor single-parent families in Massachusetts as in the nation.[8] Female headship rates and poverty rates for female heads are, however, higher for whites in Massachusetts than they are nationally. If the nation "catches up" with this trend, national poverty rates are likely to remain high and perhaps rise even if economic growth and generous social security benefits continue to reduce poverty among two-parent families and the elderly.

It is obviously difficult to project trends into the future, for either the nation or a state. General economic conditions and limited social welfare spending may bring progress against poverty to a halt, or the economy may improve and poverty rates may again head down. What seems very unlikely, though, is that the economic situation of female-headed families will improve much, or that growth in their numbers will halt, or that they will come to make up a smaller proportion of the state's poor. The most difficult problems of poverty in Massachusetts are, and are likely to remain, problems of these families.

The Dynamics of Poverty

No longitudinal data exist for Massachusetts that would allow us to describe movements in and out of poverty or the length of time people tend to remain poor. A national data set following families for fourteen years has generated considerable insight into national patterns, however, and suggests some interesting hypotheses about the dynamics of poverty in a state such as Massachusetts.[9]

One of the surprising findings from the national data (surprising at least to people who think about an "underclass" or a culture of poverty) has been the extent to which poverty is both more widespread and more short-term than people had thought. Over a twelve-year period, the panel study found that over a third of all its sample members were poor at least one year. About half of those who were ever poor were poor for only one or two years. Short-term poverty is very common.

This finding masks, however, another interesting fact. In the late 1970s, between 50 and 60 percent of those who were poor in a given year were in the midst of a spell of poverty that would last at least eight years. The average duration of a poverty spell for people poor in a given year was over ten years. Perhaps 30 percent of all poverty is accounted for by people who are more or less permanently poor.

The extent to which poverty is temporary, permanent, or middle-range obviously has important implications for public policy. It would be very interesting and useful to know these duration patterns at the state level. The characteristics of the poor provide a few hints. The national data suggest that the short-term poor have characteristics very similar to those of the population generally. The long-term poor, in contrast, are much more likely to be black or Spanish-speaking, to have low levels of education and work experience, to be elderly, or to be members of female-headed families. If these patterns hold true for Massachusetts, they suggest that a large proportion of the poor there (nearly 50 percent of whom are in female-headed households) are likely to be long-term or permanent poor.

Data on income sources and work reinforce the perception that contemporary poverty in Massachusetts poses particularly difficult problems. Table 1–2 shows some of the data. In 1975, 42

Table 1-2   Income and Work: Poor Families and Unrelated Individuals, 1975

	Poor Families (%)		Poor Unrelated Individuals (%)	
	Mass.	*U.S.*	*Mass.*	*U.S.*
Percentage with:				
Earnings	42.2%	60.2%	43.8%	38.1%
Social Security	6.7	22.2	41.7	42.8
Public assistance				
income	72.2	46.9	9.4	23.8
Percentage of heads:				
Full-time year-				
round workers	6.7	16.6		
Non-workers	66.7	50.8		
Non-workers (because				
of family				
responsibilities)	42.2	18.2		

SOURCE: U.S. Bureau of the Census, Curent Population Reports, Series P-20, No. 334, *Demographic, Social and Economic Profile of States: Spring, 1976* (Washington, D.C.: U.S. Government Printing Office, 1979).

percent of poor Massachusetts families had any income from earnings, and only 7 percent of poor family heads were year-round full-time workers. Two-thirds of all poor family heads did not work at all, with most of them reporting "family responsibilities" as their reason for not working. Seventy-two percent of poor families had some income from public assistance, including SSI. Nationally, as the table shows, much larger proportions of poor families have earnings and much smaller proportions have income from public assistance. (See Chapter 2 for more detail on work and Chapter 10 for more detail on public assistance.)

The picture for single individuals is somewhat different. In Massachusetts, a higher proportion of poor unrelated individuals have income from work and a lower proportion have income from public assistance than in the nation as a whole. This may suggest that young unattached adults are a larger proportion of poor unrelated individuals there than in the nation as a whole. However, single individuals account for less than 25 percent of the poor in Massachusetts.

These data suggest that Massachusetts may have a more persistent and less tractable poverty problem than it has had in the past. Though its poverty rates continue to be below the national average, trends in the composition of the poor, particularly the trend toward more single-parent families headed by minority and younger women, suggest that this relative advantage may not last much longer.

An Underclass?

Perhaps the most important empirical question about poverty from the point of view of public policy concerns the extent to which the poor constitute a distinct "underclass," permanently poor (or almost so) and with distinct attitudes, values, and behavior patterns that cut them off from the mainstream. Attitudes about whether poverty is a transitional phenomenon have affected policy prescriptions over the past two decades. The notion of a culture of poverty provided the intellectual rationale for the poverty programs of the 1960s. In the 1970s, however, discussion of poverty focussed on what appeared to be the short-term, temporary nature of much poverty, and welfare reformers sought passage of a negative income tax. In the 1980s, the notion of a more permanent underclass has resurfaced as the dominant definition of the poverty problem.

If there were an underclass, and if a large proportion of the poor belonged to it, policies for dealing with poverty would have to be much different than if poverty were mainly temporary income loss affecting people basically within the mainstream of the economy. Temporary poverty can be dealt with successfully by income transfers; eliminating an underclass requires changes in deep-rooted institutions and values. Policies for dealing with both simultaneously are difficult to devise.

Unfortunately, it is almost impossible to know on the basis of data we have whether and how large an underclass exists. There are some indications that poverty in the nation is more persistent than we had thought and that poverty in Massachusetts, given its structural characteristics, may be more persistent than in the nation. There are also indications that a fairly large proportion of the Massachusetts poor are neither in the labor market nor in traditional family structures. But at this point we know almost nothing about why this is so or about the way the poor perceive their world and organize their lives. It is possible that the labor market and family structure differences between some of the poor and most of the not-poor do indeed reflect differences in attitudes toward work and family responsibility that are created and reinforced by economic deprivation and by the adaptation of institutions and behavior patterns to economic disadvantage. It is also possible that what we observe is the result of a collision of basically mainstream values among the poor with hard luck and difficult circumstances.

Because of the lack of data on these issues, policymakers are in a difficult position. They must attempt to make the least harmful set of assumptions and to design policies that have the greatest chance of doing good in a situation fraught with uncertainties. As the following chapters will show, this is no easy task.

Endnotes

1. Most of the 1979 data presented in this chapter and elsewhere in the book come from U.S. Bureau of the Census, *1980 Census of Population and Housing, Supplementary Report* (Washington, D.C.: U.S. Government Printing Office, 1982). The 1980 Census was conducted in April of 1980. It collected data on income, and therefore poverty, during calendar year 1979. No more recent data are available that are broken down by state. The authors did not have access to 1980 Census computer tapes and are thus forced to rely on published tabulations.
2. As noted in the Introduction, the definition of poverty used in this chapter and generally throughout the book is the official definition used by OMB and the U.S. Bureau of Census. It is based on the "economy food plan" of the Department of Agriculture, the least costly of four nutritionally sound plans. The poverty line is determined by multiplying the cost of the economy food plan by approximately three, since surveys showed that families on the average spend about one-third of their income on food. The poverty line is adjusted annually to reflect changes in the Consumer Price Index. Income for the purposes of measuring poverty by this definition does not include non-cash assistance, most importantly food stamps, housing assistance and Medicaid. It does include all cash transfers, including Social Security, AFDC, SSI, and General Relief, as reported by survey respondents. Chapter 10 shows some of the impacts of changing the definition of poverty or poverty rates.
3. Data from U.S. Bureau of the Census, *loc. cit.*
4. The 1976 Survey of Income and Education (SIE) was a large personal interview survey of about 150,000 households, designed in such a way that reliable state level estimates could be obtained. It contained a detailed set of income questions which seemed to be quite effective in eliciting accurate information. For example, comparisons with independent estimates suggest that the SIE picked up about 94 percent of total income, including 92 percent of Social Security and 79 percent of AFDC income. The SIE, because of its questionnaire design and its use of trained personal interviewers, picked up much more income than the decennial Census and even more than the Current Population Survey (CPS). Thus the poverty rates in the SIE are low relative to those from other sources. For example, the following national poverty rates for persons were found by the Census, SIE, and CPS:

	1969	1975	1979
U.S. Census	13.7%		12.5%
SIE		11.4%	
CPS	12.1%	12.3%	11.6%

For examining the characteristics of the poor and making state–national comparisons, the SIE is the best and most accurate data source.

5. This section is based on an analysis by Beth Gelin, for her policy analysis exercise, "Poverty in Massachusetts: Trends and Implications," (Kennedy School of Government, Harvard University, 1982).

6. These data and those that follow, as well as most of the data used in Gelin's regression analysis, are from U.S. Bureau of the Census, Current Population Reports, Series P-20, No. 334, *Demographic, Social and Economic Characteristics of States: Spring 1976* (Washington, D.C.: Government Printing Office, 1979).

7. This section is based on an unpublished analysis by Mary Jo Bane of national income-poverty data collected by the Current Population Survey. These surveys differ from both the SIE and the Census, and are probably slightly less accurate than the SIE and more accurate than the Census.

8. In 1980 in Massachusetts, only about 14.1 percent of female-headed families were black, even though 53.1 percent of black families with children were female-headed. In the nation, 32.9 percent of female-headed families with children were black, and 42.1 percent of black families with children were female-headed. The above is taken from the 1980 Census provisional estimates.

9. The Panel Study of Income Dynamics had been conducted by the Survey Research Center, University of Michigan, since 1968. The analyses of the data summarized here are reported in M.S. Hill, "Some Dynamic Aspects of Poverty," in M.S. Hill, D.H. Hill, and J.N. Morgan (eds.), *5000 American Families: Patterns of Economic Progress, Vol. IX* (Ann Arbor, Michigan: Institute for Social Research, 1981) and in Mary Jo Bane and David T. Ellwood, "Slipping Into and Out of Poverty: The Dynamics of Spells," paper presented at Conference on Problems of Poverty, Clark University, August 1982.

Part One

POLICIES TO
PREVENT POVERTY

Our discussion of state policies toward the poor is divided into three parts. The first asks what state government can do to prevent poverty; the second, what it should do to ameliorate the effects of poverty; and the third, how state government should do it. In talking about what to do, we follow categories familiar in both analyzing the issues around poverty and in organizing government departments: jobs, health, education, welfare, housing, transportation, and crime. The three chapters in this part deal with policies whose objectives can be seen as the prevention of poverty—that is, helping people become capable of supporting themselves and their families at an adequate level of income through investments in job training, health, and education.

Three questions provide the themes for analysis in these three chapters:

1. To what extent do the poor suffer from poorer health, education, and employment prospects than the rest of the population?
2. To what extent do the poor have access to programs and services that address the problems?
3. What are the most effective ways to use resources on programs and services for the poor?

Employment, Health and Educational Status

All three chapters document the fact that the poor are less well off than the rest of the population in ways related to their having less

15

money. Only a tiny fraction of the poor hold year-round full-time jobs. The poor have higher mortality rates and more health problems than the population as a whole. Poor children get less schooling and do less well on measures of educational achievement than other children. The indicators examined in the three chapters all suggest a range of problems to which public policy is appropriately directed.

Access to Services

The chapters take somewhat different approaches to the question of access to services. A major finding of Chapter 2 on employment and training is that the majority of the poor cannot be expected to work: They are elderly, disabled, responsible for the care of children under six, or in school. Thus employment and training programs, however effective and important they might be, can be relevant to only a small proportion of the poor. They need to be carefully designed and directed toward the people best able to take advantage of them.

The issue of access to health and educational services, discussed in Chapter 3, is quite different. Because good health and education are important prerequisites for self-sufficiency for everyone, the question is whether the poor get their fair share of the resources devoted to improving health and education. Both Chapters 2 and 3 document inequities in access to services. Although visits to doctors and the utilization of other health services have increased dramatically among the poor in recent decades, the poor still lag behind the population, especially in preventive care and especially among children. Chapter 4, on education, shows that poor children tend to live disproportionately in cities and towns where resources for education are stretched thinnest. Thus, in both these areas, the poor seem not to have fair access to the resources and services of the society.

Programs and Their Effectiveness

The basic dilemma for policymakers in the areas of employment, health, and education, however, is that of program effectiveness. While it is easy to identify the problems of the poor and easy to identify deficiencies in the schools and programs serving the poor, it is very difficult to find programs that work well. The dilemma is particularly sharp in times of limited resources, when it is especially important to use funds carefully and effectively.

Thus all three chapters, particularly the chapter on employment, try to evaluate programs and to recommend policies that are most likely to be effective. They reach modest conclusions on program effectiveness; all three chapters find that while some programs do not seem to work very well, others in fact do. Community health centers, supported work and certain other training programs, and some approaches to compensatory education appear to be very effective. These analyses, which rely largely on national data, suggest that these approaches ought to be considered in Massachusetts and by other states as well.

Massachusetts and Other States

The basic analyses reported in these three chapters, while based primarily on Massachusetts data and experience, are on the whole relevant to other states as well. There are, however, some important demographic differences among states that affect both the definition of problems and the evaluation of policies.

Age Composition. In all states, as in Massachusetts, very high proportions of the poor are children. Our chapters place great importance on the education and health of children—a stance which should not be unique to Massachusetts. Massachusetts has unusually high proportions of elderly but low poverty rates among its elderly—a situation toward which most states are now moving. The number of elderly is a crucial determinant of Medicaid spending generally. High spending on medical care for the elderly may diminish the resources available for other groups.

Family Composition. The general historical trend toward more female-headed families and more households of people living alone (in general and among the poor) is particularly evident in Massachusetts, where only about a third of the poor are members of non-elderly male-headed families. Because female family heads with young children are not generally expected to work full time, the extent to which the poor are capable of self-support depends not only on their age but also on their family arrangements. Other states may currently have more among their poor who are able to work, but all states seem to be moving in the direction of Massachusetts.

Racial Composition. In many states, the problem of poverty is primarily a racial problem, with large proportions of blacks and Hispanics among the poor. This is not so true in Massachusetts, which has a quite small minority population. Thus our chapters do not dwell on the issue of discrimination as much as would be appropriate in other states.

Geographical Distribution. Massachusetts does not have a rural poverty problem, nor indeed much of a rural population at all. We therefore do not deal with these issues. Massachusetts is like other states, however, in the concentration of its poor population in certain cities, towns, and sections of cities. Thus our discussion of concentrations of poor children and thus of educational problems in certain school districts is quite generalizable. (Some of our particular policy recommendations on education may not be so generalizable, however, because of the state's historically peculiar governmental organization.)

These demographic differences do not, none the less, mask the fact that the problems of poverty and of finding effective programs to combat poverty are basically similar across states. If anything, Massachusetts may be a bellwether of the future for other states—a state whose demographic characteristics and economic structure are similar to those that may develop in other states. The dilemmas that state government in Massachusetts faces in understanding and dealing with its poor will also be faced by others either now or in the future.

Chapter 2

THE HOPE FOR SELF-SUPPORT

by David T. Ellwood

A familiar quotation opens Robert Taggert's exhaustive book reviewing employment and training programs in America:[1]

> *Give a man a fish and you feed him for a day;*
> *teach him to fish and you feed him for life.*

This simple proverb captures the essence of the hope of many who believe that the poor can be made self-sufficient. The critical question is: Can and should the poor be taught (or, as some argue, forced) to fish?

This chapter describes the links between work and poverty and explores policies Massachusetts might pursue to help at least a portion of the poor escape poverty through work. The discussion is divided into three main sections. The first examines the extent to which poverty is the direct result of employment problems and explores reasons that the poor do not work more:

- Families in which the head is employed full time, all year are almost never poor. Thus, in a real sense poverty is directly related to not working.
- Some 60 percent of non-elderly poor adults are either disabled, enrolled in school, or the mother of a child under six. These persons probably cannot be expected to work full time. Another 10 percent are mothers of school-age children. Thus no more than one-third of all non-elderly poor adults are likely to be available for full-time work.
- The third who are potentially employable often have little labor market experience or have histories of low-paying and sporadic work. Education and skills are often limited. As a result they face an uncertain future in the labor market.

19

Next the chapter focuses on what is known about policies that seek to help the disadvantaged in the labor market. It appears that:

- Stimulative economic policies are particularly helpful for the employable poor.,
- Regional economic development may offer some benefits to the poor. Neighborhood development looks less promising.
- Programs that offer rigorous training in basic skills such as reading and writing or in specific vocations where jobs are available seem to be particularly effective.
- Not everyone can be helped by job programs as they are now designed. New workers and displaced workers are much easier to help than those with checkered work histories.
- Programs with strong private sector links have enjoyed some success and merit particular attention in this time of fiscal conservatism. It should be realized, however, that the private sector will not be a very interested or willing participant when economic times are hard.

This chapter concludes with a special section devoted to questions surrounding workfare. It explores the rationale for workfare and its potential for aiding poor single mothers:

- Poor single mothers do not appear to work less than other mothers.
- Make-work jobs will probably not improve the long-term employment prospects of welfare mothers, but serious training programs can help.

Most of the poor are not particularly employable. But many are, and at least some can be helped. There are no easy or miracle cures. Still, government can help some persons escape poverty through work.

The Link Between Work and Poverty

Not unexpectedly the data show that the poor generally do not have full-time jobs. One is naturally led to ask why. The answer for the majority of poor persons is simply that full-time work is all but impossible because they are disabled, mothers of small children, or young people in school. There is a sizable minority of poor adults who could work more. These persons are often hampered by poor education and by limited or sporadic experience.

For the purposes of this discussion, the poor are considered to be those whose income *before* welfare payments puts them below the poverty line.[2] Welfare payments are included as income in many classifications of poverty, but since the focus here is on the potential for self-support, it seems more appropriate to consider a person's income excluding public assistance payments. The data in this section are derived from tabulations of the Survey of Income and Education (SIE), which is described in Chapter 1.

The reason most poor families are poor is that the adults in those families do not work full time, year round. Of course that is a bit like asserting that the reason some people are poor is that they do not have enough money. It may not be surprising, but it certainly is true. Table 2-1 shows the details for Massachusetts in 1974.

- *Half of the poor in Massachusetts in 1974 lived in a home where the head reported some work in 1974. But for most heads, the work was sporadic or part-time. Less than 10 percent of the poor were found in homes where the head worked full time, all year. If all heads had such complete employment, the overwhelming majority of the non-elderly poor households would have moved above the poverty line.*

Perhaps the most striking implication of the data in Table 2-1 is that persons in homes in which the head did have a full-time, full-year job are virtually never poor. Some 99 percent of persons in male-headed families escaped poverty when the head was fully employed. By contrast, some 30 percent of those in male-headed households and a shocking 75 percent of those in female-headed homes were poor if the head did not work at all. The results for families with female heads are particularly important, given the relatively rapid increase in the proportion of poor persons in female-headed households in Massachusetts.[3] If the woman did not work at all, her family was poor in three out of four cases. If she worked full time, all year, the odds of poverty fell below 5 percent. Unfortunately, two-thirds of the poor female heads did not work at all, hence their poverty.

Only 9 percent of the poor lived in homes where the head was employed full time. The numbers seem to suggest that Massachusetts could practically eliminate poverty in households with a non-elderly adult head if that adult were fully employed. A full-time, full-year minimum wage job will nearly support a family of three at the poverty line. And full-time, full-year workers almost always earn more than the minimum wage. Ob-

Table 2-1   Poverty* Rates and Distribution of Poor Persons by Work Status
of Family Head, 1974

	Poverty Rate	% of Poor Persons
Persons in families with male heads aged 16-64 (includes single male individuals)	.04	33.4%
Head worked full time:		
full year	.01	6.3
26-49 weeks	.04	8.2
Head worked part time:		
full year	.05	0.4
26-49 weeks	.25	2.2
Head worked less than 26 weeks	.20	7.8
Head did not work	.29	13.8
Persons in families with female heads aged 16-64 (includes single female individuals)	.35	55.6
Head worked full time:		
full year	.04	1.6
26-49 weeks	.45	3.5
Head worked less than 26 weeks	.61	10.3
Head did not work	.73	35.5
Persons in families with head aged 65 or older	.08	11.0

SOURCE: Tabulations of the *Survey of Income and Education (1975).*
* Poor persons are those in families whose income, excluding welfare, is below the poverty line.

viously, one "solution" to the poverty problem is to provide opportunities and incentives (including, perhaps, work requirements) for the poor to work.

Who Could Work More?

No one expects a totally disabled person to work, though some of the disabled probably could work with appropriate employment and training aid. Likewise, few believe that work—or, at least, full-time work—ought to be expected from mothers of small children. There are clearly people who do not work whom society does not expect to work even if the lack of work leads to poverty. Thus, as a first step one can ask what part of the poor population can be excused from work because their situation makes it difficult or impossible to be employed.

The elderly are the most prominent group that is not expected to work. For some time, society has accepted considerable responsibility for providing financial security for the elderly, through Social Security and public assistance. Young children are not expected to work either. In the remainder of this chapter, therefore, attention will be focused only on "working age" adults between the ages of 18 and 65.[4]

For the working-age population, disability, child-care responsibilities, and schooling can interfere with work. Table 2–2 shows the prevalence of these impediments.

> • *There are severe impediments to work for most of the poor. Over 60 percent of the non-elderly adult poor are either disabled, enrolled in school, or the mother of a child under six. Another 10 percent are mothers of school-age children.*

Overall, some 23 percent of all poor adults have some disability which limits their ability to work. Disability is most common among poor male heads, affecting nearly a third of them. It is significant, though, that a majority of those reporting some disability claim that it limits rather than prevents work. It may be that carefully constructed disability training and employment programs can substantially improve the employment prospects of this group.

Another 15 percent of poor adults are enrolled in school. While we might think that these persons could work part-time, generally we are not nearly as concerned about their poverty. They typically do not work much, but we expect they will have bright futures. They are not necessarily a group we wish would work more right now, particularly if they are not receiving welfare assistance.

Lastly, we turn to mothers. Fully one-quarter of poor adults and half of poor female heads are mothers of children under six. Realistically we cannot possibly expect full-time work from such persons. In Massachusetts, only 7 percent of all mothers (married and single) with young children work full time, all year. Even part-time work is a burden. A smaller group of mothers have a youngest child between 6 and 18; their availability for work is more ambiguous. Probably many or most could be expected to work part time. Mothers of teenagers might even be asked to work full time. Nonetheless, these persons clearly will have a more difficult time working than persons without child-care

Table 2-2 The Impediments to Work for Poor Adults by Sex of Family Head and Relationship to Head, 1975

	In Male-Headed Families			In Female-Headed Families		Living Alone	All Poor Adults
	Male Family Heads	Wives	Other Adult Family Members	Female Family Heads	Other Adult Family Members	Males and Females	
Has disability:	30.7%	16.4%	16.2%	17.3%	33.4%	29.8%	22.5%
Prevents work	(11.0)	(6.8)	(5.4)	(7.2)	(10.7)	(5.3)	(6.6)
Limits work	(19.7)	(9.6)	(10.8)	(10.1)	(22.7)	(24.5)	(15.9)
Enrolled in school	9.3	3.4	34.8	10.1	22.7	24.6	15.4
Mother with youngest child under age 6	N/A	54.6	5.7	44.9	14.8	N/A	23.2
Mother with youngest child age 6–18	N/A	11.8	0.0	25.7	0.0	N/A	9.7
Total with impediments	40.0%	86.2%	56.7%	98.0%	70.9%	54.4%	70.8%
Total without impediments	60.0%	13.8%	43.3%	2.0%	29.1%	45.6%	29.2%
Total	100.0%	100.0%	100.0%	100.0%	100.0%	100.0%	100.0%
% of All poor adults	14.8%	13.4%	4.3%	30.7%	6.4%	30.3%	100.0%

SOURCE: Tabulations of *Survey of Income and Education, 1975.*

responsibilities. We reserve a more detailed discussion of these
issues for a later section.

The results are sobering. It is true that the poverty of poor
adults is directly related to their failure to work full time, all year.
But it is equally true that for a sizable majority, full-time work is
not very feasible. The results are particularly poignant for female
heads. Nearly two-thirds of all poor female heads are either
disabled, in school, or caring for a pre-school child. It is easy to
understand why they are poor.

It appears, then, that the majority of poor adults do not work
simply because their situation precludes it. These persons can
hardly be classed as lazy or listless. Neither can failure in the labor
market be blamed for their poverty. As a result, programs aimed
at promoting full-time work will do little to help these groups.
And society can probably never require that they take full-time
jobs. Some, such as the disabled, might be helped by specialized
programs; others, such as the mothers of toddlers, might be
willing and able to work part time. Overall, however, these are
not people for whom we can expect there to be great improvement in their level of work until their situation changes.

Still, although 70 percent of poor adults have some impediment
to work, there remains a sizable minority who are not mothers
with children at home, who are not enrolled in school, and who
report no disability. Nearly 60 percent of poor male heads fall
into this category. The obvious question is, why does this group,
which appears to be fully employable, not work more or command higher pay? These "fully employable" poor and the group
of mothers who might be at least "partially employable" are the
focus of the remainder of this chapter.

Why Do the Employable Poor Not Work More?

When asked what single factor was most important in preventing
them from working more, the majority of the "fully employable"
poor pointed to an inability to find work. And while most poor
mothers reported that family responsibilities interfered, a sizable
minority of mothers with school-age children also pointed to a
lack of work. These are workers who have trouble in the labor
market.

With some risk of oversimplification, the poor with labor
market difficulties can be broken into three groups:

- *Displaced experienced workers:* Have an established record
  of sound work performance in the past and have lost their jobs

through permanent layoff or some other reason unrelated to
their performance.

- *Experienced workers with low-paying or sporadic jobs:* have
been in the job market for an extended period but have not
been able to obtain or retain a secure, well-paying job.
- *Inexperienced workers:* have little work experience and often
lack marketable skills. Some are highly motivated and job-
ready; others may have unrealistic expectations. Some are so
discouraged by repeated failures that they have stopped looking for work.

The poor are an extremely heterogeneous group, differing in
skills, confidence, education, connections, expectations, race,
sex, age, personality, and the like. But the above-listed three
categories help to isolate some critical ideas. The reasons that
each group has difficulty in the market are different, and the
prospects for helping them also differ.

The plight of displaced workers is the easiest to diagnose and
probably the easiest to improve. These workers have lost full-
time, often relatively high-wage jobs through no personal fault
because a plant has closed, markets have shrunk, or technology
has changed. They are workers with good records, but they may
have outmoded skills or they may live in a town with a locally
depressed economy.

Displaced workers sometimes stay out of work for a long
period, and they may suffer severe declines in income.[5] Still most
probably are not poor for an extended time. Although it is often
impossible to provide such workers with work alternatives as
desirable as the jobs they lost, their established work record
makes them appear to be relatively desirable employees. They
may not be able to find a job that pays as well as the job they lost,
but jobs can usually be found that will support the family above
the poverty line unless the economy is very weak. (Recall that a
full-time, year-round minimum wage job puts a family of three
above the poverty line). Most have at least 26 weeks of unemployment compensation to fall back on. In those cases where
alternatives are not readily available, retraining or relocation
offers promise—at least when the economy is strong.

But precisely because displaced workers do not typically fall
into real poverty for very long, they make up a relatively small
portion of those we classify as "the poor." Less than 5 percent of
poor adults report themselves being unemployed as a result of
temporary or permanent layoff.[6]

At the other extreme, the inexperienced consist mainly of
young people who have just reached the age when they seek

work and mothers who have previously been occupied with household duties. A surprising 25 percent of the group previously labeled the "fully employable" adult poor are young people under the age of 24. And it was shown earlier in this chapter that mothers constitute a large share of those under the poverty line. Many of these women presumably have little recent work experience.

Inexperienced workers defy easy generalizations. Some are realistic, motivated, and searching hard for work. Others want work but do not realize what is expected in the workplace. Some lack the confidence to seek a job. Still others may be only loosely interested in seeking work because they have other responsibilities (like child care) or because they do not have responsibilities (which bring financial pressures to bear). Most probably have limited knowledge of the labor market. Many have few contacts.

In this inexperienced group, one of the problems may be a lack of information on the part of employers as well as workers. Employers find it difficult to know which new workers will perform satisfactorily. As a result they must rely on the few other clues they have to judge this very heterogeneous group. They look to personal contacts or to the few characteristics that can be observed: appearance, neighborhood, sex, race, and perhaps most importantly some vague impression of the person that can be garnered from a brief interview. It probably should come as no surprise that the prejudicial attitudes of the society generally are magnified in the market for new workers. When workers have so little experience and employers have so little information, both must operate in an environment of prejudice, misconception, and often suspicion. Yet in many ways there is great hope for this group. If information and some basic skill training are provided, it seems quite likely that many of the workers can ultimately be placed in successful jobs.

Lack of information or experience is not necessarily the problem facing the last group of workers, who are somehow mired in low-paying or sporadic jobs. They have experience, but their work history is not particularly favorable. In some ways this is the most ambiguous and troubling group. It is hard to tell whether these workers have been unable to get a secure job with adequate pay because they have lacked the connections or knowledge of the job market, because they have had bad luck, or because they are workers with low self-esteem and perhaps limited motivation. They do tend to be poorly educated; half are high school dropouts. Yet the overwhelming majority of high school dropouts are not poor.[7] Some posit that a poor initial experience sets up a pattern of sporadic work and increasing alienation and depression.[8]

The prospects of this group seem gloomiest and the chance of helping them most uncertain. Some will escape on their own. Some can be helped easily. But also included in this group are the workers with the most severe labor market problems. Freeman has shown that a substantial fraction of workers with the lowest earnings will be "permanently" poor.[9] Helping these workers may require more than finding them a job or offering training. In some cases the sporadic work record may reflect failures generated by a complex set of interactions between personal characteristics and societal institutions. These failures may not be easily overcome.

Thus a small fraction, probably under 10 percent of the group of poor adults who face no impediments, are classic displaced workers. And perhaps 30 percent are inexperienced workers. Unfortunately, then, the bulk of the "employable poor" fall into the final category where causes are uncertain. The prospects for helping the employable poor are considered next.

Policies for Helping the Poor

There are two broad forms of policy intervention that could help the employable poor. One is to stimulate the private economy and to encourage job creation and expansion. Such expansionest strategies can be targeted on locally depressed geographic areas or broadly designed to increase employment in the state (or country) as a whole. The other is to provide employment and training programs which provide aid to individually troubled workers.

Stimulative Policies

Employers see persons with either limited or poor work histories as marginal workers. Even those employers genuinely interested in fair hiring are cautious. And those employers who tend to discriminate against women (and mothers) and minorities and poor persons generally are doubly disinclined to hire these groups. Thus, marginal workers are most susceptible to swings in the health of the economy.

> • *A strong and growing economy is an enormous help to the employable poor.*

Employers can and will take risks when they are desperately looking for more labor. For every point that the adult white male unemployment rate falls, two or three points are shaved off the rates for women, for minorities, for the young, and for the low-skilled.[10] The last to be hired are hired when the employer needs labor; conversely these same groups are the first to go when times get bad.

A weak economy hurts the employable poor in many ways. The blue collar jobs that the men occupy are often found in manufacturing, which is particularly sensitive to weak economic conditions. The service industries can also be hard hit. Moreover, the businesses that hire the low-skilled are often only marginally profitable, and these are prone to failure when times are bad. And the poor who live in industrial centers are always hard hit by recession. It should be remembered, however, that since the "employable poor" are but a third of all working-age adult poor persons, and since only a fraction of these can be helped with such policies, stimulative economic policies will not eliminate a very large fraction of total poverty.

Economic development is not the focus of this chapter, but it is clear that any stimulation of any state's economy is beneficial to the poor. The difficulty comes in actually generating new employment. One tool is regional economic development.

• *Although regional economic development may be an effective tool for stimulating depressed areas, its effectiveness in aiding the poor is uncertain.*

A decade ago, Lowell, Massachusetts, was a locally depressed area.[11] Now it is a nationally publicized success story. Whether such development can be reproduced elsewhere is still open to question. Lowell offered a number of advantages not always found elsewhere.

Lowell's poor are almost certainly better off today than they would have been had no economic development taken place. Other such programs will help the employable poor in those areas. Unfortunately, however, the bulk of Massachusetts' poor are probably not concentrated in a few depressed regional labor markets. Rather, they are found in poor neighborhoods within regional markets that are not particularly weak overall. Thus, we are naturally led to consider neighborhood economic development. Here there is much more reason for skepticism.

• *Neighborhood economic development—as distinct from regional development—may not be a very effective tool for aiding the poor even though the poor tend to live together in low income neighborhoods.*

The centrifugal movement of jobs from Boston toward the circumferential highway Route 128 (about 15 miles outside the city) and beyond is plainly evident to even the most casual observer. Even within the city it is painfully clear that the Roxbury community, for example, offers relatively few jobs, while other neighborhoods offer plentiful opportunities. An increasingly popular idea is to encourage firms to locate in depressed neighborhoods with economic development funds, by establishing "Enterprise Zones," or by providing tax incentives.

There is reason to be skeptical about the effectiveness of such policies. First, it has proved extremely difficult to attract businesses to ghetto neighborhoods. And even when such efforts succeed, there is reason to doubt the ability of such policies to reduce local unemployment. Normally plants hire workers from a very wide geographic area: The average worker travels at least five miles to work, and many travel three or four times that distance.[12] Thus, unless a plant departs from normal practice and instead tries particularly hard to hire local workers, the job benefits of the new plant are not necessarily concentrated in a particular neighborhood. And even if preference is shown, local residents who already have relatively good jobs may take the new jobs. The most disadvantaged of the local residents will still be left to compete in the broader labor market.

There is very little empirical evidence that neighborhood development reduces unemployment much among local residents. A recent study of Chicago found that young black workers in Chicago fared almost no better when they lived in neighborhoods near large concentrations of jobs than when they lived in neighborhoods far away from jobs.[13] While the environmental and fiscal benefits (or costs) of a new plant are quite localized, the job benefits seem to be quite dispersed. To the extent that the new plant can be induced to hire exclusively from the local community there may be some local gains. But much greater gains would probably be achieved by using the same money to encourage businesses outside the neighborhood to hire disadvantaged workers.

In sum, generalized economic growth is of considerable benefit to marginal workers. The benefits of economic development are widely spread—that of course, is part of its appeal. Nonetheless, economic expansion will not "solve" the employment problems for many of the "employable poor." Even in the best of times there are a large number of potentially employable poor persons who have no job. And even those who get jobs often find themselves mired in the same environment offering little training and few opportunities for advancement, which leaves them particularly vulnerable to the next downturn. Thus, to really improve the plight of the employable poor, the state must consider targeted employment and training programs.

Employment and Training Programs
for the Disadvantaged

There are a host of institutions that provide training in skills helpful to labor market success. We shall consider here only those specifically geared to labor market success. By way of keeping the situation in perspective, it should be noted that the overwhelmingly major part of important "training" goes on in families, schools, churches, friendships, and recreational organizations. By comparison, employment and training programs seem almost insignificant. It should thus come as no surprise that it is often difficult for a six-month training program to dramatically alter the prospects of some workers.

Schools deserve particularly close attention. The poor are on average less well educated than the population as a whole, and they probably went to disproportionately inferior schools. It may well be that the single most important thing that can be done to alleviate the long-term plight of the poor is to vastly improve school systems, particularly in depressed neighborhoods. Those issues are the subject of Chapter 4. Here the emphasis instead is on programs specifically designed to help people train for, find, and retain employment in Massachusetts.

In fiscal 1981 nearly half a billion dollars were spent on employment and training programs in Massachusetts. Table 2–3 lists these programs and reports the expenditures on each. Vocational education consumes over 60 percent of these training resources and a whopping 92 percent of all state expenditures. These programs are found almost exclusively in educational institutions, with most of the money going to high schools and some to post-secondary schools, particularly community colleges. The size of the programs is a clear reflection of their popularity. Unfortunately, their effectiveness has never been demonstrated. Studies generally find very small positive or even negative impacts of such programs on later earnings of young people, particularly men. It does appear that courses aimed at providing business/secretarial skills for women do offer some benefits.[14]

Vocational education captures virtually all state and local dollars spent on training, but the federal government has (until recently) provided considerable support for programs designed to help those who need more than in-school vocational education services. By far the largest component in 1980 was provided by

Table 2–3 Employment and Training in Massachusetts, FY 1981 (millions of dollars)

	Federal	State	Local	Total
CETA	$134.6	$0.0	$0.0	$134.6
Vocational rehabilitation	20.3	6.7	0.0	27.3
Division of Employment Security (job placement)	17.3	0.0	0.0	17.3
WIN (Work Incentive Program for AFDC recipients)	12.8	1.4	0.0	14.2
Vocational education	15.9	140.0	119.0	274.9
Adult education	2.4	3.2	0.0	5.6
All other	2.4	1.1	0.2	3.7
Total	$205.7	$152.4	$119.2	$477.3

SOURCE: *The Annual Report to the Governor on Employment and Training, Fiscal Year 1981.*

the $135 million Comprehensive Employment and Training Act (CETA) program. CETA is really a collection of programs funded through various titles of the Act and administered by local governments (the prime sponsors). By 1980 virtually every dollar spent went toward helping people whose families had low incomes. The program was the mainstay of labor market assistance for the disadvantaged. In 1981 Massachusetts CETA served over 60,000 persons, including 25,000 youths.

Labor market aid to the disadvantaged is dwindling. At one time it was estimated that the CETA program, which in fiscal year (FY) 1982 provided nearly $450 million in aid, would dwindle to just $40 million in Fiscal Year 1983. That estimate now looks unduly pessimistic, but even by 1981 the figure had fallen to just $135 million. The first cuts seemed justifiable, since much of the money was being used to subsidize public service jobs that often did not go to disadvantaged workers. Some of these jobs might have been financed by local governments anyway. The latest proposals, however, may go too far.

There is a diverse set of programs which reflect the heterogeneous nature of the population. Even though the range of options is almost infinite, job programs are usually grouped into four categories:

- *On-the-job training* (OJT) is government-sponsored, employer-based training with skills specific to the industry of the employer.

- *Classroom training* (CT) is classroom-based instruction in everything from reading and writing, to vocational skills, to job search methods.
- *Public service employment* (PSE) is fully subsidized employment with a government or non-profit agency; the tasks are comparable to those of many non-subsidized workers.
- *Work-experience* (WE) is similar to PSE except its participants typically do relatively easy tasks where close supervision is provided.

By one of those fortunate coincidences, costs of CT, OJT, and WE are almost exactly the same—between $1700 and $1800 per enrollee in Massachusetts[15] in FY 1981. Comparing the relative benefits of these programs is equivalent to comparing their relative cost effectiveness. PSE was more costly (roughly $3300 per enrollee) but that program is essentially a pure employment program and can be expected to cost more because of the salaries paid the worker-participants. Since PSE has all but vanished from the job training scene and since it was often used for less disadvantaged workers in the past, we will not discuss its impact here.

Clearly, different programs make sense for different groups. Logic suggests that displaced workers would be best served by OJT, which helps provide skills and gives them a foot in the door at a new job or in a new industry. Vocational classroom training might also be helpful if participant skills are no longer usable.

Inexperienced workers who lack understanding of the demands of work and who have no track record seem perfect candidates for WE. Those who are ready and willing to work, but who lack specific skills, can be trained in the classroom. A few might be ready to step right into OJT.

The sporadic workers are the toughest. They might potentially be helped by any of the programs. Skills come from the various forms of training: self-confidence from work experience; a job from PSE. Some may not be helped by any short-term, low-scale intervention.

This theory largely determines how people are placed. What are the results? Table 2–4 shows the estimated impact of various types of employment and training programs on the earnings of various participants in the two years after participation. Estimates are provided from two sources: a major study commissioned by the U.S. Department of Labor and conducted by Westat Inc. (DOL-Westat);[16] and a second study conducted jointly by the Congressional Budget Office and the National Commission

Table 2-4 Two-Year Earnings Gains (in 1977 and 1978) for 1976 CETA Enrollees Relative to Control Groups (National Results) (Results from DOL-Westat and CBO-NCEP)

	Classroom Training		*Type of Training Program* *On-the-Job Training*		*Work Experience*	
	DOL-Westat	*CBO-NCEP*	*DOL-Westat*	*CBO-NCEP*	*DOL-Westat*	*CBO-NCEP*
White males	$ 832	$ 600	$1,363	-$400	-$925	-$600
Minority males	349	600	1,675	3,000	- 101	600
White females	1,220	2,600	1,102	2,400	($1)	2,800
Minority females	1,178	2,200	1,924	1,600	736	1,800

SOURCES: Westat, Inc., *Impact of 1978 Earnings of New FY 1976 CETA Enrollees in Selected Program Activities, Employment and Training Administration* (Washington, D.C.: U.S. Government Printing Office, February 1981).
   Congressional Budget Office and National Commission for Employment Policy, "CETA Training Progress: Do They Work For Adults?" (Washington, D.C.: U.S. Government Printing Office, July 1982).

for Employment Policy (CBO-NCEP).[17] Although there are dis-agreements in the findings, a few generalizations can be drawn from both studies:

- No program shows dramatic gains for any group. Two-year earnings gains rarely average more than $2500 and typically are below $1500.
- Programs seem to work better for women than for men. With the exception of OJT in the DOL-Westat study, women always show higher earnings gains than men (often much higher) in any particular program.
- Classroom training is effective for white women and some-what effective for white men. OJT is effective for women; work experience is ineffective for men.

Two disagreements in the studies are troubling. DOL-Westat find that work experience is worthless not only for men but also for women. CBO-NCEP is much less favorably disposed toward OJT for men than the other study is. An examination of both methodologies along with other studies[18] does little to support the notion that the so called "work experience" programs provide many long-term benefits for anyone. Nor is OJT the great pana-cea that some regard it as being.

This is not, however, the place to carry on a detailed discussion of all the strengths and weaknesses of various programs or to examine minor changes that can improve their performance. Instead, let us try to draw a few generalizations (somewhat speculative) about the features of employment and training pro-grams that make them successful.

People struggle in the labor market when they cannot find a job that is acceptable to them. One option is to make more jobs, but most often we seek to improve the position of the individual in the existing labor market. When the problem is lack of skills, but the person is trainable, training is helpful. When the problem is that employers do not realize that a certain person will make a good worker, a program that helps the person get a foot in the door will improve the situation. But when these problems are aggravated by other, less definable problems that result in unreal-istic expectations, low self-esteem or the like, it is very difficult to improve the situation.

Programs that offer real training, either in basic reading and writing or in specific, useable vocation skills, are effective when they are rigorous and demanding. When this training is offered in such a way that the individual makes contacts with private employers who might help him or her get a job, the prospects are particularly favorable. Thus OJT seems most effective, with classroom training a close second. PSE probaby offers some on-site learning, and it offers some avenues to future public sector work. Thus for women who are more likely to fill the lower-skill clerical and service jobs in government it can be effective.

Many problems run deeper than lack of skills or lack of entry. For these people, it is not very realistic to expect our employment and training system to correct in a few short months what is the result of years of failures by other societal institutions. Even structured training programs will often fail. And putting people in a semi-structured work setting doing tasks of uncertain value seems unlikely to really improve things. Thus the so-called work experience programs do not look particularly helpful, except perhaps for people with little or no previous exposure to work.

There have been a few programs to aid the badly disadvantaged. For example, Supported Work was a program of "transitional work experience in which special features were added to the work environment to assist its employees in gaining experience with the realities of the workplace." It was tried on a predominantly black group of long-term AFDC recipients who were generally high school dropouts. It was also tried for ex-offenders (ex-cons) and youth. It used peer support structures, graduated stress, and close supervision to guide participants into successful employment experiences.

The results for the AFDC group were impressive, showing earnings gains of nearly $2500 over a group of truly random controls. But the cost was also staggering: $8200 per enrollee ($3600 went to the participants as salary). The program was less successful for ex-offenders or youth.[19]

Overall, it appears that tightly run, structured programs emphasizing traditional work skills perform best. The problem is that there are groups of disadvantaged people for whom these programs do not seem to work. Only intensive and expensive programs seem to help these persons.

What Can a State Do?

In FY 1981 over 40 percent of all the adult program CETA money spent in Massachusetts (all of which came from Uncle Sam) went to Public Service Employment. (That is no longer possible, with PSE essentially gone.) Another 40 percent went to classroom training; something over 10 percent went to work experience programs, and slightly over 6 percent went for OJT. The limited use of WE reflects adjustments that have been made in light of increased evidence that these programs are of questionable value.

Unfortunately, OJT is still the smallest component. The reasons have been alluded to already. It is hard to find employers to participate: Red tape, bad economic times, and real skepticism about the employability of the disadvantaged have hampered efforts to expand. Thus classroom training has become the primary focus of the non-PSE efforts.

Clearly, the trend away from work experience is desirable, and the programs seem to be moving in sensible directions. But the more immediate problem is the dramatic loss in federal funds. An immediate question is whether it would be worthwhile for the state to replace these funds.

From a purely fiscal national or state budget perspective, employment and training assistance for the disadvantaged rarely pays for itself. Welfare savings are typically small nationally, and are even smaller for individual states. Tax collections from low-income workers are small. Thus from a narrow fiscal standard, these programs are not winners. But then most social programs fail by this standard.

There are still compelling arguments in support of such programs. Even within a narrow cost/benefit calculation, well-managed programs seem to be justified. For a $1700 investment, returns of $1000 to $2500 are achieved within two years on both OJT and Classroom Training. After five years, it would seem to be a good value.[20] The cuts in other programs in recent years have often been justified on the basis that they discourage work and encourage dependency. Employment training programs do just the opposite. While they offer no miraculous cures, they do encourage self-sufficiency. They may stimulate feelings of confidence and self-worth in poor persons. And they symbolize society's commitment to helping persons escape poverty. It seems grossly unfair for society to criticize the disadvantaged for failing to achieve the level of work that is deemed appropriate at exactly the same time when programs which help them work more are being gutted. Whatever arguments are made against "subsidizing" the poor with cash, the appeal of investing in people and helping them pull themselves out of poverty seems powerful.

The Role of the Private Sector

Massachusetts has made a number of attempts to bring the private sector into a closer partnership with government—for example, the Bay State Skills Corporation. The federal government has mandated the creation of Private Industry Councils (PICs) to work directly with the local CETA agencies (prime sponsors) sector, particularly now that CETA funds are being cut back so severely. Local school systems are seeking increasingly close relationships also—such as the Humphrey Center in Boston.

If new relationships are to grow and flourish policymakers will have to keep several facts in mind.

- *The private sector must have something to gain if a public/private partnership is to work.*

Altruism will take employers only so far, particularly in weak economic times. If employers are going to be induced to help, there must be a minimum of red tape, and there must be either financial incentives or benefits in the form of new and better employees. That sounds obvious, but simple programs are rarely implemented.

- *Private sector firms consistently report a willingness to hire highly motivated, trainable people.[21] One of the most important roles that government can play is in screening the disadvantaged so that those ready to be strong workers will be available to employers who can be confident of their worth.*

One of the most effective programs in Massachusetts is the Hamden County Skills Center,[22] which has established a close relationship with local employers, particularly Digital. The center provides trained and trainable disadvantaged workers. Digital provides jobs and has had excellent results with these workers.

Screening has a bad name in many circles, for it implies that those who are most able are helped first. And if some are labeled as being attractive for employers, others must be labeled undesirable. Yet if one is unwilling to screen for these people, workers who have real potential may be doomed to being found guilty by association. Employers are skeptical about the disadvantaged as workers. These workers may not be hired because the employer cannot separate those who will be strong employees from those who will not.

- *Dynamic enlightened public sector leadership will be essential if a working relationship is to be developed.*

Business people mistrust government, particularly the service sector side. The most effective partnerships will be forged by those able to break down the barriers caused by past mistakes and false perception. Credibility with the business sector is critical.

• *Business will always be a fair weather partner. Efforts to include business ought to focus on growth industries.*

When firms are scrambling to get employees, they are willing to take chances to get them. The most dramatic private sector efforts of the past occurred in the late 1960s when labor was extremely scarce. When times are bad and the private sector is needed most, support is likely to evaporate. To the extent that efforts can be targeted on high-growth and cyclically insensitive industries, the partnership will be more successful.

• *Business can never take on the most disadvantaged workers.*

Business can take trainable job-ready workers and put them to work, but they will never be willing to take the hardest cases. A variety of firms motivated largely by social concerns have relocated into ghetto locations. Those that were exceptionally altruistic, hiring the least likely employees who clearly needed jobs, almost invariably failed, while those that looked for solid workers typically succeeded.[23]

Thus the public sector will always have to play the key role in programs for this group. It must screen and train the most employable and provide intensive help to the more difficult cases. But when times are bad, only the government has the capacity of providing jobs or training.

One proposal to increase labor market participation of the poor merits exceptional scrutiny because of the issues of equity and effectiveness and because it involves both poor mothers and children: workfare.

Workfare for AFDC Recipients

There are two avenues out of poverty for most single mothers: work or marriage. The pre-welfare poverty rate among non-working female-headed families is an astonishing 87 percent. This figure falls below 10 percent in homes where the single mother works full time, all year. And the poverty rate for mothers in male-headed households is just 4 percent. Massachusetts has not contemplated many policies designed to match AFDC recipients with potential mates. It has explored and continues to explore plans to put recipients to work.

Workfare can mean many things, but usually it is a plan whereby all persons who do not meet certain exemptions must engage in some sort of state-sponsored work program in order to receive welfare benefits. Typically, recipients are required to "earn" their welfare grants by working at the minimum wage rate. There are two important arguments used to justify such a program of forced work. The first arises from the presumption that people ought to take responsibility for insuring their own well-being if they reasonably can do so. When the government does provide aid to persons who might support themselves, then the recipient still ought to have responsibility for contributing as much as possible. The other justification is that such work may help people on welfare escape dependence by teaching valuable work skills and establishing a record of work experience. In the long run both the state and the recipient would benefit from this escape from welfare.

A full examination of the total effects of a mother being employed would require analysis of a host of ethical and psychological questions; those issues cannot be addressed here. Instead the question of what is the appropriate level of employment for single mothers is examined by exploring the extent to which mothers (both married and single parents) do in fact work in the state now. With the information one can better assess how reasonable it would be to ask single mothers to work as a condition for their support.

Table 2–5 compares the work behavior of single mothers and mothers who are wives by age of youngest child. Separate columns are included for all female heads and all wives and for single and married mothers in equally poor settings (excluding their earnings and welfare).

Workfare for Mothers of Pre-school Children

Two facts regarding the mothers of pre-school children emerge quite clearly from the table:

- Mothers of young children almost never work full time, 52 weeks a year. Just 7 percent of wives and 10 percent of female heads do so.
- Female heads work as much as wives do. Poor female heads work as much as poor wives.

Most mothers of small children do not work at all. In all categories roughly 60 percent do not work, even if the family is very poor and presumably badly needs the income. And less than 10 percent of these mothers are fully employed. Part-time or part-year work is somewhat more common. By and large, consistent full-time or even part-time work is the exception, not the rule, for all mothers of small children.

Table 2-5   Work Status of Female Head and Wives with Children by Age of Youngest Child and by Poverty Status (Excluding Welfare and Mother's Earnings), 1975

	Worked Full Year and Full Time (%)	Worked Part Year and/or Part Time (%)	Did Not Work (%)
Mothers with Youngest Child Under Age 6:			
All incomes:			
Female heads	10.5%	30.1%	59.4%
Wives	7.1	34.0	58.9
"Poor"*:			
Female heads	9.5	28.5	62.0
Wives	11.9	31.3	56.8
Mothers with Youngest Child Age 6–18:			
All incomes:			
Female heads	24.8	38.7	36.5
Wives	19.5	43.1	37.4
"Poor"*			
Female heads	25.5	35.6	38.9
Wives	35.2	29.8	35.0

SOURCE: Tabulations of the Survey of Income and Education, 1975.
* "Poor" means that the households income, excluding welfare payments and excluding earnings of the mother, falls below the OMB poverty line.

What is perhaps even more interesting is the fact that the work behavior of wives and single mothers is so similar, even for families in similar circumstances. Overall, female heads work as much or more than wives. And perhaps most importantly, the work of the two groups is very similar, even if we compare only mothers who have equally low incomes other than their own earnings or welfare. Female heads behave very much like poor wives who do not get welfare.

So most mothers do not work when they have small children even if the household badly needs the income. The lack of work may reflect a lack of adequate or affordable day-care arrangements, or it may be caused by a shortage of adequate jobs. But it also must reflect a widespread reluctance to work when children are still so young. When asked why they do not work, few mothers report a lack of adequate day care or an inability to find work as the primary impediment. Most cite "family responsibilities." In light of the fact that so few wives of young children work, even when the family is poor and could use the money badly, there seems little justification for forcing single mothers with children in this age group to work. And indeed the political process rarely provides much support for such proposals to put the mothers of young children on a workfare program.

Workfare for Mothers of School-Age Children

Work is much more common among mothers of school-age children. Still the basic conclusions that full-time work remains the exception and that wives and female heads behave much the same remain largely intact. One finds:

- Nearly two-thirds of mothers of school-age children do some work in the course of the year. However, full-time, year-round work is still uncommon, reaching less than a quarter of all such mothers.
- Female heads seem to work slightly more than all wives and slightly less than very poor wives. The differences are small.

The increase in work among mothers has been dramatic over the past few decades. Yet much of the increase has come not in long-term, full-time jobs but in part-time or seasonal work. By 1975 some 63 percent of mothers of school-age children in Massachusetts did some work during the year. Only a third of them worked all year in a full-time job, though. Mothers often still have responsibilities after school and during the summer unless their children are into high school or beyond.

Female heads work more than all wives on average. Full-time work is more common and part-time less common. On the other hand, it does appear that single mothers with little outside income do work somewhat less than similar mothers with husbands at home. Unfortunately the sample sizes are small and the differences are not statistically significant; therefore, one cannot be certain that they are real.

Overall the conclusion again seems to be that female heads work just about as much as wives. Thus any case for workfare based on irresponsibility or listlessness among the poor is hard to justify. It is true that welfare recipients are dependent on the state, but they are no more dependent than wives on their husbands. If one still believes that welfare mothers ought to work so as to be responsible for a greater financial burden than they are currently, one is implicitly arguing that we ought to expect more from such persons than from wives. The argument might be justified on the grounds that these persons irresponsibly divorced or became pregnant, or that it is far worse for people to rely on government than on relatives and that they therefore ought to be forced to do more. These judgments seem outweighed by the enormous difficulties such mothers face. Work is more difficult for single mothers and, as we shall see, many have serious problems that limit their market potential.

These data make it hard to justify anything more than a part-time workfare program for mothers with school-age children on the basis of equity. Perhaps full-time work might be required of those whose children are in high school, but even then the state might be imposing severe burdens on the household during the summer months. Still one cannot dismiss a workfare program if it will dramatically improve long-run prospects. And one certainly cannot dismiss a program with strong work incentives and a strong training component which encourages but does not necessarily force mothers to work.

The Employability of Welfare Mothers

Poor mothers suffer from two deficiencies: They typically lack education, and they lack experience. Table 2–6 details these shortcomings.

Roughly one-quarter of poor single mothers have a high school education and some work experience. The rest lack experience or education or both, or are disabled. It would seem that a woman with little education, little experience, and at least a certain amount of child-care responsibilities would have the least chance of landing a job of any of the poor adults. Yet in some ways the prospects for the mothers are brighter than those for the others.

The poverty of adults without child-care responsibilities can be traced directly to their inability to find or hold an adequate job. These people have in one sense already failed in the labor market, or it has failed them. Many may have been conditioned by years of failure; others may have personal characteristics that make it hard to find or keep a job. In contrast to the situation of other poor persons, it is not clear that failure in the labor market is the root

Table 2-6 Disability Status, Schooling, and Work Experience of Poor Mothers Whose Youngest Child Is Over Six (%)

Disability inhibits work	26%
Enrolled in School	2%
High school dropout, with no work in past five years	19%
High School Dropout, with work in past five years	22%
High school graduate, with no work in past five years	9%
High school graduate, with work in past five years	24%

cause of the poverty of mothers. The primary reason the mothers are not working, or at least the primary reason they have limited work experience, is that they have child-care responsibilities. Labor market difficulties may have influenced childbearing decisions and they have interfered with job-seeking efforts in the past, but overall welfare mothers do not carry with them the presumption that they already have a troubled work history.

Welfare mothers often lack any real understanding of the demands of the world of work. They lack skills and experience, and they have few contacts. Some have limited confidence in their ability to perform adequately on the job, while many have unrealistic job aspirations. Still, many are highly motivated. By most accounts many are trainable.

Employment programs seem to have achieved their greatest successes for women with little previous work experience.[24] We have noted the general agreement that on-the-job training, classroom training, and public service employment programs all have achieved moderate earnings gains for this group. Reports on work experience programs are much more mixed. Many seem to feel that these programs fail to provide a sufficiently structured environment for success and that they fail to generate many entrees into the private or public sector.

Without a doubt, welfare mothers with a long history of dependence pose the greatest problems. They often have very poor schooling; they have often done little or no work for a decade or more; and some were raised in environments without a working household member. Yet some real success has been achieved even with this group under the Supported Work program. This program provided a supportive group employment setting with close supervision, gradually escalating goals, and visible rewards (or penalties). Two-year earnings gains close to $3000 were reported relative to a perfectly matched control. Participants received $2600 less in AFDC and Food Stamps. The only drawback is the programs's $8300 price tag.[25]

For this group in particular it appears that employment programs can make a real difference. With children in the household, it is naive to expect dramatic improvements, because many women cannot or will not work full time. Still, here more than perhaps anywhere else, well-run and fully financed investments in welfare mothers can pay off. But one gets what one pays for. Most of the programs of the past have relied heavily on inexpensive and ineffective treatments. If the state is serious about having mothers take responsibility for their own support, it will have to be willing to invest more heavily in them.

Workfare therefore does offer an opportunity if it is used to invest in people. Unfortunately, the most recent workfare program proposed for Massachusetts does not provide for much investment.

Workfare in Massachusetts

In 1982, then Governor Edward King presented a proposal to require work from selected persons on the AFDC program. Recipients with school-age children were to be placed in a variety of employment programs. Refusal meant a reduction in AFDC benefits. If workfare is deemed appropriate, the design chosen by the state had some very desirable features and some very questionable ones. The plan called for first attempting to place the mothers in private jobs. During a period of job search, mothers participated in "job clubs" where the searchers meet periodically to share experience, offer support, and learn certain job-search skills. If attempts at private sector placement failed, most recipients were to be placed in work experience programs such as those described earlier. A few were put in Supported Work programs.

From what we have seen, the emphasis on an initial attempt at private placement and the use of Supported Work programs seems likely to enhance the future employment prospects of recipients. These programs thus are more than a penalty for receiving aid; they may also offer longer-term aid to the recipients.

By contrast the work experience component appears unlikely to enhance future employment prospects for these women. Consequently this part of the program must be sold strictly on the basis of an argument that society has a right to expect work from such mothers in exchange for its assistance payments. Indeed since much of the work performed by any unwilling workers is likely to be of minimal real value, one could argue that the use of a WE-based workfare plan is essentially a plan to extract a penalty from women who have been unable (or unwilling) to find ways to support the family without resorting to welfare.

Such a penalty is judged fair by some. After all, other members of society must work or suffer financially. On the other hand, it does mean that we are expecting more work from single mothers than we do from wives. The dependence of the family may reflect the failure of the father to provide his share of support rather than inappropriate work effort on the part of the mothers. Given the high cost of workfare programs, there is some evidence that investing the same amount of money in child support enforcement would be much more beneficial to state budgets.

Ultimately one's position on workfare must reflect one's personal values regarding the appropriateness of work for mothers and the legitimacy of welfare aid for poor single mothers. Workfare may be most palatable and most cost-effective when there are strong programs that will in fact help the mother to become self sufficient and where the work she is required to do is of clear value to society. Although the motivations for more extreme policies may be defensible, simply penalizing mothers for wanting to be home seems needlessly vindictive. Far preferable would be a concerted effort to provide superior programs offering effective training and placement. These programs would not be mandatory for most mothers, but they would provide a strong work incentive in the sense that women starting to work would not lose $1 in benefits for each $1 they earned. Until recently these incentives were present. As a result of the latest round of Reagan budget cuts, it is frequently the case that after a few months a woman will lose more in benefits when she goes to work than she will gain in earnings.

Conclusion

A dangerous stereotype of the poor seems to be emerging: the poor person as a listless individual milking the government while living in another culture. And his or her face is usually black. Undoubtedly there are many who fit parts of that stereotype. but the poor are caught in a terrible bind caused by misperception and a weakened economy. Benefits are being cut because the public believes that many poor people are abusing the system by not working, yet most poor people cannot realistically work full time. Those who can work often have serious problems in the labor market. Whatever the reasons for their problems, these persons fare much worse when the economy is weak; accordingly they are working even less now.

Government can help. The economy can be strengthened. Rigorous employment and training programs which have a strong training component and which keep an eye on placement help some workers. The private sector could be induced to do more, but we must have realistic expectations. The employable poor are not a cross section of middle class residents who have had a bit of bad luck. Some need nothing more than a chance, but many are the product of failures, both personal and institutional, that have created problems not easily overcome. Improving our schools may do more than any single employment plan ever can. Still the ultimate goal must be to help those who can become self-sufficient to do so. Abandoning efforts designed to help the disadvantaged find and take advantage of job opportunities would not be an effective way to achieve that goal.

Endnotes

1. Robert Taggart, *A Fisherman's Guide. An Assessment of Training and Remediation Strategies* (W.E. Upjohn Institute for Employment Research, 1981).
2. For a discussion of different definitions of poverty, see Chapter 1 of this volume. The definition used here differs from the standard OMB definition which includes welfare payments as income.
3. See Chapter 1 of this volume.
4. Many persons under 18 and over 65 are working or looking for work. The employment problems facing such persons can be severe. Nonetheless nearly all teenagers are at home and rely heavily on the income of others. Most persons over 65 do not work and instead rely on Social Security, pensions, savings, and other sources of support.
5. Louis Jacobson and Janet Thomason, *Earnings Loss Due to Displacement* (Virginia: Public Research Institute, Center for Naval Analyses, 1979).
6. Tabulations of Survey of Income and Education. This figure may understate the importance of displaced workers among the poor. The question of whether a worker is on layoff is asked at the time of the survey, whereas poverty is measured over the previous year. Some persons who were poor in the past year may have since found jobs and thus no longer show up as on layoff. On the other hand, such workers no longer need help.
7. The poverty rate among male household heads who are high school dropouts is 10 percent. The poverty rate for male heads is 5 percent.
8. Peter Doeringer and Michael Piore, "Low Income Employment and the Disadvantaged Labor Force," *Internal Labor Markets and Manpower Analysis*, (Lexington, Mass.: D.C. Heath and Company, 1971), Chapter 8.
9. Richard Freeman, "Troubled Workers in the Labor Market," *National Commission for Employment Policy, Seventh Annual Report: The Federal Interest in Employment and Training*, Report No. 13 (Washington, D.C., (October 1981).
10. Kim Clark and Lawrence Summers, "Demographic Differences in Cyclical Employment Variation," *Journal of Human Resources*, Vol. XVI, No. 1, (Winter 1981).
11. Michael Piore, "Jobs and Training," in Samuel H. Beer and Richard E. Barringer, eds., *The State and the Poor* (Cambridge, Mass.: Winthrop Publishers, Inc., 1970).
12. David T. Ellwood, "The Mismatch Hypothesis: Are There Teenage Jobs Missing in the Ghetto?" (Cambridge, Mass.: National Bureau of Economics Research, Working Paper No. 999, April 1983).
13. *Ibid.*

14. National Commission for Employment Policy, *The Federal Role in Vocational Education*, Reports No. 12 and 13 (Washington, D.C., 1981).
15. Massachusetts State Employment and Training Council, *The Annual Report to the Governor on Employment and Training, Fiscal Year 1981* (Boston, Mass., 1982).
16. Westat, Inc., *Impact of 1978 Earnings of New FY 1976 CETA Enrollees in Selected Program Activities, Employment and Training Administration*, (Washington, D.C., February 1981).
17. Congressional Budget Office and National Commission for Employment Policy, "Ceta Training Progress: Do They Work For Adults?" (Washington, D.C., July 1982).
18. A good review of other studies can be found in Michael Borus, "Assessing the Impact of Training Programs," in Eli Ginzberg, (editor), *Employing the Disadvantaged* (New York: Basic Books, 1980).
19. Judy Gueron, "The Supported Work Experiment." in Eli Ginzberg, (editor), *loc. cit.*
20. The more accurate and sophisticated calculation would have to take account of the possibility of "crowding out." It is possible that some trainees are simply pushing others out of jobs rather than filling new ones. If this is so, the societal gain will be less than the private gain to the trainee.
21. Vice President's Task Force on Youth Employment, *Private Sector— Education Roundtable Series, Final Report* (Brandeis University: Center for Public Service, October 1979).
22. Olivia Golden, "Economic Development and Inner City Unemployment: The Opportunities and the Limits," Policy Analysis Exercise (John F. Kennedy School of Government, Harvard University, April 1981).
23. *Ibid.*
24. Congressional Budget Office and National Commission for Employment Policy, *loc. cit.*
25. Gueron, *loc. cit.*

Chapter 3

HEALTH CARE AND THE POOR

by David Blumenthal and David Calkins

An examination of the health and health care of Massachusetts'
poor illustrates dramatically the old maxim that yesterday's solutions in social policy are often today's problems. Over the last
fifteen years, the nation as a whole has undertaken a major effort
to improve the health status of the poor. Massachusetts and its
citizens have participated fully in that effort. Though incomplete, the evidence indicates that the state's poor have realized
health benefits comparable to, if not greater than, the nation's
poor as a whole.

Nonetheless the health-related difficulties of the state's poor
seem in some ways just as troubling today as they did 15 years
ago. Programs inaugurated to address those difficulties in the
mid-1960s are increasingly attacked in the 1980s as excessively
costly and inefficient. The Medicaid program in particular has
become so expensive that it threatens to undermine public support in Massachusetts, as in many states, for an array of health and
social welfare efforts. In addition, despite what seems a substantial investment by the state in health care programs for the poor,
considerable disparities persist between poor and non-poor in
health status and access to health services. This raises the question
of whether the return on existing public programs justifies their
current and projected costs.

Accordingly, policy problems related to the health care needs
of the poor remain front and center on Massachusetts' social
welfare agenda. In this chapter we will examine those policy
issues in three general sections. First we will consider the current
health status of the poor, their access to needed health services,
and the changes that have occurred in these variables over the

past ten years. In the second section we will examine the record of existing public health care programs and identify those that hold substantial promise for addressing remaining disparities between the poor and non-poor in health status or access to services. We also will consider some suggestions for making existing programs more effective and/or efficient. Finally, we will formulate some general recommendations concerning health policy toward the state's poor in the 1980s.

Two qualifications should be kept in mind as the discussion proceeds. First, data related specifically to the health care problems of the poor in Massachusetts are relatively sparse. Consequently this chapter draws liberally on nation-wide data to reach conclusions about the health and health care of the state's residents. Fortunately, what state-specific data are available indicate that, for the most part, Massachusetts has followed national trends. Second, the discussion here is focused primarily on acute medical care, de-emphasizing long-term care and mental health services, as well as services provided by health professionals other than physicians and nurses (for example, dentists, optometrists, podiatrists, and pharmacists).[1]

Health and Health Services Among the Poor

Health Status

A review of national data concerning the health status of the poor supports two conclusions. First, the health status of the poor has improved since 1970, and has improved faster than that of the non-poor. Second, despite these improvements, the poor remain considerably less healthy than the non-poor. Limited data suggest that Massachusetts is in line with national trends.

Traditional indicators of health status can be grouped into two broad categories: measures of morbidity and measures of mortality. We will consider overall morbidity and mortality data for the poor as well as data for one especially vulnerable group: infants and children. Mortality data are not reported by income. Therefore in analyzing mortality (and occasionally morbidity) data we use race as a proxy for income. Though necessary, the use of race-related data creates special problems in this state, where so many of the poor are white (see Chapter 2).[2]

Overall Population.   National data show that mortality rates for blacks are declining more rapidly than those for whites. From 1970 to 1978 the age-adjusted mortality rate for black males dropped 15.6 percent, while that for white males dropped only 13.5 percent. Similarly, the age-adjusted mortality rate for black females declined 20.1 percent, while that for white females declined only 15.2 percent. Nonetheless, the age-adjusted mortality rate for black males is still 44.0 percent greater than that for white males, and the rate for black females 52.9 percent greater than that for white females.

National data on morbidity suggest only small, inconsistent changes in recent years. For example, between 1974 and 1979 the proportion of low-income persons reporting their health as fair or poor declined from 24.7 to 22.5 percent. Among low-income persons, however, the number of restricted-activity days increased from 25.7 in 1974 to 30.6 in 1979, and the number of bed-disability days increased from 9.9 in 1974 to 10.6 in 1979. All of these indices remain about twice as high as those for persons in the highest income category.[3]

A 1978 survey of Boston elderly suggests that income-related differentials in morbidity in Massachusetts may be similar to those in the nation as a whole. Among persons living alone, 51 percent of the low-income group rated their health as fair or poor, compared with 40 percent of the high-income group. Similarly among persons living with a spouse, 47 percent of the low-income group reported their health as fair or poor, compared with 30 percent of the high-income group.[4]

Infants and Children. There has been significant progress in the health status of poor infants in Massachusetts as measured in terms of infant mortality. Between the years 1970–1972 and 1976–1978, infant mortality for blacks fell 34.0 percent. This compares with a reduction of only 27.7 percent for whites during the same period and with a reduction of only 22.0 percent for blacks in the nation as a whole.

Data on low-birth-weight infants also suggest improved health status among Massachusetts' poor. Weighing less than 2,500 grams, such neonates are substantially more vulnerable to early death and long-term disability. Between the years 1970–1972 and 1976–1978, the frequency of low-weight births among the state's blacks fell by 16.2 percent. This compared with a reduction over the same period of only 10.3 percent among whites and of only 5.1 percent among blacks nationally.

These signs of improvement should not, however, obscure the persistent disparities in health status between poor and non-poor infants in Massachusetts. Black mothers are still 86.9 percent more likely than white mothers to deliver infants weighing less than 2,500 grams. Black infants are 75.0 percent more likely than

white infants to die in their first year of life. The death rate for
black infants in the state exceeds the overall rate of infant mortality in most industrialized nations.[5]

Access to Health Services

There is no single, agreed-upon definition of access to health
services. Some analysts distinguish between "potential" and
"realized" access. *Potential* access is measured in terms of service
availability, both physical and financial. *Realized* access is measured in terms of service utilization—ideally, adjusted for need.[6]

While measures of service availability or utilization are useful
for comparing access among various population groups and
monitoring trends in access over time, such measures do not tell us
whether individuals or groups have appropriate access to health
care services. Such a determination requires that we compare
measured access with need. Unfortunately, standards defining
appropriate access levels for given population groups remain
controversial.

In the absence of generally accepted norms, evidence that the
poor have less access than the non-poor does not prove that
access among the poor is inadequate. In fact, some observers
argue that the poor now have achieved an absolute level of access
that equals or exceeds their needs, and that remaining disparities
between the poor and non-poor no longer have policy significance. This position shifts to the poor and their advocates the
burden of proving that current levels of access are inadequate—
an extremely difficult task given prevailing uncertainties about
how much care is truly enough.

A more generous view is that, given persistent gaps in health
status between the poor and non-poor, the burden of proof
should fall on policymakers to demonstrate that access is adequate. At a minimum, persistent disparities in access should raise
concern that the poor may not be receiving necessary services.

Availability. Over the past fifteen years both the federal and
state governments have committed substantial resources to improving the physical and financial availability of health services.
This investment has coincided with substantial growth in service
availability. For example, between 1970 and 1980 the supply of
active, non-federal physicians in Massachusetts increased 34.7
percent.[7]

Nonetheless, the state continues to list 17 communities with
populations over 1,000 as Medically Underserved Areas. The
ratio of primary care physicians to population for communities

throughout the state is directly correlated with town per capita income. In 1977 the ten towns with the highest per capita incomes had an average of 1.0 primary care physicians (that is, family physicians, internists, and pediatricians) per 1,000 residents, compared with 0.6 in the ten towns with the lowest per capita incomes. The financial availability of health services for the poor will be discussed in the review of the Medicaid program later in this chapter.

Utilization.   While the data are incomplete, public health care programs seem to have enjoyed some success in overcoming disparities in health service utilization between the poor and non-poor, both nationally and in Massachusetts. The best available information concerns physician services. National data show a steady increase in physician utilization by the poor. Between 1970 and 1980 the physician visit rate for low-income individuals increased 13.2 percent. This is in contrast to an increase of only 4.3 percent in the overall physician visit rate. In 1980 low-income individuals made 25.0 percent more visits per capita than the overall population.[8]

Recent data suggest a similar pattern of physician utilization in Massachusetts. For example, in the 1978 survey of Boston elderly cited earlier, Branch found that among persons living alone, the low-income group made 6.0 physician visits per year while the high-income group made only 4.5 physician visits per year.[9] Similarly, in a 1980 survey of Massachusetts adults, Lambert and his colleagues found that 70 percent of low-income respondents had seen a doctor within the past six months compared with 60 percent of high-income respondents.

Encouraging as these data are, they should be interpreted with caution. Most analyses of national data indicate that if one adjusts for health status, the poor continue to utilize fewer physician services than the non-poor. Kleinman, for example, using data from the 1976–1978 National Health Interview Survey (NHIS), found that persons with family incomes below $7,000 made 7 to 44 percent fewer physician visits per year than persons of comparable health status with family incomes of $14,000 and above.[10]

The place of physician visits by the poor is also of interest, since it may have implications for both service cost and quality. Nationally, the poor are more likely to use hospital outpatient departments or emergency rooms for their care. In 1980 these sources represented only 12.9 percent of visits by the overall population but 19.4 percent of visits by low-income persons.[11]

Perhaps because of their increased reliance on episodic care in institutional settings, poor adults nationally utilize fewer preventive services. For example, poor women are less likely to have had a recent Pap smear or breast exam than non-poor women. Low-income pregnant women are less likely to receive prenatal care during the first trimester of pregnancy. Poor men are less likely to have had a recent blood pressure measurement.[12]

Given the relatively high proportion of children among the poor in Massachusetts (see Chapter 2), the utilization of health services by children should be of special concern to policymakers in this state. National data show that physician visits by low-income children (birth through age 5) increased from 4.6 per person in 1970 to 5.2 per person in 1980. Nonetheless, low-income children continue to make fewer physician visits per person per year than children overall (5.2 versus 6.7).[13]

These differences between high- and low-income children become even more striking if one adjusts for health status. For example, using data from the 1975–1976 NHIS, Kovar found that children (birth through age 18) from low-income families made only 72 physician visits per 100 bed-disability days, whereas children from high-income families made 98 physician visits per 100 bed-disability days.[14]

Discrepancies in place of physician visit by income groups are greater for children than for the population as a whole. In 1980, 30.5 percent of physician visits by low-income children (birth through age 5) were to hospital outpatient departments and emergency rooms, compared with only 13.1 percent of visits by all children.[15]

Low-income children receive fewer preventive services than the overall population. Of particular concern is a lower rate of immunization against childhood infections.[16]

Health Care Programs for the Poor

Massachusetts' Current Portfolio

Using somewhat generous standards to determine which state health care programs (excluding mental health) are poverty-related, we can estimate total state expenditures on health care for the poor at about $1.07 billion for fiscal year (FY) 1981, the last year for which complete figures are available. That figure, which includes federal monies channeled through the state, constitutes approximately 15 percent of the total state budget and about 98 percent of all state health care expenditures, which total $1.09 billion.

A review of the state expenditures on health care for the poor makes one thing very clear: At 88 percent of the total, Medicaid dwarfs all other programs on the list. Indeed, the 15 percent annual growth in Medicaid expenditures nearly equals the annual commitment to all other poverty-related health programs combined. Like most of the states, Massachusetts finds Medicaid to be a sizable, growing, and largely uncontrollable portion of its total expenditures. It is appropriate, therefore, that we begin our program review with a discussion of Medicaid.

Medicaid

Program Characteristics. The Medicaid program was established in 1965 with enactment of Title XIX of the Social Security Act. Medicaid is managed and financed jointly by the state and federal governments. States have considerable discretion with regard to program policy, and Massachusetts has used that discretion to fashion a program that is relatively generous in certain respects but relatively austere in others.

With respect to eligibility, the Massachusetts program is for the most part fairly generous.[17] In FY 1979 there were 597,179 average monthly Medicaid beneficiaries in Massachusetts, a total exceeded by only four states. Massachusetts extends Medicaid coverage to a number of groups that need not be covered under federal law, including two-parent families in whom the head is unemployed and the "medically needy." In only one major respect is Massachusetts eligibility policy relatively restrictive: The payment (income) standard for AFDC eligibility is only $5,334 per year for a family of four, 57 percent of the federal poverty standard. The AFDC payment standard has not been raised since July 1980, despite an 18 percent increase in the cost of living. In FY 1979 Massachusetts ranked fourteenth nationally in terms of AFDC payment standard.[18]

Like eligibility policy, Medicaid benefits policy in Massachusetts is fairly generous.[19] Massachusetts places no limit on the scope of services (for example, the number of hospital days or physician visits) for required benefits. In addition Massachusetts provides virtually all optional benefits without limitation as to scope of service or requirement of beneficiary cost sharing.

The relative generosity of Massachusetts' treatment of Medicaid eligibility and benefits contrasts sharply with its restrictive policies toward reimbursement of Medicaid service providers. Federal law requires that hospitals, nursing homes, and home care programs be reimbursed at "reasonable cost" (as under Medicare), unless the federal government approves an alternative method. For several years Massachusetts has had a federal waiver of the "reasonable cost" requirement to allow reimbursement of these providers based on a negotiated rate. More recently, in response to the adoption of Chapter 372 of the General Laws, Massachusetts was granted permission to pay hospitals for Medicaid services on a prospective basis. Under the terms of this new waiver, Medicaid will pay less than other payors for comparable services, and should realize substantial savings.

Massachusetts has been relatively restrictive in its reimbursement of physicians as well. States have greater discretion in reimbursing physicians than institutional providers of services, and Massachusetts is one of 10 states that have used that discretion to reimburse physicians according to a fee schedule. In 1979 Massachusetts Medicaid fees for general practitioners averaged 57 percent of Medicare fees. Thirty-eight states paid their physicians more generously than Massachusetts.[20]

Costs.   From FY 1970 to FY 1980, Medicaid expenditures in Massachusetts rose from $253 million to $903 million. During FY 1979 Massachusetts ranked sixth nationally in total Medicaid expenditures. However, in terms of expenditures per recipient, Massachusetts ranked only thirty-seventh.[21]

Four factors affect total Medicaid expenditures: (1) size of beneficiary population, (2) range and scope of covered services, (3) utilization of services, and (4) cost per unit of service. The number of average monthly Medicaid beneficiaries increased only 26.0 percent (from 455,300 to 573,500) between FY 1970 and FY 1975, and actually dropped 1.2 percent (from 573,500 to 566,900) between FY 1975 and FY 1980. Similarly, apart from the addition of intermediate care facilities (ICFs) as an optional service in 1972, there have been few changes in covered services. It follows that most Medicaid cost increases in recent years must be attributed to increased utilization and/or increased cost per unit of service consumed by Medicaid beneficiaries.

Inpatient hospital and nursing home services account for the bulk of Medicaid costs (72.9 percent of total expenditures in FY 1980). In recent years there has been an increase in both the utilization and unit cost of these services. Unfortunately, in the absence of a Medicaid Management Information System, documentation of these trends has been somewhat fragmentary.

Data on acute hospital utilization are available for 1979 and 1980. They show an increase from 1.6 to 1.8 in inpatient days per Medicaid beneficiary. Data on expenditures for acute hospital services are unavailable; between 1979 and 1980, however, the hospital room component of the Consumer Price Index increased 13.1 percent.

Data on chronic hospital and nursing home utilization and expenditures are available for 1978 and 1980. Over this two-year period chronic hospital days per Medicaid beneficiary increased from 1.7 to 2.0, and the average per diem payment to chronic hospitals by Medicaid increased from $75.55 to $92.65. Similarly, the average number of days in a skilled nursing facility (SNF) or ICF per beneficiary increased from 17.9 to 19.9, and the average per diem payment to these facilities increased from $19.63 to $25.18.

Since Medicaid is merely a purchaser (and not a direct provider) of health care services, Medicaid expenditures are influenced heavily by the characteristics of the overall health care system in the state. Historically, Massachusetts has been a high-cost state for health care. In 1980 per capita expenditures for health care in Massachusetts were $1,315, compared with $1,053 in the United States as a whole. This is explained in part by a greater supply of hospital beds and greater use of hospital services, and hence greater hospital expenditures per capita than for the overall U.S. population. Massachusetts also has a greater supply of nursing home beds per 1,000 population age 65 and over than the United States as a whole.[22]

Impact. Medicaid was enacted in part to improve access to health care services and, ultimately, health status for the poor. Has it succeeded? It has, indeed, provided many poor with financial access to services. Because of categorical and income-related exclusions, however, almost two-thirds of the poor nationally are ineligible for Medicaid. Data on the extent of Medicaid coverage among all poor in Massachusetts are unavailable, but it has been estimated that in 1980, 28 percent of poor children in Massachusetts remained uncovered by Medicaid.[23]

Medicaid has had a significant impact on physician utilization by the poor. National data show that Medicaid beneficiaries use more physician visits than similar individuals not on Medicaid, even after adjustment for health status.[24]

Nevertheless, Medicaid has not succeeded in bringing beneficiaries into the "mainstream" of American medicine. A 1975 study showed that only 14 percent of poor persons with Medicaid coverage (in the five communities surveyed) reported a private physician as their usual source of care, compared with 41 percent of the poor covered by private insurance. This pattern of care results in part from physician non-participation in Medicaid. Nationally, about 20 percent of office-based physicians see no

Medicaid patients. Sixteen percent of office-based physicians account for 60 percent of office visits by Medicaid beneficiaries.[25]

Even when Medicaid beneficiaries do see private physicians, the quality of services they receive may be below average. Nationally, physicians whose practices are 50 percent or more Medicaid patients are disproportionately aged, general practitioners. As compared with other physicians, they are less likely to be board-certified or to have hospital affiliations. In some states foreign medical graduates provide a disproportionate share of physician services received by Medicaid beneficiaries.[26]

Physician non-participation in Medicaid should be a matter of some concern to state policymakers, for reasons both of access and cost. When services are unavailable from private physicians, the only alternative may be more costly hospital outpatient departments or emergency rooms. At some hospitals in this state the cost to Medicaid of an outpatient visit may be as much as $100.

Assessing the impact of Medicaid on the health status of the poor is difficult. As we have seen, the health status of the poor nationally and in Massachusetts has improved, although the poor still lag behind the non-poor. The magnitude of the Medicaid program relative to other public health efforts suggests that much of this improvement can be attributed to Medicaid. It is likely, however, that a number of societal forces unrelated to health care (for example, education, health and safety regulations) also have played a role.

Policy Implications. The magnitude of Medicaid expenditures creates strong pressures for Medicaid cost containment. As federal and state authorities continue to seek Medicaid savings, a number of critical points should be kept in mind.

First, as we have seen, rising Medicaid costs are due principally to increased utilization of health care services and increased unit costs for these services. These trends are endemic to the health care system generally, in which Medicaid participates as a relatively small purchaser of care. Efforts at Medicaid cost containment are more likely to succeed, therefore, if they are accompanied by more general efforts at reforming the health care system. In this respect, the enactment of Chapter 372, which establishes for all payers a system of prospective reimbursement for hospital services, represents a healthy development. The full effects of Chapter 372 remain to be defined. Certain aspects of the law may encourage discrimination against Medicaid patients.[27] Nonetheless, Chapter 372 at least recognizes the advantages of seeking Medicaid cost containment as part of generic reform in the organization and financing of health care services.

Secondly, we also have seen that, while Medicaid has provided the poor with increased access to health care services, gaps in access between the poor and non-poor remain. Medicaid cost containment efforts may expand these gaps. Such efforts must be targeted, therefore, toward reduction in the utilization of services that are either unnecessary or marginally important for maintaining the health of beneficiaries. As we shall see, the experience of community health centers (CHCs) and health maintenance organizations (HMOs) in serving Medicaid patients offers the hope that such targeted program changes may be achievable.

Medicaid expenditures may be cut through reductions in eligibility, benefits, utilization, or unit costs of services (that is, payments to providers). However, reductions in eligibility or benefits tend to impede access indiscriminately. Furthermore, savings from such policy changes might be limited.[28] It seems prudent, therefore, to focus our discussion on cost-containment strategies that seek to decrease utilization and/or payments to providers.

One way to limit utilization is through regulation of beneficiary or provider behavior. Massachusetts has implemented a variety of such regulatory measures: Professional Standards Review Organizations, utilization review, prior approval (for example, for dental care), preadmission screening (for example, for nursing home care), and second opinions (for example, for elective surgery). Many of these measures have been shown to be effective in reducing Medicaid expenditures.

Continued regulatory efforts should focus on those beneficiaries and providers who account for the largest volume of Medicaid expenditures. Among beneficiaries, the elderly and the disabled were responsible for 71.8 percent of expenditures in FY 1980. Among providers, hospitals and nursing homes accounted for 80.4 percent of expenditures in the same year.

Beneficiary cost sharing has been proposed as a means to decrease Medicaid utilization and expenditures. States currently have the authority to require co-payments from the categorically needy for optional services and from the medically needy for all services. Massachusetts does neither. Studies in the United States and Canada indicate that co-payments can lead to decreased utilization of physician services, especially by the poor. Data from a 1972 Medicaid co-payment experiment in California, however, suggest that decreased utilization of physician services may be associated with increased utilization of hospital services and hence higher total expenditures.[29]

An alternative approach is to eliminate provider incentives to deliver unnecessary services. Members of HMOs generally use fewer hospital days per capita than non-members but receive health care that is comparable in overall quality. This lower level of utilization may be due in part to the fact that HMO physicians are at risk for costs which exceed annual payments from HMO members. Studies suggest that enrollment of Medicaid beneficiaries in HMOs can result in decreased Medicaid expenditures.[30] Massachusetts currently contracts with only 4 of the 16 HMOs in the state to provide services to 3,500 Medicaid beneficiaries. Medicaid beneficiaries represent only 1.8 percent of HMO enrollees in the state.

In 1979 Massachusetts initiated a case management program on a demonstration basis. This program utilized a primary care network (PCN), a variant of the HMO model, to provide services to Medicaid beneficiaries. The state contracted with one hospital-affiliated health center, three CHCs, two hospital outpatient departments (acting as a single site), and one private group practice to serve 2,842 AFDC recipients. Under this program beneficiaries were "locked in" to a particular site. This site authorized all non-emergency services received by enrollees. Two sites were at risk for expenditures above a fixed amount. Evaluation at the close of the demonstration in 1981 showed that expenditures at three of the six sites were below levels experienced prior to the implementation of case management. The recently disbanded Commonwealth Health Care Corporation, a PCN built around Boston health centers and teaching hospitals, had proposed enrolling all AFDC beneficiaries in Boston in an expanded case management network.

The long-run prospects for case management are uncertain. The experience in other states has been mixed. For example, the Group Health Plan of Northeast Ohio has been relatively successful, while United Health Care (UHC), a PCN in Washington, Utah, and California, was forced to close in June 1982 because of large deficits. Several factors accounted for UHC's failure, including the inability or unwillingness of primary care physicians to police the practice behavior of specialists.[31] The Massachusetts case management program experienced some of the same problems faced by UHC. Nevertheless, the case management approach deserves a full and careful trial. Like HMOs, primary care networks may be capable of selectively reducing utilization of unnecessary or marginally useful Medicaid services, thus reducing costs without jeopardizing the health status of beneficiaries.

The Massachusetts case management initiative has been criticized because it limits the freedom of Medicaid beneficiaries to choose where they will receive care. It requires beneficiaries to obtain primary care services only from participating primary care physicians. Other services may be obtained from any Medicaid provider but must be authorized by the primary care physician.

Case management does impose constraints on freedom of choice by Medicaid beneficiaries which are not encountered by privately insured individuals, but such constraints may be justified by two considerations. First, as we have noted, physician non-participation in Medicaid already constitutes a de facto limitation on beneficiary freedom of choice. Second, if case management is effective in reducing the rate of growth in Medicaid expenditures, it may be an attractive alternative to the more extreme limitations on freedom of choice now permissible under waiver authority provided by the Omnibus Budget Reconciliation Act of 1981. California, for example, has used this authority to establish a Medicaid "czar" to contract with providers on a competitive bid basis. Only those providers receiving contracts will be eligible for Medicaid reimbursement.

As noted above, Massachusetts historically has been rather aggressive in limiting provider reimbursement. Chapter 372 will result in additional reductions in reimbursement to hospitals. Conceivably, additional reductions in physician fees also might be possible. The consequences of such payment limitations, however, deserve careful consideration.

Reductions in payments to physicians may mean that fewer physicians will be willing to serve Medicaid beneficiaries. Past studies suggest that a 10 percent cut in Medicaid fees results in a 7 percent reduction in the physician participation rate. Furthermore, reduction in physician payments may result in little reduction in total Medicaid expenditures. In the absence of prospective reimbursement, physicians may compensate for a reduction in payments for individual services by increasing service volume. This has been the response to limits on physician fees in Canada.[32]

While we thus far have emphasized Medicaid cost containment, state policymakers should not lose sight of other policy goals, such as providing access by the poor to needed health services. As we have noted, many of the poor in Massachusetts are ineligible for Medicaid. To some extent this is the result of categorical restrictions imposed by federal law, but it is also a function of income eligibility standards, some of which are set by the state (for example, the AFDC and medically needy standards). Raising the AFDC payment standard would increase the proportion of poor with financial protection against the cost of illness. While such a change in the AFDC standard would increase Medicaid costs, any increased expenditures might be partially offset by cost-containment efforts of the types discussed in previous sections.

Long-Term Care. In a discussion of Massachusetts Medicaid policy, long-term care merits particular attention for two reasons. First, long-term care services consume nearly half of all Medicaid resources. SNF and ICF services accounted for 34.6 percent of Medicaid expenditures in Massachusetts in FY 1980; chronic hospitals accounted for 12.7 percent and home health services for 1.4 percent. Second, the population that is the principal consumer of long-term care services—namely, the elderly—is growing rapidly. Between 1970 and 1979 the overall population in Massachusetts increased only 1.4 percent, while the population age 65 and over increased 12.3 percent. The demand for nursing home and other long-term care services, and Medicaid payment for those services, will continue to increase in the years ahead.

Though long-term care is often equated with chronic hospital or nursing home care for the elderly, it is in reality a continuum of services provided to all functionally disabled individuals. In addition to chronic hospital and nursing home care, services may include adult day care, home health and homemaker services, hospice care, meals, and congregate living programs. Although the elderly consume the majority of these services, many physically or mentally disabled persons (for example, persons with severe mental retardation or spinal cord injury) also may need long-term care.[33]

In Massachusetts, Medicaid expenditures for chronic hospital and nursing home care historically have dwarfed those for other long-term services. For example, in FY 1980 these institutional providers received 97.2 percent of Medicaid payments for long-term care services.

Partly because non-institutional services are thought to be less costly, several recent reviews of long-term care needs and services nationally have recommended increased development and use of community-based alternatives to institutional care for persons in need of long-term care services.[34] Such alternatives can be justified in that they allow functionally disabled persons to remain with families and maintain maximum independence. However, it is as yet unclear whether the provision of more community-based services can reduce total long-term care expenditures.

Several factors may mitigate against any substantial savings from expanded use of community-based services. First, there may be a substantial queue of persons awaiting nursing home beds. Even if a few nursing home beds could be emptied by shifting patients to community-based care, these beds would soon be filled. Several studies of expanded use of home health services, in fact, fail to demonstrate any reduction in nursing home use. In addition there are many functionally disabled persons who do not require nursing home care but who might use community-based services were they available. In 1977 only 24.1 percent of persons who were dependent on others for help with activities of daily living or mobility resided in institutions. Finally, a few studies indicate that persons receiving community-based services may live longer. Desirable as this may be, total health care expenditures over an extended lifespan may be greater.[35]

Future long-term care policy will benefit from two national research activities funded by the Department of Health and Human Services (DHHS). The National Long-Term Care Channeling Demonstration seeks to coordinate long-term care services through a central agency. Several project sites combine case management with the authority to purchase services. Expenditures per beneficiary are limited to 60 percent of area SNF and ICF costs. The Social Health Maintenance Organization Demonstration attempts to extend the financial principles of HMOs to long-term care. Under this demonstration beneficiary expenditures for both acute and long-term care services are subject to a fixed budget.[36] Policymakers should examine the outcome of these studies carefully.

Community Health Centers

Program Characteristics. CHCs provide comprehensive health services to low-income populations and have been promoted through federal grant support since the mid-1960s. Expenditures by the federal government on CHCs totalled $330 million in FY 1980.[37]

The state of Massachusetts has 70 health centers, of which 33 are located within the Boston metropolitan area. In FY 1980 these centers received approximately $9 million in federal grants, including about $7 million under authority contained in Section 330 of the Public Health Service Act.

In Massachusetts, as in most states, state government has played a subsidiary role in supporting CHCs. Federal monies have gone directly to CHCs without passing through state coffers. While the state has funded centers indirectly through Medicaid payments (which totalled about $20 million in 1981), direct state support in the form of grants and contracts has been minimal.

In the near future, however, state government may need to show more interest in CHCs. One reason is that other sources of financial support for CHCs are in jeopardy. In FY 1982 federal grants to CHCs under Section 330 were reduced by a full 26 percent to $244 million. Massachusetts' allocation has fallen from $7 million in FY 1980 to a projected $3.6 million in FY 1982, a 50 percent reduction in two years. While it is not yet known precisely which centers will bear the brunt of these reductions, a study of Boston's CHCs estimated that about 20 percent of the city's centers will lose all their federal funds, 20 percent will lose about 40 percent, and an additional 20 percent will face lesser reductions. Exacerbating the impact of these funding reductions is the fact that local support for CHCs is projected to decrease by about 25 percent as a result of Proposition 2½, the state's tax-limiting law. Health center advocates thus have been turning to state government in an effort to prevent feared center closures.[38]

Costs. Because of their age, number, and importance to the War on Poverty, CHCs are a comparatively well-studied social innovation. Early, incomplete research seemed to show that CHCs were relatively costly compared with the traditional health care system. A number of recent investigations indicate, however, that they may be cost-effective, primarily because they reduce the utilization of certain expensive services. For example, Hocheiser and his colleagues found a 38 percent reduction in the use of emergency room visits in a community served by a CHC. Klein found a 50 percent reduction in hospital days utilized by children cared for in a CHC. Freeman and Goetch found that hospital admission rates were 31 percent lower among patients using CHCs as their primary source of care and that total utilization of hospital days was 50 percent lower. After adjusting for age, sex, race, education, income, insurance coverage, and health status, hospital admission rates were even more markedly reduced—to 50 percent of non-CHC users.[39]

These findings concerning utilization suggest that total expenditures per patient may be reduced by CHCs, and at least one study demonstrates this to be true. JRB Associates found that Medicaid expenditures for beneficiaries using a CHC for at least 50 percent of their care were 30 percent lower than for Medicaid beneficiaries using other sources of care. Hospital admission rates and total hospital days were reduced by 48 percent and 40 percent respectively.[40]

The ability of CHCs to realize savings in providing health care to poverty populations should not be surprising. While CHCs do collect fees for some patients (chiefly Medicaid), in Massachusetts these account for only 27 percent of total revenues. For the most part, centers must operate on a fixed, annual budget provided by grant support or other revenues unrelated to services rendered. They have fewer incentives as institutions, therefore, to overutilize services; and individual physicians, since they are salaried, are similarly insulated from incentives which may encourage excessive utilization.

Impact.   CHCs seem to do more than reduce the utilization and cost of health services. They also seem to improve the health status of the populations they serve. Several studies demonstrate the effectiveness of CHCs in reducing morbidity in poor populations. A classic study by Gordis found that the incidence of rheumatic fever fell by one third in census tracts served by a Baltimore CHC but remained unchanged in other poor neighborhoods of the city.[41] (Rheumatic fever is a preventable complication of strep throat infections.)

CHCs also have demonstrated a significant impact on infant mortality. Anderson and Morgan found a dramatic fall in infant mortality (from 46.9 to 28.3 per thousand over a four year period) in an Alabama county served by a CHC; in neighboring counties infant mortality rates were unchanged during the study period. In New York City Gold found a 41 percent reduction in perinatal mortality over a four-year period in a community served by a CHC, and prematurity rates there fell 20 percent.[42]

In Massachusetts the Office of State Health Planning has credited CHCs with helping to reduce infant mortality rates in certain low-income neighborhoods of Boston. For example, between 1972 and 1979 infant mortality rates in Charlestown fell by 74.5 percent, in South Boston by 47.5 percent, and in Roslindale by 54.2 percent. Statewide, the reduction in infant mortality was 28.5 percent during this same period.

Policy Implications.   CHCs are not without problems as instruments for delivering health care services to the poor. It is widely acknowledged, for example, that some centers suffer from low productivity and inadequate management. Nevertheless, the evidence suggests that, in general, CHCs are a cost-effective means of providing health care services to the poor. A convincing argument can be made, therefore, that the state should insure the continued survival of existing CHCs and perhaps expand their number and/or capacity. Such assistance can be justified by the potential savings in Medicaid expenditures from expanded Medicaid enrollment in CHCs. For example, if the JRB Associates study is accurate, the state could realize savings of up to $7.5 million annually by enrolling an additional 50,000 AFDC recipients in CHCs.[43]

Health Care Programs for Pregnant Women, Infants, and Children

Massachusetts invests more state resources in health programs for mothers and children than in any health program or set of programs other than Medicaid. In 1983 the Department of Public Health (DPH) expects to spend over $32 million on a series of initiatives designed to improve the health status of pregnant women, infants, and children. Of these funds roughly $24 million will be provided by the federal government. Because of changes in federal law, however, the state will have more discretion in the expenditure of these federal funds than ever before.

A discussion of all the maternal and child health programs funded or administered by the state is beyond the scope of this chapter, but two sets of initiatives deserve special mention because of their size or pending changes in the manner of their administration. These are the Special Supplemental Food Program for Women, Infants and Children (WIC), and activities funded under Title V of the Social Security Act, commonly referred to as the Maternal and Child Health Program.

The Special Supplemental Food Program for Women, Infants, and Children. Inadequate maternal and infant nutrition is a well-established cause of adverse health outcomes among mothers and infants, including low birth weight, as well as maternal, neonatal, and infant mortality. In 1972 the federal government initiated the WIC program to provide supplemental food and nutrition education to women and infants regarded as high-risk. The program is available to low-income women who are pregnant, post-partum or lactating, and to infants and children up to age five. Families with incomes up to 195 percent of the poverty level are eligible. Massachusetts will receive $15.1 million through WIC in 1982. Monies are distributed by the state DPH to health centers and poverty agencies around the state. An estimated 16 percent of eligible women and children are served in the state.

The WIC program was one of the few federal social welfare programs to survive the 1981 budget cuts unscathed. A chief reason was its apparent success in affecting health outcomes. Several studies, including at least two done exclusively in Massachusetts, have demonstrated that infants of mothers enrolled in

WIC programs fare better than those born to non-WIC mothers. For example, Kotelchuck and his coworkers found that WIC participants in Massachusetts had 21 percent fewer low-birth-weight infants and experienced significantly fewer neonatal deaths. The difference between WIC and non-WIC participants was largest for subgroups considered at highest risk: teenagers, unmarried mothers, black and Latin mothers, and mothers without high school degrees. Similarly, Kennedy found that the incidence of low-birth-weight infants among WIC participants in the state was significantly lower than among non-WIC mothers using the same health facility.[44]

A number of factors suggest that the WIC program in Massachusetts is highly cost-effective. First, nutritional supplements and prenatal care are relatively inexpensive, while the cost of caring for low-birth-weight infants is high. In addition, inadequate nutrition and poor prenatal care are highly correlated with life-long problems, such as learning disabilities and mental retardation, whose costs to society are substantial. Finally, no intervention saves more potentially productive years of life than one which prevents neonatal or infant mortality.

Despite its apparent effectiveness, the WIC program does not reach all eligible individuals in Massachusetts. State officials consider 17 cities and towns in the state with populations greater than 1000 to have unmet needs for WIC services. While all WIC funds are currently provided by the federal government, nothing would prevent the state from supplementing this program with its own funds to increase the percentage of high-risk mothers and children receiving nutritional support.

Title V and the Maternal and Child Health Block Grant. Since 1935 Title V of the Social Security Act (commonly known as the Maternal and Child Health Program) has supported activities aimed at improving the health of mothers and children. In recent years Congress has steadily relaxed federal control over the use of these funds. Until 1981, they were disbursed through loosely monitored state formula grants. Under the Omnibus Budget Reconciliation Act of 1981, Title V was lumped with six other federal programs in a Maternal and Child Health Block Grant. Simultaneously, appropriations for the programs included in the Block Grant were cut dramatically. In FY 1983 the federal government is expected to provide Massachusetts $7.2 million under the Maternal and Child Health Block Grant. This represents a reduction of 12 percent from the level of $8.2 million provided in FY 1981.

Since three quarters of the Block Grant monies support projects previously funded under Title V, the performance of Title V activities is highly relevant to policy decisions concerning the use of Maternal and Child Health Block Grant funds. In Massachusetts Title V funds have supported primary care, dental care, family planning, detection and follow-up of high-risk pregnancies, school health programs, adolescent health programs, provision of hearing aids to children, and adolescent pregnancy programs. In evaluations in other locales certain of these activities have been found to have a positive effect on health status. For example, prenatal services can reduce neonatal mortality. Similarly, programs that seek out women with high-risk pregnancies and refer them to tertiary centers for care may improve neonatal survival.[45] However, the effectiveness of the programs in place in Massachusetts has not, to our knowledge, been directly assessed.

The relative absence of good evaluations of Title V activities poses difficult problems for state policymakers. The target populations for these activities have conspicuous unmet needs. Evidence supports the efficacy of certain services provided through such programs. Many other initiatives funded under Title V, such as outreach services for pregnant adolescents and efforts to reduce long-term disability among low-birth-weight infants, have a compelling logic.

Yet, at a time when state discretion in the use of funds is increasing and state resources are strictly limited, the available evidence provides little basis for setting priorities among competing activities. In 1983 DPH proposes to support more than 15 different programs with Maternal and Child Health Block Grant funds. Policymakers should ask whether concentrating maternal and child health expenditures on a more limited set of programs might be more effective in reducing morbidity and mortality among the state's low-income mothers and children. The Senate Ways and Means Committee, for example, has made a convincing case for the importance of screening Massachusetts children for evidence of excessive exposure to lead. A recently published study suggests that screening for lead poisoning may be highly cost-effective,[46] but the relative value of this program compared to the many others funded by the state government is difficult to assess.

Clearly, improved evaluation of existing programs is essential for policymaking in the future.

Conclusions and Recommendations

The health status of the poor in Massachusetts has improved over the past decade, but the poor remain substantially less healthy than the non-poor. Although black infant mortality has declined, black infants are still more likely than white infants to die in their first year of life. Low-income elderly in Boston are more likely than high-income elderly to report their health as fair or poor.

Access to health services for the poor also has improved over the past decade, but the poor continue to have less access to health services than the non-poor. While physician utilization by the poor has increased, low-income children continue to make fewer physician visits per year than high-income children. At all ages the poor continue to lag behind the non-poor if one adjusts for health status. The poor are more likely than the non-poor to be deficient in the use of preventive health services. The poor continue to face both financial and physical barriers to care. Many of the poor lack Medicaid coverage, and many poor communities are deficient in primary health care services.

Existing programs have been successful in increasing utilization of health services among the poor. There is good evidence that some of these programs also have improved the health status of the poor and decreased health care costs. Nationally, Medicaid beneficiaries use more physician visits than similar individuals not on Medicaid, even after adjustment for health status. Physician non-participation in Medicaid, however, has kept the poor out of the "mainstream" of American medicine. Several studies show a reduction in morbidity, mortality, and hospital utilization in communities served by CHCs. Locally, CHCs may have contributed to reduced infant mortality during the past decade in such Massachusetts communities as Charlestown, South Boston, and Roslindale. There are fewer low-birth-weight infants and fewer neonatal deaths among low-income women participating in WIC in Massachusetts than among similar women not in the program. This difference is largest among high-risk subgroups: teenagers, unmarried mothers, black and Latin mothers, and mothers without high school degrees. Certain services supported by Maternal and Child Health Block Grant funds, such as special care for women with high-risk pregnancies, are known to be effective. However, there has been no comprehensive evaluation of the programs receiving Block Grant funds in Massachusetts.

As the above conclusions suggest, program expansion in some areas could yield further gains in access or health status. Our review also indicates that reforms in selected programs could reduce the cost of health services for the poor. Accordingly, the following recommendations seem appropriate.

1. *Enroll more Medicaid beneficiaries in HMOs.* Very few Medicaid beneficiaries in Massachusetts are enrolled in

HMOs. The state should seek a substantial increase in Medicaid HMO enrollment in the immediate future.

2. *Pursue existing experiments with case management and primary care networks.* Existing experiments with case management programs and primary care networks should be nurtured and evaluated carefully by state health policymakers. Restrictions on freedom of choice should be minimized, and quality of care should be monitored closely.

3. *Provide more community-based alternatives to institutional long-term care services.* While it is not clear that more community-based services (such as home care, adult day care, and congregate housing) will mean reduced Medicaid expenditures, additional community-based services can be justified on the grounds that they will maximize independence among the state's functionally disabled population. The impact of any expansion of community-based services on demand for long-term care services, and hence on Medicaid expenditures, should be monitored carefully. Ongoing national long-term care demonstrations may offer important lessons to state health policymakers.

4. *Provide financial and managerial assistance to existing CHCs.* The state should underwrite existing CHCs threatened by federal cutbacks. The cost of doing so would be no more than a few million dollars, and some of that money could be recouped in Medicaid savings. Also, the state should assist health centers in improving the efficiency of their operations. This might be accomplished by providing technical or managerial aid. Close cooperation with representatives of CHCs would be necessary in the design of such initiatives.

5. *Develop new CHCs in underserved communities.* The state should consider working with local governments to establish CHCs in communities designated as Medically Underserved Areas. There is a reasonable likelihood that such an initiative would accelerate the decline in state infant mortality rates and reduce remaining disparities in health status between the poor and non-poor.

6. *Increase the number of high-risk women, infants, and children served by WIC.* Only a small fraction of eligible women in Massachusetts currently participate in WIC. State resources should be used to reach some of the eligible women not currently participating in the program. An expanded WIC program might accelerate further the decline in rates of infant mortality and low-weight births among the poor. WIC programs should be located in CHCs to facilitate the provi-

sion of prenatal services and general pediatric care to high-risk mothers and children.

7. *Develop better data on the health and health care of Massachusetts' poor.* The development of health care policy for the poor in Massachusetts is severely handicapped by lack of essential data, including income-specific information on such basic matters as mortality, morbidity, health insurance coverage, and utilization of health services. In addition, the state lacks information necessary to evaluate rigorously the performance of key health care initiatives, including Medicaid and many maternal and child health care programs. Until such data become available, it will be impossible to determine how best to improve the health and health care of Massachusetts' poor.

Endnotes

1. Though mental health services are not discussed in this chapter, they are an important part of the state budget. In FY 1981 Massachusetts spent $458 million on mental health services. The poor benefited substantially from these expenditures, though it is not possible to specify the exact amount spent on mental health services for low-income residents.

2. Using race or ethnicity as a proxy for income has a number of other pitfalls. Racial or ethnic groups may differ in their genetic predisposition to certain health problems. Also, changes over time in the comparative health status of different racial and ethnic groups in fact may result from alterations in the relative distribution of incomes within such groups.

3. Office of Health Research, Statistics, and Technology, Public Health Service, U.S. Department of Health and Human Services, *Health, United States, 1980* (Washington, D.C.: U.S. Government Printing Office, 1980). Also, Office of Health Research, Statistics, and Technology, Public Health Service, U.S. Department of Health and Human Services, *Health, United States, 1981* (Washington, D.C.: U.S. Government Printing Office, 1981).

4. L.G. Branch, *Boston Elders: A Survey of Needs, 1978* (Boston, Mass.: City of Boston Commission on Affairs of the Elderly/Area Agency on Aging, Region VI, 1978).

5. Office of Health Research, Statistics, and Technology, *op. cit.* (1980 and 1981).

6. L.A. Aday, R. Andersen, and G.V. Fleming, *Health Care in the U.S.: Equitable for Whom?* (Beverly Hills, Calif.: Sage Publications, 1980).

7. J.N. Haug, G.A. Roback, and B.C. Martin, *Distribution of Physicians in the United States, 1970: Regional, State, County, Metropolitan Areas* (Chicago, Illinois: American Medical Association, 1971). Also, C.N. Bidese and D.G. Danais, *Physician Characteristics and Distribution in the United States, 1981 edition* (Chicago, Illinois: American Medical Association, 1982).

8. Unpublished data from the National Health Interview Study (1970 and 1980), used by permission of the National Center for Health Statistics.

9. L.G. Branch, *op. cit.*

10. J.C. Kleinman, M. Gold, and D. Makuc, "Use of Ambulatory Medical Care by the Poor: Another Look at Equity," *Medical Care* (1981: 19: 1011–1029).
11. Unpublished data from the National Health Interview Survey (1980), used by permission of National Center for Health Statistics.
12. L.A. Aday *et. al., op cit.* Also, D.M. Makuc, "Changes in Use of Preventive Health Services," Office of Health Research, Statistics, and Technology, *op. cit.* (1981: 41–46).
13. Unpublished data from the National Health Interview Survey (1970 and 1980), used by permission of the National Center for Health Statistics.
14. M.G. Kovar, "Health Status of U.S. Children and Use of Medical Care," *Public Health Reports* (1982: 97: 3–15).
15. Unpublished data from the National Health Interview Survey (1980), used by permission of the National Center for Health Statistics.
16. Office of Health Research, Statistics, and Technology, *op cit.* (1981).
17. Under federal law two population groups are eligible for Medicaid: the categorically needy and (at state option) the medically needy. The categorically needy include persons eligible for Aid to Families with Dependent Children (AFDC) or Supplemental Security Income (SSI). The medically needy include persons who meet the categorical requirements for AFDC or SSI but whose incomes are above the relevant eligibility standards. Such individuals become eligible for Medicaid after they "spend down" to a state eligibility standard. In Massachusetts this standard is currently $5,340 per year for a family of four. States may modify the number of Medicaid eligibles by altering eligibility for either AFDC or the medically needy program. Eligibility for SSI is determined by federal law, although states have the option of limiting Medicaid eligibility to persons who would have met the more restrictive state Medicaid eligibility standards in place prior to 1972.
18. D.N. Muse and D. Sawyer, *The Medicare and Medicaid Data Book, 1981* (Washington, D.C.: U.S. Government Printing Office, 1982).
19. Under federal law Medicaid benefits are divided into two categories: required (which include hospital, physician, laboratory, x-ray, skilled nursing facility, and home health care services, as well as early and periodic screening, diagnosis and treatment services for persons under age 21) and optional (which include intermediate care facility services, prescription drugs, and some 30 other services). States must provide all required benefits but may limit the scope of service (i.e., they may place a ceiling on the number of physician visits or hospital days for which reimbursement will be provided). States may provide optional services at their discretion and may both limit the scope of service and require beneficiary cost sharing.
20. J. Holahan, *A Comparison of Medicaid and Medicare Physician Reimbursement* (Washington, D.C.: Urban Institute, 1982).
21. D.N. Muse and D. Sawyer, *op cit.*
22. Office of Health Research, Statistics, and Technology, *op. cit.* (1981).
23. Office of the Assistant Secretary for Health and Surgeon General, Public Health Service, U.S. Department of Health and Human Services, *Better Health for Our Children: A National Strategy. The Report of the Select Panel for the Promotion of Child Health to the United States Congress and the Secretary of Health and Human Services. Volume III: A Statistical Profile*

(Washington, D.C.: U.S. Government Printing Office, 1980).

24. K. Davis, M. Gold, and D. Makuc, "Access to Health Care for the Poor: Does the Gap Remain?" *Annual Review of Public Health* (1981: 2: 159–182).

25. L.M. Okada and T.T.H. Wan, "Impact of Community Health Centers and Medicaid on the Use of Health Services," *Public Health Reports* (1980: 95:520–534). Also, J.B. Mitchell and J. Cromwell, "Large Medicaid Practices and Medicaid Mills," *Journal of the American Medical Association* (1980: 244: 2433–2437).

26. J.B. Mitchell and J. Cromwell, *op. cit.* Also, J. Studnicki, R.M. Saywell, and W. Wiechetek, "Foreign Medical Graduates and Maryland Medicaid," *New England Journal of Medicine* (1976: 294: 1153–1157). Also, B.B. Perlman, A.H. Schwartz, J.C. Thornton, *et al.*, "Medicaid-Funded Private Psychiatric Care in New York City," *New England Journal of Medicine* (1978: 299, 230–234).

27. Under Chapter 372, Medicaid reimburses hospitals at a lower rate than other payers. Thus hospitals have a disincentive to care for Medicaid patients.

28. B. Spitz and J. Holahan, *Modifying Medicaid Eligibility and Benefits* (Washington, D.C.: The Urban Institute, 1977).

29. R.G. Beck, "The Effects of Copayment on the Poor," *Journal of Human Resources* (1974: 9: 129–141). Also, J.P. Newhouse, W.G. Manning, C.N. Morris, *et al.*, "Some Interim Results from a Controlled Trial of Cost Sharing in Health Insurance," *New England Journal of Medicine* (1981: 305: 1501–1507). Also, M.I. Roemer, C.E. Hopkins, L. Carr, and F. Gartside, "Copayments for Ambulatory Care: Penny-Wise and Pound-Foolish," *Medical Care* (1975: 13: 457–466).

30. H.S. Luft, "How do Health-Maintenance Organizations Achieve Their 'Savings'?" *New England Journal of Medicine* (1978: 298: 1336–1343). Also, C. Gaus, B. Cooper, and C. Hirschman, "Contrasts in HMO and Fee-for-Service Performance," *Social Security Bulletin* (1976: 39(5): 3–14). Also, N.A. Fuller, M.W. Patera, and K. Koziol, "Medicaid Utilization of Services in a Prepaid Group Practice Health Plan," *Medical Care* (1977: 15: 705–737).

31. B. Spitz, "Primary Care Networks and Medicaid: A Background Paper," presented at the National Governors' Association Conference on Primary Care Networks/Case Management Systems (New Orleans, La., December 2, 1981).

32. I.L. Burney, G.J. Schieber, M.O. Blaxall, and J.R. Gabel, "Medicare and Medicaid Physician Payment Incentives," *Health Care Financing Review* (1979: 1(1): 62–78). Also, J. Holahan, B. Spitz, W. Pollack, and J. Feder, *Altering Medicaid Provider Reimbursement Methods* (Washington, D.C.: The Urban Institute, 1977).

33. W.G. Weissert, "Long-Term Care: An Overview," in Office of the Assistant Secretary for Health, Public Health Service, U.S. Department of Health, Education, and Welfare, *Health, United States, 1978* (Washington, D.C.: U.S. Government Printing Office, 1978: 91–109).

34. U.S. General Accounting Office, *Entering a Nursing Home—Costly Implications for Medicaid and the Elderly* (Washington, D.C.: U.S. Government Printing Office, 1979). Also, Office of the Secretary, Department of Health and Human Services, *Report of the Under Secretary's Task Force on Long-Term Care* (Washington, D.C.: U.S. Department of Health and Human

Services, 1981). Also, *Final report of the 1981 White House Conference on Aging* (Washington, D.C.: U.S. Government Printing Office, 1982).

35. U.S. General Accounting Office, *The Elderly Should Benefit from Expanded Home Health Care, But Increasing These Services Will Not Insure Cost Reductions* (Washington, D.C.: U.S. Government Printing Office, 1982).

36. *Ibid.*

37. K. Davis, "Primary Care for the Medically Underserved: Public and Private Financing," in *Changing Roles in Serving the Underserved: Public and Private Responsibilities and Interests* (Washington, D.C.: American Health Planning Association, 1981: 27–50).

38. K. Davis, *Ibid.* Also, P. Smith, "How Should Advocates of Low-Income People Respond to Reduced Federal Funding for Boston's Neighborhood Health Centers?" Master's thesis (Cambridge, Mass.: John F. Kennedy School of Government, 1982).

39. L.I. Hochheiser, K. Woodward, and E. Charney, "Effects of the Neighborhood Health Center on the Use of Pediatric Emergency Departments in Rochester, New York," *New England Journal of Medicine* (1971: 285: 148–152). Also, M. Klein, K. Roghmann, K. Woodward, and E. Charney, "The Impact of the Rochester Neighborhood Health Center on Hospitalization of Children, 1968 to 1970," *Pediatrics* (1973: 51: 833-829). Also, K. Davis, *op. cit.*

40. B.C. Duggar, B. Balicki, S. Lazarus, *et al.*, *Final Report for Community Health Center Cost-Effectiveness Evaluation* (McClean, Va.: JRB Associates, Inc., 1980).

41. L. Gordis, "Effectiveness of Comprehensive Care Programs in Preventing Rheumatic Fever," *New England Journal of Medicine* (1973: 289: 331–335).

42. K. Davis and C. Schoen, *Health and the War on Poverty: A Ten-Year Appraisal* (Washington, D.C.: The Brookings Institution, 1978). Also, K. Davis, *op. cit.*

43. B.C. Duggar *et al.*, *op. cit.*

44. M. Kotelchuck, J. Schwartz, M. Anderka, and K. Finison, *1980 Massachusetts Special Supplemental Food Program for Women, Infants, and Children (WIC) Evaluation Report* (Boston, Mass.: Commonwealth of Massachusetts, 1981). Also, E. Kennedy, S. Gershoff, *et al.*, "The Effect of Supplemental Feeding on Birthweight," paper presented at the annual meeting of the American Public Health Association, (1979).

45. J. Harris, "Prenatal Medical Care and Infant Mortality," conference paper no. 84 (Cambridge, Mass.: National Bureau of Economic Research, 1981). Also, F. Goldman and M. Grossman, "The Responsiveness and Impacts of Public Health Policy. The Case of Community Health Centers," paper presented at the annual meeting of the American Public Health Association (1981). Also, J.C. Sinclair, G.W. Torrance, M.H. Boyle, S.P. Horwood, S. Saigal, and D.L. Sackett, "Evaluation of Neonatal-Intensive-Care Programs," *New England Journal of Medicine* (1981: 305: 489–494). Also, R.L. Williams and P.M. Chen, "Identifying the Sources of the Recent Decline in Perinatal Mortality Rates in California," *New England Journal of Medicine* (1982: 306: 207–214).

46. D.M. Berwick and A.L. Komaroff, "Cost Effectiveness of Lead Screening," *New England Journal of Medicine* (1982: 306: 1392–1398).

Chapter 4

PRIMARY AND SECONDARY EDUCATION AND THE POOR

by Rosemary C. Salomone

In the past decade educational governance in this country has undergone a dramatic transformation. The roles played by federal, state, and local governments and the goals established by the political process have changed. The 1960s ushered in a new era of federal policymaking through a series of grants aimed at narrowly defined populations and programs. The 1970s witnessed an increase in state control, building on the federal base of the 1960s, as state legislatures and education agencies became increasingly involved in the daily work of local school districts. State administration of federal categorical grants, requirements for educational accountability, and state programs for children with special needs all give evidence of growing state intervention in establishing educational goals and priorities. During the 1970s, state aid for local schools rose by $27.3 billion, while local support increased by only $19.7 billion. Stated differently, state aid increases surpassed local revenue increases by nearly 50 percent during those years.[1] The current political and economic climate points to an even stronger leadership role to be played by state legislatures and departments of education in the years ahead.

This increase in state responsibility and control comes at a low point in the history of American public schooling. In recent years, a number of forces have coalesced so as to divert public attention and financial resources away from public education, particularly

NOTE: The author wishes to acknowledge the assistance of Robert O. Harrison, a doctoral candidate at the Harvard Graduate School of Education, who served as research assistant on this project.

75

with regard to poor children. The federal government is with-drawing incrementally the meager 8.1 percent of educational revenues it provided in FY 1982[2], weakening the legal mandate to serve disadvantaged populations, retreating from the enforce-ment of that mandate, and shifting policymaking to the state and local levels through grant consolidation with weakened fiscal controls. Changing demographics and middle class flight have left the public schools of the older cities with a poor and politi-cally powerless clientele. The failure of the system to adequately prepare students for the working world has eroded the confi-dence of its public constituency. Increased pressure for direct and indirect aid to non-public schools threatens to divert addi-tional funds from the public school sector. Voter-initiated prop-erty tax limitations (such as Proposition 2½ in Massachusetts) have diluted the primary source of revenue for school systems and have resulted in reduced educational services, particularly in communities with low property wealth.

Within this adverse climate of weakened voter confidence and decreased federal and local support, state governments are strug-gling to redefine their role in educational governance. Depending on their individual political culture,[3] some states will respond apathetically to the present crisis in public education; others will seize the opportunity to examine the piecemeal legislation of the past decade and to design comprehensive legislative policy and administrative programs for a public school population that has grown increasingly poor and linguistically diverse in composition.

From the current political and social context emerge three issues that will dominate the question of educating the poor in the 1980s:

1. *Governance.*   Local tax limitations and federal cutbacks have placed state governments in a pivotal role with regard to educational finance and governance. States are struggling to redefine their role vis a vis local communities while, within state government itself, legislatures and departments of education must develop new strategies for joint efforts toward meeting state objectives.

2. *Equity.*   Overall declining resources must now be directed to communities and populations with the most severe fiscal and educational needs. Communities differ widely in their ability to supplement state education funds from local sources, in the cost of providing educational services, in the range of other public services that compete with education for local dollars, and in the educational needs of students. On this last point, it is widely accepted that in order to afford the racial, ethnic, and linguistic

minorities which increasingly dominate urban schools equal access to educational opportunity, additional funds and unique instructional services are required.

3. *Effectiveness.* The public has become increasingly intolerant of the perceived waste of already strained tax dollars. There are those who believe that public schooling has suffered largely from mismanagement and a lack of standards against which achievement may be measured. States must now exercise stronger leadership in instructional design and management to assure program effectiveness.

This chapter looks at one state, Massachusetts, and suggests strategies for addressing the issue of educating the poor. The recommendations are, of course, applicable elsewhere as well. The following discussion is based upon three premises, the first two of which have received broad support in the recent literature on effective schools[4] and the last of which is founded in state constitutional law and the court opinions of the school finance reform movement. The first premise is that all children can learn—that every child, regardless of socio-economic background, can benefit from quality education. Second, the public educational system has developed organizational and instructional strategies for providing effective education for poor children. Third, the ultimate legal responsibility for providing an adequate and appropriate education for all children lies at the state and not the local level.

It is proposed here that Masssachusetts approach the problem of achieving educational excellence for poor children from two vantage points. It is recommended, first, that the state legislature assume a more active role in resource allocation, tempered by fiscal constraints, to assure that state funds are in fact expended at the local level to meet the state-identified needs of the poor and, second, that the state education department assume a stronger leadership role with regard to instructional design, comprehensive program planning, and overall accountability.

Educational Governance

While the major educational equity initiatives of the past two decades have resulted primarily from federal action, educational authority does not stem from the federal Constitution but is rather reserved to the states under the Tenth Amendment. The states have assumed the responsibility for operating an educational system at the public expense through variously worded state constitutional provisions guaranteeing a "thorough and efficient," "ample and sufficient," or "free public" education to children within a given age range. Through enabling legislation, states have established an administrative superstructure to oversee this charge and have delegated responsibility for the daily operation of educational programs to local school districts. In fact, all states except Hawaii designate school districts as agents of the state. In Massachustts educational authority and responsibility are derived from Part Two, Chapter V, Section II of the state constitution which reads in part:

> ... it shall be the duty of legislatures and magistrates, in all future periods of the Commonwealth, to cherish the interests of literature and the sciences, and all seminaries of them; especially the university at Cambridge and grammar schools in the towns. . . .

The constitution guarantees that educational opportunities and advantages will be disseminated generally among all public school students in the state. Chapter 15 of the state laws establishes a Department of Education to operate under the supervision and control of a state Board of Education. The latter is granted broad regulatory and enforcement powers over education in the state, including the establishment of minimum educational standards, the planning and approval of federal programs, the recommendation of changes in the state aid formula, and the withholding of state and federal funds from school committees found in non-compliance with the law and regulations. Finally, Chapter 71 of the state law obligates every town to maintain a sufficient number of free public schools and to provide instruction in a broadly defined list of designated areas.[5]

The state's political culture has been dominated by a strong predilection for local control. Until it was recently withdrawn by Proposition 2½, individual school districts enjoyed fiscal autonomy and local communities bore the major burden of financing public education. In fact, in FY 1982 the state's share of education costs was only 38.4 percent as compared with an average of 49.0 percent across the other 49 states, ranging from 6.9 percent in New Hampshire to 87.1 percent in Hawaii.[6]

The education clause contained in the state constitution as stated above provides an ambiguously worded mandate to the state legislature with regard to the maintenance of a public school system. Part One, Articles, I, VI, and VII of the Declaration of Rights of the Massachusetts Constitution further guarantees the equal protection of the laws to all. It can be argued that while the state legislature may delegate to cities and towns the authority to maintain the daily operation of public schools, it may not delegate the ultimate responsibility. If, in fact, the state is responsible for educating all the children within a given age range who reside within its borders, the next question is how much education is the legal entitlement of each child.

This latter argument shifts the focus of school finance from disequalization to deprivation, from equality of expenditures to "appropriateness" and "adequacy" of services, two concepts that have received considerable attention in the educational debate of recent years. The implication here is that equal dollars are insufficient to meet the high-cost educational needs of children. Incident to poverty is educational deprivation. And overlapping with the poor is a significant population of linguistic minority and handicapped students. Finally, the poor must be granted access to the benefits and protection provided for all.

School Finance Reform and the Search for Equity

Education in this country has developed largely as a matter of national concern, state responsibility, and local function. Beginning in the 1960s with Lyndon Johnson's "War on Poverty," the national concern was directed toward the economically and educationally impoverished condition of minority groups whose interests traditionally had been neglected by an anti-urban bias in state legislatures.[7] Head Start programs provided pre-school education to poor children between the ages of three and five years. Title I of the Elementary and Secondary Education Act of 1965 provided remedial instruction in reading and mathematics to economically and educationally disadvantaged students. The Bilingual Education Act of 1968 served as a stimulus for local school systems to develop model projects to meet the educational needs of linguistic minorities. The rationale underlying these federal efforts was as follows: Educational failure is disproportionately the experience of the poor and is correlated with adult poverty. The poor tend to reside in certain geographic areas. A disproportionate number of underachievers are members of racial minorities who have historically suffered from neglect, discrimination, and disenfranchisement. Extra governmental assistance would afford these groups equal access to educational opportunity. Finally, it was believed that federal initiative would stimulate the development of similar poverty programs among states.[8]

While the federal share has never reached 10 percent of overall education revenues, the federal initiative has stimulated debate on the educational needs of the poor and has served as the engine for the state school finance reform movement. In the late 1960s, reformers began to examine the larger context of local-state school finance and found wide interdistrict disparities in per pupil expenditures as a function of disparities in property wealth and taxing power. In states such as Massachusetts, which traditionally has relied on the local property tax as the primary source of educational revenue, interdistrict disparities in property wealth became of particular concern for those seeking quality education for the poor as well as for those seeking tax reform. Reform advocates observed that taxpayers in property-poor communities had to exert a higher tax effort (tax rate) in order to generate a given number of education dollars as compared with property-rich communities. In many communities low property wealth was correlated with low resident income. The ability of taxpayers in these communities to support higher property tax rates resulted in lower revenue receipts for educational services.

Federal funding initiatives have sought to erase the effects of poverty per se and to break the link between social class and the opportunity to enjoy the benefits of a free society. Equal educational opportunity has been defined as the *end* and the allocation of additional resources as the *means*. State initiatives at meeting needs of the poor, however, are carried out in a more politically complex climate of competing goals, a narrower tax base, and larger portions of overall revenues at stake. The goals of state school finance reform in general have been to achieve equity not only for students but also for taxpayers.

Equity is a broad concept encompassing justice, equality, humanity, morality, and right. It is abstract and not easily definable. It is concerned with group, not individual, rights and is based on a system of distributive justice. As used in school finance reform parlance, equity looks toward identified groups: children and taxpayers residing in property-poor, high-need, and high-cost communities. The "equitable" distribution of resources is based on more than mere property values. Equity with regard to students recognizes that school districts vary as to the costs in purchasing a given amount of school services (cost differentials); as to the competing demands of other public services such as health and police and fire protection, particularly in urban areas (municipal overburden); and as to the needs of high-cost populations including low-achieving and low-income students, linguistic minorities, and the handicapped (needs differentials). Fair treatment for all may require some inequalities in the distribution of resources. School finance reformers have suggested that educational equity can be achieved by "leveling up"—that is, by infusing more state tax revenues into education, by reallocating state revenues at the existing appropriation level, or in the extreme by "recapturing" funds (redistributing revenues raised by wealthy districts beyond a certain level to poor districts).

The early reform efforts of the 1970s targeted additional state aid to low-wealth, high-need school districts through "leveling up." Large budgeted surpluses in states such as California helped reformers realize their equity goals.[9] However, in the depressed fiscal climate of recent years, "leveling up" to achieve educational equity demands new and/or larger sources of state revenue, while reallocation at existing appropriations levels remains politically unpopular and "recapturing" funds politically unthinkable.

In some respects, Massachusetts has assumed a leadership role in the search for equity. The state was one of the first to adopt a racial imbalance act. Its legislation (Chapter 766) providing for the needs of handicapped students has not only served as a model for national initiatives but guarantees more comprehensive services and protections than the federal law. Massachusetts was one of the first of sixteen states to mandate bilingual education for linguistic minority students, a mandate not clearly defined in federal law. In addition to legal mandates, the state has attempted to achieve a more equitable distribution of state funds for education through legislative reform. As will be demonstrated, however, the financing scheme has fallen short of its equity goals.

Educational Effectiveness

The fundamental question underlying the discussion which follows is how to design state-level policies that will provide poor children with resources that effectively support learning. The myriad of cost-benefit studies on education conducted in the past fifteen years have yielded inconclusive findings on this point. Based on economic models, these studies have sought a relationship between school resources and student achievement. Findings indicate little or no correlation between such input measures as teacher experience, quality of facilities, or per pupil expenditures, on the one hand, and student performance on standardized achievement tests on the other.[10] Other studies have found a relationship between smaller class size and higher student achievement levels.[11] More recent research has broadened the definition of education resources or inputs to include characteristics of teachers and classmates, indicators of teacher quality, the amount of time devoted to given learning tasks such as basic skills, and the implementation of specific instructional techniques. Preliminary findings indicate that the primary determinants of school effectiveness are teachers and students, while physical facilities, class size, curricula, and instructional strategies can be viewed as secondary resources. It has been observed that students learn more when they spend more time "on task" at basic skill development and that disadvantaged students who attend schools that serve a significant number of children from higher socio-economic backgrounds demonstrate higher achievement levels. Students also learn more when they are taught by talented, highly motivated teachers who believe that their students can learn.[12]

What we have learned from the quantitative research on school effectiveness is that schools do make difference. What remains inconclusive from research findings, however, is whether additional financial resources are crucial to realizing that difference. The lack of consensus on this issue has fueled the fires of discontent among those who believe that public schooling, particularly in urban areas, has suffered largely from mismanagement coupled with a complexity of social problems the system is ill-equipped to handle. It must be recognized that some school systems are indeed mismanaged. It must also be recognized that public schools are called upon to serve an increasingly high-cost population of economically disadvantaged, handicapped, and linguistic minority students and to provide a range of services beyond mere instruction, including counseling, vocational training, and nutrition.

A 1982 report published by the Massachusetts Advocacy Center highlights a broad spectrum of educational problems pertaining specifically to poor children in the state.[13] In 1980, although blacks comprised 6 percent of the overall school population and 7.9 percent of the special education population statewide, only 2.4 percent of students enrolled in pre-school special education were black. The annual dropout rate for high school students was 20 percent for fiscal years 1979–1980, with 25 percent of that group having left school for economic reasons. In Boston the dropout rate between 9th and 12th grades during those years was 47 percent. Statistics demonstrate a marked disparity in suspensions by racial group. For blacks the rate is 10.7 per hundred, while for white students the rate is only 4.63. Public school attendance in Boston is the lowest of the 13 largest urban school districts in the country, with an average daily attendance of only 81.8 percent during the 1980–1981 school year. Data on student achievement is equally revealing. For the 1980–1981 school year, 9th, 10th, and

11th grade students in Boston were reading on the average at least two and a half years below grade level as measured by standardized test scores. Reading scores for grades three through eleven in Boston had been below the national median for the previous nine years. During the 1980–1981 school year, one out of five black students and one out of four Hispanic students, as compared with one out of ten white students, failed to meet local standards in basic skills.

These sobering truths have eroded public confidence in the schools and have led to the search for educational alternatives outside the public school system. However, the cost society will bear from disinvesting in public education may be far greater than additional expenditures. The economics and political benefits to be gained by society at large from a system of free and effective public education aimed at producing self-sufficient, productive, and informed citizens capable of participating in the political process have long been recognized.[14] It now rests with the state to develop financial, organizational, and instructional strategies to meet both the individual and societal goals of public schooling.

Rich Towns, Poor Towns

Before proceeding to any discussion of educational services to the poor, some guidelines must be established to identify the population under discussion. Since state education funds are allocated to local school districts whose boundaries are largely coterminous with towns or cities, it is the school district which typically serves as the unit of analysis.

School districts can be labeled rich or poor on several factors: on the basis of the number and percentage of students eligible to participate in the school lunch program, on the basis of income levels as a measure of the community's ability to exert a given local tax effort to finance the schools, and on the basis of property wealth as a measure of a community's ability to generate local revenue to operate its school system. Viewed in the aggregate, these various measures clearly indicate that poverty is concentrated in certain areas, particularly in urban centers, and that school-age children comprise a sizable segment of the poor population.

Low-Income Students

Public and private schools throughout the state annually report the numbers of low-income students based upon any of four

criteria including school lunch participation, status as a state
ward, membership in a family receiving AFDC payments, and
established poverty guidelines. School lunch participation, however, serves as the most commonly used criterion. During the
1980–1981 school year a total of 152,589 children were identified
as low-income by the state's 436 local and regional school districts. Table 4–1 indicates the numbers and percentages of low-
income children residing in the 12 school districts with the highest
percentages of low-income students statewide. These twelve
districts include 54.4 percent of all such students throughout the
state. Of the 83,073 low-income students within that group, 39.5
percent attend schools in Boston.

Income as a Measure of Poverty

According to data drawn from the 1980 Census (see Chapter 2), a
total of 532,458 persons, or 9.6 percent of the Massachusetts
population for whom poverty status is determined, had a 1979
income below the poverty level: 26.3 percent, or 140,277 of
these individuals, were between the ages of 15 and 17 years. For
the 12 school districts identified by school lunch data as low-income, the percentage of persons with income in 1979 below the
poverty level was considerably higher than statewide. For exam-

Table 4–1   Distribution of Low-Income Children in School Districts with 20
Percent or More Low-Income Membership.

	Net Average* Membership (NAM)	Total Low-Income Membership	Percentage Low-Income Membership
Boston	67,747.8	32,828	48.5%
Springfield	25,527.2	10,660	41.8
Holyoke	7,753.5	3,182	41.0
Lawrence	9,812.5	4,010	40.9
New Bedford	16,006.5	5,020	31.4
Lynn	13,256.3	3,891	29.4
Worcester	22,685.2	6,637	29.3
Fall River	14,209.7	4,029	28.3
Lowell	14,614.5	3,911	26.8
Somerville	9,266.4	2,281	24.6
Cambridge	8,869.3	2,155	24.3
Brockton	19,140.4	4,469	23.3
Total	228,889.3	82,073	Average 36.3

SOURCE: *1980–81 Distribution of Low-Income Children,* Massachusetts Department of
Education, Bureau of Data Collection and Reporting.
* Average number of students in attendance throughout school year.

ple, Boston shows a percentage of 20.2; Holyoke, 19.3; Lawrence, 19.3; and Springfield, 17.8. The average percentage below the poverty line for all 12 districts combined was 15.8, or 1.6 times the statewide percentage of 9.6.[15] The forgoing data indicate that poor children, as identified by several poverty indices including family income, are concentrated in significant numbers in certain communities. Providing additional state aid to such communities compensates for their relative inability to support high property tax rates and assists them in meeting the high-cost needs of their disadvantaged student population.

Property Wealth and the Ability to Support Schools

Property wealth is determined by equalized assessed valuations per capita. In a financing system where 53.8 percent of educational revenues in FY 1982 were derived from local sources and where the local property tax serves as the primary means of generating local school funds, the equalized assessed valuations of real property serve as a significant measure of a community's ability to support its schools. In FY 1982 the equalized valuation per capita among the 351 school districts in Massachusetts ranged from a low of $6,209 in Chelsea to a high of $392,560 in Rowe. Included within this range are the 17 school districts at the uppermost extreme with equalized valuations per capita above $50,000, many of them resort towns with high property wealth and low year-round population.[16] Even excluding these figures, equalized valuations per capita in the 334 remaining districts in FY 1982 still covered a range of $42,898. Property wealth has been linked with expenditures per pupil and has been seen as a measure of a community's ability to finance public schools through the local property tax. Some communities, therefore, are more fiscally able to support educational services than others. This issue will be addressed in the following discussion of school finance, particularly in the context of interdistrict disparaties in wealth and expenditures.

Financing Educational Services in Massachusetts

Massachusetts, as many other states, has undertaken a series of legislative initiatives in its quest to achieve a more equitable distribution of state funds for education and ultimately to assure that adequate educational services are provided to all students. However, the issue of school finance reform in Massachusetts, as elsewhere, has been rendered more complex in recent years by an adverse political and economic climate. Any state initiatives to increase state funding for education must take into consideration the loss of federally earmarked funds for the poor as well as reductions in local revenues, particularly in low-wealth communities. If poor children are to receive effective instruction, allocation strategies must be developed at the legislative level to assure that the educational needs of this population continue to be met.

General Aid to Education

Recognizing inadequacies of the existing school finance scheme in its stated purpose to equalize educational opportunity as well as tax burdens across school districts, the Masachusetts legislature in 1978 revised the school aid formula with the added legislative purpose of reducing reliance upon the local property tax in financing public schools.[15] Several aspects of the present formula deserve particular note with respect to the education of the poor.

First, the formula has never been fully funded. The goal of 50 percent state funding has never been reached. For FY 1982 the state contribution amounted to 38.4 percent of overall educational expenditures. Secondly, the present formula fails to earmark funds specifically for educationally and economically disadvantaged students. Using the weighted pupil concept, state aid is determined each year by multiplying the number of full-time equivalent (FTE) students in special education, vocational education, bilingual education, and regular day programs by the average per pupil cost statewide for each category of service. In addition, a low-income weighting of 0.2 is used to reflect the high cost needs of Chapter 1 (formerly Title I) eligible students.[18] While the low-income weighting demonstrates a state legislative concern for poor children, the legislation provides no safeguards to assure that state funds are in fact expended on these students at the local level. Unlike states such as Connecticut, Maryland, Michigan, New York, Rhode Island, Texas, Utah, and Wisconsin, which have included a non-supplantation provision within their compensatory education legislation,[19] Massachusetts has failed to impose any fiscal or programmatic constraints to assure that school districts provide additional services to the population of poor whose members generate the additional revenues.

It must be underscored that poor students lose more than other identified groups under such a system of weightings combined with non-earmarking of education funds. While federal and state legal mandates assure that handicapped and linguistic minority students receive increased expenditures and services, there exists no similar legislation protecting the educational rights of the poor. As special and bilingual education costs have mounted, school districts have channelled a disproportionate amount of state and local aid into these programs to assure legal compliance. In fact, in Massachusetts the state subsidy for special education is direct. Chapter 766, lacking a separate state appropriation, is funded off the top of the regular local educational aid budget, thus directly reducing the amount of state funds remaining to support the equalization formula. Given local cutbacks and federal reductions in Chapter 1 programs, school districts are hard pressed to provide the basic skills remediation typically needed by that segment of poor students who are not identified for special or bilingual education.

A third aspect of the present formula that works against poor communities is the hold harmless provision. High-wealth districts are guaranteed to receive no less than 107 percent of their adjusted state education aid as received in FY 1979. This provision has severely undercut the equalizing effect of the formula. Approximately 85 percent of local school districts in FY 1980 were identified as hold harmless. These districts represent high property valuation per capita and typically demonstrate fewer weighted FTE pupils (high-cost special, bilingual, and low-income pupils drive the weighted FTE's up) and high per pupil expenditures. It has been argued that hold harmless provisions such as the one operating under the present Massachusetts formula do not result in a windfall to high-wealth districts but merely compensate for inflationary costs and thereby maintain level per pupil funding. But this argument is vitiated when one considers that these same districts are experiencing declining enrollments and, with traditionally lower property tax rates and higher full-market value assessed valuations, are feeling a lighter pinch from Proposition 2½ decreases in local revenues. It cannot be disputed that hold harmless school districts are receiving funds that would have been allocated to low-wealth school districts absent the 107 percent guarantee.

Finally, a preliminary analysis of school district data reveals that the current state finance formula has failed to reach its legislative goal of equalizing tax burdens across the state. This failure relates directly to taxpayer equity but may well become a student equity issue in the context of local fiscal retrenchment. In fact, several noteworthy observations can be made from the data presented in Table 4–2.

First, in order to maintain per pupil expenditures at a given level, low-wealth districts must exert a higher school tax effort consistently and at the average rate of 4.93 as compared with high-wealth districts. A comparison of overall tax rates is even

Table 4-2 Comparison of Low and High Property Wealth School Districts by Fiscal Ability, Tax Effort, and Expenditures

| Property Wealth | City/Town | Fiscal Ability | | Tax Effort | | | Expenditure per Student (NAM) |
| | | Median Family Income in 1979 Dollars* | Equalized Assessed Valuation per Capita† | Equalized Tax Rate‡ | | | |
				Total	School	%	
Low	Worcester	$18,120	$ 8,832	$ 66.00	$20.34	32%	$2,410.87
High	Belmont	27,719	22,789	37.69	14.61	41	2,458.52
Low	Brockton	18,606	9,784	56.00	23.29	41	2,002.71
High	Essex	18,992	22,158	26.39	11.75	45	2,002.25
Low	Holyoke	16,854	8,588	42.84	10.20	24	1,895.42
High	Plymouth	20,118	27,283	33.00	12.59	38	1,909.15
Low	Somerville	18,220	8,454	66.14	13.33	20	2,114.04
High	Braintree	24,810	20,998	42.18	16.92	40	2,180.45
Low	Cambridge	17,845	13,544	70.28	18.47	26	3,474.56
High	Rowe	21,875	392,560	6.80	1.51	22	3,543.91
Low	Fall River	14,810	6,394	61.76	12.64	20	2,048.21
High	Otis	16,964	49,107	16.17	7.91	49	2,050.49
Low	Lawrence	15,457	8,160	48.87	10.30	21	2,013.25
High	Sunderland	17,746	14,442	16.44	9.24	56	1,979.74
Low	Lowell	17,942	8,239	53.18	10.13	19	1,947.46
High	New Marlborough	16,161	41,250	11.67	6.46	55	1,970.09

Low	Lynn	18,458	9,256	80.84	17.46	22%	2,078.43
High	Tyringham	21,563	47,442	9.50	3.78	40	2,109.97
Low	New Bedford	14,430	7,535	54.08	9.96	18	1,886.13
Low	Springfield	16,607	8,633	57.50	11.04	19	1,891.04
High	Sandwich	22,348	46,625	15.00	8.23	55	1,914.29
Low	Boston	18,606	9,306	114.73	19.79	17	3,154.85
High	Wellesley	36,745	29,501	30.50	15.02	49	3,295.16
Average (High)		$22,276	$ 64,293 (with Rowe) / $ 32,160 (without Rowe)	$ 22.31	$ 9.82	45%	$2,310
Average (Low)		$17,163	$ 8,894 (with Rowe)	$ 64.35	$14.75	23%	$2,243
Difference		$ 5,113	$ 55,399 (with Rowe) / $ 23,266 (without Rowe)	$-42.04	$-4.93	22%	$ 67

*Summary of Social and Economic Characteristics, 1980 (U.S. Census Bureau, 1982).

†School Revenues and Expenditures in Massachusetts Cities and Towns: Fiscal Year 1979–1980, Massachusetts Department of Education, Bureau of Data Collection and Reporting.

‡1979–1980 Year-End Report, Management Information for School Committees, Massachusetts Association of School Committees.

more striking, with taxpayers in low-wealth districts paying taxes at a rate of 42.04 higher than those in high-wealth districts. Using average family income as a measure of a community's ability to bear a given tax burden to support its schools, it is clear that the taxpayers in the low-property-wealth districts presented in Table 4–2, with a combined median family income of $5,113 below those in high-property-wealth districts, have fewer income dollars with which to support the public school system.

A second observation to be drawn from the data relates to "municipal overburden." According to this concept, urban school districts must compete with the high tax demands of other public services such as police, fire, and sanitation. These latter services receive broad constituent support among the general population of users. The public schools in the cities, on the other hand, are progressively declining in constituent support while serving a larger clientele of the poor—a group with marginal political power. As Table 4–2 indicates, the school tax in high-wealth suburban school districts represents, on the average, 22 percent more of the overall tax rate as compared with school tax rates in low-wealth urban districts. A larger proportion of property tax revenues in cities such as Worcester, Brockton, Holyoke, and Somerville must be allocated to meet critical demands for other essential public services. As low-wealth districts annually reduce their typically high tax rates by 15 percent until the rate of 2.5 percent of full market value of all taxable property is reached under Proposition 2½, the drain on school services may reach critical proportions. As discussed in the following section on the impact of Proposition 2½, first-year data indicate that school services in general have been reduced disproportionately as compared with other municipal services.

Municipal overburden is not factored into the current school finance formula in Massachusetts, but pre-Proposition 2½ data indicate that it does reduce the local revenue available for school services. And post-Proposition 2½ data further reveal that the problem has become magnified. Caught in the squeeze between high demands from other public services and reduced tax revenues on the local level and by cutbacks in aid for the disadvantaged at the federal level, poor children who typically reside in low-wealth and municipally over-burdened cities stand to lose the benefits of even basic instructional services.

Effects of Proposition 2½ on School Services

The state of Massachusetts is a prime example of what has been called the "new politics of state education finance," a tug of war between student equity and taxpayer equity. With the advent of the taxpayers' revolt in recent years, these interests no longer converge. When viewed within the context of a strong tradition of local control, on the one hand, and a state-level commitment to protect special group interests on the other, the statutory changes effected by Proposition 2½ make a significant impact upon the entire system of educational governance in the state. Looking at it from a broader policy perspective, Proposition 2½ and its aftermath provide some revealing insights into the inevitable consequences of taxing and spending limitations in the absence of a booming state economy.

Proposition 2½ is directly linked to education of the poor in several ways. First, it requires communities to reduce their property tax rates by 15 percent annually until they reach 2½ percent of full market value. In a state where the local property tax serves as the primary source of education aid (53.8 percent in FY 1982), such severe reductions in tax rates must inevitably result in reduced services, particularly in communities characterized by low-wealth and high-tax effort. Of the 351 cities and towns in the state, 182 were required to reduce property taxes in FY 1982, with further reductions in 34 communities during FY 1983. According to the Department of Revenue estimates, approximately 11 of these will be required to reduce local levies up to 15 percent more in FY 1984.

Second, Proposition 2½ repealed "fiscal autonomy" under which school committees traditionally had exercised the power to determine local school budgets unilaterally. Repeal of this provision effectively places final approval of school budgets with the local legislative body, where education will be weighed in the balance with other public services. It has been argued that "fiscal autonomy" serves as a safeguard against supplantation of state education funds at the local level. Any local attempt at supplantation of state funds forces the locality to compensate for the difference with local revenue, hardly a winning proposition. The repeal of "fiscal autonomy" with its potential danger of supplantation promises to bear most heavily on low-wealth districts characterized by high competing demands for police, fire, and other public services.

Finally, Proposition 2½ prohibits the state from mandating new local services unaccompanied by the additional revenues needed for compliance. This provision limits the authority of the state legislature and department of education to mandate in the future specific programs and levels of service for state-identified populations as it has for the handicapped and limited-English-proficient students. These restrictions are prospective and will be discussed in further detail relative to the state's basic skills program.

Aside from its potential impact on educational governance, Proposition 2½ has had a direct impact on school budgets and services, with the severest cuts evidenced in low-wealth, high-need districts. The results of several studies support this conclusion. Based upon a survey of 132 cities and towns, including only 6 of the 21 communities with populations over 50,000 and excluding the three largest cities, the percentage by which preliminary 1982 budgets fell below 1981 budgets was found to range between 3.7 percent in the smallest communities and 9.6 percent in the largest.[20] A survey conducted by the Massachusetts Municipal Association on the first-year impact of 2½ on 75 cities and towns representing a cross-section of municipalities provides additional data on municipal service cutbacks. The report divides the group into 42 Moderate Impact and 33 Severe Impact Communities, the latter having rolled back their property tax levies by 10 percent or more and having made significant reductions in personnel. As can be seen from Figure 4-1, fire and police protection, which represent public services of broad usage across the population, received the lowest proportionate cuts. Schools, libraries, and recreation, on the other hand, were reduced by 9.9, 14.6, and 25.8 percent respectively. As stated in the report, Proposition 2½ has had the most severe impact in communities with the

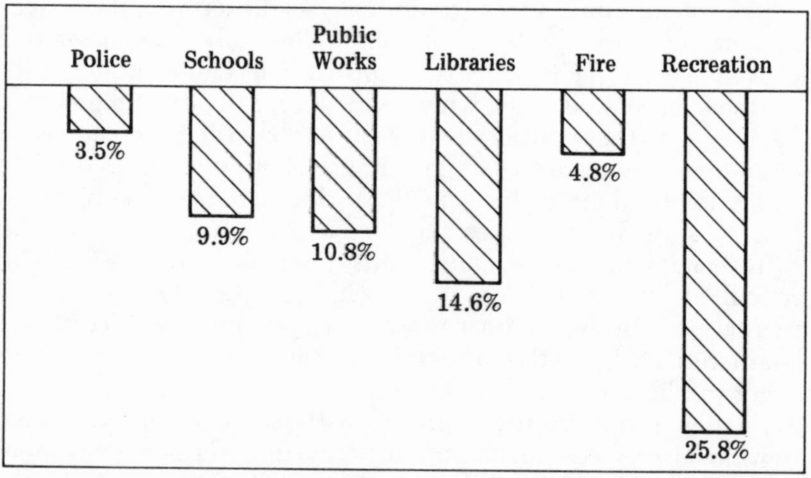

Figure 4-1   Municipal Budget Cuts by Department in Severe-Impact Communities. *Source: Report on the Impact of Proposition 2½* (Boston, Mass.: Massachusetts Municipal Association, January 1982).

densest population and the poorest inhabitants.[21] As the figures indicate, those districts have made disproportionately high reductions in services which the poor are less able to purchase in the open market—that is, education, library books, and recreation. The decision of local officials to protect public safety and to cut those areas considered less critical is understandable, but the potential impact of such reductions upon the overall educational development of poor children should not be underestimated.

According to another study that specifically examined the impact of Proposition 2½ on public education in the state, total local education appropriations were reduced on the average by 9.4 percent, as were instructional appropriations, while administrative services were reduced on the average by 6.8 percent. [22] As indicated in Table 4–3, the most severe reductions were made by cities, with 37.5 percent making severe cuts in total education appropriations as compared with 25.3 percent of suburbs, 24.3 percent of towns, and 12.5 percent of resorts. The higher percentages of fixed municipal expenses for debt payment and pensions (which typically burden cities) necessitate deeper cuts in other services when forced by fiscal cutbacks. However, cities are also characterized by high percentages of low-income students whose educational needs are costlier (remedial programs, bilingual instruction, counseling, and food services) and on whom educational cutbacks have a severe impact. In fact, as Table 4–3 further indicates, the highest incidence of severe cuts made by cities was in instructional appropriations (53.1 percent) and teaching workforce (56.0 percent), the two budget items that relate most directly to the quality of educational services, as compared with only

Table 4–3 Percentage of School Districts Making Severe* Reductions in Education Services

	Cities	Suburbs	Towns	Resorts
Total local appropriations	37.5%	25.3%	24.3%	12.5%
Administrative appropriations	40.6	33.7	27.0	12.5
Instructional appropriations	53.1	29.1	24.3	0
Percentage of teaching workforce reduced	56.0	31.4	39.3	0
Percentage of schools closed	40.6	40.2	40.5	0

SOURCE: Edward P. Morgan, *Public Education and the Taxpayers' Revolt: The Causes and Consequences of Proposition 2½ in Massachusetts,* unpublished paper (May 1982). *"Severe" was defined as exceeding the median reduction among all districts reducing budgets. Cut-off points for each item were: Total—9.4%; Administrative—6.8%; Instructional—9.4% Workforce—13.4%; School Closings—14.3%.

40.6 percent having made severe reductions in administrative appropriations.

Finally, the constraints 2½ has placed on the revenue-raising capability of cities and towns have encouraged many communities to consider alternative revenue sources. Since local governments in the state are prohibited from imposing any local taxes other than the property tax, one of the only alternative revenue sources is user fees and charges.[23] According to a survey conducted by the Massachusetts Association of School Committees, in FY 1982, 99 communities initiated user fees for such services as athletics, extra-curricular activities, use of buildings, driver education, and instrumental music lessons.[24] Data collected by the Impact 2½ Project for case studies of 13 communities indicate an increase in fees charged for school lunches, transportation, and athletics programs. In Springfield the school lunch charge was increased by 25 percent, while Framingham school lunch fees increased from $0.40 in 1980, to $0.75 in 1981, to $1.25 in 1982. In a brief survey of 31 other cities and towns conducted by the town of Arlington, nearly half the communities surveyed stated that they already had or were considering a system of athletic fees. One school superintendent estimated that an average family with two children to bus, each of whom participated in one after-school activity, might be forced to spend $300 a year in user fees.[25] Obviously, such fees can price poor children out of educational services and particularly out of enrichment programs which they lack the resources to purchase in the marketplace.

Tax revolts in general, and Proposition 2½ in particular, have the potential of bearing negatively or positively on the quest for student equity in school finance reform: negatively by withdrawing the power of low-wealth communities to exert greater tax effort without a voter override and thereby linking school expenditures to property wealth by means of a fixed tax rate, or positively by forcing the state legislature to respond with additional equalized aid. Unlike other states where school finance reform has been used as a vehicle for tax reform, in Massachusetts the two represent clearly competing interests. Proposition 2½ has placed the issue squarely in the state legislature and added a factor to be considered in the equalization debate. Any new aid distributions must take into account local revenue losses resulting from Proposition 2½.

Improvement of Basic Skills: A Race and Poverty Issue

As stated earlier, economic and educational deprivation typically go hand-in-hand. The educational needs of poor children are more severe and costlier to meet than those of the general school population and cover a broad range of services, including remedial instruction, special education, bilingual education, career guidance, and vocational education.

The state of Massachusetts has provided for all the above except the first through a system of weightings within the Chapter 70 formula. Massachusetts presently does not provide, either legislatively or administratively, for a state compensatory education program aimed at providing remedial instruction to economically disadvantaged students. The problems inherent in such a gap in state funding have been highlighted in recent years by federal cutbacks in Chapter I funds for remediation and by the State Board of Education's attempt to impose a statewide basic skills improvement policy without the requisite state or local funds for effective implementation.

Any serious discussion of raising overall student achievement levels must consider the link between compensatory or remedial education and basic skills improvement, the correlation between low achievement and race or poverty, and the cooperative roles to be played by the state legislature and department of education in the implementation of a statewide policy to improve basic skills.

Federal Compensatory Aid

Title I of the Elementary and Secondary Education Act was enacted in 1965 as a categorial grant with the stated legislative purpose of providing "financial assistance to local educational agencies serving areas with concentrations of children from low-income families," and this purpose has continued into the 1981 amendments.[26] Over the years, however, Congress has enacted periodic amendments to the original legislation imposing fiscal constraints on local school districts as to expenditure of federal funds and defining the role of state departments of education in compliance monitoring, rulemaking, evaluation, and technical assistance. With the stated purpose of eliminating unneccessary and unproductive paperwork, of freeing schools from unnecessary federal control, and of protecting state and local personnel from overly prescriptive regulations, Chapter 1, as enacted in 1981, effectively places increased responsibility on the states for assuring that federal funds are expended on the intended target population of poor children and that effective educational programs are designed to meet their needs.

The Chapter 1 allotment for the State of Massachusetts for FY 1983 was $53 million. The 1981 legislation reduced the allowable allocation for state education department administration from

1.5 to 1.0 percent of the total state allocation. This grants the state an administrative budget of $530,000 to oversee a program serving approximately 60,000 students with a full-time local staff of approximtely 4,500 teachers, administrators, and aides. According to state education department sources, the decrease in state administrative funds resulted in five fewer staff positions, with a total of eight professionals remaining in the regional centers during the 1982–1983 school year. The lack of specificity in Chapter 1 has made states more fearful of audit exceptions.[27] Massachusetts, as many states, has given priority in allocating staff time to monitoring legal compliance. As a result, technical assistance in instructional programming has been left largely to the local school districts. However, many districts have cut resource staff positions under Proposition 2½ cutbacks and now lack such expertise in reading and math skill development.

State Compensatory Programs

As of 1982, 15 state legislatures had initited compensatory education programs with statutory provisions describing the types of services to be provided, the children to be served, and procedures for monitoring and program evaluation. Most of these are patterned after the federal Chapter 1 program and a few states explicitly tie their programs to Chapter 1. State compensatory programs vary widely as to student eligibility criteria, local school district requirements for use of funds, and funding approaches. Most states target funds to low-achieving students as measured by local or statewide achievement tests, while some states give priority to Chapter 1 eligible schools, using Chapter 1 poverty criteria. Most states have also established minimum requirements for the use of state funds.

Typically school districts must submit an annual plan describing how compensatory funds will be used. California, Connecticut, New York, and Rhode Island require consolidated applications for federal Chapter 1 and state compensatory funds. In fact, New York guidelines stipulate that Chapter 1 state compensatory funds be coordinated with locally funded remedial services as a comprehensive instructional program. The state education department in New York has developed guidelines related to local planning, staff development, and instructional content of remedial programs in reading, writing, and mathematics. Connecticut requires that, while funds are allocated on the basis of achievement scores, at least 75 percent of program funds must be expended on economically as well as educationally disadvantaged students. Finally, as for funding approaches, some states allocate funds on the basis of a flat grant per identified child, others on a pupil-weighting system, and still others as project grants that are either competitive or non-competitive.[28]

Minimum Competency Testing

Within the past decade, achievement test scores and anecdotal accounts of high school graduates who can barely read or write have given rise to a movement to improve school accountability and to ensure that students master certain minimal skills before receiving a high school diploma. To date, at least 36 states have established a program of minimum competency testing, approximately half of which use or plan to use test results to award a high school diploma. Others use the test scores to identify students in need of remediation.

Those programs that condition the receipt of a diploma or promotion on passing of the test are vulnerable to legal challenge. Opponents of minimum competency tests have noted the disproportionate numbers of minority students failing such tests and argue that the tests are racially and culturally biased. They further claim that certain of the tests do not reflect what is actually being taught in the schools and therefore lack curricular validity. Finally, critics maintain that competency tests must provide due process protections—that is, they must be phased in over time in order to give students adequate notice of the requirements for receipt of a high school diploma or promotion.[29]

Basic Skills Improvement Policy in Massachusetts

Massachusetts is among the 36 states identified as having initiated some form of competency testing program. That program clearly reflects the state's efforts to raise student achievement and instructional effectiveness within a strong political culture of local control and without additional funds to achieve policy objectives.

Pursuant to the State Board of Education *Policy on Basic Skills Improvement* (adopted in August 1978) and to the Board regulations (promulgated the following January), school districts were required to develop basic skills improvement program plans by August 1, 1980 for implementation during the 1980–1981 school year. Such plans were to include the skill areas of reading, writing, and mathematics for three grade levels: early elementary (K-3), later elementary (4-6), and secondary (7-12). School districts were required to submit to the State Education Department at the end of the 1980-1981 school year detailed data on student achievement and the testing instruments used.

The primary purpose of the *Policy* was "to assist all students to achieve mastery of basic skills prior to high school graduation through the provision of appropriate curriculum, instruction, and evaluation." The *Policy* was further designed to encourage local autonomy and flexibility in deciding minimum standards and evaluation instruments. At best, the program has heightened public awareness, has forced school districts to take initial steps toward addressing the problem, and has minimally strengthened the Department of Education's role in establishing accountability standards to improve instructional effectiveness throughout the state. At worst, the program has generated invalid comparisons among districts; has led to erroneous conclusions among educators, legislators, and the general public as to student achievement throughout the state; and has identified problems in individual students, schools, and districts that remain unremedied in the absence of additional funds.

Certain aspects of the testing program are particularly problematic and limit the utility of the data collected. First, the policy permits districts to establish their own minimum standards for assessing achievement. Therefore, a high failure rate in a given district may be a function of higher minimum achievement standards as compared with districts imposing lower standards. Secondly, districts may administer the tests at any grade within each of the three designated levels. Students tested in grade 4 are likely to achieve a lower score than those tested in another district in grade 6, even on the same test. Third, districts using the same test may use different sections or subtests within an achievement battery, yet state education department printouts do not include this information. Fourth, districts are not required to administer the tests at any given point in the school year. Even within the same grade, students tested in June can be expected to achieve higher scores than those tested on the same test in another district in September. Finally, the policy permits students to be exempted from the tests if they are identified for special education services or as having limited English ability. Districtwide scores therefore become partially a function of the willingness of school administrators to exercise this discretion and exclude these students from the testing program. For some districts, students of limited English ability represent a sizable percentage of the over-

all school population and their exclusion or inclusion can significantly skew scores in one direction or the other.

The lack of statewide minimum standards, evaluation instruments, testing periods, and designated grades for testing precludes any valid interdistrict comparison of basic skills testing
data. Therefore, the relative need for remediation programs
throughout the state cannot be identified on the basis of poverty
indices such as property or income wealth or on the severity of
Proposition 2½ reductions. It is well understood, however, that
poverty is related to race, and comparisons can be drawn among
racial/ethnic groups both statewide and within a given school
district.

As Table 4–4 indicates, not only is there a striking disparity in
the faiure rate on basic skills standards between minority and
white students, but that disparity increased between 1980–1981
and 1981–1982. Between the first and second years of the basic
skills improvement program, the overall percentages of students
not achieving minimum standards rose from 21 to 28 percent
among blacks, from 24 to 29 percent among Hispanics, and from
12 to 14 percent among "others," while that figure decreased
from 9 to 8 percent among white students. It is also clear that the
higher the grade level, the higher the failure rate for all four
racial/ethnic groups in both testing years.

As Table 4–5 indicates, testing data from several of the low-
wealth districts identified earlier in Table 4–2 reveal similar disparities. These represent urban school systems with high percentages of Chapter 1 eligible schools and proportionately large
Chapter 1 allocations from the federal government.

Furthermore, the potential effectiveness of the basic skills program has been undercut severely by state and local funding
limitations. At the state level, Proposition 2½ constrains the state
from prospectively mandating services at the local level without
providing the necessary funds from state coffers. The state therefore cannot mandate that local districts provide remediation
along with the basic skills testing program unless the state is
willing to provide the necessary funds. And given the severity of
local cutbacks, particularly in those low-wealth communities
most severely impacted by Proposition 2½, the ability of local
school districts to allocate funds for remedial instruction remains
questionable.

In Massachusetts, federal Chapter 1 programs in fact serve as
the sole source of funds specifically earmarked for the disadvantaged and for reading and math remediation. It can reasonably be concluded from the foregoing data that these programs

Table 4-4 Percentage of Students Not Achieving Minimum Standards in Basic Skills by Grade Level and Ethnic Group, 1980–1981 and 1981–1982

Grade Level	Black		Hispanic		White		Other*	
	1980–81	1981–82	1980–81	1981–82	1980–81	1981–82	1980–81	1981–82
K–3	17%	27%	18%	25%	8%	6%	8%	13%
4–6	22	24	24	29	9	8	9	10
7–12	23	32	29	32	11	10	18	18
Total	21	28	24	29	9	8	12	14

SOURCE: *Basic Skills Improvement Policy*, First Annual Report (December 1981) and Second Annual Report (February 1983), Massachusetts Department of Education.
*"Other" includes persons of American or Alaskan Native heritage and persons of Asian or Pacific Islander heritage.

Table 4-5   Percentage of Students Not Achieving Minimum Standards in Basic Skills by Ethnic Group in Select Low-Wealth School Districts, 1980–1981, and 1981–1982

School District	Black		Hispanic		White		Other	
	1980–81	1981–82	1980–81	1981–82	1980–81	1981–82	1980–81	1981–82
Boston	26%	28%	25%	25%	12%	14%	7%	9%
Cambridge	31	26	28	24	2	23	9	19
Lynn	21	21	22	21	9	7	18	14
Springfield	24	18	27	25	10	7	NA*	27
Worcester	21	29	26	35	7	13	20	22

SOURCE: Bureau of Research and Assessment, Massachusetts Department of Education.
*Across all children tested, none were classified as "other."

have proved inadequate in closing the achievement gap between the disadvantaged and the larger population. Two state-level solutions to the problem deserve serious consideration. One is to infuse additional state funds into remedial instruction to offset recent federal cutbacks and to increase present service levels. The other is to increase the capacity of the state education department to improve ovreall program effectiveness. Underlying both is a need to develop a comprehensive statewide basic skills program.

Federal Education Block Grants and Desegregation

In 1981 Congress enacted Chapter 2 of the Education Consolidation and Improvement Act, which merged 28 discretionary programs into one education block grant to be awarded to the states based on school-age population figures.[30] The legislative purpose of the consolidation was to reduce administrative and paperwork burdens, to permit the development of programs in accordance with the educational needs and priorities of state and local agencies, and to vest responsibility for the design and implementation of programs in local school districts.

While the block grant legislation has, in fact, granted greater discretion to local school officials, which is viewed by many as a positive effect, it has also resulted in a twofold negative impact on educational services, particularly in communities with large minority populations. First, the consolidation has diverted funds from the public school to the private school sector; second, it has eliminated the Emergency School Aid Act (ESAA), which provided funds for desegregation efforts. Those school districts that formerly received sizable grants under ESAA now receive only a proportionate share of the local state allocations. These adverse results stem from both the state formula implementing the law and the provisions of the law itself.

Under the legislation, each education department may retain 20 percent of the state allocation for its own use and must distribute at least 80 percent to local school districts on a formula basis in proportion to their relative student enrollments in public and nonpublic schools. Each state is required to devise its own allocation formula to take into account the needs of high-cost students such as those from low-income families. In Massachusetts the allocation formula recommended by the Governor's advisory council (as mandated by law) and implemented by the State

Education Department is as follows: 40 percent based on the number of students in each school district, including public and nonpublic schools; and 60 percent based on the number of low-income students in each school district. "Low-income" is defined using the same criteria as eligibility for Aid to Families with Dependent Children (AFDC).[31]

The Massachusetts formula is an attempt to strike a balance between the interests of urban school systems and those of school systems that have lost the competitive edge they formerly enjoyed by writing strong grant proposals for such programs as ESEA Title IV C, which provided grants for educational innovation. According to the Council of the Great City Schools, however, merger of ESAA desegregation funds into the block grant has resulted in considerable losses to large-city school districts with their disproportionate number of poor and minority students.[32] In fact, ESAA represents the only consolidated program that was formerly tied to a specific population and to the federally defined goal of promoting equal educational opportunity; all other programs were tied to the improvement of instruction.

Unlike a majority of the states, which turned a disinterested ear to the problem facing former ESAA recipients, the Massachusetts legislature responded to the loss in ESAA funds in FY 1983 with an additional allocation of approximately $500,000 under the state's Chapter 636 desegregation program. As Table 4–6 indicates, however, the state allocation fell short of total replacement of ESAA funds. As a result, urban school districts were forced to absorb even further cutbacks in service beyond those imposed by Proposition 2½.

Table 4–6 Comparison of FY 1982 ESAA Grants and FY 1983 Additional State Allocation Under Chapter 636

District	ESAA Grant FY 1982	Chapter 636 Additional Aid FY 1983	Difference
Cambridge	$350,000	$ 90,800	−$259,200
Holyoke	387,000	100,000	− 287,000
Lawrence	295,000	70,000	− 225,000
Lowell	225,000	99,896	− 125,104
Springfield	—	80,000	+ 80,000
Worcester	100,000	100,000	—

SOURCE: Informal Telephone Survey of Federal Grant Directors (October 1982).

Table 4-7 Comparison of Federal Funds Allocated to Public and Non Public Schools in Select Low-Wealth Districts Under Block Grants in FY 1983 with Funds Allocated Prior to Consolidation in FY 1982.

| | FY 1982 (categorical grants) | | | | FY 1983 (block grants) | | | |
| | Public | | Nonpublic | | Public | | Nonpublic | |
District	$	% total	$	% total	$	% total	$	% total
Boston	$536,221	(81.4)	$123,500	(18.6)	$1,011,068	(77.5)	$294,180	(22.5)
Brockton	109,214	(89.9)	12,250	(11.1)	177,573	(89.9)	19,861	(11.1)
*Cambridge	744,299	(95.5)	34,701	(4.5)	85,000	(80.4)	20,668	(19.6)
Fall River	90,000	(81.8)	21,000	(18.2)	136,000	(79.5)	35,000	(20.5)
*Holyoke	445,548	(99.0)	4,452	(1.0)	106,354	(83.0)	21,804	(17.0)
*Lawrence	284,000	(96.3)	11,000	(3.7)	118,277	(82.1)	25,736	(17.9)
*Lowell	332,072	(96.9)	10,332	(3.1)	119,397	(76.3)	37,034	(23.7)
Lynn	46,273	(91.2)	4,469	(8.8)	149,289	(89.2)	18,007	(10.8)
New Bedford	122,037	(95.7)	5,482	(4.3)	173,513	(88.8)	21,900	(11.2)
Somerville	33,885	(88.2)	4,540	(11.1)	87,925	(84.5)	16,100	(15.5)
Springfield	137,000	(83.0)	28,000	(17.0)	343,000	(80.3)	84,000	(19.7)
*Worcester	775,000	(96.9)	25,000	(3.1)	268,000	(89.9)	30,000	(10.1)

SOURCE: Informal Telephone Survey of Federal Grant Directors (October 1982).
*School Districts receiving Desegregation Grants in FY 1982 under the Emergency School Aid Act.

The termination of ESAA as a separate categorical grant and its subsequent merger into the block grant has therefore spread the funds available more thinly across the state and across given districts. The losses experienced by urban districts have been magnified further by another provision of Chapter 2 whereby funds must be spent "equitably" on public and private school students, according to U.S. Department of Education regulations. This requirements is met by equal expenditures per student, as compared with public school expenditures within the district and by equitable services to meet the needs of the non-public school population.[33] In Massachusetts 60 percent of education block grant funds are allocated to school districts on the basis of numbers of low-income students. Private schools within each district receive a per capita proportion of the district's allocation without demonstrating proof of a low-income student population. Of the 28 previously separate programs, only ESEA Title IV B, which provided funds for educational and library materials and equipment, had previously benefited private school students. Now the private schools may share equitably in the entire state allocation, which decreased from $16 million in FY 1982 (prior to consolidation) to $10 million in FY 1983. As a result, private schools in some communities received a windfall in block grant funds in FY 1983.

Table 4–7 compares the total dollars and percentage of district-wide allocations received by public and nonpublic schools in Massachusetts under categorical aid prior to the merger in FY 1982 and under block grants in FY 1983 in select low-wealth school districts. These figures indicate that non-public schools in all districts, with the exception of Brockton, have increased their share of districtwide funds under block grants. Those districts that were recipients of ESAA funds in FY 1982 demonstrate the highest proportionate gains to the private schools and the most severe porportionate losses to the public schools.

The negative impact of the federal block grant legislation on educational services to the urban poor cannot be overlooked. While representing only .045 percent of total education expenses in the state of approximately $2.2 billion (estimated for FY 1983), a sizable portion of block grant funds prior to consolidation were channelled through ESAA and were specifically earmarked to provide educational services to minority students. The net reduction in desegregation aid throughout the state, combined with severe cutbacks in local aid under Proposition 2½ calls for strong state commitment and leadership in meeting the needs of the urban poor.

Conclusions and Recommendations

This chapter began by outlining three critical concerns facing the education of the poor in the 1980s. What clearly has emerged from the analysis that followed is the need for a state mandate to address those concerns. It is recommended that the state legislature and department of education join forces in developing a comprehensive statewide plan for financing, integrating, and managing educational services to the poor. Such a plan might include the following elements.

1. Governance.   The state legislature should consider legislative alternatives to the present system of financing education in the state, with the objective of achieving a more equitable distribution of resources. Morever, the state education department, with financial support from the legislature, should assume a stronger leadership role by establishing state-wide minimum achievement standards and by providing expert assistance to school districts in instructional design, program implementation and evaluation, and comprehensive school-based planning.

2. Equity.   The Chapter 70 state aid formula should be revised and complementary legislation enacted to address the following issues:

- *Full funding:* In order to decrease dependency of local school expenditures on the property tax, the state aid percentage should be increased to 50 percent.

- *Hold harmless:* The present provision at 107 percent of FY 1979 allocations dilutes the equalizing effect of the formula. A phasedown of hold harmless guarantees over a reasonable period would target additional aid to low-wealth districts and allow hold harmless communities to plan for any consequential effects.

- *Aid to cities:* In order to target additional aid to the urban poor, municipal overburden and cost differentials should be factored into the state equialization formula.

- *Earmarking of funds:* To avoid supplantation at the local level, legislation should be enacted requiring cities and towns to reallocate state education funds directly to local school districts and further requiring school districts to expend state aid on state-identified target groups in the same proportion as allocated through the state aid formula.

- *State aid for desegregation:* The legislature should continue to allocate increased aid to school districts undergoing voluntary desegregation in order to compensate for losses under the merger of ESAA into the federal education block grant.

3. Effectiveness. The state legislature and department of education should join together in an effort to improve instructional effectiveness and student achievement by addressing the following issues:

- *State compensatory aid:* Legislation should be enacted whereby the 0.2 poverty weighting in the current Chapter 70 formula is replaced with a state allocation for basic skills remediation. Funds would be allocated to school districts based on numbers of students failing to meet statewide minimum standards.
- *Statewide minimum standards:* If the state of Massachusetts is to develop an accountability program aimed at improving school effectiveness and raising student achievement levels, serious consideration must be given to the establishment of statewide minimum achievement standards, with students throughout the state tested on a state-developed or state-determined standardized test, at given grade levels and at a given point in the school year. Care must be taken that test items are not racially or culturally biased against minority students and that the skills tested are included in the prescribed state curriculum for the particular grade level (that is the test must have curricular validity). Implicit within this last requirement is greater state level regulation over the basic instructional program throughout the state, which represents a radical departure from the culture of local control that has dominated the state up to the present. If the state is to assume the primary role in funding educational services, however, it is reasonable for the state to demand higher levels of accountability for expenditures and for overall school performance. On the other hand, the state should view statewide standards not as a punitive measure with regard to students but as a means of early diagnosis of student learning problems and as a vehicle for fine-tuning the instructional program.
- *State leadership in program coordination:* Additional state aid should be allocated to the state education department for providing technical assistance to local school districts in the development of comprehensive school-based plans for coordinating Chapter 1 services with those to be provided under the state's basic skills program. Additional funds would allow the state agency to hire field-based staff with expertise in basic

skills development and instructional management to advise school districts throughout the state on integrating federal and state remediation programs into the overall instructional program. Program coordination should aim at minimizing instructional fragmentation and staff/student isolation while maximizing overall program effectiveness.

Endnotes

1. A. Odden, and J. Augenblick, *School Finance Reform in the States: 1980* (Denver, Colo.: Education Commission of the States, April 1980), p. 26.
2. E.K. Adams, *A Changing Federalism: The Condition of the States* (Denver, Colo.: Education Commission of the States, April 1982), p. 56.
3. See L.M. McDonnell and M.W. McLaughlin, *Education Policy and the Role of the States* (Santa Monica, Calif.: The Rand Corporation, May 1982) for a discussion of state political culture and how it influences state action relative to local school districts.
4. See G. Weber, *Inner-City Chidlren Can Be Taught to Read: Four Successful Schools* (Washington, D.C.: Council for Basic Education, 1971); W.B. Brookover and L. W. Lezotte, *Changes in School Characteristics Coincident with Changes in School Achievement* (Lansing, Mich.: Michigan State University, 1977); and M. Rutter *et al.*, *Fifteen Thousand Hours* (Cambridge, Mass.: Harvard University Press, 1979).
5. The elementary and secondary education system in Massachusetts is composed of 436 school districts, of which 351 are coterminous with cities or towns. Of that number, 297 operate instructional programs, while the remaining 54 are either members of fully organized regional school districts or have entered into cooperative agreements with neighboring school districts. In addition there are 52 regional academic districts that provide instruction either in all grades or only on the high school level to students from two or more towns. Three independent vocational districts operate under the control of boards of trustees in three cities, while 27 regional vocational districts provide occupational instruction to high school students from two or more cities or towns. Finally, three counties operate agricultural schools for secondary students.
6. E.K. Adams, *op. cit.* pp. 56–9. For FY 1982 the percentage distribution of dollar revenues from all sources for elementary and secondary education in Massachusetts was 7.8 percent federal, 38.4 percent state, and 53.8 percent local. National figures were 8.1 percent federal, 49.0 percent state, and 42.9 percent local. In FY 1981 Massachusetts ranked 10th among the states in its reliance on local revenues to fund education and 40th in its support of education from state revenues.
7. M. Gittell, "Localizing Democracy Out of Schools, *Social Policy,* 12 (Sept. –Oct. 1981), pp. 4–11.
8. R.C. Salomone, "Equal Educational Opportunity and the New Federalism: A Look Backward and Forward, *Urban Education,* 17 (July 1982), pp. 213–32.

9. See R. Elmore and M. W. McLaughlin, *Reform and Retrenchment: The Politics of California School Finance Reform* (Cambridge, Mass.: Ballinger Pub. Co., 1982) for a thorough discussion of the legal and political aspects of school finance reform in California.

10. See E.A. Hanushek, "Throwing Money at Schools," *Journal of Policy Analysis and Management*, 1 (Fall 1981), pp. 19–41, for an analysis of 130 separate analyses of determinants affecting educational performance.

11. See G.V. Glass and M.L. Smith, "Meta-Analysis Research on Class Size and Achievement," *Educational Evaluation and Policy Analysis*, 1 (January–February 1979), pp. 2–16 for an analysis of 80 evaluations of the effect of class size on achievement.

12. R.J. Murnane, "Interpreting the Evidence on School Effectiveness," *Teachers College Record*, 83 (Fall 1981), pp. 19–35.

13. *Massachusetts: The State of the Child* (Boston, Mass.: Massachusetts Advocacy Center, 1982).

14. In a 1982 decision upholding the right of illegal alien children to a free public education, the United States Supreme Court recognized the importance of education in the preservation of our political fabric. Distinguishing education from other governmental benefits, the Court stated, "Both the importance of education in maintaining our basic institutions, and the lasting impact of its deprivation on the life of the child, mark the distinction....we cannot ignore the significant social costs borne by our Nation when select groups are denied the means to absorb the values and skills upon which our social order rests." Plyler v. Doe, 102 S.Ct. 2382, 2397 (1982).

15. *Summary of Social and Economic Characteristics: 1980* (U.S. Census Bureau, 1982).

16. *1981–1982 Valuation Ratios*, Massachusetts Department of Education, Bureau of Data Collection and Reporting. The 17 districts with equalized valuations per capita above $50,000 in FY 1982 include Chatham, Chilmark, Eastham, Edgartown, Gay Head, Gosnold, Mashpee, Mount Washington, Nantucket, New Ashford, Oak Bluffs, Orleans, Rowe, Tolland, Truro, West Tisbury, and Worthington.

17. *Taxes, Schools, and Inequality in Massachusetts: Chapter 70 and School Finance* (Massachusetts Department of Education, June 1977).

18. The Boverini-Collins school aid formula, which continues to remain operative, is as follows:

$$\text{School Aid} = (1 - P \ \frac{\text{Ev/capita-L}}{\text{Ev/capita-S}}) \ (\text{FTE}_{W-L}) \ (\frac{C_R-S}{\text{FTE}_{R-S}})$$

where,
   P = local support percentage (determined annually depending upon the ratio of Chapter 70 aidable expenditures to local appropriations);
   Ev/capita–L = equalized property valuation per person in the LEA;
   Ev/capita–S = equalized property valuation per person in the state;
   $\text{FTE}_{W-L|}$ = total need in weighted full-time equivalent students in LEA in current fiscal year;

C_{R-S} = current state operating expenditures for regular day programs excluding transportation, regional school districts, food, and capital outlays;

FTE_{R-S} = total FTE students in regular day programs in the state.

Pupil weights based on statewide average costs are as follows:

Regular day program	1.0
Transitional bilingual program	1.4
Special education (except residential)	4.0
Special education (residential)	6.3
Vocational education	2.0
Low-income pupils (additional weight)	0.2

19. *1978–79 State Compensatory Education Program Characteristics and Current Funding Levels for Sixteen States* (Denver, Colo.: Education Commission of the States, November 1979).

20. K.L. Bradbury and H. F. Ladd, with C. Christopherson, "2½: Initial Impacts, Part II," *Impact 2½*, 24 (April 15, 1982), pp. 1, 6.

21. Of the 75 communities in the survey, the average population in the Severe Impact Group was 31,150, while it was only 9,530 in the Moderate Impact Group. Average per capita property valuation was $23,529 in the Moderate Impact Group and only $13,151 in the Severe Impact Group.

22. E. P. Morgan, *Public Education and the Taxpayers' Revolt: The Causes and Consequences of Proposition 2½ in Massachusetts*, unpublished paper (May 1982).

23. Proposition 2½ prescribes a limit on user fees. Section 11 of the article states, "No city, town, county, district, public authority or other governmental entity shall make any charge or impose any fee for goods provided or services rendered in excess of the cost of furnishing such goods or providing such services."

24. *The Impact of Proposition 2½ on the Schools* (Boston, Mass.: Massachusetts Association of School Committees, Inc., 1982).

25. P. L. McCarney, "User Fees and Charges Under Proposition 2½ in Massachusetts," *Impact 2½*, 36 (October 15, 1982), pp. 1–2.

26. The Education Consolidation and Improvement Act of 1981 was enacted as part of Subtitle D of the Omnibus Budget Reconciliation Act of 1981 (P.L. 97–35). Chapter 1 of the Act replaces Title I of the Elementary and Secondary Education Act of 1965 and provides federal aid on a formula basis for remedial instruction to economically and educationally disadvantaged students.

27. "Shifts in Chapter 1 Policy Worry State Directors," *Education Week*, 11 (October 25, 1982), p. 8.

28. C. K. McGuire, *State and Federal Programs for Special Student Populations* (Denver, Colo.: Education Commission of the States, April 1982).

29. See M. McClung, "Competency Testing Programs: Legal and Educational Issues," *Fordham Law Review*, 47 (1979), pp. 651–712; S. G. Christie and J. A. Casey, "Heading Off Legal Challenges to Local Minimum Competency Programs," *Educational Evaluation and Policy Analysis*, No. 5 (1983) pp.

31–42. In the precedent-setting case of *Debra P. v. Turlington,* 644 F. 2d 397 (5th Circuit 1981), the appeals court affirmed the district court's finding that Florida's functional literacy test was racially discriminatory and culturally biased. The appeals court remanded the case for clarification on whether vestiges of segregated schools remained in Florida and for further proof that the material tested was indeed taught. In May 1983 the district court concluded that the test met the appeals court standard on curricular validity and that the graduating class of 1983 no longer "shoulders the burden of years of inferior education," No. 78–892-Civ-T-GC (M.D. Fla. May 4, 1983).

30. States received $512 million in categorical aid in FY 1981 through the 28 programs now combined in Chapter 2. Emergency School Aid Act funds for desegregation accounted for $149 million of that figure. In FY 1983 states received only $455 million through the block grant legislation.

31. The Massachusetts formula grants a greater weight to poverty than other states. Colorado allocates only 16 percent of the LEA funds on the basis of low-income students. North Carolina allocates 30 percent of the LEA funds on number of students eligible for free lunch. Several states such as New York, on the other hand, equalize Chapter 2 aid based on district wealth and use the same aid ratio now used in their general state operating aid formula. The New York state aid formula uses a system of weightings for high-cost students, with the last group weighted at .25. New York does not include a low-income factor per se in its formula.

32. According to preliminary estimates, the following cities have experienced severe reductions in federal aid under block grants: Atlanta (–39.5%), Chicago (–30.5%), New Orleans (–65.4%), Boston (–24.3%), St. Louis (–86.2%), New York City (–40.5%), Buffalo (–87.6%), Cleveland (–80.6%), Philadelphia (–47.9%), Dallas (–62.4%), Seattle (–82.7%), and Milwaukee (–65.6%). *City School Desegregation and Block Grant Legislation: A Report to the House Subcommittee on Civil and Constitutional Rights of the Committee on the Judiciary* (Washington, D.C.: Council of the Great City Schools, 1982), pp. 7–8.

33. Chapter 2 of the Education Consolidation and Improvement Act of 1981, *Federal Register,* Vol. 47, No. 146 (July 29, 1982), p. 32,891. (Note: 32,891 refers to one page.)

Part Two

POLICIES TO AMELIORATE POVERTY

Although policies to make people self-supporting or to keep them that way are clearly the most effective long-term approach to poverty, short-term approaches are needed as well. Many poor people cannot be expected to work. For these people and for those moving toward self-support, the primary goal of state policy is to provide the support they are unable to provide for themselves.

The most straightforward way to provide support is to provide cash assistance, and the first chapter in this part deals with the income security system. It describes the successes of social security and other programs in providing income support for the elderly and disabled, and it identifies the more troubling problems implicit in the program of Aid to Families with Dependent Children. The other chapters in this part discuss policies that can be seen—at least arguably—as contributing both to the prevention of poverty and to its amelioration. In our judgment, though, transportation, housing, and crime-control policies are best thought of as policies whose primary function is to make the lives of the poor more palatable.

The Basic Dilemma: Targeting on the Poor

All the chapters in this part, like those of the first part, face the question of how best to use limited resources to improve the lot of the poor. In these policy areas, however, the dilemmas that policymakers must deal with are somewhat different than those

in employment and training, health, and education, where a
primary worry was whether it was possible to design programs
that effectively improved prospects for self-support. Here the
most basic question is whether resources meant to improve the
lives of the poor actually go to the poor—the question of targeting.

Transportation provides perhaps the best example of this
dilemma. Subsidies for mass transportation are often advocated
as a way of aiding the poor. In contrast, policies that impose costs
on automobile owners, such as mandatory vehicle inspections
and high-cost required insurance, are thought not to affect the
poor—if the question is thought about at all. Chapter 6 shows,
however, that many of the benefits of mass transportation subsidies go to the middle class. At the same time, because the poor,
like the rest of the population, rely on the automobile for most of
their transportation, the high costs of automobile ownership are
in fact a heavy burden on the poor. The question thus arises as to
whether there are not more efficient ways of alleviating the
transportation problems of the poor than the policies we are now
following.

The same question is raised, especially in the areas of income
security and housing, by programs for the elderly. It is often
thought that helping the elderly is a good way of helping the poor.
Most of the elderly, however, are not poor. Thus elderly housing
(a large proportion of subsidized housing) is often occupied by
people who are not poor, and the majority of Social Security
expenditures (by far the largest income security program) go to
people who are relatively well off. That we devote so many
resources to the elderly may be one reason that other groups seem
to be shortchanged. There is a substantial shortage of affordable
rental units for families, especially the female-headed families
with children that are such a large fraction of the poor. And the
benefits that these families receive from Aid to Families with
Dependent Children most often leave them below the poverty
line. Our analyses of both these issues raise questions about the
possible reallocation of resources to direct them more precisely at
the poor.

A different kind of targeting issue is raised in our discussion of
crime. The poor are not only disproportionately committers of
crime but also disproportionately victims of crime. The poor also
suffer—like the rest of us—as much from the fear of crime as
from its actual effects. While reforms of the criminal justice

system to protect the rights of the accused are often linked in the public mind with anti-poverty efforts, policing practices that control crime and alleviate fear could well be far more important in improving the lives of the poor.

Massachusetts and Other States

The chapters in this part, like those in the first part, focus on the poor in Massachusetts and on the programs that Massachusetts has established for the poor, but the analyses have general relevance for other states as well. All states have programs in these areas, all have limited resources to spend on them, and all are faced with the basic dilemma of how to attack poverty most directly and effectively.

Historical, geographical, and demographic differences among states, however, have important influences on some aspects of the policy problems. Many of the demographic differences noted in the introduction to Part One are relevant here as well; the age and family composition of the poor, for example, determine the relative importance of AFDC versus other income-transfer programs and of family versus elderly housing. That Massachusetts is a highly urbanized state affects both its problems and its potential solutions in transportation, housing, and crime. In more rural states, for example, the poor may be even more dependent on automobiles than they are in Massachusetts. In states with substantial proportions of rural poor, crime is likely to be somewhat less of a problem, and housing problems somewhat different.

Other important differences include the facts that Massachusetts is relatively generous with regard to public assistance, has well developed—if old—systems of public transportation, and has a quite large stock of public housing. Thus while the general description of problems and analysis of solutions in these chapters are often relevant to other states, specific policy prescriptions may be unique to this state.

Chapter 5

INCOME TRANSFERS
AND THE POOR

by Mary Jo Bane

If poverty simply means that some people have less money than others, a logical solution to the problem of poverty would be to transfer money from the non-poor population to the poor. Indeed, income transfers are—and have long been—the crucial governmental policy mechanism for alleviating poverty. But of course the matter is not so simply dealt with. Does *everyone* who is poor need and deserve transfer payments? How much money should be transferred, and under what conditions? Is there a danger of too many people ending up being transferees rather than transferors? If so, what do we do then?

This chapter looks at these questions in the context of the income transfer system of Massachusetts. Cash assistance or "welfare" programs are a large and controversial share of the state budget. Controversy arises, on the one hand, because the numbers are large, relative both to the total state budget and to welfare spending in other states. At the same time, real dollar spending on cash assistance has fallen during the last few years, both absolutely and as a share of the state budget. Average benefit levels have fallen in real terms as inflation has outstripped benefit increases, raising questions about the adequacy of the system for meeting the basic needs of the Massachusetts poor. Adding to the rancor of the debate is the question of whether welfare may be part of the problem of poverty rather than part of its solution, by providing disincentives to working and encouragement for breaking up families.

These controversies arise in the form of disagreements about benefit levels, eligibility rules, work requirements, and child support enforcement. They reflect, though, a profound dilemma inherent in welfare systems between generosity and compassion for the unfortunate, on the one hand, and the need for a fair system of incentives and encouragements for independence and private responsibility on the other. The dilemma is not solvable. At best, policy can achieve a sensible balancing of admirable but contradictory goals.

This chapter takes a somewhat unconventional approach in its attempt to work through the welfare dilemma by looking at welfare programs as part of a larger income security system that is basically defined by the principles embodied in the Social Security Act. The argument is that the values, goals, and basic operating tenets of the social security system (what I call the "social security ideal") are the right ones for thinking about income security programs generally, including those of the state welfare system. Accordingly the chapter looks at the major welfare policy issues and choices facing the state in terms of their compatibility with this ideal.

The chapter begins by describing the overall income security system and the place of state cash assistance programs within it. The "social security ideal" is then discussed and data are presented to suggest that the system is working pretty well in fulfilling its goals for most of the needy groups in the population. I then argue that the income security system for female-headed families with children (mainly AFDC) is a major area in which the "welfare reality" is inconsistent with the social security ideal. The chapter next looks at the major policy choices in AFDC in terms of progress toward the ideal, and concludes that encouraging parental responsibility through child support and work programs should be the major goal of welfare proposals.

The Income Security System

What we can call the public income security system in the United States is made up of a large number of state and federal programs that replace income lost through retirement, unemployment, or disability, or that provide basic income to those in need. Some of these programs, such as Social Security and unemployment compensation, are usefully thought of as social insurance, while others (those colloquially known as welfare) are more accurately described as cash assistance based on need rather than other principles of entitlement.

Principles Underlying the System

Because the "income security system" is made up of many programs, legislated at different times and for different purposes, it is difficult either to define the goals of the system or to see how these goals are being met. A good place to start, however, is with the principles embodied in the Social Security Act, which remains the basic legislation authorizing not only the social security system but also the major cash assistance programs for the poor (as well as Medicare, Medicaid, Social Services, and some other programs).[1] Those principles best reflect, I believe, the goals and values that most Americans believe ought to govern programs for assisting the poor and the dependent.

One of the basic assumptions behind the Social Security Act is that citizens should be insured against some circumstances that are beyond their control. Old age, disability, injury, unemployment, and death, or desertion by a bread-winning spouse,[2] are all uncontrollable conditions and can leave people destitute. A contributory insurance system in which all participate can protect against the inability to work through the collective sharing of risks. The Social Security Act established a national insurance system designed to be consistent with the American values of self-reliance and family support. In exchange for contributions from working citizens to the system, each contributor and his or her family would be insured against income loss due to misfortune or age.

For most people, who spend most of their lives as workers or as spouses or children of workers, this social insurance system will be sufficient to support them during the times they cannot support themselves. The designers of the social security system saw, however, that there would likely be some people in some situations who would need assistance outside of, or in addition to, the basic social insurance programs. The legislation thus includes several programs that provide assistance with eligibility based on need rather than on contributions. These were originally seen as programs that would diminish in importance, and perhaps even disappear, as coverage under the social security system expanded. The programs included assistance, based on low income rather than on contributions, for the elderly, blind, and disabled who had not made sufficient contributions to the social security system to provide them adequate benefits. (These programs, originally state-run, later became the Supplemental Security Income program.) The Social Security Act also authorized a program of Aid to Dependent Children (later AFDC) for widows whose spouses had not been covered under social security and for what was predicted to be a very small group of women and children who had been deserted.

The basic ideas, therefore, were that workers were responsible for their own and their families' support; that insurance against old age, disability, unemployment, injury on the job, and death of a bread-winning spouse would get most people through most of the circumstances that would otherwise leave them poor; and that welfare and income supplement programs, with eligibility based on need, would fill the few gaps in the system. It is consistent with the thinking behind the Social Security Act (though it has not always characterized attitudes historically) that most of the programs for the poor be generous and relatively easy to get. The programs were designed for people who were genuinely unable to support themselves; since the size of the potential client population was expected to be small, the cash assistance programs could afford to be generous.

These basic notions—self-reliance, insurance, and appropriately directed compassion—continue to describe the way most Americans think income transfer programs ought to work. They are appropriate principles to use in examining and evaluating the way the income security system in fact works.

Spending on Income Security

Three needs-based cash assistance programs are of major concern to the state: (1) Aid to Families with Dependent Children (AFDC), (2) Supplemental Security Income (SSI), and (3) General Relief (GR). These three programs for the poor require state appropriations of funds and, to some extent, state policy decisions about program design and operation. These three programs, however, are but a small part of an overall system of income security provided to Massachusetts residents, most of which is federally funded and most of which is not directed specifically at the poor. To think sensibly about the state programs, it is important to understand this overall system.

One perspective on the income security system comes from data on spending in Massachusetts on the various programs. Table 5–1 shows spending in 1977 on the following components: Old Age and Survivors Insurance (OASI—Social Security) pay-

Table 5-1   Income Security Spending in Massachusetts, Selected Programs
(millions of dollars)

	1969	*1977*	*1980*
Old Age and Survivors Insurance	—	2132.1	—
Disability Insurance	—	247.1	—
Unemployment Insurance	—	332.6	—
Veterans Benefits	—	300.5	—
SSI (federal)	102.2	103.1	118.6
SSI (state supplement)	—	114.0	122.2
Aid to Families with Dependent Children	128.1	466.6	489.3
General Relief	21.4	45.6	46.5
CPI	110.0	183.4	240.0

SOURCES: *Social Security Bulletin: Annual Statistical Supplement, 1977–1979*, and
Massachusetts Department of Public Welfare, *Statistical Supplement to the Annual
Report.*

ments to retired Massachusetts residents and their surviving
spouses; Disability Insurance payments to the covered disabled
among Massachusetts residents; Unemployment Insurance payments; Veterans Pensions and disability payments; federal payments to the low-income elderly and disabled under the
Supplemental Security Income (SSI) program; state supplements
to the elderly and disabled under SSI; state and federal payments
under AFDC to families with dependent children; and state
payments under the General Relief (GR) program. State spending on the three needs-based cash assistance programs (SSI,
AFDC, and GR) is shown for 1969 and 1980 as well.

The table shows several important facts about the current
income security system.

- *The vast bulk of the spending is, and has been, on social security,
unemployment and veterans benefits, not on programs that are
normally thought of as "welfare".*

Social security accounted for 64 percent of total spending on
income security in the state in 1977. Unemployment and veterans
benefits accounted for another 17 percent. Spending on these
programs has grown extremely rapidly over the last two decades.

- *Welfare programs (cash assistance programs directed specifically at
the poor, with eligibility based on need) have grown substantially
over time, but remain a small part of total transfer payments.*

The basic state welfare programs (AFDC, SSI, and GR) cost $658
million in 1980, up from $252 million in 1969. This expenditure

Table 5-2 Social Insurance and Public Assistance Recipiency in Massachusetts Households, 1975

		PERCENTAGE WITH ANY INCOME FROM:		
	% of house-holds	SSI, unemp. ins. or veterans benefits	AFDC SSI or UA	Food Stamps
Poor Before Transfers:	21.1%	70.5%	32.5%	21.4%
Non-elderly, non-disabled male-heads:				
with children	6.3	51.0	49.0	42.9
with no children	8.2	54.0	9.5	12.7
Non-elderly non-disabled female-heads:				
with children	15.2	12.8	82.1	71.8
with no children	5.3	48.8	7.3	12.2
Disabled family heads	9.2	56.3	63.4	49.3
Disabled primary individuals	6.1	63.8	31.9	14.9
Elderly family heads	19.9	100.0	9.1	0.6
Elderly primary individuals	29.8	98.3	20.9	1.7
All:	100.0	45.2	9.6	6.8
Non-elderly, non-disabled male-heads:				
with children	29.7	31.0	5.2	6.4
with no children	25.6	31.7	2.2	1.7
Non-elderly, non-disabled female-heads:				
with chidren	5.2	19.4	57.1	50.3
with no children	8.7	25.9	4.1	2.5
Disabled family heads	7.1	55.6	19.3	16.2
Disabled primary individuals	2.6	48.4	16.8	8.4
Elderly family heads	11.9	91.5	8.3	0.7
Elderly primary individuals	9.3	92.0	14.2	1.5

Households = 3654
Poor before transfers = 772

SOURCE: Tabulations from the Survey of Income and Education.

level accounted for about 12 percent of the total state budget in 1980, a substantial but not overwhelming amount.

• *State spending on welfare programs, in real terms, grew very little during the 1970s.*

State spending on SSI, AFDC, and GR was lower in real terms in 1980 than in 1977, and up only about 20 percent from 1969. The welfare programs are a smaller share of the state budget now than then.

Despite their relatively small share of total income security spending and of the state budget, cash transfer programs for the poor are among the most controversial in the state budget. This is partly because AFDC and SSI recipients are also eligible for Medicaid, the costs of which, as discussed in Chapter 3, are very difficult to control. Controversy also arises, however, because it is hard to judge how effectively the programs are meeting the overall goals embodied in the principles behind Social Security.

The System in Practice

To what extent do income security programs, as they exist in Massachusetts in the early 1980s, meet this "social security ideal?" Let us consider a tentative answer to this extremely difficult question: "Very well indeed for most of poor and dependent groups; less well for the single families who are the basic clients of AFDC."

Tables 5-2 and 5-3, calculated from the 1976 Survey of Income and Education,[3] show some of the data on which this judgment is based. Table 5-2 shows the proportion of people who receive income from the social insurance programs (Social Security, unemployment insurance, and veterans benefits), from needs-based cash assistance or welfare (AFDC, SSI and GR), and from food stamps. Data are given for all Massachusetts households and separately for elderly, disabled, and male and female-headed families with and without children. Table 5-3 shows the proportions of people, by categories, whose incomes fall below the poverty line when income is defined before any transfers;[4] after social security, unemployment, and veterans benefits; after AFDC, SSI, and GR; and after food stamps. The table thus shows how many households were moved out of poverty in 1975 by the various income security programs. The next sections of this chapter use the data to discuss, first, the experience of the elderly and the disabled and then, briefly, that of non-disabled two-parent families. The remainder of the paper examines AFDC and the situation of single parent families.

Table 5-3   Poverty Rates Among Persons in Massachusetts, 1975

	Before All Transfers	After SS, UI, VA, Pre-welfare	After All Cash Transfer, Including AFDC, SSI, and UA	After Food Stamps	% Population
Non-elderly non-disabled in male-headed families:					
with children	5.9	4.3	3.2	2.6	49.0
with no children	6.0	3.0	2.9	2.6	20.6
In female-headed families:					
with children	65.3	59.4	47.3	37.6	7.1
with no children	15.6	11.6	10.7	10.2	5.3
Non-elderly disabled:					
in families	25.9	15.0	9.7	8.4	5.3
not in families	21.3	11.1	6.6	5.3	1.0
	50.0	35.2	25.9	25.5	
Elderly:					
in families	36.8	2.3	1.0	0.8	7.9
not in families	67.3	24.9	17.5	17.5	3.3
All	16.4	9.5	7.3	6.2	100.0

NOTE: N = 10529

The Elderly and Disabled

Tables 5–2 and 5–3, and other research as well, tell what is basically a success story about the elderly and disabled.

> *Nearly all households headed by elderly and about half of all households headed by disabled persons (defined as being limited in the amount they can work) receive income from social insurance.*

Over 90 percent of the elderly receive social insurance income, almost entirely Social Security Old Age and Survivors Insurance. They receive substantial sums: In 1975 the average income from Social Security for the elderly was slightly above the poverty line. About half of households headed by the disabled receive social insurance income, both Social Security Disability and veterans benefits. The average income received is considerably less than that received by the elderly. Many of the disabled, however, are only limited in the amount they can work rather than kept from working entirely. These households receive substantial income from earnings.

> *Relatively low proportions of elderly and disabled households receive income from public assistance or food stamps.*

Not quite a fifth of disabled households and less than 15 percent of elderly households received income from SSI. This is no doubt primarily because these households receive sufficient income from Social Security and other sources to make them ineligible for welfare. About two-thirds of the elderly and disabled who were still poor after Social Security had income from public assistance (now shown in the table). This fact suggests that some people in these categories did not know about SSI and general assistance, or chose not to participate. Very low proportions of the elderly and disabled, including only about a third of the post-transfer poor, reported income from food stamps. This low participation rate among eligible elderly and disabled is a phenomenon found nationwide in the mid-1970s. Food stamp participation rates in the 1980s are much higher.

> *Social insurance is very effective in moving the elderly out of poverty.*

About a third of all households headed by a disabled person were poor before transfers. Social insurance brought over a third of the pre-transfer poor above the poverty line. After public assistance, poverty rates for disabled families were very low, but poverty rates were about 25 percent for disabled primary individuals. The category of disabled primary individuals includes people now living in the community who would once have been, and who perhaps were in their own past, institutionalized in mental institutions or other custodial facilities. This could be, therefore, an extremely disadvantaged group, which would make the decrease in poverty rates more impressive.

In short, the social insurance system seems to be an important source of income for the elderly and disabled and is quite effective in moving the income of those groups above the poverty line. The welfare system, primarily SSI, seems to be mostly a gap-filling program for the elderly, the disabled, and the poor in male-headed families. In combination with social security, it fulfills the goal of income support relatively effectively.

Recent and proposed changes in federal and state policy are not likely to change this overall evaluation. No important cuts in Social Security have been enacted, nor are they likely to be. Although state supplements to the needs-based SSI for the elderly, blind, and disabled have not increased as rapidly as inflation over the past few years, SSI benefits remain above the poverty line and the recent extension of food stamp eligibility to SSI recipients makes up for part of the real benefit decline.[5]

The policy issues in SSI are not particularly difficult, though of course decisions must be made about benefit levels and costs. SSI is conceptually relatively easy because its recipients, poor elderly and disabled, are quite clearly deserving of public compassion. There is thus a fair amount of sentiment for keeping benefit levels reasonably generous (within some cost constraints) and harrassment reasonably low. (Medicaid is the overwhelmingly difficult issue for this group.) The program fits well within the social security ideal, as described earlier, and thus works relatively smoothly.

Male-Headed Households

The previous tables show several interesting facts about non-elderly non-disabled male-headed households.

- *Surprisingly large proportions of the non-poor have income from social insurance.*

Almost 30 percent of non-elderly, non-disabled, non-poor households have social insurance income. Some of this is unemployment compensation. Most of it, however, seems to be income from veterans benefits, in amounts that average $1500 or so for male-headed families.

- *Poverty rates for male-headed households are very low.*

Even before any transfers, only about 6 percent of the people living in male-headed households were poor. Of the pre-transfer poor in these households, many received income from transfers. Households with children, many of which are quite large, were much more likely to receive public assistance income and food stamps. (Male-headed households with children can receive AFDC under the AFDC Unemployed Parent Program and also as payments for some step and foster children). Transfers are quite effective in moving these households out of poverty to a poverty rate after food stamp transfers of only 2.6 percent.

The policy issues for male-headed households in Massachusetts are raised partly around the AFDC program and partly around General Relief. (Most of the transfers to male-headed families without children and some to families with children come from General Relief.) Current Massachusetts eligibility for General Relief is limited to individuals who are medically certified as disabled. Benefit levels are low and, with food stamps, provide a minimal subsistence level. There is not much sentiment for changing this program dramatically.[6] If benefit levels were high, the General Relief program might raise serious work incentive issues. As it is, however, the program remains small, acting as a gap-filler of last resort.

Single-Parent Families and AFDC

In contrast to the elderly and disabled, for whom the data suggest that the income transfer system is working reasonably well, female-headed households (especially those with children) seem, on the basis of the data shown in Tables 5–2 and 5–3, to be in trouble. The Social Security system is not meeting their income support needs. AFDC, far from "withering away," is an important income source. And the households remain poor.

• *Relatively small proportions of female-headed families with children have income from social insurance.*

About 30 percent of female-headed families with children and 13 percent of those pre-transfer poor had income from social insurance, presumably Social Security survivors and dependents benefits primarily but also unemployment and disability insurance. Social insurance income for those who did receive it was quite substantial and probably kept its recipients off welfare.

• *A very large proportion of all female-headed households with children receive substantial amounts of income from public assistance and food stamps.*

Almost 60 percent of all female-headed households with children (82 percent of those households who were pre-transfer poor and 18 percent of those not pre-transfer poor) had at least some income from public assistance, almost entirely AFDC. Half of all female-headed families with children had income from food stamps.

> • *Though cash transfers move a large number of female-headed families out of poverty, 40 percent remain poor after all transfers.*

More than two-thirds of all female-headed families with children were poor before transfers. Social insurance moved about 9 percent of the pre-transfer poor in this group above the poverty line. Public assistance, primarily AFDC, moved 20 percent of the pre-welfare poor in the group out of poverty. Food stamps moved 20 percent of the pre-food stamps poor above the poverty line. Even the post-food-stamps poverty rate was almost 40 percent for this group, a higher rate than that for any other group.

These data do not, of course, prove that the system is working badly. They do, however, raise important questions, both conceptually about how to think about the system and empirically about other data that might clarify the issues. The next section will discuss the questions of whether the Social Security ideal can be applied to single-parent households and how it can be modified to reflect changing family structures and attitudes. It will then look at additional data, partly Massachusetts but mainly national, to see whether the ideals are being met.

Dependent Children and the Social Security Ideal

One question is whether the Social Security ideal, as described earlier, is even applicable to contemporary female-headed families with children. It can be argued that the Social Security Act, with its focus only on survivors benefits for widows, did not anticipate the massive changes in family structure that have taken place during the past 25 years. The dramatic increases in divorce, separation, and birth outside of marriage have produced large numbers of dependent children not insured by survivors benefits. These children, it can be argued, are just as entitled to parental care as children whose fathers are deceased, and their mothers, just as much as widows, need public support to enable them to remain out of the labor market and to provide good care for their children. A large AFDC program is thus inevitable and necessary.

Despite this argument, however, the basic tenets of the Social Security ideal—self-support, insurance, and gap-filling—ought to be as applicable to female-headed families with children as to other groups. For all but widows, for whom survivors benefits are available, two parents are alive and responsible for the support of children. When parents live together, they divide up caretaking and wage-earning responsibilities in some way acceptable to both of them. The same time and money resources are potentially available for these same tasks when the parents live apart, although the split-up families, of course, lose some economies of scale. The decision to separate or not to marry is presumable made with the knowledge that it is more difficult and costly to maintain two households and with acceptance of these difficulties and costs.

It may seem that the society's increased tolerance of individual freedom in choices about marriage and living arrangements implies tolerance of individual choices not to support and care for children. But this does not follow. While liberal divorce laws and public attitudes, which are not likely to change, indeed mean that couples can separate from or not marry each other without public sanction, they do not mean that parents have public sanction to divorce their children or abdicate the responsibilities they take on when they have children. The law and public attitudes are quite clear that parents retain their basic caretaking responsibilities for minor, dependent children.

If most Americans believe that the basic responsibility for the support and care of children belongs to parents, whether they live together or apart, then public programs have a basically supplementary role:

1. To insure against the insurable (death of the spouse, unemployment, and disability— in the Social Security tradition.
2. To encourage, indeed enforce, parental responsibility; and to help make it possible for parents to exercise that responsibility through the provision of employment and training opportunities and the operation of a fair and efficient system for assessing and collecting child support from non-custodial parents.
3. To fill in, with generosity and compassion, in cases of real hardship (genuine desertions); and to supplement when necessary the resources of poor parents who are making their best effort to be self-sufficient—perhaps even enough public support that mothers can be full-time parents when children are very young.

Changing Roles of Men and Women, Fathers and Mothers

Although our notions of parental responsibility and of the basically supplementary role of public support for children remain consistent with the ideals of the Social Security Act, American attitudes about the appropriate roles of men and women have changed dramatically over the past several decades. This section will argue that the income security system has not coped adequately with these changing attitudes and has, as a result, burdened itself in many ways with the worst of both worlds.

The old notion of the appropriate division of labor between men and women was that fathers were breadwinners while mothers took care of children. Almost no married mothers, especially of young children, worked in the paid labor force. Partly because of the lack of economic opportunities for women, rates of divorce and of births to unmarried women were low. When marriages did break up, it was assumed that the father would continue to support the family through alimony and child support payments while the mother would remain at home caring for children. Alternatively, the mother and her children could move in with the mother's family and be supported by her father.

Over time, both attitudes and behavior changed dramatically. More and more women, including mothers of young children, entered the paid labor force. By 1981, 48 percent of the unmarried mothers of pre-school children and 63 percent of mothers of school-age children were in the labor force.[7] In two-parent families, husbands and wives increasingly shared both breadwinning and child-care responsibilities. Women increasingly saw themselves, and were seen by men, as at least partly responsible for the financial support of their families.

The increased economic opportunities and perceived economic responsibilities of women also affected the division of labor and responsibility after marital separation or unmarried childbirth. The number of divorced, separated, and unmarried women with children increased dramatically, at least partly because work and welfare broke the complete dependence of women on men for support. The earnings capabilities of women began to be taken into account in child support awards. Some women, especially those initiating a divorce or choosing to have children outside of marriage, increasingly saw themselves as primarily responsible for the financial support of their children, whether through work or through the welfare payments to which they were entitled as mothers. Some men, especially those who saw themselves as victims of divorce or beneficiaries of unmar-

ried fatherhood, agreed. The new norms of increased sharing of
responsibility which had begun to develop within two-parent
families were difficult to apply outside of marriage.

The best public response to the changing roles of men and
women as they affect the support of dependent children would
be a system that assessed, enforced, and when necessary supplemented the support responsibilities of both mothers and fathers.
Both men and women would be expected to contribute, as they
do in two-parent families; courts would define and enforce the
contributions; and the welfare system would take them into
account in determining benefits. The worst public response
would be a system in which neither mother nor father had clear
responsibilities and the state would take over for both. Though
such a system would not be consciously advocated by anyone,
there are some indications that our current welfare system works
just that way for many people.

The Worst of Both Worlds

One piece of evidence comes from data on income sources of
female-headed families with children. Table 5–4, again tabulated
from the SIE, shows the average proportion of total income from
various sources for Massachusetts households in 1975. This table,
as well as other data, suggests some interesting hypotheses about
the responsibilities of mothers, fathers, and the state; about the
ambivalence in the current system; and about the difficulty of
working out an appropriate allocation of the support responsibility for children.

• *Mothers' work is the most important non-welfare income source for
female-headed families with children.*

Table 5–4 **Proportions of Income from Various Sources in Female-headed
Families with Children, 1975**

	AFDC recipients (%)	Not recipients (%)
Earnings	18.4%	65.4%
Social insurance	0.4	13.7
Public assistance	66.2	—
Child support and alimony	1.8	13.9
Food stamps	12.4	1.5
Other	0.7	5.6
Percentage of all female-headed families	57.1%	42.9%

The table shows that 65 percent of the total income of non-welfare recipients and 18 percent of that of welfare recipients came from earnings, most of which resulted from mothers' work. Average annual earnings for those who had earnings were $5558, or about 130 percent of the 1975 poverty line for a family of three. As Chapter 2 shows, women who work full time are able to keep their households out of poverty. They are also able to keep off welfare or to get off the roles relatively quickly. We know from national data that most of the women who go on welfare remain on the rolls only a short time. One estimate suggests that only about 10 percent of those who ever go on welfare can be described as welfare dependent, relying on welfare for a substantial proportion of income over a long period of time.[8] While remarriage is the route off welfare for many women, work is fully as important.

For those who are on welfare, though, work makes a trivial contribution to income. Caseload data suggest that only about 20 percent of AFDC recipients work. Table 5-4 shows that less than a fifth of the total income of welfare recipients comes from their own and others' earnings. These data suggest that a substantial number of the women on the welfare rolls at any given time are not in a "transition" situation—that is, they are not gaining the work experience and gradually building up the earnings that would enable them to move from reliance on welfare to reliance on earned income. Rather, they are caring for their children and relying on the state to bear the major financial responsibility for their children.

• *The state and federal governments are ambivalent about requiring or even encouraging mothers to work.*

That many welfare recipients do not work is not necessarily morally reprehensible, and indeed is quite consistent with the attitude toward mothers' work that seems to be embodied in the welfare system. The original purpose of the AFDC program and the state programs of widows' benefits before it was to support mothers so they could stay home and take care of their children. Despite the increasing numbers of mothers in the labor force, there is still considerable sentiment that this is appropriate and that mothers, at least mothers of young children, ought not to be forced into the labor market. Combined with the fact that day care for young children is extremely expensive, these sentiments have led to the exemption of mothers of pre-school children from all work requirements under AFDC and Food Stamps and the partial exemption of mothers of school-age children.

Moreover, the incentives for AFDC mothers to work are small, especially after the recent Reagan Administration changes in AFDC rules. After four months of the program, AFDC benefits are reduced dollar for dollar for all earnings. A strict limit on the amount that can be deducted from income for work expenses before benefits are calculated makes work a losing proposition for most AFDC recipients. It is perhaps less surprising that few AFDC recipients work than that so many single mothers do. The welfare system and the society are profoundly ambivalent about the relative importance of the economic support and the child-care responsibilities of mothers.

• *Fathers' contributions are depressingly small.*

Perhaps the most important fact shown by Table 5–4 is the small proportion of income that comes from child support and alimony for both welfare-recipient single mothes and those who do not receive welfare. Only 23 percent of female-headed families with children reported receiving *any* income from child support. The average amount received by those who reported any child support income was $2160, which is equivalent to about 20 percent of the average earnings of 25- to 34-year old male workers. In interpreting these figures it is important to remember that child support income is probably underreported in this survey. It is also important to remember that the particular men in question may be less well educated, more often unemployed, and more generally disadvantaged than male workers generally. Nonetheless, it is hard to believe that 77 percent (or even 50 percent, to make an extremely liberal adjustment for underreporting) of fathers are unable to make any contribution to their children's support. And it is hard to believe that an overall average contribution of $498 per year, or 4.4 percent of average male earnings (or even double that), represents a full and fair exercise of fathers' responsibilities. To the extent these figures do indicate an abdication of responsibility and to the extent the welfare system permits or encourages it, the state has a serious problem.

• *The state has great difficulty in assessing and enforcing fair contributions from fathers.*

Child support enforcement programs have been a high priority for both federal and state efforts over the past few years. They have been reasonably successful in paying for themselves, in increasing collections somewhat, and probably in discouraging some families from applying for welfare. In the way they operate, however, they would seem to reinforce the notion that the state, not the parents, is primarily responsible for the support of children: The state collects the money from the fathers and puts it in the treasury; the benefits received by children do not increase because of contributions by their fathers; neither fathers, mothers nor children see any direct benefits to the children as a result of the fathers' efforts. Indeed, the state's child support enforcement efforts may discourage direct contributions from fathers, both because they collect money that might otherwise go directly to children and because they provide some incentive for fathers to avoid contact with their families so as to avoid being caught. That child support enforcement efforts are pretty much limited to AFDC families further reinforces the notion that what the state is really worried about is reducing the costs of exercising its responsibility for children instead of helping parents exercise their responsibilities.

Moreover, the AFDC child support enforcement effort operates, as it must, through the court system. Although this is the basic mechanism in all the states through which child support payments are assessed and enforced, it is cumbersome in the extreme and quite arbitrary as well. Individual judges make individual deteminations of what fathers ought to pay,. based in many cases on subjective judgments about the abilities of the mothers and fathers and the needs of the children. Fathers may often resist paying child support, in many cases because they rightly perceive that money for the children goes through the mothers, and they have, after all, just broken up with those mothers—often with considerable rancor. When payments are not made, the mother or the welfare department must go to court, get a court order, and then try to get the order enforced. There is nothing routine, and not much that is fair, about the process. For these and other reasons, the child support system as a whole seems to work badly.

• *State welfare benefits seem both overly large, relative to other sources, and overly stingy, relative to need.*

Table 5-2 shows that almost 60 percent of female-headed households with children in 1975 received income from welfare. Table 5–4 shows that welfare recipients received the overwhelming proportion of their income (79 percent) from AFDC and food stamps, with only about a fifth of their income from earnings and almost nothing from social insurance, child support, or other sources. Other data, both state and national, show that most of the people on welfare at a given point in time are in the midst of a long spell.[9] Caseload data from the Massachusetts welfare department show that the average recipient has been on the rolls 3.6 years, implying (with a stable caseload) an average completed spell of welfare recipiency of about 7.2 years. Most of the welfare dollars go to long-term recipients with little other income.[10]

These data suggest that welfare is for many people a more important income source than would seem consistent with the social security ideal. The data are not, however, conclusive on this point. It could be that even in long-term, high-welfare cases, AFDC is simply filling in on a temporary basis while parents are, for reasons of unemployment, disability, or commitment to full-time mothers' care for very young children, unable to fully meet their support responsibilities. For most single parents, this is undoubtedly the case. Nonetheless, it seems foolish to deny the possibility that the state is taking over for irresponsible parents in at least some cases and that it is widely perceived as doing so in many.

Perhaps for these reasons, AFDC benefit levels are far from generous. Table 5–3 showed that, even after AFDC and food stamp income, the poverty rate for female-headed households with children was almost 40 percent. This rate is not surprising: Benefit levels are below the poverty level. In 1980 the AFDC needs standard and benefit level for families with no other income was $445 for a family of four in Massachusetts, or 79 percent of the poverty line. A family receiving the maximum benefit was eligible for about $97 in food stamps, bringing their income to about 87 percent of the poverty level. Housing and fuel assistance, which are unevenly distributed, probably pushed some fraction of recipients above the line. Benefit levels, further, have deteriorated over time, rising only from $314 to $345 (maximum benefit for a family of four with no other income), or 10 percent, between 1970 and 1981. Over this same period, the cost of living has gone up 134 percent. Real benefit levels have therefore fallen by 40 percent since 1970.[11]

The Welfare Problem

Looking at the issues and the data in terms of parental responsibilities suggests a new way of conceptualizing the welfare problem. The problem is not primarily, as is often claimed, that welfare breaks up families, although it is true that limiting eligibility for AFDC to families without resident fathers would seem to provide an incentive for fathers to leave. Moreover, when taken in combination with food stamps, energy assistance, housing assistance, and medical assistance, welfare benefits in Massachusetts are indeed relatively generous—especially compared with what a disadvantaged young man or woman can earn through work.

Research on the effects of welfare benefit levels on family break-up and on teen-age pregnancy gives some indications of a relationship. Taken as a whole, it seems to show that higher benefits have almost no relationship to marital separation or unmarried pregnancy and some discouraging effects on remarriage. The negative income tax experiments seem to show that it is the existence and ease of income support payments that permit higher family break-up rates rather than either the benefit level or the limitation of income support to one-parent families.[12] Certainly the numbers of divorces, births out of wedlock, and single-parent families grew dramatically over the same period during which welfare programs became more easily accessible and more generous.

Nonetheless it is not clear what states either can or will want to do about this issue. Reasonably compassionate states are not likely to abolish their programs or reduce benefits dramatically. Even if they did, and even if marital breakup declined as a result, it is not clear that this would result in greater human happiness or better-off children. Americans no longer believe that men and women are forever bound to each other, however much pain a marriage inflicts. The psychological research evidence, moreover, suggests that children in unhappy two-parent families may be as much damaged as children with single parents. So the issue is not whether the existence of welfare supports marital break-up per se.

Nor is the issue welfare dependence, in any simple sense. Welfare dependency, as the term is usually used, occurs because mothers are unable or unwilling to work. This may be perfectly appropriate and consonant with the goals of the system, at least when children are very young. It is not at all clear that single mothers should be expected to work more than married mothers; indeed, since they lack a partner to share child care, they might more reasonably be expected to work less.

The real welfare problem is thus better conceptualized as a problem of parental responsibility. If parents were expected to bear reasonable support responsibilities for children, whatever their marital status, the state would have no reason to care what marital arrangements adults made. And if the state were sure that both parents were indeed meeting their responsibilities, it could afford to be generous in supplementing the efforts of those parents unable to fully meet their children's needs. The current system seems to embody ambivalence about all three roles: mother's, father's, and state's. The challenge for the future will be to sort these roles out and to build them into the design of the AFDC system.

Current Policy Decisions Facing Massachusetts

The major policy questions for the welfare system in Massachusetts over the next few years fall into three categories: (1) welfare benefit levels, (2) work incentives and requirements, and (3) child support enforcement. These questions will exist, albeit in different form, whether or not the "new federalism" achieves its goal of turning back the AFDC program to the states, although solutions may be easier to implement if the state can control the AFDC program rules. Two of these issues, benefit levels and requirements and incentives for mothers to work, seem to be relatively easy—at least in theory. Far more difficult problems are raised by child support and the more general issue of fathers' responsibilities.

Benefit Levels

As noted earlier, combined benefit levels from public assistance are generally not now high enough to move families with no other income above the poverty line. Moreover, the adequacy of benefit levels has deteriorated over the past few years as benefit levels have remained constant in the face of high inflation. Politically, raising benefit levels seems to be a hopeless cause, although the legislature did approve a supplemental $75 lump-sum clothing allowance for FY 1983 and the governor proposed a $125 clothing allowance for FY 1984. The main reason is presumably cost, even though AFDC costs have not risen much in recent years and even though the cost of raising benefit levels to the poverty line would not be a substantial percentage increase in the total state budget (perhaps $320 million if other things remained constant, half of which would be federally reimbursed). The cost problem is complicated by the fact that cash assistance programs are run by the same department that administers Medicaid, which is almost twice as expensive as all the cash assistance programs taken together. With the costs of Medicaid rising rapidly, apparently without much hope of real cost control, both the department and the legislature seem to feel compelled to make cuts in the other major DPW programs—especially AFDC.

Even with a stabilized or falling caseload (which AFDC has), allowing real benefit levels to fall is necessary to achieve the desired savings.

Perhaps if caseloads continue to fall and if the Medicaid budget were either brought under control or divorced from the welfare issue, increases in benefit levels could be entertained. Simple compassion for the unfortunate children who are, after all, the reason for the AFDC program, would seem to require this. Using inadequate benefit levels as the major mechanism for inducing mothers to work or to remarry, for families to stay together, or for fathers to pay child support seems a particularly blatant case of punishing the children for the sins of their parents. While it is probably not wise to make AFDC benefit levels overly generous, to the extent of providing serious incentives for families to break up, it is not clear what "overly generous" means—and the state is almost certainly a long way from being there.

Work Requirements and Incentives

At the federal level, work incentives have been all but eliminated from the AFDC program. Federal law now sets a gross income ceiling on AFDC eligibility, eliminates the 30 and a third rule for keeping earned income after four months on the program, and places a ceiling on the deduction from income for work-related expenses. These legislative changes resulted in almost everyone who worked being cut off the AFDC rolls in the fall of 1981. At that time, Massachusetts DPW officials predicted that half of those who were cut off would respond to the negative incentives by stopping work and coming back on welfare. Interestingly, however, this has not happened; only two percent of the cases have reappeared on welfare.[10] Apparently those who were cut off did not, for whatever reason, find it in their interests to do what would appear to be the rational thing. This casts some doubt on the importance, perhaps even the appropriateness, of financial incentives for working.

Nonetheless, it seems both inequitable and foolish to have a welfare system under which a family receives no benefit from going to work. It seems contrary to the purposes of the AFDC system to *require* mothers of pre-schoolers to work or to require mothers of school-age children to work full time. On the other hand, most low-income mothers who are not welfare recipients *do* work. Women have at least partial responsibility for the economic support of their children. Moreover, if welfare recipients are ever to become self-supporting, it is important that they develop and maintain attachments to the labor force. For these reasons, even though mothers of young children should probably not be required to work, they probably should be encouraged to work—or at least not discouraged. Mothers of school-age children should perhaps be required to work part time and should certainly be strongly encouraged to work.

The federal removal of all incentives to work thus seems a step in entirely the wrong direction, but at this point there is not much that a state can do about it. The state can, and should, advocate change in that law and should insist on more sensible rules if the program is indeed turned back to the states under the new Federalism proposal. States should also do everything possible to provide employment opportunities and supplementary services for mothers along the lines described in Chapter 2, and should pay attention to affirmative action and equal-pay requirements.

Child Support and Fathers' Responsibilities

Substantial child support enforcement programs have been part of both federal and state law and budget proposals for several years. These efforts represent a step—if a small one—in the right direction, and should continue. But the state should not rest content with its current program. This is the area in which new policies are most needed and creative policy thinking most called for.

Child support enforcement cannot be seen as solely a problem of the welfare department nor, indeed, solely a problem of the state. The state needs to think about how to rationalize and simplify the whole procedure, an undertaking that will require participation by the court system as well as by various agencies of the executive. One possibility is to design a uniform schedule for child support awards based only on the number of children and on the actual or expected earnings of the father.[11] Another part of a reformed system might be the automatic withholding of child support payments from fathers' wages, with processing and transmittal of the payments by the state. This would be a radical change but one worth considering.

There are some things that the welfare department could consider doing to clarify its own role in child support. To the extent it collects payments from fathers, whether under the present system or under a more extensive effort, it could pass the money on to the children's families with a clear indication that it came from the fathers. Welfare checks or stubs could perhaps show the expected as well as the actual contributions of fathers and mothers. The amount paid under welfare could then be shown to consist of two parts: one to make up the difference between contributions and needs; and one to advance to the children the amount expected to be paid, but not actually collected from the parents. This latter part might even be listed as a loan by the state on the part of the parents, and could be continuously tallied as an obligation due the state. The "loan" would be expected to be paid back as a percentage of earnings when parents were able to do so.

The state also needs to think about work requirements and programs for fathers to reinforce their ability and obligation to pay child support. It is not easy to figure out how to implement such requirements. But under a comprehensive child support program the state could perhaps assess awards on the basis of minimal expected earnings rather than actual earnings. It could then require (or at least strongly encourage) fathers not making these contributions to register for work, to enroll in training programs, or to participate in workfare programs.

Obviously these proposals raise serious implementation issues and would require considerable work to get the details straight.[13] The most troublesome issue is raised by the fact that a large minority of welfare recipients have never been married, making the assignment of parental responsibility extremely difficult. But because the issues are so important, these or similar proposals are at least worth considering.

Summary

The cash assistance programs commonly referred to as welfare are only a small, though controversial, part of the overall income security system supporting Massachusetts residents. For the elderly and disabled the system has been remarkably successful in moving recipients out of poverty, with minimal harrassment or political controversy. For single-parent families, a large and growing proportion of the state's poor, the system has been less successful. Many of these families receive a large proportion of their income from AFDC, and most of those who do live in poverty.

To make progress on the AFDC problem, the state should clarify and strengthen its role in both enforcing and supplementing parental responsibility for children, including three types of actions:

1. The state should do all it can within the limitation of federal regulations to provide incentives and opportunities for AFDC recipients to work.

2. The state should continue to strengthen its child support enforcement activities and should experiment, on a pilot basis, with more radical approaches to this problem.
3. The state should raise AFDC benefit levels to provide a more adequate standard of living for these poor families.

The magnitude of the AFDC problem should be neither exaggerated nor diminished. AFDC is but a small part of the state budget and a small part of the total income security system supporting Massachusetts residents. The dollars at stake are not large. At the same time, however, the controversy generated by AFDC reflects the troublesome reality that children without parental support are a large proportion of the state's poor, and it also exposes the conflicting values that reality calls forth. The dilemma for the state is how to encourage parental support for children while ensuring the children's care. These problems cannot be easily solved, but they must be addressed.

Endnotes

1. The original legislation was passed in 1935, and it has been amended many times. A compilation of all the titles of the act in effect in October 1980, with all amendments up to that time, was published by the U.S. Senate Committee on Finance as Committee Print 96–39, "The Social Security Act and Related Laws, November 1980 Edition." The Social Security Bulletin, published monthly by the Social Security Administration, periodically publishes summaries of the legislation.
2. The system in fact developed over time; not all of these circumstances were insured against by the original SSA. I avoid those details for the sake of simplicity in describing the system.
3. Under-reporting of income from cash assistance programs is a relatively serious problem in the SIE, as it is in all household surveys—of which the SIE seems to be as good as any. Estimates made by comparing reported income with program data suggest that nationally about 92 percent of Social Security and about 79 percent of AFDC income were reported by respondents to the SIE. A recent study of non-cash benefits suggests that about 79 percent of food stamp income was reported by respondents to that CPS survey, which was similar to the SIE. David Ellwood's study in Maryland comparing the SIE to program data found that average benefit levels were on the whole reported correctly but that about 20–25 percent of recipients simply did not report receiving benefits. The same seems to have been true of reports on food stamps in the recent CPS survey: only about 77 percent of recipients reported receiving benefits. The food stamp problem may be worse in the SIE than the CPS because the program was less visible in 1975 than in 1981.
4. The "poverty line" here is that defined in the Introduction and Chapter 1: the Census Bureau/OMB standard of need.

5. In 1981 the federally set SSI benefit for an individual with no other income was about 73 percent of the poverty line. Massachusetts supplemented those benefits to bring elderly, disabled, and blind recipient individuals to 111 percent, 107 percent, and 117 percent of the poverty level, respectively. Food stamps, for which Massachusetts SSI recipients became eligible in 1981, could bring them slightly higher.

6. In 1981 general assistance benefits for individuals with no other income were about 50 percent of the poverty line; food stamps could bring them to 75 percent.

7. A. S. Grossman, "More Than Half of All Children Have Working Mothers," *Monthly Labor Review*, 105 (February 1982), pp. 41–43.

8. L. Rainwater, "Persistent and Transitory Poverty: A New Look," Joint Center for Urban Studies of MIT and Harvard University, Working Paper No. 70 (June 1981).

9. People who are on welfare at any point in time look different from people who never go on welfare because long-termers are over-represented at any point in time, simply because they are long term. An analogy to a hospital may be helpful in understanding this. Most admissions to the hospital are of people who will only stay a short time; chronic care patients are only a small proportion of admissions. At the same time, chronic care patients can end up occupying most of the beds in the hospital on any given day, and utilizing most of the hospital's resources, simply because the chronic care patients who are admitted stay a long time.

10. Office of Research and Statistics, *Social Security Bulletin, Annual Statistical Supplement, 1977–79*, U.S. Department of Health and Human Services, Social Security Administration (1980).

11. Office of Research and Statistics, *AFDC Standard for Basic Needs, July 1979*, ORS Report D-2, U.S. Department of Health and Human Services, Social Security Administration (November 1980). SSA #13-11924. (Corresponding reports for the years, 1968–1980).

12. S. Danziger, G. Jakubson, S. Schwartz, and E. Smolensky, "Work and Welfare as Determinants of Female Poverty and Household Headship," *Quarterly Journal of Economics* (August 1982), pp. 519–534. Also K. A. Moore-M.R. Burt, *Private Crisis, Public Cost, Policy Perspectives on Teenage Childbearing* (Washington, D.C.: The Urban Institute, 1982). Also, I.V. Sawhill, G. E. Peabody, C. A. Jones, and S. B. Caldwell, *Income Transfers and Family Structure* (Washington, D.C.: The Urban Institute, September 1975).

13. The Poverty Research Institute at Wisconsin has worked out an elaborate and interesting scheme for child support in that state. It too is worth consideration by other states.

Chapter 6

TRANSPORTATION AND THE POOR

by Jose A. Gomez-Ibanez

It is often argued that lack of mobility prevents poor people from participating fully in society. Low incomes discourage the poor from owning automobiles, for example, and low-cost and convenient public transportation is not always available, especially as jobs and residences have been decentralizing to the suburbs. Inadequate transportation may contribute to other more basic problems of the poor, such as unemployment, poor housing, inadequate health care, or reduced educational opportunity.

As in most states, Massachusetts and its local governments offer a variety of programs designed, at least in part, to help poor people with transportation problems. Over $200 million dollars per year is spent to subsidize low fares and extensive service on publicly operated mass transit systems (that is, bus, subway, and commuter rail lines). In addition, reduced mass transit fares, special door-to-door van services, and other forms of assistance are provided for elderly and handicapped travellers, in part because many elderly and handicapped persons are thought to be poor. Finally, some health, employment, and social service agencies either reimburse transportation expenses or operate special transportation services for their low-income clients.

Despite our limited understanding of the transportation problems of the poor and the need for government assistance, the available data suggest three important conclusions. First, transportation is a serious problem for the poor, even if it does not rank as high among their concerns as employment, housing, health, or education. A majority of poor households rely on the automobile

143

Policies to Ameliorate Poverty

Table 6-1 Travel Patterns by Household Income in U.S. Metropolitan Areas, 1977–1978[a]

	Less than $6,000	$6,000–$10,000	$10,000–$15,000	$15,000–$20,000	$20,000–$25,000	$25,000 and over	All Incomes
Relative daily miles of travel per person	1.00	1.46	1.74	2.03	1.97	1.84	N.A.
Relative daily trips per person	1.00	1.19	1.30	1.42	1.40	1.56	N.A.
Average trip length (miles)	4.4	5.4	6.3	6.3	6.2	5.2	N.A.
Share of trips by mode (percent):							
Auto driver	37.5	47.4	51.3	54.2	52.2	56.3	51.3
Auto passenger	28.7	30.0	32.7	31.4	31.0	30.7	31.0
All auto	66.2	77.4	84.0	85.6	86.2	87.0	82.3
Transit	6.9	4.8	3.0	2.5	2.4	2.3	3.4
Taxi	0.5	0.3	0.2	0.2	0.1	0.2	0.2
Walk	23.4	13.7	10.0	7.7	7.2	7.3	10.7
Other[b]	3.0	3.8	2.8	4.0	4.1	3.2	3.4
All modes	100.0	100.0	100.0	100.0	100.0	100.0	100.0
Percentage of households with at least one motor vehicle[c]	53.7[d]	82.6[e]	93.3	97.1		97.7	84.7
Average age of autos owned (years)[c]	8.38[d]	7.23[e]	6.54	6.04		< 5.56[f]	6.40

a. All data except vehicle ownership and age statistics are adapted from John Pucher, Chris Hendrickson, and Sue McNeil, "Socioeconomic Characteristics of Transit Riders: Some Recent Evidence," *Traffic Quarterly* 35 (July 1981): 461–483.

b. Includes trips by bicycle, motorcycle, moped, commercial truck, and school bus.

c. Data for all U.S. households from J. Richard Kuzmyak, *Household Vehicle Ownership*, Report No. 2 of *1977 Nationwide Personal Transportation Study* (Washington, D.C.: U.S. Government Printing Office, 1980), pp. 66 and 94.

d. For households with incomes below $5,000.

e. For households with incomes between $5,000 and $10,000.

f. Households with incomes of $25,000–$35,000, $35,000–$50,000, and over $50,000 own autos with average ages of 5.56, 5.32, and 4.58 years, respectively.

for transportation, but auto expenses absorb 20 to 40 percent of their incomes. Other poor households rely on public transportation, but it often does not serve all of their needs. Second, some of the existing transportation programs that are thought to help the poor are relatively inefficient and ineffective, particularly mass transit subsidies and special assistance for elderly and handicapped travellers. Finally, much could be done to improve the effectiveness of current transportation programs with little or no increase in cost. The most promising possibilities include policies to increase the availability of automobiles to poor people, to target mass transit subsidies to low-income riders, and to use specialized transportation services more selectively.

Transportation Problems of the Poor

Travel Patterns of the Poor

The transportation problems of the poor are reflected, albeit crudely, in their travel patterns. Although comprehensive travel data for Massachusetts residents are not available, the statistics on all U.S. metropolitan residents in Table 6–1 are probably representative of conditions in Massachusetts, especially since 87 percent of Massachusetts' poor live in metropolitan areas.

The statistics in Table 6–1, which include only local or intrametropolitan trips,[1] show that persons with 1977–1978 household incomes below $6,000 per year travel about half as many miles as higher-income individuals, both because they make fewer trips and because their average trip is shorter. Lower trip-making rates among the poor are not necessarily indicative of lack of access to adequate or affordable transportation per se but may be due in part to the fact that many poor people are unemployed (often because they are retired or are single parents with children) and thus make fewer commuting trips. Whether employed or not, poor people also have less income to spend on shopping, receation, health care, and other activities that typically require transportation services.[2]

Although poor people rely less on automobiles for transportation than higher-income groups, the automobile is still by far their most important mode of transportation. While 82 percent of trips by all 1977–1978 metropolitan residents were made either as an automobile driver or passenger, residents with incomes below $6,000 made 66 percent of their trips by autos and those with incomes between $6,000 and $10,000 used autos for 77 percent of their trips (see Table 6–1). A surprising 54 percent of all metropolitan households with 1977–1978 incomes below $5,000 own at least one motor vehicle, while 83 percent of households with incomes between $5,000 and $10,000 own one or more vehicles.

Auto ownership does not necessarily imply a lack of transportation problems, of course, since owning and operating an automobile is a severe financial burden for a low-income household. Although poor people economize on auto expenses by owning older automobiles (Table 6–1) and by driving them fewer miles per year, the annual cost of owning and operating an automobile absorbs 20 to 40 percent of their incomes (two to three times the percentage paid by non-poor households).[3] By the same token, lack of an automobile does not necessarily suggest obvious transportation difficulties, because many auto-less persons get rides with friends or relatives and, particularly in urban areas, find public transportation and walking acceptable alternatives for many types of trips.

Walking and mass transit (for example, buses, streetcars, and subways) are the second and third most important transportation modes after the private automobile for all income groups, including the poor. Not surprisingly, the poor rely on these modes more than others do: Walking and transit account for only 10.7 and 3.4 percent, respectively, of trips by all metropolitan households but 23.4 and 6.9 percent of trips by households with 1977–1978 incomes below $6,000. The concentration of poor people in central cities, where walking and transit are more feasible, facilitates their use of these modes. Reliance on transit and walking may be particularly high in Massachusetts since so many of its poor households live in or near central cities.[4]

Poor people also use taxis more frequently than other income groups. Persons in households with 1977–1978 incomes under $6,000 accounted for only 12.2 percent of trips by all modes but 26.8 percent of taxi trips.[5] Taxis, far from a luxury for the poor, represent an economical alternative to automobile ownership when used occasionally for trips where walking or public transportation are not convenient.

In short, the travel patterns of the poor differ from those of other income groups, but not strikingly so. It is difficult to determine, moreover, the extent to which these differences reflect inadequate transportation rather than other problems and circumstances of the poor. It may be unrealistic, for example, to expect that special transportation programs to aid the poor would ever increase their trip-making or auto ownership rates to levels found among the remainder of the population, for several reasons. The poor tend to live in central cities where auto ownership is less important. They also have less income to spend on activities such as recreation and shopping that tend to involve travel, and they are less likely to be employed and have regular commuting needs.

A remarkable implication of the travel statistics, however, is that the cost of automobile ownership may be the single most important transportation problem of the poor. The dependence of the poor on automobiles is striking, especially given the auto's high costs and the fact that many poor live in metropolitan areas where walking and public transit are often feasible travel options. Poor households clearly attach great value to the automobile's convenience and versatility.

The relatively high level of private auto use also contrasts sharply with the conventional wisdom that mass transit subsidies are important aids to the poor. While the poor rely more heavily on mass transit than high-income travellers, transit still accounts for only 7 percent of all trips by metropolitan households with 1977–1978 household incomes below $6,000.

Equally important, the willingness of many poor households to pay the high costs of auto ownership, despite low transit fares, suggests that transit subsidies might be better used to support more convenient and extensive transit service than to lower the fares. What makes the automobile worth its high cost to many poor families is that it can go anywhere at any time. While public transportation may have an advantage of low fares, it also does not go all the places one might wish to travel. It is possible that poor people may suffer more from transit service cuts than from fare increases, since the former may make it more difficult for poor households to avoid the high costs of auto ownership.

The Handicapped, the Elderly, and Poverty

Some poor people may face special transportation problems because they are elderly and handicapped as well. Transportation planners have made special efforts to solve the transportation problems of the handicapped and elderly, in part because many of them are thought to have low incomes.

Approximately 413,000 Massachusetts residents had some form of physical or mental disability that impaired their mobility in 1975. The transportation handicapped are an extremely diverse group with a variety of different disabilities and mobility problems. Among those with chronic problems, for example, approximately 13,300 persons were wheelchair-bound, 13,400 used a walker, and 166,000 required special shoes, canes,

Table 6-2 Estimates of the Number of Massachusetts Residents Who Are Poor, Elderly, or Have a Handicap that Affects Mobility, 1975*

Age and Handicap	Poor	Not poor	Total
Elderly only (not handicapped)	9,600	383,100	392,700
Elderly and handicapped	27,400	206,900	234,300
Handicapped only (not elderly)	36,800	142,100	178,900
Neither elderly nor handicapped	330,900	4,563,200	4,894,100
Total	404,700	5,295,300	5,700,000

Brace totals — Poor: 37,000 (elderly only + elderly and handicapped); 64,200 (elderly and handicapped + handicapped only). Not poor: 590,000; 349,000. Total: 627,000; 413,200.

* Estimates for 1975 prepared by the author assuming that the proportion of elderly and non-elderly poor persons who are handicapped in Massachusetts is the same as in an 1969–70 nationwide survey reported in Transportation Research Board, *Transportation Requirements for the Handicapped, Elderly, and Economically Disadvantaged*, National Cooperative Highway Research Program, Synthesis of Highway Practice, Report No. 39 (Washington, D.C.: Transportation Research Board, 1976), pp. 8, 10, 11, and 13.

crutches, braces, or an artificial leg or foot to walk. In addition, there were approximately 63,000 persons with a vision problem, 10,000 who were deaf, and 101,300 with other disabiities such as arthritis that affected their mobility.[6]

Approximately 627,000 Massachusetts residents were over 65 years old in 1975. Since many transportation handicaps are associated with old age, it is not surprising that the handicapped and elderly groups overlap. In fact, although only 11 percent of Massachusetts' general population is over 65 years old, more than half of Massachusetts' handicapped are elderly. Persons who are both elderly and handicapped are also more likely to be poor. As Table 6–2 shows, in 1975 approximately 12 percent of the elderly handicapped were poor, compared with only 6 percent of all elderly.

On the whole, however, the overlap between the elderly and the handicapped population and the poor is much more limited than commonly supposed, particularly in Massachusetts where elderly poverty rates are slightly below those for the nation as a whole. The vast majority of Massachusetts elderly (94 percent) and handicapped (84 percent) are not poor. Moreover, 82 percent of Massachusetts' poor are neither elderly nor handicapped.

The travel patterns of the handicapped and elderly differ from those of the general population. As with the poor, however, it is difficult to determine the extent to which the differences stem from transportation difficulties or other more basic problems. Both handicapped and elderly people average only about one-third as many trips per day as the general population,[7] for example, but most elderly and handicapped persons are not employed[8] and their poor health, infirmities, and related problems restrict their social and recreational activities and associated travel demands.

If availability of an automobile is used as the measure of transportation problems, most handicapped people do not experience serious difficulties. According to a 1978 survey, the handicapped relied on the automobile for almost the same share of their total trips as the general population (71 versus 78 percent of trips), although the handicapped are more likely to travel as passengers than drivers.[9] Approximately 41 percent of the urban handicapped well enough to leave their homes had driver's licenses, and 66 percent lived in a household with at least one automobile.[10] Thus, perhaps one-half to two-thirds of the Massachusetts handicapped have ready· access to automobiles, and possibly more if rides from relatives and friends are considered.

The elderly also rely heavily on the private automobile, with almost the same share of trips by automobile, mass transit, and taxi as the general population.[11] Although the elderly are more likely to travel as auto passengers than drivers, approximately 83 percent of all men and 56 percent of all women aged 65 to 69 are licensed to drive.[12] Gerontologists expect these percentages to increase in the future due to improvements in the health of the elderly and the increasing numbers of elderly persons who grew up when auto ownership and licensing was nearly universal.

Many handicaps are also not so severe as to preclude the use of public transportation. Persons who use wheelchairs or have difficulty walking, climbing steps, or standing in a moving vehicle may find conventional mass transit inaccessible. For the vision- or hearing-impaired and for many persons with minor mobility problems, however, transit is still a useful option. As a result, in urban areas where service is available, handicapped people use transit for about the same proportion of their trips as the general population does.[13]

These statistics clearly indicate that the elderly and the handicapped are an extremely diverse group for whom a variety of transportation programs may be of use. In particular, the high proportion of both elderly and handicapped people that can and do use private automobiles and conventional mass transit services suggests that many would benefit from programs that make automobiles more affordable and extend or maintain conventional transit services. Specialized and costly transportation services, such as door-to-door vans, may be needed for only a small minority.

More important for our purposes, however, the small proportion of the elderly and the handicapped who are poor implies both that many of the benefits of transportation programs targeted to the elderly and the handicapped may go to people who are not poor and that programs targeted to the elderly and the handicapped are no substitute for programs targeted to the poor.

Transportation as a Cause of Other Poverty Problems

Another troubling possibility is that lack of mobility may contribute to other problems of the poor such as unemployment, inadequate housing, or poor health care. Inadequate transportation may make it difficult for poor people to find and hold jobs, particularly since employment has been shifting to the suburbs where transit service is not as good. Inadequate transportation may also limit the places people look for housing, as well as their opportunities for health care, education, training, and social services.

The relationship between transportation and unemployment was a particular focus of concern after the 1965 riot in Watts, a minority neighborhood in central Los Angeles. The McCone Commission, appointed to investigate the riot, found that frustration over lack of jobs was the primary cause and hypothesized that lack of adequate public transportation between Watts and suburban job centers was a major contributor to neighborhood unemployment. These findings stimulated the federal government to sponsor experimental "reverse commuter" bus routes between low-income neighborhoods and suburban employment sites in Boston and 13 other cities during the late 1960s.

The results of these demonstrations were largely disappointing. Low patronage and high deficits caused local authorities to discontinue most of the experimental routes after federal funding ran out. In the Boston area, for example, the two routes operated by the Massachusetts Bay Transportation Authority (MBTA) to industrial complexes along Route 128 (the circumferential highway about 15 miles outside the city) attracted only about 60 passengers per day and incurred operating deficits of $4.75 per passenger trip—far above the average deficit per passenger on the remainder of the MBTA's transit routes at that time.[14] There was little evidence that the routes significantly increased employment for low-income job seekers, so the cost per new job placement was probably extraordinarily high. Surveys typically revealed that 25 to 50 percent of the riders were newly hired, for example, but there was a strong suspicion that most of these workers would have been able to commute to their jobs by other means or that they had the skills and experience to find comparable jobs elsewhere if the bus service had not been available.[15]

Several other studies conducted since the demonstration program also suggest that transportation is a relatively minor cause of unemployment among the poor, especially when compared with racial discrimination or lack of skills, education, or affordable day care. Surveys show that very few low-income people cite transportation problems as the principal reason they are unemployed or no longer looking for work.[16] Studies also reveal no difference in the unemployment rates among neighborhoods located far or close to major employment centers, once the effects of the education and race of the neighborhood residents are taken into account.[17]

Given the weak link between transportation and employment, reverse commuting bus routes are probably worthwhile only where the average costs can be substantially reduced by serving other travellers in addition to low-income commuters on the same bus route. An express bus route connecting the Chicago subway system with O'Hare Airport was probably the demonstration program's only success, because it served airport travellers and employees as well as low-income workers bound for plants around O'Hare. As a rule, however, transportation appears to be a far less efficient way of reducing unemployment among low-income persons than job training, day care, or improved education.

Far less is known about the relationship between inadequate transportation and the health, education, or housing problems of the poor. These problems may be more important than employment in Massachusetts, since non-working mothers and their small children make up such a high proportion of Massachusetts' poor. As with unemployment, however, inadequate transportation is almost certainly not the principal culprit and perhaps not even an important cause of these problems. To the extent that transportation does contribute to these problems, moreover, the preferred remedies would probably still be more affordable automobiles and more extensive transit coverage, perhaps supplemented by special efforts by social service agencies to locate their clinics, training centers, and offices in low-income neighborhoods and to reimburse or provide transportation for clients facing special mobility problems.

In summary, the poor are surprisingly mobile. The majority own or have access to automobiles, and many of those who do not own autos reside in metropolitan centers where conventional mass transit, taxis, and walking are reasonable alternatives for many trips. Some of the poor face special mobility problems because of age or disability, but they account for only 18 percent of all Massachusetts poor and many of them have access to private automobiles or can use conventional mass transit services. Although we know relatively little about the link between transportation and other more basic problems of the poor, the evidence strongly suggests that transportation is not a major cause of unemployment and probably not a major contributor to housing, education, or other problems as well.

Nevertheless, transportation is still a serious problem for the poor. Auto ownership is a crushing economic burden for many poor households, especially when one considers that many must also spend 40 to 50 percent of their income on rent alone (see Chapter 8). And while many can escape the burden of car ownership by living in cities and relying on public transportation, public transportation may not serve all their trips. Efforts by the state to make automobiles more affordable and available, to maintain transit service in metropolitan areas, and to provide specialized services for the minority who cannot use automobiles or transit would clearly be of great assistance to the poor. Unfortunately, some of the present transportation programs in Massachusetts are not as helpful to the poor as they might be.

Current Transportation Programs

Three Massachusetts transportation programs are thought to be most useful to the poor: (1) subsidies to support conventional mass transit systems, (2) special services for elderly and handicapped travellers, and (3) special transportation services provided to low-income clients of social service agencies.

Conventional Mass Transit

Subsidies to support mass transit services are the most expensive of these programs, with a total cost to the state and its cities and towns of around $245 million in fiscal 1980.[18] If the experience of the 1970s is a reliable guide, moreover, the cost of these subsidies will increase at about twice the rate of inflation during the 1980s due to a combination of rapidly rising operating costs, stable ridership, and relatively modest fare increases.

Approximately 92 percent of the subsidy dollars are used to support service in the Boston metropolitan area, which also has about 89 percent of the state's transit riders.[19] As Table 6–3 shows, the bus, streetcar, rapid transit, and commuter rail lines operated in metropolitan Boston by Massachusetts Bay Transportation Authority (MBTA) incurred an operating deficit of $223 million in 1980, based on operating expenses of $303 million and passenger revenues of $80 million. Approximately 52 percent of the MBTA's operating deficit was funded by the state and 35 percent by the 79 cities and towns in the MBTA district. The federal contribution of 13 percent is expected to decline in the future with proposed federal budget cuts. The operating deficit averaged 80 cents per ride, of which 70 cents was paid by either the state or its cities and towns.

Outside metropolitan Boston, transit service is provided by 14 Regional Transit Authorities (RTAs). The RTAs' fixed-route bus service cost $26.2 million in 1980 while generating passenger revenues of $7.6 million. The $18.6 million operating deficit was financed approximately 50–25–25 percent by federal, state, and local governments, respectively. The operating deficit amounted

Table 6-3 MBTA Operating Results by Mode, 1980[a]

	Total system	Bus only	Rail transit and streetcar only	Commuter rail only
Operating expense ($m)[b]	$303.3	$121.3	$120.2	$61.9
Passenger revenue ($m)	$ 80.2	$ 28.2	$ 38.0	$14.0
Operating subsidy ($m)[c]	$223.1	$ 93.1	$ 82.1	$47.9
Passengers (millions)[d]	279.1	145.6	125.0	8.5
Operating cost/passenger	$ 1.09	$ 0.83	$ 0.96	$7.28
Revenue/passenger	$ 0.29	$ 0.19	$ 0.30	$1.65
Operating subsidy/passenger	$ 0.80	$ 0.64	$ 0.66	$5.63

[a] Unpublished MBTA data for calendar year 1980 adjusted by the author.
[b] Operating expense is net of non-passenger operating revenue.
[c] Excludes payments on MBTA bonds which amount to $32 million in 1980.
[d] These are unlinked trips.

to 53 cents per ride, half of which was paid by the state and local governments.[20]

Transit subsidies are viewed not only as measures to help the poor but also as means to reduce the excessive traffic congestion, air pollution, and energy consumption caused by private automobiles. But the experience of transit subsidies in achieving these other goals has been disappointing, largely because they have been relatively unsuccessful in attracting travellers from automobiles. In Boston, for example, the mass transit operating deficit increased from approximately $80 million in 1971 to $223 million in 1980, while passenger revenues remained relatively constant at $50–$60 million per year. The operating aid was used to maintain existing service and keep the fare at 25 cents,[23] despite rapid inflation in operating costs. In as much as the consumer price index more than doubled between 1971 and 1980, retaining the 25 cent fare amounted to reducing the fare by half (in real dollars) over the course of the decade. Despite this substantial decline in price, ridership on the MBTA remained stable or declined slightly throughout the 1970s. In late 1980 and 1981, when financial realities finally forced the MBTA to raise fares, the response in ridership and auto usage was also relatively small.[25] When MBTA bus fares increased by 100 percent and rail fares increased 50 percent in August 1981, for example, MBTA ridership fell by only 10 percent and car usage in the metropolitan area increased by at most 0.5 percent.[22]

Viewed as a means to help the poor, the current transit subsidies are neither very effective nor very efficient. Since transit accounts for only a modest fraction of the trips by poor people, many low-income travellers receive little assistance. Equally important, since poor people account for only a small fraction of transit riders, much of the subsidy goes to riders who are not poor. Granted poor people use transit more intensely than other income groups. Although only 6 percent of Boston households had incomes below $5000 in 1978, these households accounted for 10 percent of all MBTA rapid transit riders in the same period. Nevertheless poor people clearly make up a small minority of Boston's transit riders; 80 percent of the MBTA's rapid transit ridership came from households with incomes of $8000 or more in 1978 and 50 percent from households earning more than $15,000.[23]

The share of the subsidy that goes to poor riders is even smaller than these aggregate statistics suggest, moreover, because low-income ridership tends to be concentrated on transit services where the subsidy per rider is comparatively small. Riders on the

MBTA's commuter rail system have much higher incomes than the riders on bus or rapid transit lines, for example, because the commuter rail system serves distant suburbs that tend to be wealthier. The average subsidy per trip on the commuter rail system was $5.63 in 1980, however, while the subsidy per bus or rail transit ride was less than 70 cents (Table 6–3).

Even within the bus and rapid transit systems, moreover, poor people tend to use services that are subsidized less. Poor people tend to ride shorter distances, for example, largely because they live closer to the metropolitan center. Approximately 75 percent of the work trips made on Boston's buses and streetcars by households with 1978 incomes below $6000 were less than 5 miles long, while less than 20 percent of such work trips by households with incomes above $15,000 were so short.[24] MBTA bus and rapid transit fares do not vary with distance travelled, unless a transfer is required,[25] so that travellers making short trips tend to pay more per mile travelled than others. Since the MBTA's cost per trip is probably roughly proportional to the distance travelled, short-distance travellers, such as the poor, probably require less subsidy than long-distance travellers.[26]

Moreover, poor people probably ride more during the off-peak hours than the peak or rush hours, because the majority of the poor are unemployed and many do not have cars that they can use for shopping and other types of trips generally made during the off-peak.[27] Although passenger loads are heavier during the peak, the cost of providing a bus- or train-mile of service is also much higher in the peak.[28] As a result, on most transit systems the average subsidy per traveller is typically higher in the peak than the off-peak.[29]

The extension of the MBTA's rail lines farther into the suburbs over the past decade probably has made the distribution of transit subsidies even less progressive. The combined operating and capital deficits on these rail transit extensions is almost surely far greater than the deficits on the bus lines they replaced. And since these extensions service Boston's outer suburbs, they are mainly patronized by higher-income travellers.

Of course, the small fraction of transit subsidy that goes to poor riders may understate the advantages of transit assistance to the poor if the subsidies are financed out of relatively progressive taxes. Some analysts argue that the poor may benefit overall from transit assistance because they pay even less in transportation taxes than they receive in transit subsidy.[30] This argument is less convincing in Massachusetts than it may be in other places, however, because a large portion of the state's transit subsidies are financed out of sales and property taxes that are less progressive.

More important, these calculations usually equate the benefits to riders with the subsidy received by the transit system, an assumption that is questionable because some of the subsidy may be absorbed in higher wages, inefficient labor and management practices, or unproductive services rather than passed on to patrons.[31]

Another more convincing line of argument is that poor riders may benefit from transit service they do not patronize heavily. Poor riders might be willing to pay something to maintain the option of using services they patronize only occasionally or not at all, for example, if the availability of an extensive transit route system and service during most hours of the day would help them avoid the high cost of owning an automobile. Even considering this option value, however, the poor account for such a small percentage of total ridership that the benefits to poor riders probably amount to only a small fraction of the subsidy cost. As we shall discuss later, moreover, there are ways to target transit subsidies more directly to low-income riders while still preserving, and perhaps even expanding, the transit network that many of them depend on.

Special Elderly and Handicapped Programs

The MBTA and the 14 RTAs all have special programs to assist elderly and handicapped riders, partly to meet requirements for federal transit aid. A 1974 amendment to the Urban Mass Transportation Assistance Act requires that all transit agencies receiving federal aid, including the MBTA and the RTAs, charge elderly riders half fare or less. Section 504 of Rehabilitation Act of 1978 also requires that no person be excluded by reason of a handicap from participation in any federally subsidized program. To meet Section 504 requirements the MBTA has developed plans to construct elevators in its heavily used subway stations and has placed an initial order for 110 buses equipped with wheelchair lifts to be deployed on selected routes. In addition, the MBTA offers discount fares to the handicapped and operates a special door-to-door handicapped van service (called "The Ride") in some parts of Boston, Cambridge, and Somerville. All fourteen RTAs also offer lower fares to the handicapped, and most supplement their conventional fixed-route bus service with door-to-door van service for handicapped riders and, in a few cases, the elderly as well.

The cost of the MBTA and RTA special elderly and handicapped programs is relatively high. Fare discounts to the elderly and handicapped probably increased the fiscal 1980 operating deficits of the MBTA and the RTAs by around $4 million, for example, because fare reductions did not produce an equivalent increase in elderly and handicapped riders.[32] Deficits on the door-to-door handicapped and elderly services offered by the RTAs amounted to $2.6 million in 1980, for an average subsidy per passenger of $2.89. The MBTA's "The Ride" operated at a loss of about $1 million, or $11.35 per passenger trip, in 1981. If the MBTA goes ahead with plans to buy lift-equipped buses and to install elevators in important rapid transit stations, the annual operating and amortized capital costs may be as high as $5 to $10 million.[33] Although a substantial portion of the capital costs for these modifications are likely to be financed by federal grants, these federal funds could conceivably be used elsewhere on the MBTA system.

Other state and local agencies also provide special transportation services for the elderly or the handicapped. The Massachusetts Rehabilitation Commission finances vehicle modifications to enable handicapped Massachusetts residents to drive their own automobiles and vans and also operates special van services to pick up clients attending its workshops or programs. At the local level, many municipal governments operate small fixed-route or door-to-door van services for senior citizens, often funded with federal community development block grants.

Finally, a large number of private social service agencies, churches, and charitable groups operate special transportation services for the elderly or the handicapped, often with state or federal aid. The Massachusetts Executive Office of Transportation and Construction administers federal grants authorized under Section 16(b)2 of the Urban Mass Transportation Assistance Act to pay up to 80 percent of the capital cost of vans or other vehicles purchased by private non-profit groups to provide transportation for the elderly or the handicapped. The Massachusetts Department of Elder Affairs and the U.S. Department of Health and Welfare distribute federal funds to private agencies to pay for elderly transportation for medical trips under Titles XIX and XX of the Social Security Act and Titles IIIb and IIIc of the Older Americans Act. These non-profit agencies carry substantially more passengers than the special elderly and handicapped services offered by the MBTA or the RTAs; the 17 private agencies receiving Section 16(b)2 assistance in the Boston metropolitan area carried approximately two million passenger trips in 1979, or about twenty times as many as the MBTA's "The Ride."[34]

The most obvious possible drawback of these special elderly and handicapped programs is that many of the beneficiaries may not be poor since, as explained earlier, only 6 percent of the elderly and 16 percent of the handicapped in Massachusetts are poor. But the participants in most of these programs appear to be substantially poorer than the elderly and the handicapped population as a whole, largely because the special services offered are not very convenient. The van services are probably used only by those with few transportation alternatives, for example, since they often serve only a limited number of destinations, require reservations made days in advance, and may not be very reliable. Over 60 percent of the riders on van services receiving 16(b)2 grants in metropolitan Boston had 1979 household incomes below $4,000.[35] Similarly, only a small fraction of the eligible elderly population ever registers for the MBTA's discount fare identification cards, which suggests that those who take the time to register probably have lower than average incomes.

Despite the fact that many of the beneficiaries of these programs may be poor, most of the poor are neither elderly nor handicapped and thus do not benefit from these programs. The high cost per ride of some elderly and handicapped services compounds this difficulty: To the extent that costly elderly and handicapped programs compete for funding with programs to assist the poor, the poor may be short-changed even more. Improving the efficiency of these programs and targeting them to the most needy elderly and handicapped would be clearly beneficial.

The most wasteful of the elderly and handicapped programs are the plans to install lifts in transit stations and buses. These lifts are necessary for only a very small minority of the handicapped, primarily those who are confined to wheelchairs or use walkers, and even for these people the modifications are of questionable value. Getting to the transit station or the bus stop will still be difficult, especially in the winter. Since only about 10 percent of the buses will be lift-equipped, handicapped riders may also be forced to wait a long time for a lift-equipped vehicle. Finally, lift-equipped buses are not only substantially more expensive to buy and operate, but unreliable and difficult to maintain. The experience of other cities with lift-equipped buses and elevators shows that they are used by only a small number of handicapped riders and the cost per trip is extraordinarily high.[36] Providing wheelchair-bound persons with door-to-door van services, taxi vouchers, or automobiles specially modified so that they can drive, may be far more reasonable alternatives.

Some of the door-to-door van services for the elderly and the handicapped are also relatively costly, particularly those operated by the MBTA and the RTAs. At $3 to $12 per ride, the RTA and MBTA van services are probably more expensive than private taxis. Although cost data are not available, van services operated by non-profit agencies may be far less expensive because they use lower-paid or volunteer labor.[37] While some special van services are desirable for certain elderly and handicapped groups, such as those confined to wheelchairs, they clearly should be used selectively.

Other Social Service Agency Programs

Massachusetts social service agencies provide a variety of other transportation programs for their low-income clients in addition to the elderly and handicapped services, although the extent of this aid is difficult to estimate because transportation expenditures are often not listed separately in their budgets. One example is the Massachusetts Rehabilitation Commission, whose programs for its handicapped clients were described earlier. Under the Medicaid program, the state and the federal government also pay the costs of certain medical trips for low-income Massachusetts residents; in addition to emergency ambulance services, the Massachusetts Medicaid program reportedly reimburses nearly $10 million per year in client taxi and van fares. Some job training programs apparently provide transportation or reimburse clients for travel expenses to and from training locations. An increasing number of state and local social service agencies contract with the 14 RTAs to provide some special door-to-door services for their clients.[38]

In addition, many social service agencies may reduce the transportation problems of their clients indirectly by locating offices in low-income neighborhoods. One of the important benefits of community health centers, discussed in Chapter 3, may be increased accessibility to health care. Similarly, the location of welfare, employment and multi-service centers in low-income neighborhoods may be extremely useful.

It is difficult to evaluate the effectiveness of these special programs because we know so little about them or the importance of improved accessibility to social service clients. They are appealing in principle, however, since they can be targeted to low-income groups and tailored to very specific mobility problems.

Better Ways to Help the Poor

Improving Auto Availability

The most obvious shortcoming of current transportation programs is that they do little to increase the availability of the most

important mode of transportation for the poor: the private automobile. While a majority of Massachusetts' poor households
probably already own cars, the cost is a severe financial burden.
Many poor households without cars or licensed household
members might become motorized with a little assistance from
the state.

One possibility would be to subsidize the expense of owning
and operating an automobile, much as we now subsidize mass
transit fares. The cost would not necessarily be prohibitive, especially if viewed as an alternative to other less effective transportation programs for the poor. If only *half* of the funds used to
subsidize mass transit in Massachusetts were used instead to
subsidize the costs of automobiles for poor people, for example,
the state could buy every poor family in Massachusetts a new car
every six years or give each poor family $830 every year towards
the cost of owning and operating an automobile.[39] These calculations, while interesting, probably do not reflect political realities.
But it is striking that we are willing to heavily subsidize mass
transit, which probably accounts for less than 10 percent of all
trips by poor households, and are reluctant to subsidize automobiles, which account for over 60 percent of poor travel.

On a more practical note, however, the state already regulates
the cost and availability of automobiles in a variety of ways, and a
little sensitivity to the problems of the poor might be of great
assistance. One area where the state is already active, for example, is automobile insurance. The Registry of Motor Vehicles
requires all motorists to carry minimum insurance coverage and
the Insurance Commissioner regulates the rates charged for different types of coverage. While mandatory minimum insurance
provides many important benefits to motorists, the annual premium can be as much as several hundred dollars per car. Direct
subsidies to the poor to offset the cost of mandatory coverage
might make car ownership much more managable for many poor
households. Less attractive for a variety of reasons is the possibility of setting low "lifeline" rates for mandatory coverage and
allowing the insurance companies to cross-subsidize the resulting
losses by charging higher premiums for expanded coverage.[40]

Modifications to the vehicle inspection program are another
potential source of assistance. The annual safety inspection may
be a burden to the poor (and others) with little safety benefit,
since there is little difference in accident rates in states with and
without inspections.[41] To meet requirements of the Clean Air Act,
moreover, the state added an annual air pollution emissions
inspection beginning in 1983. Owners of vehicles badly out of

compliance with emissions standards are required to perform indicated maintenance, up to a maximum cost of $100 per vehicle or 10 percent of the car's book value (whichever is less), and then have their vehicles retested. The results of pilot programs in other states suggest that the benefits from the reductions in automotive emissions may be smaller than the costs of the inspections.[42] Since poor people tend to own older and poorly maintained automobiles, assistance with the repair costs or a more forgiving inspection policy for old cars would be helpful.

The state's policies toward driver licensing might also be modified to encourage low-income persons, the elderly, and the physically handicapped to get licenses or keep their licenses longer. Such a policy might pose safety problems because many elderly and handicapped have slower reflexes, poorer vision, and other problems. Measured by the number of accidents and fatalities per vehicle-mile, however, elderly drivers are among the safer driving groups, in part because they recognize their limitations and compensate by driving less at night and staying on familiar roads.[43] Special instruction for elderly drivers, limited licenses (perhaps for daytime or local driving only), and subsidized driver education for low-income persons might increase the number of licensed drivers without creating a safety hazard.

Finally, the Massachusetts Rehabilitation Commission's program of subsidizing vehicle modifications to enable disabled persons to drive should be continued and perhaps expanded for low-income clients. This program provides far more mobility at a much lower cost per trip than other alternatives such as special van services or the installation of lifts in transit stations and vehicles.

Using Transit Subsidies More Effectively

Current transit subsidy programs could also be reformed to benefit the poor. The most needed change is to keep fares low for poor riders while allowing fares to rise for others. Such a policy would insure that low fares were targeted to the riders who need them most. But equally important, the revenue from increased fares paid by other passengers would allow the transit system to maintain or expand the extensive service coverage that is so important to auto-less households.

One way to target low fares to the poor is to subsidize poor users directly. Poor families could be issued discount fare identification cards like those currently used by elderly and handicapped MBTA riders. Alternatively, to avoid the possible stigma of an identification card, poor families could be sold monthly transit passes or a supply of transit tokens at a discounted price. The administrative costs of certifying eligible households could be reduced by using participation in Food Stamps or other welfare programs as the criterion. Misuse of identification cards or resale of tokens could be minimized by using identification cards with photos or limiting the token sales per family. Direct subsidy schemes of this type are being used for conventional transit service in at least three U.S. metropolitan areas and for elderly or handicapped taxi service in nine other communities.[44]

An alternative means of targeting fares is to keep them low on only those services the poor patronize most heavily. For example, fares could be raised on commuter rail, during the peak period, and for longer-distance trips and be kept low during off-peak hours, for short trips, and on routes that serve low-income neighborhoods. The administrative problems of collecting fares that vary by time of day or distance travelled can often be minimized by careful fare structure design. The MBTA might vary fares by distance, for example, by reducing the current base subway and bus fare below current levels while collecting double or triple fares from passengers boarding at the outer stops of long rail and bus lines. The MBTA already collects double fares at the outermost stations of two rail transit lines, so there is precedent for expanding and refining this practice.

A recent study in Atlanta demonstrated that direct user subsidies are more effective and efficient in reducing fares for the poor than varying fares by type of route, time of day, or distance. Low-income riders receive 100 percent of the assistance with direct user subsidies but only 50 to 77 percent of the assistance with other alternatives. Moreover, 70 to 80 percent of all the poor transit riders were thought likely to participate in a direct user subsidy program, while most other schemes benefited a smaller percentage of poor riders. Because direct user subsidies are more efficiently targeted, less revenue is lost, the fares for other riders do not have to rise as much to compensate for the losses, and the effective average subsidy per poor rider can be greater.[45] Although no comparable study has been done in Boston, the advantages of direct user subsidies are probably similar to those found in Atlanta.

Even if direct subsidies to poor users are adopted, however, fares should also be varied by distance traveled, time-of-day, and particular routes as the best means of recouping the subsidy cost or raising additional revenues from other riders. Since marginal costs are higher on long-distance, peak, and commuter rail trips, for example, higher fares for these services would be desirable. More important, the long-distance and peak ridership is generally less sensitive to fare increases both because the riders tend to have higher incomes and because traffic congestion makes auto use a less satisfactory alternative to transit during the peak period. As a result, selective fare increases by distance, time or day, or route hold the promise of generating the greater increases in passenger revenue and losing fewer riders than an across-the-board increase in the base fare.

Raising additional revenue from other riders is important because low fares for poor should not come at the expense of reduced services. Some services that are very lightly patronized by the poor might be safely cut back, such as the commuter rail system. But significant cuts in service to inner-city neighborhoods or in the evening and midday hours should probably be avoided, since these are probably extremely important for families who are trying to avoid the expense of owning an automobile.

Service might even be expanded selectively in unserved low-income markets. Careful experimentation with bus routes connecting inner-city neighborhoods and suburban employment centers might be useful, for example, despite the disappointing results of the demonstrations during the late 1960s. Although the ridership and the benefits from these services will not be very high, these services may still be worthwhile if the costs can be kept low, for example, by using the usually empty return trips of express buses carrying suburbanites to downtown jobs. Hartford, Connecticut recently experimented with routes of this type with some success.[46]

Selective Use of Special Services

Although increasing auto use and maintaining extensive conventional transit service are the best ways to help a great majority of the poor, at least two groups will still face transportation problems that require additional special assistance. First, some rural or suburban auto-less poor households may need special assistance because conventional transit systems can not hope to serve all types of trips, especially in low-density areas, without imposing astronomical burdens on the taxpayers. Second, special aid will also be needed for a small number of handicapped poor with disabilities that prevent them both from using conventional mass transit and from driving even specially modified automobiles.

Since special services such as door-to-door vans are relatively costly, however, it is crucial that they be targeted only to the minority of the poor that cannot depend on autos or conventional transit. Transportation services or travel expense in reimbursements provided by health, manpower, and other social service agencies may already be reasonably well targeted, since they are offered only to low-income clients and presumably tailored to specific mobility problems. Many of the van services provided by transit agencies or municipal governments are, however, available to all elderly and handicapped persons. While the limited availability and low quality of some of these services now effectively discourage their use by all but the poorest elderly and handicapped riders, it may be more sensible to upgrade the quality of service but restrict eligibility to the severely disabled and to travel by other poor households to destinations not served by conventional transit.

In addition, the state should explore ways to reduce the cost per ride on these special services. One possibility is more heavy reliance on van services operated by non-profit private agencies such as the current 16(b)2 operators, since they probably have lower costs than the van services provided by transit agencies. An even more promising possibility is contracts with private taxi companies to provide service; a number of studies have shown that special elderly and handicapped van services often cost more than the fares charged by taxis for comparable trips. Both the goals of targeting the services to those who need them, most and reducing costs might be best served by issuing taxi vouchers or script to a limited number of eligible households. Ten U.S. cities (including Lawrence, Massachusetts) have experimented successfully with similar taxi voucher systems for the elderly and handicapped.[47]

In summary, transportation is a serious burden for many poor households, even if it is not at the top of the list of their problems. The state can do much to help the poor with their transportation problems at little cost to taxpayers, moreover, by redirecting and targeting some of the funds spent on existing transportation programs for the poor. Efforts to relieve the economic burden of auto ownership and to increase driver licensing among poor households are perhaps most important, since the private automobile is by far the poor's most dominant transportation mode. Existing mass transit subsidies should also be redesigned so that the low fares are targeted to the minority of riders who are poor and so that extensive transit service is maintained. Finally, costly special door-to-door services should be reserved only for the handicapped poor who can use neither automobiles nor conventional mass transit.

Endnotes

1. "Local trips" are defined as trips of less than 50 miles (one way) that do not involve an overnight stay.
2. The argument that inadequate transportation is a relatively minor cause of the low trip-making rates of the poor is also supported by some evidence on trip-making rates by low-income households facing different levels of transportation service or prices. For example, a survey of low-income families without autos in Brooklyn found that average daily trips declined by only about 10 percent for families that live 3000 rather than 1000 feet away from the subway station: John C. Falcocchio, Louis J. Piguataro, and Edward J. Cantilli, "Modal Choices and Transportation Attributes of Inner-City Poor." *Transportation Research Record* no. 403 (1976), p. 9.
3. National consumer expenditure surveys reveal that households with 1972–1973 incomes below $3000 spent an average of 27 percent of their post-tax income on transportation (almost all of it on automobiles), while all households spent an average of only 17 percent. See U.S. Bureau of Labor Statistics, *Handbook of Labor Statistics*, Bulletin No. 2070 (Washington, D.C.: U.S. Government Printing Office, 1980), pp. 368–374 and John R. Meyer and Jose A. Gomez-Ibanez, *Autos, Transit and Cities* (Cambridge, Mass: Harvard University Press, 1981), p. 242.
4. In 1975, 44 percent of Massachusetts' poor lived in central cities (compared with only 26 percent of the total Massachusetts population). Another 43 percent of the poor lived in metropolitan suburbs, many in communities close to the central city (such as Cambridge or Somerville) which enjoy extensive transit service.
5. John Pucher, Chris Hendrickson, and Sue McNeil, "Socioeconomic Characteristics of Transit Riders: Some Recent Evidence," *Traffic Quarterly* 35 (July 1981), p. 464.
6. In addition, another 31,800 were institutionalized and 14,200 were suffering from a variety of acute conditions. These statistics for Massachusetts were estimated by the author using the nationwide rates of disabilities among elderly and non-elderly persons found in Transportation Systems Center, *The Handicapped and Elderly Market for Urban Transportation*, report no. PB-224-821, prepared for the Urban Mass Transportation Administration (Springfield, VA: National Technical Information Service, 1973), p. 6.
7. U.S. Department of Transportation, Federal Highway Administration, *A Life Cycle of Travel by the American Family*, Report No. 7 of the *1977 Nationwide Personal Transportation Study* (Washington, D.C.: Federal Highway Administration, 1981), pp. 14 and 35; and Grey Advertising, Inc., *Summary Report of Data from the National Survey of Transportation Handicapped People*, report for the U.S. Department of Transportation, Urban Mass Transportation Administration (Washington, D.C.: U.S. Department of Transportation, 1978), p. 38.
8. Most unemployed handicapped people cite their disability or illness as the reasons that they do not work; only 2 percent list transportation as a m ajor reason. Grey Advertising, Inc., *National Survey of Transportation Handicapped People*, pp. 23–25.

9. *Ibid.*, p. 25.

10. *Ibid.*, p. 65.

11. U.S. Department of Transportation, Federal Highway Administration, *Mode of Transportation and Personal Characteristics of Tripmakers*, Report no. 9 of the *(1969) Nationwide Personal Transportation Study* (Washington, D.C.: U.S. Federal Highway Administration, 1973), p. 31.

12. In that same year 69.3 percent of all men and 32.7 percent of all women aged 70 and over were also licensed to drive; see U.S. Department of Transportation, Federal Highway Administration, *Characteristics of 1977 Licensed Drivers and Their Travel*, Report no. 1 of the *1977 Nationwide Personal Transportation Study* (Washington, D.C.: Federal Highway Administration, 1980), p. 9.

13. Grey Advertising, Inc., *National Survey of Transportation Handicapped People*, p. 65.

14. John L. Crain, *The Reverse Commute Experiment: A $7 Million Demonstration Program*, report prepared for the U.S. Department of Transportation, Urban Mass Transportation Administration, (1980), pp. 6, 9, and 14; and Charles S. Greenwald and Richard Syron, "Increasing Job Opportunities in Boston's Urban Core," *New England Economic Review* (January/February 1969), pp. 30–40.

15. John F. Kain and John R. Meyer, "Transportation and Poverty," *The Public Interest* (Winter 1970) pp. 80–81.

16. In a special 1970 census of employment of residents of low-income areas, less than 0.5 percent of those who said that they were not in the labor force but wanted, might have wanted, or would have wanted a regular job reported that transportation problems were the principle reason they were not looking for work. See U.S. Department of Commerce, Bureau of the Census, *Employment Profiles of Selected Low-Income Areas, United States Summary—Urban Areas*, Vol. PHC(3)-1 of *1970 Census of Population and Housing* (Washington, D.C.: U.S. Government Printing Office, 1972), p. 64.

17. The most complete of these studies of unemployment rates, by David Ellwood, compares different neighborhoods in the city of Chicago; see David T. Ellwood, "The Mismatch Hypothesis: Are Teenage Jobs Missing in the Ghetto?" National Bureau of Economic Research working paper (Cambridge, Massachusetts, 1983). Although there is little evidence that proximity to jobs significantly affects unemployment rates, Quentin Gillard argues that proximity may affect the wage rates of those who are employed. Gillard finds higher incomes among suburban than central city residents who are employed; See Quentin Gillard, "Reverse Commuting and the Inner City Low-Income Problem," *Growth and Change* 10 (July 1979): 12–17.

18. This figure includes approximately $194 million in operating assistance and $32 million in fixed charges for the MBTA for calendar year 1980, plus $18.6 million in operating assistance for the 14 RTAs for fiscal 1980.

19. the MBTA carried approximately 279.1 million unlinked passenger trips in calendar 1980, while the 14 RTAs carried 34.8 million passenger trips on fixed-route service in fiscal 1980.

20. Commonwealth of Massachusetts, Executive Office of Transportation and Construction, "Regional Transit Authority Operations Report," publication no. 12438-37-225-6-81-CR, pp. 14-15.

21. Rail rapid transit fares were raised to 50 cents in July 1980, raised to 75 cents in August 1981, and then rolled back to 60 cents in May of 1982. Bus fares were kept at 25 cents until August 1981, when they were raised to 50 cents.

22. (Boston) Central Transportation Planning Staff, *Final Environmental and Socioeconomic Impact Report of the MBTA Fare Increase* (Boston: Central Transportation Planning Staff, 1982), pp. 63, 69. For a more complete discussion of recent attempts to use transit subsidies to reduce auto use see John R. Meyer and Jose A. Gomez-Ibanez, *Autos, Transit, and Cities*, esp. pp. 39–55.

23. These statistics are for rail rapid transit lines only, since comparable figures for bus ridership are not available yet; see Michael Carakatsane and Lawrence Tittemore, *MBTA Systemwide Passenger Data Collection Program, Volume 1-Rapid Transit System*, Central Transportation Planning Staff, Technical Report no. 24 (Boston, 1981), p. 79.

24. Special tabulation of the 1978 Annual Housing Survey computer tapes prepared by John Pucher of the Department of Urban Planning at Rutgers University under contract to the U.S. Urban Mass Transportation Administration.

25. Exceptions include the outermost stations on the MBTA's Red and Green Lines, where double fares are required for inbound passengers. Free transfers are also allowed between rail transit lines.

26. Data on costs and revenue by length of trip are not available for Boston, but a study of three California transit systems shows that the operating subsidy increases with trip length. Robert Cervero, "Flat versus Differentiated Transit Pricing: What's a Fair Fare?," *Transportation* 10 (1981) 211–232, esp. 223.

27. Data on peak and off-peak ridership by income in Boston are not readily available, but national statistics and data for other U.S. transit systems show that off-peak ridership is disproportionately poor; see John Pucher, Chris Hendrickson, and Sue McNiel, "Socioeconomic Characteristics of Transit Riders," p. 470.

28. Costs are higher because the number of vehicles and other capital requirements are determined by peak needs and because transit labor agreements restrict management flexibility in assigning operators to peak shifts and require premium pay for peak work. For a more complete explanation of the higher costs of peak service see John R. Meyer and Jose A. Gomez-Ibanez, *Improving Mass Transit Productivity*, report prepared for the U.S. Department of Transportation, Urban Mass Transportation Administration, 1977.

29. Data on peak and off-peak subsidies are not available for Boston; typical results for other systems can be found in Robert Cervero, "Flat versus Differentiated Transit Pricing," pp. 225–227.

30. This argument has been made most forcefully by John Pucher in a variety of articles including John Pucher, "Equity in Transit Finance," *Journal of the American Planning Association* 47 (October 1981): 387–407.

31. This proposition is difficult to demonstrate empirically, but it is striking that before the advent of federal transit subsidies the rate of growth in transit wage rates was generally slower or comparable to that of general manufacturing wage rates, while after subsidies became available transit wage

increases outstripped those in manufacturing; see John R. Meyer and Jose A. Gomez-Ibanez, *Autos, Transit and Cities*, pp. 48–49.

32. This figure assumes that 10 percent of the RTA's and MBTA's riders are elderly and handicapped, each elderly or handicapped patron paid half the average fare of $0.29 per rider, and the fare discounts encouraged only small increases in ridership.

33. Estimates of the cost of installing elevators in an existing subway station range around $2 million, while a wheelchair lift is estimated to increase the annual capital, operating, and maintenance costs of a bus by around $2000. Assuming 20 stations will be modernized, that the elevators will last 20 years with negligible operating costs, and that 200 buses will be lift-equipped, the total cost would amount to $4.9 million per year. If the federal government paid 80 percent of the capital costs but none of the operating cost, the cost to the MBTA would be roughly $1 million per year. For estimates of the costs of elevators or lifts in stations and buses see U.S. Congressional Budget Office, *Urban Transportation for Handicapped Persons: Alternative Federal Approaches* (Washington, D.C.: U.S. Government Printing Office, 1979) and U.S. Department of Transportation, Transportation Systems Center, *The Accessible Fixed-Route Bus Service Experiment*, TSC Urban and Regional Research Series, Report no. UMTA-MA-06-0049-81-7 (Cambridge, Mass: Transportation Systems Center, 1981).

34. Central Transportation Planning Staff, *An Evaluation of the 16(b)2 Program in the MAPC Region*, (Boston, December 1980), pp. 14–15.

35. *Ibid*, p. 32.

36. John R. Meyer and Jose A. Gomez-Ibanez, *Autos, Transit and Cities*, p. 251; U.S. Congressional Budget Office, *Urban Transportation for Handicapped Persons: Alternative Federal Approaches;* and U.S. Department of Transportation, Transportation Systems Center, *The Accessible Fixed-Route Bus Service Experiment.*

37. These labor economies may be partly offset by higher capital costs per ride, however, since the non-profit agencies probably use their vehicles less intensively.

38. Social service agencies reimbursed $400,000, or 17 percent, of the cost of special door-to-door services operated by the RTAs in fiscal 1980.

39. In 1980 approximately 146,000 poor households resided in Massachusetts. Transit subsidies in that year amounted to $245 million, or $1678 per poor household. Since a basic subcompact car cost about $5000 in 1980, buying every poor household a new car every six years would cost only $122 million per year, or $833 per poor household.

40. Since the lifeline rates would apply to all households, they would be substantially more costly than direct subsidies to the poor. Moreover, if insurance companies were forced to cross-subsidize the losses on lifeline rates with higher rates on supplementary coverage, many middle-income motorists would probably be forced to substantially reduce their insurance protection.

41. W. Mark Crain, *Vehicle Safety Inspection Systems: How Effective?* (Washington, D.C.: American Enterprise Institute, 1980), esp. pp. 20–36.

42. Benefits exceed costs for inspections only if one uses extremely optimistic estimates of the value of the benefits gained from emission reduction and if one ignores the costs of the inspections to motorists in the form of lost time and inconvenience. See Lawrence J. White, *The Regulation of Air Pollution Emissions from Motor Vehicles* (Washington, D.C.: American Enterprise Institute for Public Policy Research, 1982), pp. 105–106.
43. The accident rates for elderly drivers are about the same or slightly lower than the general driver population, depending upon the exact measure used. Elderly drivers have poorer safety records than drivers in their 40s and 50s but substantially better records than drivers in their teens or 20s; see John R. Meyer and Jose A. Gomez-Ibanez, *Autos, Transit and Cities*, p. 247.
44. In Sacramento, California and Arlington, Virginia, for example, the county welfare departments offer transit subsidies of this type for low-income persons. Direct subsidies for elderly and handicapped riders have been used for bus and taxi service in Danville, Illinois and for taxi service in at least nine other communities. See Mary E. Lovely and Daniel Brand, "Atlanta Transit Pricing Study: Moderating the Impact of Fare Increases on the Poor," *Transportation Research Record*, no. 857 (1982); and Bruce D. Spear, "User Side Subsidies: Delivering Special Needs Transportation Through Private Providers," *Transportation Research Record*, no. 850 (1982).
45. The Atlanta study used Food Stamp eligibility as the criterion for low incomes; see Lovely and Brand, "Atlanta Pricing Study."
46. Helen M. Kemp, "A Report on Connecticut Transit's Reverse Commutation Program," Connecticut Transit, October 1981.
47. Bruce D. Spear, "User Side Subsidies."

Chapter 7

STATE HOUSING POLICY AND THE POOR

by John M. Yinger

The Massachusetts State Government has a long history of improving housing opportunities for poor households. Many poor families now live in state housing projects originally built for veterans in the early 1950s, and state programs to build elderly housing and scattered-site family housing, plus programs to provide rental and mortgage assistance, received funding throughout the 1970s. Recent legislation has established programs for weatherization and heating fuel assistance. Over the last few years, however, both economic conditions in the housing market and federal housing policy have changed rapidly, with important consequences for the housing opportunities of poor households and for the design of state housing policy in the 1980s.

This chapter reviews the latest evidence on housing conditions for the poor in Massachusetts and discusses the implications of this evidence for state housing policy. The chapter is organized around four issues: (1) conditions in the private housing market, (2) the condition of existing public housing, (3) the displacement of poor households by rent increases or condominium conver-

NOTE: In preparing this paper I have received valuable suggestions and information from many people. I would particularly like to thank Larry Antin, Rachel Bratt, Elaine Fersh, Joseph Flatley, John Kain, John Loehr, Wayne Sherwood, Harry Spence, John Washek, and the participants in the Kennedy School Faculty Study Group on the State and the Poor. I have not always taken their good advise, however, and the reader should not assume that any of these people agree with what I have written.

sion, and (4) discrimination against poor minority households. My analysis reveals that on each of these issues the poor would benefit from major changes in state housing policy and in particular from a more effective use of existing housing resources. The state should expand the housing available to the poor and improve neighborhood conditions by subsidizing the rehabilitation of deteriorated units and the reclaimation of abandoned units; it should provide rental assistance to make existing housing affordable to the poor; it should implement a comprehensive program to preserve existing public housing; it should develop focused policies to protect the poor from displacement; and it should eliminate the discriminatory barriers that limit the housing opportunities of poor minorities.

Housing Conditions for the Poor in the Private Housing Market

Most poor people in Massachusetts are served by the private housing market, which includes privately owned housing supported by government subsidies. In this section we document recent trends in conditions facing the poor in the private housing market. We also untangle the causes of these trends and draw some conclusions for state housing policy.

Evidence

Housing conditions are notoriously difficult to measure. We know that many poor families in Massachusetts, like similar families in other states, live in deteriorated and even unsafe housing. Furthermore, we can observe some neighborhoods in which a large portion of the housing appears to be in severely run-down condition. But to compare housing conditions across cities or across time, we must rely on data concerning a few housing characteristics that can be objectively measured, such as lack of plumbing or rental payments as a percentage of income. These data obviously cannot fully describe the housing problems of the poor, but they do reveal the extent of a few key problems and indicate some broad trends in housing conditions.

Published data on housing conditions by income class can be found in the 1970 and 1980 U.S. Census of Housing and the 1975 and 1977 Annual Housing Survey (AHS). Most of the data for Massachusetts are from the two largest metropolitan areas in the state, Boston and Springfield, so our discussion will focus on these two areas. This focus provides a reasonably accurate picture of housing conditions for the poor in the state: About half of the poor people in Massachusetts in 1980 lived in the Boston metropolitan area and about one-quarter lived in the central cities of Boston and Springfield.

These two data sources tabulate housing characteristics by household income class but not by poverty status, which depends on family size as well as on income. Consequently, we examine housing conditions of households in the lowest-income classes as an approximation for the housing conditions of poor households. We compare households reporting 1969 incomes below $5,000 with households reporting 1976 incomes below $7,000; in real terms (that is, after dividing by the consumer price index) these two cutoffs are about the same. The 1976 cutoff is slightly above the 1976 poverty line for a family of four ($5,815), so that some larger poor families and some smaller near-poor households are included in our comparisions.

The most basic indicators of inadequate housing are incomplete plumbing facilities and overcrowding (defined as more than one person per room). Tables 7–1 and 7–2 show the percentage of poor households that, according to these standards, did not have adequate housing in 1970 and in 1977. These tables reveal that housing quality for poor households has been improving in Massachusetts. In every case (Boston and Springfield, metropolitan area and central city, majority and minority households, owners and renters) the percentage of poor households lacking plumbing or facing overcrowding declined from 1970 to 1977.

A closer look at these tables reveals that severe housing problems are confined largely to poor renters and fall into two classes. First, lack of a complete kitchen or of some plumbing confronts a small proportion of poor renters, regardless of whether they live in central city or suburb or whether they belong to the majority or to a minority group. Second, overcrowding and deteriorated neighborhood conditions are problems of all renters, primarily in central cities, but they are particularly severe for poor minorities. In Boston, for example, the incidence of both overcrowding and deteriorated neighborhoods is three times as great for poor black renters as for all poor renters. Furthermore, the incidence of these two problems among minorities is striking: 10.6 percent of poor black renters and 12.4 percent of poor Hispanic renters live in overcrowded conditions, and 45.5 percent of poor black renters and 39.1 percent of poor Hispanic renters live in neighborhoods with abandoned or boarded up units.[1]

Table 7-1 Percentage of Households with Selected Housing Problems in the Boston Metropolitan Area 1970 and 1977

| | Renters | | | | Minority Renters in Central City | | | | Owners in Central City | |
| | Metropolitan Area | | Central City | | Black | | Hispanic | | | |
	Poor	Non-Poor	Poor	Non-Poor	Poor	Non-Poor	Poor	Non-Poor	Poor	Non-Poor
1970:										
Incomplete plumbing	7.9%	2.7%	9.6%	4.2%	6.2%	2.8%	5.9%	2.9%	3.5%	1.3%
Overcrowded	4.2	7.3	5.6	8.8	9.1	16.0	18.7	17.8	2.7	7.4
(Poor/non-poor share)	34.5	65.5	40.9	59.1	52.2	47.8	41.3	58.7	19.2	80.8
1977:										
Incomplete	5.4	1.5	5.8	2.3	5.9	1.4	3.8	3.8	0.8	0.4
Overcrowded	3.0	3.5	4.7	4.4	7.7	8.6	13.2	7.7	0.8	5.4
Incomplete kitchen	2.9	0.6	3.5	0.9	3.0	0.0	1.9	3.8	0.0	0.2
Abandoned units nearby	19.1	9.9	32.2	22.3	46.2	40.7	41.5	26.9	19.5	18.4
(Poor/non-poor share)	35.8	64.2	44.3	55.7	54.7	45.3	67.1	32.9	21.0	79.0

SOURCES: 1970 Census of Housing; 1977 Annual Housing Survey.
NOTE: "Poor" defined as all households with incomes below $5000 in 1969 or $7000 in 1976.

Table 7-2 Percentage of Households with Selected Housing Problems in the Springfield Metropolitan Area, 1970 and 1975

| | Renters | | | | Owners | |
| | Total | | Minority | | Total | |
	Poor	Non-Poor	Black	Hispanic	Poor	Non-Poor
1970:						
Incomplete plumbing	7.3%	2.0%	2.5%	—	3.0%	0.6%
Overcrowded	4.0	8.7	16.0	—	1.3	6.4
(Poor/non-poor share)	40.2	59.8	100.0	—	15.1	84.9
1975:						
Incomplete plumbing	4.8	1.4	—	5.7	0.0	0.0
Overcrowded	3.2	3.7	—	20.0	0.5	4.0
Incomplete kitchen	5.5	1.4	—	8.5	0.0	0.1
Abandoned units nearby	14.8	9.9	20.7	25.7	4.8	3.9
(Poor/non-poor share)	46.8	53.2	100.0	100.0	18.0	82.0

SOURCES: 1970 Census of Housing; 1975 Annual Housing Survey.
NOTE: "Poor" defined as all households with income below $5000 in 1969 or $7000 in 1974.

Table 7-3   Rent Burdens by Income Class in Boston and Northeast, 1970–1980

	Boston Metropolitan Area				Boston Central City					Mass. Renters		Northeast Renters	
	All Renters		Black Renters		All Renters			Black Renters	Hispanic Renters				
	1970	1977	1970	1977	1970	1977	1980	1977	1977	1970	1980	1970	1980
Upper boundary of income class[a]	13.2%	9.4%	14.5%	14.8%	13.3%	13.2%	—	16.5%	—	—	—	12.4%	8.3%
Median rent burden[b]	35+	50+	35+	50+	35+	50+	—	50+	—	—	—	35+	60+
Upper boundary of income class	22.3	25.1	26.6	37.3	22.9	32.7	23.2	41.1	44.2	—	20.9	33.8	33.6
Median rent burden	35+	50+	35+	50+	35+	50+	35+	50+	50+	—	35+	35+	49
Upper boundary of income class	43.5	38.0	48.3	49.7	39.3	45.3	46.8	54.7	67.0	—	43.5	41.4	47.3
Median rent burden	35+	41	35+	36	25-34	39	35+	36	41	—	35+	20-24	33
All households, Median rent burden	20-24	22	25-34	28	20-24	27	20-24	29	37	—	20-24	20-24	27

SOURCES: 1970 Census of Housing; 1977 Annual Housing Survey; 1980 Census of Housing; 1980 Annual Housing Survey.

a Upper boundary of each income class is stated as a percentage of total households—e.g., in the first column, the first class consists of the poorest 13.2% of households and the next class consists of households in the bottom 22.3% of the income distribution but not in the bottom 13.2%.

b Rent burden is defined to be gross rent—i.e, rent plus utilities paid by the tenant—as a percentage of total money income.

Rent burden, that is, the percentage of income spent on housing, is another widely used indicator of housing conditions. Table 7–3 shows gross rent, which is rent plus utilities and heat paid by the tenant, as a percentage of income in Boston and in the Northeast. These rent burdens are shockingly high for poor households. In 1977 the median household in the bottom third or so of the renter income distribution devoted over half of its income toward housing. Because the highest category in the 1970 data is 35 percent or more, it is difficult to compare rent burdens across different years. Nevertheless, several pieces of information indicate that rent burdens rose significantly during the 1970s, particularly for poor households. The median rent burden in the second fifth or so of the renter/income distribution rose from 25–34 percent to 39 percent in Boston and from 20–24 percent to 33 percent in the Northeast. It is reasonable to conclude that the bottom fifth of the renter income distribution experienced a similar jump in its rent burden.[2]

Energy prices, particularly for fuel oil, the primary source of heat in Massachusetts, have risen much faster than prices in general. The resulting rapid increase in heating bills has made a large contribution to the growth in rent burdens, particularly for poor households. In the Northeast in 1978, households with incomes below 75 percent of the poverty line spent 26 percent of their income on heating fuel alone and 41 percent of their income on all home energy. Households between 75 and 125 percent of the poverty line spent 9 percent of their income on heating fuel alone and 16 percent of their income on all home energy.[3]

All else equal, an increase in the cost of housing will induce some households to move into lower-quality units. How then can we explain the fact that housing quality for the poor has improved at the same time that the cost of housing for the poor has gone up? The answer to this puzzle is that the provision of public and subsidized housing allowed low-income households to move out of the worst housing in the state.[4] As shown in Table 7–4, Massachusetts had only 10,800 units of privately owned subsidized housing in 1970. Over the course of the next decade, however, about 59,000 subsidized housing units were constructed and 39,000 existing units obtained a new government subsidy. In addition 35,300 units of publicly owned housing were built, mostly for the elderly.

Eligibility for this subsidized housing is tied to income, so many of the tenants are poor or near poor. According to the AHS data for the Boston metropolitan area in 1977, 84 percent of the tenants in subsidized housing had incomes below $10,000 and 57

Table 7-4 Subsidized Housing and Public Housing in Massachusetts and in Boston, 1970–1983 (thousands of units)

	Massachusetts		Boston	
	1970[a]	1983[b]	1970[c]	1980[c]
Constructed subsidized housing:				
State	0.0	32.0	0.0	5.3
Federal	8.9	36.7	6.8	19.0
Total	8.9	68.7	6.8	24.3
Rental subsidies to existing housing:				
State	0.0	5.0	0.0	0.0
Federal	1.9	36.0[d]	0.0	3.2
Total	1.9	41.0	0.0	3.2
Subtotal—subsidized housing:				
State	0.0	37.0	0.0	5.3
Federal	10.8	72.7	6.8	22.2
Total	10.8	109.7	6.8	27.5
Public housing:				
State	29.3	48.3	3.0[e]	3.5[e]
Federal	17.6	33.8	12.2[e]	14.2[e]
Total	46.9	82.2	15.2	17.7
Grand total: subsidized plus public housing:				
State	29.3	85.3	3.0	8.8
Federal	28.4	106.5	19.0	36.4
Total	57.7	191.9	22.0	45.2

a Estimated by the author from information in "Housing Needs in Massachusetts," Massachusetts Executive Office of Communities and Development (September 1978).

b Figures from Massachusetts Executive Office of Communities and Development.

c Figures from Rolf Goetze, "Boston's Housing in the 1980s: Challenges and Opportunities" (Boston Redevelopment Authority, September 1980).

d Author's estimate based on a figure of 34.8 on 1/1/81.

e State/federal breakdown estimated by the author on the basis of information from the Boston Housing Authority.

percent had incomes below $5,000. These percentages are slightly higher in the central city. Nevertheless, most poor households in the private market are on their own; roughly one third of these poor households are assisted by government subsidies.[5]

Directions for State Policy

The evidence reveals that high rent burdens constitute the main housing problem for the poor in the private housing market in Massachusetts. In addition, many poor households (disproportionately minorities) live in overcrowded conditions. In this section we will discuss state policies for alleviating high rent burdens and for improving distressed neighborhoods. State policies to deal with overcrowding and the concentration of poor minorities in distressed neighborhoods are discussed later in the section on discrimination.

The evidence on rent burdens for the poor is striking. Despite large increases in public and subsidized housing in Massachusetts, most of the state's poor households must find housing in the private housing market without any assistance from government subsidies and therefore must devote over half their income to housing. Energy costs are expected to continue to rise faster than prices in general during the 1980s.[6] Hence, rent burdens for poor households are likely to continue to grow.

The urgency of this affordability problem has been heightened by the recent withdrawal of the federal government from the subsidized housing business. The Reagan Administration has cancelled over half of the 700,000 federally subsidized housing units in process or under construction throughout the nation. After 1983 only 10,000 federally subsidized units will be built each year, all for elderly and handicapped, compared with over 110,000 units built in both 1980 and 1981.[7] In the near future at least, relief must come from the state.

Policymakers in Massachusetts are fortunate in having a range of policies with which to alleviate the high rent burdens of the poor. In particular, four different types of policies are available: (1) constructing publicly owned housing for poor households, (2) subsidizing the construction of privately owned housing for poor households, (3) subsidizing the rents paid by poor households for existing housing, and (4) helping poor households lower their energy costs. In this section we describe existing policies of each type, determine which policies the state has emphasized in recent years, and suggest a new emphasis for the 1980s.

Massachusetts already has constructed over 48,000 units of public housing. (The condition of this existing stock is discussed in the next section.) Additional public housing can be constructed under two programs, both established by the Acts of 1966.

Under Chapter 705, the Family Housing Program, local housing authorities receive funds from the state to build, buy, and/or rehabilitate single-family houses or small apartment buildings for use as low-income family housing. In addition, the state provides rent subsidies to keep the rents for this housing at a reasonable percentage of tenants' incomes. The program emphasizes scattered site development—that is, separate, small buildings often in suburban locations. By FY 1982 this program had created 832 housing units and another 164 units are expected to be built during the next fiscal year.[8]

Chapter 667, the Elderly Housing Program, provides housing for the elderly. Again, the state assists local authorities in obtaining such housing and in keeping rent burdens at reasonable levels. Over 25,000 housing units have been built under this program and 1033 more units are planned for FY 1983.[9]

The Massachusetts Housing Finance Agency (MHFA), also established by the Acts of 1966, makes low-interest loans to developers for the construction or rehabilitation of apartment buildings, as long as at least 25 percent of the units are for low-income households. In practice, approximately 37 percent of the units have been designated for low-income households. MHFA loans are financed by the sale of tax-exempt bonds, which have relatively low interest rates and which enable the state to give developers a substantial interest subsidy. MHFA units for low-income households may also receive direct subsidies through other federal or state programs. In 1983, for example, 1,978 MHFA units will also receive state subsidies through the Chapter 707 program, which is discussed below. About 50,000 units of multi-family housing have been financed by the MHFA, and, as of August 1982, the MHFA had $530 million in loans outstanding on 15,543 units including 7,410 units for low-income households.[10]

Chapter 707, the Rental Assistance Program, is the state's program of the third type—that is, it provides rental subsidies to low-income households. Chapter 707 was also set up in 1966. Local housing authorities or nonprofit organizations help eligible households find suitable housing and the state pays enough of the rent to keep rent burdens at a reasonable level. In FY 1983, 6,981 households are expected to be subsidized through this program.[11]

Finally, the state has several programs to offset the high cost of energy. In FY 1982, $17 million was appropriated to help low-income households pay their fuel bills. Another $2.5 million was appropriated to pay the principle and interest on bonds to finance home weatherization efforts.[12]

Over the past several years, state housing policy has emphasized Chapter 667. Since 1975, construction awards for almost 10,000 units of Chapter 667 housing have been awarded, compared with awards for less than 400 units of Chapter 705 housing. Furthermore, the state's annual spending on Chapter 667 (operating subsidies plus interest and principal on construction bonds) is roughly $56 million, compared with $6 million for Chapter 705 and $19 million for Chapter 707.[13] In 1982 state policy makers debated a new housing package. Although no agreement was reached, all the proposals contained at least $80 million for new construction and two or more times as much money for the construction of Chapter 667 units as for Chapter 705 units. Funding for Chapter 707 is included in the state budget, not in a separate housing package, and the increase in the amount appropriated for this program in 1982 ($2.7 million) was swamped by the proposed increases in new construction (an annual cost of about $13 million). Indeed, the annual cost of the proposed new Chapter 667 and Chapter 705 units would be almost as high as the total amount spent on Chapter 707.

The obvious question at this point is whether the recent emphasis on new construction in general and on Chapter 667 in particular is the most cost-effective way to help the poor. Table 7–5 provides some helpful evidence, namely the average annual construction and operating subsidies for state housing programs. In 1980, Chapter 707 cost $2475 per unit, Chapter 705 cost $4718 per unit, and Chapter 667 cost $3827 per unit. Comparable MHFA subsidies are not available.[14]

Table 7–5 Annual Costs of Various State Housing Programs, 1980 (thousands of dollars)

Program	Annual Cost of Construction Loans	Operating Subsidies	Administrative Costs	Total Costs
Ch. 707	—	$2292	$183	$2475
Ch. 705	$3695	840	183*	4718
Ch. 667	3306	338	183*	3827

SOURCE: Byron J. Matthews, "Cost Comparison of Various Housing Subsidy Approaches," Executive Office of Communities and Development Memorandum (April 6, 1981).
* Under Ch. 707, an 8% administrative fee is paid to the local housing authority that administers the program. Administrative costs for Ch. 707 and Ch. 667 are not indicated on the EOCD memorandum, and are therefore assumed to be the same as for Ch. 707.

These numbers must be interpreted with care. First, the programs differ in ways other than costs. In particular, Chapter 705 and Chapter 667, unlike Chapter 707, add units to the housing stock and can provide low-income housing in suburban locations where it has not existed before. Indeed, the state has encouraged the latter course. Executive Order 215, signed by Governor Edward King in 1982, denies community development assistance to any city or town that does not accept its fair share of low-income housing.

Second, Table 7–5 does not reveal the time dimension of the subsidies under the various programs. The construction subsidies are average annual payments of principal and interest over the life of the construction bonds. Because serial bonds are used, the actual payments are higher in the early years of the bond issue than in the later years. With a 9 percent, 20-year serial bond issue, for example, the annual payment is 14 percent of the construction cost in the first year but less than 5.5 percent of this cost in the last year. Hence, the first-year cost of the construction subsidy is considerably higher than the amount in this table. On the other hand, payments on the construction bond are fixed at the time of construction and, unlike the operating subsidy, do not rise with energy and maintenance costs. It follows that once a Chapter 705 unit has been built, its total cost will grow less rapidly than the cost of a Chapter 707 unit.[15] Finally, we do not know how these program costs have changed since 1980 or how they will grow in the future; since both construction and energy costs have been growing faster than inflation and are likely to continue to do so, however, it seems unlikely that the relative costs in Table 7–5 will change significantly.

Third, the operating subsidies required for a particular housing project depend on the incomes of the tenants. For all these programs, the state pays the difference between a fair market rent and 25 percent of the tenant's income. Hence, if the recipients of Chapter 707 subsidies are poorer than the tenants of Chapter 705 projects, the average operating subsidies will be higher for Chapter 707. But it is difficult to determine whether this is true. Chapter 707 and 705 have the same eligibility requirements and the same tenant selection procedure, so one might argue that tenant incomes will also be the same and that the observed difference in operating subsidies is caused by the higher operating costs of Chapter 707 housing. In my view, however, another explanation is more likely. The eligibility requirements of the two programs are two or three times the poverty line, so only about 20 percent of the eligible households are poor.[16] Furthermore, Chapter 705 units are in scattered site developments in suburban locations, which are less accessible to poor households than the more central locations where Chapter 707 subsidies are used. Thus, I suspect that tenants in Chapter 707 housing are poorer than tenants in Chapter 705 housing and that the difference in operating subsidies for the two programs largely reflects this difference in tenants' incomes. The same argument applies to Chapter 667 housing; to a large degree, the low operating subsidies of the program probably reflect the relatively high incomes (relative to poor people, that is!) of the tenants.[17]

This analysis leads to several conclusions about the trade-offs facing state policy makers. First, for any given amount spent on housing, one can reach two or two and one-half times as many households with Chapter 707 as with Chapters 705 or 667.[18] In other words, Chapter 707 is much more cost-effective than are the other programs for alleviating the primary problem facing poor households today—namely, high rent burdens. Accordingly, the emphasis of state housing policy should change: New state housing funds should be devoted primarily to alleviating rent burdens for many poor households, not to providing new housing for a few. As explained earlier, the cost disadvantage of constructed housing gradually declines as payments on construction bonds decline, and eventually it may be reversed. But this potential long-run advantage cannot help poor families pay for housing in the 1980s.

Second, Chapter 707 helps the poor find housing where it currently exists, whereas Chapter 705 and to some extent Chapter 667 have been used to provide low-income housing in locations where it did not previously exist. Because of the high eligibility limits, however, this difference implies that Chapter 707 is more effective in reaching the poor than are the other programs. Although the eligibility standards are the same, Chapter 707 is more accessible to the poor. Again, a change of emphasis toward Chapter 707 and away from Chapter 705 and 667 is warranted. Furthermore, the limited evidence suggests that Chapter 667 is particularly ineffective in reaching the poor. Although Chapter 667 housing may be desirable for other reasons, state policymakers should not delude themselves into thinking that it is a cost-effective way to help the elderly poor.

The poor would also benefit from two changes in all the existing programs. As noted, the eligibility limits are well above the poverty line, and housing is given on a first-come, first-served basis. The poor would therefore benefit from new rules to give them preference in the tenant selection procedure. Also as noted recently constructed state public housing apparently is not accessible to the poor. To the extent that the state builds more public housing, therefore, the poor would benefit from a shift toward more central locations for this housing.

In addition, an increased emphasis on rehabilitation may allow the state to improve the housing stock more than rental assistance typically does without raising costs to the level of new construction.[19] This change could be accomplished within the confines of current law. Chapters 705 and 667 can be used to acquire existing housing, and Chapter 707 subsidies can be adjusted to reflect rehabilitation expenditures by a landlord. Furthermore, in 1981 MHFA lending authority was extended to housing rehabilitation projects. Indeed, MHFA interest subsidies and Chapter 707 rent subsidies may prove to be a powerful combination for providing rehabilitated housing for the poor. If the state shifts toward rehabilitation, it must be careful to keep rehabilitation costs low so that many households can be assisted and to improve program targeting so that assistance goes to those most in need.

The state must also determine the appropriate role for energy assistance. We have seen that energy costs are an important component of the affordability problem for the poor. One obvious way to ease this problem, therefore, is to help ease the burden of energy costs. The state can provide relief either through direct assistance with energy bills or by promoting energy-conserving investments. The most immediate relief comes from direct assistance. However, the pay-off from investment in energy-saving products is often very rapid. Even with a short time horizon, therefore, energy-saving investments may be more cost-effective than direct assistance. Although no existing data provide information on the potential savings from energy-conserving investment in housing occupied by the poor, it seems likely that these savings are substantial.[20]

As noted earlier, the state has committed $17 million for a direct energy assistance program and $2.5 million for a weatherization program, but many of these funds have not yet been spent. Rapid implementation of and continued support for these programs would make a significant contribution to reducing the high burden of energy costs on poor and near-poor households.

Now let us turn to the second major housing problem for the poor, namely their concentration in deteriorated neighborhoods. To some degree, state housing programs for rental assistance and for construction give poor households more choice and thereby help them move to less deteriorated neighborhoods. A more direct approach, however, is to give aid directly to poor neighborhoods. Although neighborhood policy is primarily the responsibility of city governments, the state can play an important role by assisting financially pressed cities in dealing with key neighborhood problems.

So far, state neighborhood assistance has focused on a few programs that work in somewhat deteriorated but fairly cohesive neighborhoods. For example, the state recently provided $1.5 million for the Neighborhood Housing Services (NHS) program. This community-based program stimulates revitalization by providing rehabilitation loans and by promoting the cooperation of homeowners, banks, landlords, and businesses. NHS has been successful in neighborhoods that are not severely distressed and that begin with a critical mass of resident and business commitment. Although a few poor people live in such neighborhoods, the most severely distressed neighborhoods—that is, the ones with large concentrations of poor people—do not meet these conditions and therefore will not be aided by NHS.[21]

Massive revitalization of the most distressed neighborhoods is undoubtedly beyond the state's capacity, but the state can help to alleviate the most acute problems in these neighborhoods, such as arson or the use of abandoned property for criminal activities. Many people have advocated a "triage" strategy which involves giving up on the worst neighborhoods and concentrating assistance on those neighborhoods in which it will generate the most revitalization. This strategy is a disaster for the poor. The alleviation of acute problems would benefit the residents of a distressed neighborhood even if it did not stimulate massive revitalization. Thus, a shift of emphasis toward programs that deal with acute problems in distressed neighborhoods would help poor people. For example, the City of Boston is now faced with a serious arson problem in distressed neighborhoods. Financial assistance from the state could make a major contribution toward eliminating this problem. Or the state could help finance the securing and eventual rehabilitation of abandoned buildings.

In summary, the policy recommendations made here have a common theme: The state should make better use of existing housing resources. Housing construction programs are expensive and, as currently operated in Massachusetts, do not reach the people most in need. The most cost-effective way to help the poor is through increased funding of programs to rehabilitate existing housing, to reclaim abandoned housing, to provide rental assistance, and to promote weatherization.

The Condition of Public Housing

Over 80,000 households, about half elderly, live in public housing throughout Massachusetts. Consequently, housing conditions for the poor depend heavily on the fate of existing public housing. In large cities, where public housing is concentrated, a majority of the public housing units are federally sponsored. For example, Boston has about 18,000 occupied units, of which over three quarters are federal. Throughout the state, however, one-third of the family projects and over 60 percent of the elderly projects are sponsored by the state.[22]

Evidence

Both the physical condition and the demographic character of public housing projects vary considerably. Most of the elderly projects and a few of the family projects are fairly new and in good condition. On the other hand, about 15,000 housing units in state family projects were built around 1950 and several federal projects were built even earlier. Not surprisingly, these older units often exhibit run-down conditions and inefficient energy systems. In addition, some projects are filled with some of the poorest and most disadvantaged of the state's citizens. According to the 1977 AHS for the Boston metropolitan area, 57 percent of the tenants in public housing had incomes below $5,000 and 81 percent had incomes below $10,000. In addition, a 1978 survey of ten state-aided family projects found that the mean household income in a project ranged from $4145 to $9742.[23]

The most severe problems are concentrated in the large family projects in large cities. Indeed, the extent of poverty and deterioration in some of these projects is startling. A survey of 23 large family projects (both state and federal) in Boston in 1978 found that 84 percent of the households were headed by non-elderly single parents—almost always female. Furthermore, almost half (47 percent) of the project residents were children under 18. The median project had an average family income of $4,830, with only 14 percent of its adult residents employed. Forty-one percent of the household heads were black, 12 percent were Hispanic, and three quarters of the projects were very segregated with over 90 percent white residents or over 90 percent minority residents.[24]

As shown in Table 7–6, tenants' characteristics in these 23 projects have changed during the 1970s. In particular, the percentage of single-parent families and the percentage of minorities have

increased substantially. The population also appears to be somewhat more stable, with only 32 percent staying less than 5 years.
Thus, because of poor conditions in the private housing market
and the shift of many elderly households from family housing to
elderly housing, the concentration of long-term, severely disadvantaged tenants in these projects has increased.

The extent of deterioration in the large, family projects is
revealed by the vacancy rate, which, as shown in Table 7–6, has
now risen to an astonishingly high level. These vacancies do not
represent a lack of demand for the units; in fact, almost every
project has a long waiting list. Instead, these vacancies reflect
both a legacy of neglect and the high cost of returning units to
habitable condition. A vacant unit is more susceptible than is an
inhabited unit to damage through leaks or by vandalism; in a few
projects, units are often vandalized as soon as they become
vacant. The increase in the vacancy rate in the late 1970s reflects
BHA's inability to keep up with this destructive cycle. Currently,
however, the BHA secures units as soon as a household moves out
and is gradually rehabilitating its vacant units. Most of the units
now vacant require only modest rehabilitation, but a significant
number require major repairs. The situation is similar, although
less severe in other cities. One study found long waiting lists in
other cities with many vacant units and counted 180 mothballed
units in Cambridge.[25] Hence, even with good management, it will
take a long time and a great deal of money to eliminate the sad
paradox of high vacancy rates and long waiting lists.

Most of the family public housing units are also in large, hard-
to-heat buildings, often with ancient heating systems. In 1978 at

Table 7-6 Vacancies and Population Characteristics in the 23 Largest Family
Public Housing Projects in Boston, 1969–1982

	1969	1975	1979	1982
Percentage non-elderly single-parent households	44.0%	72.3%	84.3%	n.a.
Percentage black and Hispanic[a]	33.1	43.6	53.0	45.1%
Percentage of households in project less than 5 years[b]	n.a.	42.6	32.0	n.a.
Vacancy rate[c]	n.a.	7.6	28.3	28.0

SOURCE: Boston Housing Authority.
[a] Includes a few other nonwhites; "1982" entry is for September 1981.
[b] Entry is percentage for the median project.
[c] Does not include Columbia Point Project, which had a 74 percent vacancy rate in January 1982, in part because of extensive rehabilitation.

least 10 of the 23 large family projects in Boston had their original heating equipment, and 31-year-old boilers are still used in some state projects in Haverhill and Lowell. In Worcester, Springfield, Holyoke, and Chicopee, the heating pipes in the state family projects are over 30 years old and not insulated.[26] Not surprisingly, therefore, energy costs are a large percentage of the operating expenses for public housing, and the rapid rise in energy prices over the past fifteen years has hit public housing very hard. This problem is particularly severe in Massachusetts, which has the highest energy costs in the nation. In fact, in FY 1981 the BHA spent over half of its operating budget on heat, and the Lowell and Fall River authorities spent over 40 percent of their budgets on heat.[27]

Directions for State Policy

A substantial portion of the poor households in Massachusetts are served by federal and state public housing. Under current economic conditions, these households would not be served by the private housing market—at least not without devoting most of their income toward rent—and new housing for the poor is not economically viable without an enormous state subsidy. Furthermore, many of the poor households in public housing face discrimination in the private housing market because they have children, because they are female-headed, and/or because they belong to a minority group. It follows that the preservation of existing public housing must be the top priority of state housing policy toward the poor.

Federal public housing projects are threatened with severe cutbacks in their support from the federal government. The large public housing authorities (PHAs) in the state, a majority of whose units are federal, are in a particularly precarious position. Federal subsidies are essential to these PHAs for covering the gap between rental receipts and operating expenses. In fact, federal subsidies covered three quarters of the operating costs for the BHA and approximately one-half of the operating costs for the PHAs in Lowell and Fall River.[28] Furthermore, the trend toward more disadvantaged tenants and the rapid growth in energy costs both magnify the need for subsidies. In the 18 largest PHAs in the nation, rental income rose only 12 percent from 1968 to 1977 while operating costs grew 124 percent. The situation was even worse for the BHA, whose rental income fell by 14 percent and whose operating expenses grew by 138 percent.[29]

Despite the urgency of the need, however, every one of the

Reagan Administration's budgets has proposed to cut subsidies to public housing. According to one estimate, the Reagan proposal for FY 1983 covered only 60 percent of the needs of large PHAs.[30] A cutback of this magnitude would have a devastating impact on public housing. So far, Congress has rejected the Administration's proposed cuts in public housing subsidies. More cuts will undoubtedly be proposed, however, and Massachusetts should join other states in lobbying against them.

As noted earlier, over one-third of the 42,400 family units and over 60 percent of the 47,400 elderly units in Massachusetts are state-supported. These units receive almost $60 million per year in state subsidies. In addition, the state periodically has issued bonds to finance rehabilitation of family housing projects.[31] Operating subsidies are essential to state public housing projects, just as they are to federal projects. Because the tenants are poor and rents are kept at a reasonable portion of their incomes, rental receipts cannot be expected to cover the high cost of heating and maintaining the public housing units.[32] Without adequate subsidies, therefore, housing authorities would have to move toward market rents or stop providing necessary maintenance. As shown earlier, market rents place an extreme burden on poor tenants. And as the condition of many of the family housing projects demonstrates, neglected maintenance inevitably leads to the need for large rehabilitation expenditures.

Although large operating subsidies will continue to be necessary, they can be controlled to some degree through better management, through project rehabilitation and upgrading, and through improvement of the neighborhood environment in the projects. Indeed, these three issues are the key to a cost-effective state policy toward public housing.

Several management practices mandated by current state law unnecessarily boost the cost of running public housing and hence raise the operating subsidy the state must pay. For example, housing authorities must now pay their maintenance employees 80 percent of the pervailing wages for construction workers. This rule leads to maintenance wages that are much higher than the wages of maintenance employees in the state personnel system and much higher than the guidelines developed by HUD. BHA estimates that switching to the HUD guidelines would save almost one million dollars per year. The current rule is too generous and should be reformed.

A second example is that the state simply pays the heating bill for state housing projects. If a housing authority devises ways to save one dollar on its heating bill, its subsidy is cut by exactly one dollar. Thus, authorities have no incentive to cut heating costs, for none of the savings show up in their budgets. In federal projects, authorities are allowed to keep some of the savings they generate through energy-conservation measures. A similar rule has been proposed for state projects and it should be implemented.

Another policy that has been called management reform is the recent state decision to limit the increase in the non-utility component of state subsidies to 4 percent per year. This policy is designed to force PHAs to come up with better management techniques. In my view, however, this policy is so harsh that its primary effect will be to cause undermaintenance and thereby to exacerbate PHAs long-run financial difficulties.

Operating and maintenance expenses are closely linked with upgrading and rehabilitation expenditures. Not only does continued maintenance preserve housing and postpone major rehabilitation, but upgrading and rehabilitation can substantially cut needed operating expenses. Thus, in many cases, upgrading is a very good investment and, particularly with energy-saving improvements, can even save money for the state. For example, one survey of state projects found that $18,500 for upgrading the boilers in a Haverhill project would save $20,000 in energy costs the first year alone; $125,000 for replacing the hot water system and insulating the pipes at Boston's Commonwealth project would save $150,000 per year in heating costs; and energy-saving investments in projects in Waltham, Milford, and Malden all lowered energy costs by about 40 percent—more than expected in each case.[33]

Chapter 490 of the Acts of 1980 enables $90 million to be raised through long-term tax-exempt bonds for the modernization of state public housing projects. A substantial portion of this money is set aside for energy conservation measures. These funds will allow local housing authorities to upgrade a few large projects, but futher funds, both for rehabilitation and for energy conservation, are needed. This need is widely recognized, but state policymakers could not agree on a funding package for 1982. Breaking this stalemate and authorizing further funds for revitalizing public housing should be a high priority in 1983 and in the years beyond.

Finally, state policy must recognize that public housing has a neighborhood dimension. Because the large family projects house very poor and disadvantaged people, they sometimes provide a very impoverished neighborhood environment. Criminals prey on the residents and make use of or vandalize the vacant units. Residents are isolated from surrounding neighborhoods and hence from networks that might alert them to jobs or training opportunities. Many neighborhoods in the private housing market contain poor people, but none of them has the impersonal environment or the concentrated isolation of three or four thousand people in poor single-parent families that characterize the state-created neighborhoods in the large family public housing projects.

State housing policy should address these problems not only to improve the opportunities and quality of life of the residents of public housing projects but also to lower the costs of running public housing. Increasing the involvement of public housing tenants in decisions about their projects will give them stronger incentives to maintain their units and to conserve energy. Increasing tenants' knowledge of training and educational opportunities will help some of them find jobs and hence will lead to more rental revenues. And increasing project security will lower the costs associated with crime.

The state recently has entered this field by financing several neighborhood-type projects for local housing authorities. In 1981, for example, $2 million was appropriated for the Supportive Services Program. Local housing authorities will use these funds to improve the delivery of employment and social services to project tenants. With its share of this money, the BHA is assisting tenant organizations in several projects to expand the access of tenants to education, training, and day care. This approach is particularly promising because it both strengthens tenant involvement and capacity and improves services for tenants. The state also finances, through the Department of Public Works, a BHA effort to find jobs for public housing tenants through the Supported Work Program. This program, modeled after a successful federal program, provides jobs and training for people with little or no experience in the labor force. The state should continue to support programs like these.

In summary, any state housing policy for the poor must begin with the preservation of existing state public housing. In recent years, the state has provided some badly needed funds for rehabilitation of family housing projects and has begun to recognize the neighborhood dimension of public housing projects. But the state has yet to develop a comprehensive, farsighted policy toward public housing. As long as the projects face unreasonable management constraints, operate ancient heating systems, contain severely dilapidated units, and possess poor neighborhood environments, the subsidy costs to the state will be high and the state will be tempted to restrict subsidies. And as long as local housing authorities are pressed by inadequate subsidies, they will be unable to provide necessary maintenance or to create better neighborhood environments. Both the poor and taxpayers in general would benefit from enough state funding for public housing to break this vicious cycle.

Displacement of Poor Households

The phenomenon of displacement has received a great deal of attention in recent years. This section briefly explains the causes of displacement, examines the evidence on displacement of poor households in Massachusetts, and considers several options for state policy.

Causes

Displacement occurs whenever a household is forced to move from its dwelling because of circumstances beyond its control. Because a forced move may involve considerable hardship, particularly for a poor or elderly tenant, displacement has long been a concern of policymakers. In recent years, attention has focused on displacement caused by large rent increases or by condominium conversion. At other times, displacement caused by landlords' abandonment of their buildings and by urban renewal have been of more importance. In this section, we will restrict our attention to the former two types of displacement.

Displacement in American cities in recent years has been caused primarily by the baby boom and by the continuing strength of office employment. Because of the baby boom, many new young adult households have entered the housing market. These households, like previous cohorts of young adults, prefer to live in the city. The office sector has provided jobs for many of these young adults, thereby pulling them toward center city neighborhoods near office jobs and providing them with income to outbid current residents for housing in many neighborhoods. The strength of these displacement pressures should diminish as the baby-boom bulge in household formation tapers off in the late 1980s.[34]

These forces have been magnified—but not caused—by condominium conversion. Because property taxes and mortgage interest are deductible on the federal income tax, many households find owning a housing unit financially preferable to renting. Central city condominiums allow young adults to take advantage of these tax provisions without having to buy a single-family house or leave the city. These tax provisions are more favorable the higher a household's income. Low-income households may not be able to afford the down payment necessary to take advantage of the tax provisions, and low-income households have low marginal tax rates so that the tax deductions do not reduce their tax payments very much.[35]

The tax advantages of condominiums were boosted by inflation during the 1970s. Inflation pushes households into higher tax brackets and therefore increases the value of deductions. Furthermore, housing prices rise along with other prices so that a homeowner gets a capital gain that is not available to a renter. On the other hand, recent high interest rates boost the real value of a household's monthly payments in the early years of its mortgage, thereby preventing many households from becoming homeowners.

Unfortunately, displacement is extremely difficult to measure. To begin with, renter households are very mobile. According to the 1980 Census, about one-third of all renters in Massachusetts (and in the Boston metropolitan area) move every year. Hence, many renters would leave their apartment within a year even without large rent increases or condominium conversions. It is hard to argue that people who would have moved anyway are being displaced. Furthermore, one cannot determine when a rent increase is large enough to force a household to move. After all, many renters already pay 50 percent of their income for housing, so how can an increase from 30 to 35 percent be said to "force" a household to move? Finally, even if we could agree on the magnitude of a rent increase that constitutes displacement, rental transactions are not recorded in any systematic fashion so that displacement from rent increases cannot be observed. The result of this measurement difficulty is that most studies focus on condominimum conversion, even though it may be only a small part of the problem.

Evidence

A study of condominium conversion in Boston found that only 5 percent of the units converted between 1970 and 1980 had previously been low-rent apartments—that is, apartments where poor people might have lived. This result is not surprising, given that most of the condominium conversion has been in Back Bay and Beacon Hill, areas of the city where few poor people live. In fact, virtually all of the low-rent apartments were in rooming houses, an unusual feature of these neighborhoods. So far in Boston, therefore, the poor people displaced by condominium conversion have mainly been residents of rooming houses.[36]

Another study tracked former tenants from apartments converted to condominiums in Cambridge in 1978. This study found that 7.7 percent of the former tenants had incomes below $5,000 and 23.1 percent had incomes between $5,000 and $10,000. Most of these low-income tenants were elderly. Because elderly people are not very mobile and therefore would not have moved without conversion, it appears that condominium conversion in Cambridge did displace a significant number of poor people.[37] This higher rate of apparent displacement in Cambridge arises because conversions in Cambridge took place in much more heterogeneous neighborhoods than Back Bay or Beacon Hill.

We are led to the obvious conclusion that condominium conversion does not necessarily displace poor people, although it may under some circumstances. Unfortunately, we simply do not have the data to determine whether the circumstances leading to displacement of poor people are widespread in Massachusetts. My own guess is that in most places, the first units to convert are middle- to high-rent units in desirable neighborhoods. If demand for condominiums persists, however, conversion may spread to lower-rent units in less desirable neighborhoods—that is, to units in which poor people sometimes live. One cannot determine whether this will occur without forecasting the demand for condominiums and determining the neighborhoods into which they are likely to spread.[38]

Some evidence suggests that over the next decade many poor elderly renters in two- to four-family buildings may be displaced by rent increases rather than by conversion. Many of these buildings are owned by couples nearing retirement who have a low interest mortgage or have paid off their mortgage altogether. These resident-owners often sell their buildings upon retirement, so that ownership passes from a household with a low or no mortgage payment, and often with personal ties to the elderly tenants, to a new owner who must support a mortgage at a current higher interest rate and who does not have ties with the tenants. The result can be a dramatic increase in rents and, hence, displacement of the elderly tenants. Although it is difficult to determine the magnitude of this problem, one study of Boston concludes that over the next few years this type of displacement could be more important than displacement from condominium conversion.[39] Furthermore, it may be a particularly frequent type of displacement of the poor, because many of the affected elderly tenants may be poor.

Directions for State Policy

Although displacement is difficult to measure, the available evidence indicates that many poor households may be displaced so that some state action is called for. However, designing appropriate anti-displacement policy is even more difficult than measuring displacement, partly because of disagreement about the degree of protection the state should provide and partly because the market forces that cause displacement are so powerful. The state must also decide whether to intervene in the housing market directly or to pass regulation authority on to local governments.

In my view, a successful anti-displacement policy must obey two rules. First, it must be focused on those households the state wishes to protect. Second, it must not alter the incentives of landlords and developers in ways that ultimately hurt the groups one is trying to help. For example, a blanket ban on condominium conversion violates the first rule. Most condominium conversions do not involve displacement, let alone displacement of poor or elderly households. A blanket ban therefore causes far more disruption of the housing market than is needed to prevent displacement. Furthermore, a blanket ban cannot turn off the underlying market forces and may simply cause them to spill over into other types of housing; young adult households denied the opportunity to purchase a condominium may decide to purchase 2-family houses instead, resulting in an increase in displacement of tenants in those houses. A policy that prohibits condominium conversion only for apartments inhabited by the poor and elderly violates the second rule because it gives landlords an incentive to discriminate against poor and elderly tenants. A landlord who expects to convert to condominiums sometime in the future will not want to have poor and elderly tenants around to complicate that process.[40]

To keep this discussion in perspective, remember that our goal is to protect the poor from displacement. The state may also want to develop procedural safeguards for all tenants and to provide minimal regulation of housing market transactions, but these broader policies raise issues well beyond the scope of this chapter. We want here only to identify focused policies that protect the poor and the elderly without giving undesirable incentives to landlords and developers.

At present Massachusetts has no policy to prevent displacement of the poor or to ease its burden. Rent-control legislation has given a few cities the authority to regulate condominium conversions, but no state-wide policies have been enacted.[41] Nevertheless, focused anti-displacement policies without undesirable incentives could be designed.

First, the state could encourage long leases for poor and elderly tenants. A lease provides legal protection against displacement; no tenant can be displaced until his or her lease runs out. The state could therefore protect poor and elderly tenants by rewarding, through direct payments or tax breaks, landlords who provide long leases for such tenants.[42]

Second, the state could finance local agencies that provide relocation assistance to displaced poor and elderly households and that protect the right of poor and elderly tenants. Relocation assistance would ease the transition for tenants who are displaced. It is important that this assistance come from the state, not from the converter or new owner. If a converter has to pay relocation assistance to poor or elderly tenants, then landlords who expect to convert will avoid renting to poor or elderly households. It might be desirable for converters to pay a fee for every conversion, but it would not be desirable for them to pay relocation assistance only to poor and elderly tenants. An agency that provides relocation assistance could also make certain that the rights of poor and elderly tenants are respected.

Third, the state could reactivate and expand a 1981 demonstration program that allowed PHAs to prevent the displacement of low-income elderly tenants. Under this program, which was part of the Chapter 667 Elderly Housing Program, PHAs purchased condominiums being created from apartments inhabited by elderly tenants; these condominiums then became part of the public housing stock and the tenants did not have to move. This program received $1 million in state funds. It deserves further funding and should be expanded to include apartments inhabited by any low-income families.[43]

Discrimination Against Poor Minority Households

We have already shown that the two largest minority groups in the state, blacks and Hispanics, have a greater incidence of housing problems than do majority households. To some degree, this situation arises because blacks and Hispanics are over-represented among low-income households. But it also reflects housing market discrimination against these groups. This section reviews the evidence on the importance of discrimination in Massachusetts. As before, we do not have data for the entire state, but a focus on Boston is reasonable because almost three quarters of the poor blacks and Hispanics in the state in 1980 lived in the Boston metropolitan area. We conclude with some suggestions for policy at the state level.

Evidence

Without discrimination, we would expect households with the same incomes to live in housing of the same quality. Tables 7-1 and 7-2 demonstrate that this expectation was not met in Massachusetts in 1970; discrimination was clearly at work. Even within a given income class, black and Hispanic households have a higher incidence of housing problems than do majority households. As noted earlier, the incidence of overcrowding is particularly striking for poor, minority households.

Households tend to cluster around their places of employment. Hence, without discrimination we would expect that minority and majority households with the same incomes would live the same distances from workplaces. Table 7-7 demonstrates that this expectation was also not met in the Boston metropolitan area in 1970. Discrimination confined blacks to the central city. Indeed, non-poor black households were much more likely to live in the central city than were poor majority households.

Finally, in a competitive, nondiscriminatory housing market, the price of housing of equivalent quality would be the same for

Table 7-7   Percentage of Households That Live in the Center City, Boston Metropolitan Area

	Renters			Owners		
	White	*Black*	*Hispanic*	*White*	*Black*	*Hispanic*
1970:						
Poor*	40.9%	89.1%	n.a.	17.3%	74.8%	n.a.
Non-poor	32.1	84.7	n.a.	11.3	68.1	n.a.
1977:						
Poor	40.4	88.0	100.0	19.9	75.0	33.3%
Non-poor	21.0	72.2	100.0	8.8	69.5	42.9

SOURCES: 1970 Census of Housing; 1977 Annual Housing Survey.
*"Poor household" defined as a household with an income below $5,000 in 1970 or $7,000 in 1977.

all buyers at all locations. In a careful study of housing prices, Schafer demonstrated that this was not true in the Boston metropolitan area in 1970. Because of discrimination, the price of equivalent housing was higher in largely black than in largely white neighborhoods. Furthermore, within a given neighborhood, blacks paid more than their white neighbors for equivalent housing.[44]

This evidence demonstrates conclusively that the Boston metropolitan area entered the 1970s with a strong legacy of discrimination in housing. The next question to ask is whether the 1970s brought a reduction in this discrimination. If discriminatory barriers dropped we would expect that, within an income class, the disproportionate incidence of housing problems among minorities would decline during the 1970s. Tables 7–1 and 7–2 demonstrate that this expectation was not met. In 1977, blacks and Hispanics were still three times as likely as majority households to live in overcrowded dwelling units or in deteriorated neighborhoods. Furthermore, Table 7–7 shows that the concentration of blacks and Hispanics in the central city changed hardly at all from 1970 to 1977. We are led to the conclusion that, as of 1977 at least, powerful discriminatory barriers were still at work in the Boston metropolitan area.

Two studies provide more recent and more direct evidence about discrimination in the Boston metropolitan area. These studies make use of a survey technique called a fair housing audit, in which a black person and a white person who have been carefully matched according to their economic and family characteristics successively visit a landlord or real estate broker. The two teammates then record the information they received and the way they were treated so that discrimination—that is, less complete information or less favorable treatment for the minority auditor—can be measured.

The first study was carried out in 40 large metropolitan areas in 1977.[45] High levels of discrimination were found virtually everywhere, including Boston. The study focused on discrimination in the provision of information about the availability of housing. In Boston the probability that a black apartment seeker visiting a single rental agent would encounter discrimination was between 24 and 46 percent. Similarly, the probability that a black house seeker would encounter discrimination was between 10 and 43 percent. The information presented in this study does not allow us to pin down this probability exactly, but there can be no question that the level of discriminatory treatment in Boston was very high.[46]

The second study was carried out in the City of Boston in 1981.[47] This study found that black housing seekers were told about far fewer available housing units than were their white teammates. On average, black apartment seekers were told about .64 apartments and whites were told about 1.85 apartments (76 percent more than their black teammates). In other words, a black apartment seeker would have to visit seven rental agents to learn about the same number of apartments as a white learns about in four visits. In 36 percent of the cases, blacks were not told about *any* available units, whereas their white teammates were told about 1.2 units on average. The racial information gap was large for apartments in all price ranges, including the lowest. Furthermore, this study found some evidence when they were shown apartments at all, blacks were steered to different units than whites: 51 percent of the units seen by blacks were not shown to their white teammates. Similar results were found for black house seekers.

Directions for State Policy

This evidence leads to the inescapable conclusion that housing discrimination has not disappeared in Massachusetts; indeed, it may not even have lessened. Because of discrimination in access to information, minority households must search for housing much harder than majority households. The burden of this extra search is particularly heavy for poor minority households whose housing choices are already severely constrained.

Because so many poor minority households rely on the private housing market, the prevention of discrimination by landlords and real estate brokers must be a central part of the state's anti-discrimination policy. State law explicitly prohibits racial and ethnic discrimination in housing, and the Massachusetts Commission Against Discrimination (MCAD) has primary responsibility for enforcing this law. The MCAD investigates complaints of discrimination and attempts to negotiate a settlement between the parties involved. In cases where discrimination is found and a settlement cannot be reached, MCAD has the power to levy fines of up to $1,000.

MCAD's complaint-processing capabilities have improved over the past few years. A logical next step in the development of this agency would be a boost in its investigative capability. Fair housing agencies in several other states have found that fair housing audits are a cost-effective investigative technique, and MCAD should regularly employ this valuable tool.

Although complaint-processing is an important part of any anti-discrimination strategy, any process that leaves initiative in the hands of the victim is limited. The state should empower MCAD to carry out less restricted law enforcement activities, such as systematic fair housing audits that are not tied to complaints. Furthermore, the negotiating position of MCAD is severely limited by the low limitation on fines. Discriminators do not need to settle because the fine is small and the probability is low that a victim will go through a lengthy, expensive civil suit. Therefore, the state should also raise the maximum fine to a level, at least $10,000, that represents a serious deterrent.

The state can also prevent discriminatory behavior through its administration of subsidized housing programs. For example, developers that receive MHFA loans must meet several anti-discrimination guidelines. Although the presence of many minority tenants suggests that discrimination is not a serious problem in subsidized housing, to my knowledge, no careful analysis of this topic has been carried out.

Summary

Massachusetts has been fairly generous in providing housing opportunities for the poor. Given the severity of rent burdens for many poor households and the deteriorated condition of many family public housing projects, a continuation of or growth in this support for housing is warranted.

Over the past few years, the emphasis of state housing programs has been on housing construction. For the most part, this new housing has not been for the poor; indeed, under current conditions building housing for the poor is not a cost-effective policy. A shift away from construction toward rental assistance, rehabilitation, and energy conservation would better serve the interests of the poor. In addition, the poor in severely distressed neighborhoods would benefit from state funding for city programs to deal with acute neighborhood problems.

The state pays a substantial subsidy to state-supported public housing projects. Because so many poor people live in public housing, this subsidy is a key ingredient of state housing policy for the poor. Subsidy costs could be cut substantially by a series of management reforms and by energy-saving investments. The money saved by these policies could be used for further energy conservation, for apartment rehabilitation, and for improving the neighborhood environment in the projects. These investments would offer substantial returns to public housing tenants and lower the state subsidy in the long run.

State policies could help prevent the displacement of some poor households and ease the burden of displacement on others. These policies should be carefully designed so that they are focused on the poor and do not give landlords an incentive to discriminate against the poor.

Finally, the state does not have any effective policies for enforcing anti-discrimination laws, despite strong evidence of widespread discrimination. Extensive use of low-cost investigative techniques and higher fines for discriminators would greatly expand the housing opportunities of poor minority households.

Endnotes

1. The AHS contains information on numerous other indicators of housing quality; however, either their incidence is very low or they are problems that are equally likely to hit the nonpoor and the poor. For example, only 2 percent of poor renters in Boston lack regular heat. And exposed wiring, leaks in the roof, holes in the wall or floor, broken plaster, peeling paint, and presence of rodents are problems that are only slightly more common for the poor than for other households. The poor may be much more likely to face several of these problems at the same time, but the published data from the AHS do not indicate whether or not this is true.

2. The data in Table 7–3 overstate the growth in rent burdens to some degree because they do not reflect the growth in in-kind income, such as food stamps. There can be no doubt, however, that rent burdens are very high for the poor, regardless of how income is measured.

3. These figures, which are calculated from the 1978 national AHS, are reported in Raymond J. Struyk, "Home Energy Costs and the Housing of the Poor and of the Elderly," unpublished manuscript (1981).

4. During the 1970s rents grew less rapidly than inflation. From 1969 to 1976, for example, the rental component of the CPI increased only 32 percent, whereas the CPI as a whole increased 55 percent. One might argue, therefore that during the 1970s the poor faced declining relative prices for housing and responded by moving to better housing. If one assumes that a decrease in the price of housing leads to a large increase in housing quality, so that total spending on housing increases, then this argument is consistent with a rising rent burden. However, this view founders on two points. First, the above rental index does not include household payments for heat, the cost of which has risen faster than inflation. For example, the heat and utilities component of the CPI increased 76 percent from 1969 to 1976. And in Boston in 1970, 30 percent of renters pay for heat themselves; see Karen Buglass *et al.*, "Characteristics of Boston's Population and Housing: 1980," Boston Redevelopment Authority (1981). Second, the assumption that housing quality is very

responsive to a drop in price is contradicted by virtually every study on the topic; see Stephen K. Mayo, "Theory and Estimation in the Economics of Housing Demand." *Journal of Urban Ecoomics,* (July 1981), pp. 76–94.

5. The 1980 Census counted 206,200 poor households in Massachusetts. Suppose that three quarters of the 88,200 public housing units are inhabited by poor households. Then 206,200 – (.75) (82,200) = 144,550 poor households must rely on the private market. Now if half the 109,700 households in subsidized housing are poor, then slightly over one-third (54,850/144,550) of the poor households in the private housing market are assisted by government subsidies. This estimate is very rough but is consistent with a 1978 estimate that three quarters of all public and subsidized private housing units are inhabited by households below a low-income standard, which is somewhat above the poverty line. (See "Housing Needs in Massachusetts," Executive Office of Communities and Development 1978).

6. One expert forecasts rising relative rents. See Anthony Downs, *No Vacancy: Rental Housing in the 1980s* (Washington, D.C., The Brookings Institution, forthcoming). Downs also discusses forecasts of energy costs.

7. The cuts proposed by the Reagan Administration are discussed in Henry J. Aaron, "Nondefense Programs," in *Setting National Priorities,* edited by J.A. Pechman (Washington, D.C.: The Brookings Institution, 1982). Some members of this administration have proposed a national housing voucher plan. Given the budget-cutting approach of the Administration and the high cost of such a plan, it seems highly unlikely that a voucher plan will be passed in the near future.

8. Figures on Ch. 705 are from The Massachusetts Senate Ways and Means Committee (WMC), Bill No. 1900, June 1982.

9. Figures on Ch. 667 are from WMC, *op. cit.* A similar but much smaller program, Ch. 689, provides housing exclusively for the handicapped.

10. Figures on MHFA are from "Policy Report #3: Public Authorities," in WMC, Bill No. 2222, June 1981; the number of double subsidies is from WMC, Bill No. 1900, June 1982; figures on outstanding loans are from MHFA Housing List, August 1982.

11. Figures on Ch. 707 are from WMC, Bill No. 1900, June 1982. The Massachusetts Home Mortgage Finance Agency should also be mentioned. MHMFA, which was recently merged with MHFA, makes low-interest mortgage funds available to participating banks. The banks in turn provide these funds as mortgages for households with moderate incomes. MHMFA loans, like MHFA loans, are obtained through the sale of tax-exempt bonds. The subsidy in MHMFA mortgages is not great enough to make them accessible to poor households, so that MHMFA is not discussed in the text.

12. These programs were slow to get off the ground. As of January 1982 less than 500 households had been served by the first program and weatherization bonds have not yet been authorized. See WMC, Bill No. 1900, June 1982.

13. Accurate information on annual spending for housing programs is difficult to obtain because spending for construction programs takes the form of principal and interest on bonds and the bonds are not always issued in the year they are authorized. The figures in the text add the state's annual appropriations and the estimated annual cost of housing bonds authorized

since 1966. In estimating the annual cost of each bond, I assumed that the bonds were issued in the years they were authorized, that all bonds were 20-year serial bonds, and that all bonds paid average interest rates for the year in which they were sold. Because of these simplifying assumptions, the estimates are only rough approximations.

14. The memorandum cited in Table 7–5 also calculates a $2,545 annual subsidy cost for MHFA units that receive no federal assistance. This figure is not comparable to the others, however, because most of the units in a MHFA project are not for low-income households and because it reflects both the MHFA interest subsidy and Ch. 707 rent supplements for some units. Some people argue that MHFA interest subsidies do not require an appropriation. This argument is incorrect; using for housing finance its limited ability to borrow deprives the state of the opportunity to undertake other capital projects.

15. The memorandum cited in Table 7–5 argues that a Ch. 705 unit built today will be as cheap as a Ch. 707 subsidy in 8 to 10 years. This argument implicitly assumes that tenants in the two programs have the same incomes. The costs of the two programs converge much more slowly if this difference reflects differences in tenants' incomes. With a 6 percent inflation rate, for example, the costs converge in 13 yers under the equal-income assumption but do not converge for 21 years, after the construction bonds are paid off, under the assumption that operating subsidies would be the same if tenant incomes were the same. In either case, the poor have a long time to wait for the arrival of the cost advantage of Ch. 705.

16. The income limits for state housing programs vary somewhat by city, but are approximately equal to $15,000 for a family of 3 and $11,000 for a one-person household. The 1980 Census counted 439,000 families below $15,000 and 601,300 unrelated individuals below $10,000. Hence, the number of households in poverty (206,200) is about 20 percent of the number of eligible households (1,041,200).

17. Because Ch. 667 units tend to be smaller than units in the other two programs, their operating expenses may be somewhat lower. However, the available evidence suggests that Ch. 667 tenants tend to be closer to the income limits and hence require smaller subsidies than tenants of the other programs; Ch. 667 is the most suburbanized program and hence the least accessible to poor people, and some Ch. 667 tenants are former homeowners with substantial assets. Note that tenant incomes in all these programs could be determined through a survey, but to my knowledge, this information is not currently available.

18. If the operating subsidy difference between Ch. 707 and 705 reflects only operating costs, then Ch. 707 can serve 1.9 (4718/2475) times as many households. If this difference reflects only differences in participant incomes, then Ch. 705 costs $3695 + $1191 + $183 = $6170 to serve the same income tenants as Ch. 707, and Ch. 707 can serve 2.5 (6170/2475) times as many households.

19. Several studies, which are based on the Experimental Housing Allowance Experiment, indicate that rental assistance has little impact on the overall quality of the housing stock. It may allow some poor households to move to

better housing, but in a tight housing market these moves take place at the expense of other poor households, who are left with the worst housing. For a review of these studies, see Eric Hanushek and John M. Quigley, "Consumption Aspects," in *Do Housing Allowances Work?*, edited by K. L. Bradbury and A. Downs (Washington, D.C.: The Brookings Institution, 1981).

20. For a review of some evidence on this point, see Struyk, *op cit.* A recent survey in Somerville found that low-income households were just as likely as high-income households to use inexpensive energy-saving products, such as weatherstripping or caulking, but that low-income households were much less likely to buy expensive energy-saving products such as storm windows. These results suggest that programs to assist the poor with major energy-saving investments could have large payoffs. See H. Kim, *et al.*, "Study of a Community Energy Business in Somerville," Program in city and Regional Planning (Harvard University, 1982).

21. For a discussion of the type of neighborhood served by NHS, see William A. Moss, "Describing Target Neighborhoods: Neighborhood Housing Services, 1978" (Washington, D.C.: U.S. Department of Housing and Urban Development, 1980).

22. For sources on the number of public housing units, see the notes to Table 7–6.

23. "OPPD Survey of Rents, Utility Costs, and Incomes in State-Aided Public Housing," Massachusetts Executive Office of Communities and Development (January 3, 1979).

24. Demographic information on Boston's family projects is from "State of the Development Report" (BHA, 1979). In 1977 the 18 largest PHAs in the country served people who were equally disadvantaged: 83 percent of the households had a single parent, 48 percent of the households contained minors, the average household income was $4033, and 87 percent of the households belonged to a minority group. See Robert Kolodny, "Exploring New Strategies for Public Housing Management," U.S. Department of Housing and Urban Development (July 1979).

25. "Policy Report #8: Public Housing in Massachusetts," in WMC, Bill No. 2222, June 1981.

26. Condition of heating systems obtained from BHA and the WMC, *op. cit.*

27. For energy costs as a percentage of expenditures, see "Survey of Housing Authority Budgets for 47 Large Housing Authorities," Citizens Housing and Planning Association (April 3, 1981). For documentation of high heating costs in Massachusetts, see Cornelia Patten, "National Trends in Fuel Prices and Their Relationship to Public Housing Operating Subsidies," Research Report #82–1, Council of Large Public Housing Authorities (1982).

28. Figures on federal subsidies are from Citizens Housing and Planning Association, *op. cit.*

29. Information on rent and expenses is from Kolodny, *op. cit.*

30. The impacts of proposed federal cutbacks are documented in Citizens Housing and Planning Association, *op. cit.*

31. Figures on public housing subsidies are from WMC, Bill No. 1900, June 1982. The subsidy for FY 1983 is expected to be about $79 million.

32. Because the construction bonds on Ch. 200 housing are virtually paid off, these units require a lower subsidy than units in other programs. According

to the memorandum cited in Table 7–5, the capital cost of a Ch. 200 unit is now $423 per year and the operating subsidy is $2014, for a total of $2437 per unit. This memorandum also estimates the annual cost of rennovation—that is, the principal and interest on rennovation bonds, at $573. Hence, a rennovated Ch. 200 unit costs $3010 per year—far less than the cost of a newly constructed unit.

33. These examples of energy-saving investments are from WMC, "Policy Report #8: Public Housing in Massachusetts," in Bill No. 2222, June 1981.
34. For additional discussion of the causes of displacement, see Anthony Downs, *Neighborhoods and Urban Development* (Washington, D.C.: The Brookings Institution, 1981).
35. For a review of the link between taxes and homeownership, see Frank DeLeeuw and Larry L. Ozanne, "The Impact of the Federal Income Tax on Investment in Housing," *Survey of Current Business* (1979), pp. 50–61.
36. Bonnie Heudorfer, "Condominium Development in Boston," Boston Redevelopment Authority (1980). I suspect but cannot prove that many former rooming house residents are now among Boston's homeless citizens.
37. Betty J. Desrosiers, *et al.*, "Condominium Conversion in Cambridge," Cambridge Community Development Department (1978). Note that former tenants are often difficult to locate; accordingly the sample size in this study is small and its conclusions should be interpreted with care. For further discussion of the situation in Cambridge, see Herman B. Leonard, "Regulation of the Cambridge Housing Market: Its Goals and Effects" (Cambridge Chamber of Commerce, 1981).
38. An analysis of this type was carried out for Cambridge by Bowman *et al.*, "Condominiums in Cambridge: Forecast of Conversions and Alternatives for the City," Workshop Report, Department of City and Regional Planning (Harvard University, 1980).
39. Callans, *et al.*, "Displacement in Boston's Appreciating Neighborhoods," Workshop Report, Department of City and Regional Planning (Harvard University, 1981).
40. One provision of Boston's 1983 condominium ordinance provides another example: Elderly and handicapped tenants can stay in their apartments for two years after conversion is announced (four years if the landlord fails to find them a comparable apartment), whereas other tenants can only stay one year. This provision protects current elderly and handicapped tenants but gives landlords a strong incentive to discriminate against elderly and handicapped tenants searching for housing.
41. Acton, Brookline, Cambridge, and Somerville require permits for condominium conversion. The State gave Acton the specific authority to regulate conversions; the regulations in the other cities are based on rent-control-enabling legislation. In 1982 a bill to give all cities and towns the power to regulate conversions received widespread support bu did not pass. For other discussions of policy toward condominium conversions, see Leonard, *op. cit.*, and Bowman, *et al.*, *op. cit.*
42. Consider the following income tax deduction: A landlord pays taxes on the net rental income from an apartment. To encourage long leases, the State could provide an income tax deduction equal to 10 percent of this net rental

income from apartments with poor or elderly tenants for every year of the lease above one year. Under this scheme, a landlord would pay no taxes on income from qualifying apartments whenever the lease is for eleven years or longer.

43. The average price of condominiums purchased under this program was about $36,500. Experience with the program led Bryon J. Matthews, Secretary of the Executive Office of Communities and Development, to recommend that it be made a "permanent feature of Chapter 667." See "Summary of the One-Year Condominium Demonstration Program," Executive Office of Communities and Development (May 27, 1981).

44. Robert Schafer, "Racial Discrimination in the Boston Housing Market," *Journal of Urban Economics* (1979), pp. 176–96.

45. Ronald E. Wienk, Clifford E. Reid, John C. Simonson, and Frederick J. Eggers, *Measuring Racial Discrimination in American Housing Markets* (Washington, D.C.: U.S. Department of Housing and Urban Development, 1979).

46. In the results reported in the text, the higher figure is the actual probability that the black will encounter unfavorable treatment. However, some of this unfavorable treatment may be due to random variation in the behavior of rental agents rather than to systematic discrimination. The smaller figure takes out the maximum number of cases that could be due to random behavior and is therefore a lower-bound estimate on the probability of encountering discrimination.

47. Judith D. Feins, Rachel G. Bratt, and Robert Hollister, "Final Report of a Study of Racial Discrimination in the Boston Housing Market" (Cambridge, Massachusetts: Abt Associates, 1981).

Chapter 8

CRIME AND THE POOR

by Susan Estrich

There is little question that crime will be one of the major issues that state government attempts to address in the 1980s. In recent years victimization rates, fear, and measures of concern about crime have increased steadily. Crime has emerged in Massachusetts as the number one or number two issue on virtually every recent public opinion and political poll. Whereas in past years people tended to view at least their own neighborhoods as safe, today—no matter where they live—Massachusetts residents increasingly believe that they are in danger. And whereas in past years people tended to think politicians could do little actually to reduce crime, today they are demanding action.

Unlike some other areas covered in this book, then, there is no need to convince either the public or elected officials that crime is a problem that must be addressed. But if we can be sure that policymakers will be addressing themselves to crime, we can hardly be certain that their priorities will be the same as those of our poorest population.

The purpose of this chapter is to examine the problem of crime in Massachusetts from the particular perspective of the poor, to evaluate the way our system responds to that problem, and to suggest areas of potential improvement. One conclusion is inescapable: For our poorest citizens, crime is a major fact of day-to-day life.

Defining the Problem

Surely one of the reasons that crime is as important an issue politically as it is in Massachusetts is the fact that it touches

Table 8–1 Victimization by Family Income in Massachusetts, 1980 (Rate per 100 Population)

Crime	Under 3,000	3,000– 4,999	5,000– 7,499	7,500– 9,999	10,000– 11,999	12,000– 14,999	15,000– 19,999	20,000– 24,999	25,000– 49,999	Over 50,000
All crimes of violence:	9.637	6.737	2.713	2.562	.0	2.597	3.925	2.306	4.455	1.040
Rape	.882	.0	.432	.0	.0	.0	.0	.0	.0	.0
Robbery	1.537	.0	.387	.856	2.849	.293	.225	.214	.822	.0
Assault	7.218	6.737	1.894	1.706	2.135	2.304	3.700	2.092	3.633	1.040
Personal crimes of theft:	16.455	9.060	6.821	7.859	7.834	7.834	7.834	7.831	10.146	21.109

SOURCE: Bureau of Justice Statistics, 1980 National Crime Survey.

Table 8–2 Household Crime Victimization by Family Income in Massachusetts, 1980 (Rate per 100 Households)

Crime	Under 3,000	4,999	7,499	9,999	11,999	14,999	19,999	24,999	49,999	Over 50,000
Burglary	14.639	11.351	7.631	7.981	10.242	7.507	4.046	6.586	6.447	10.759
Household larceny	7.507	9.851	11.173	5.684	8.430	13.256	13.881	10.306	10.306	7.628
Auto theft	1.294	.818	4.094	1.270	1.270	2.325	2.675	6.080	6.430	5.133

SOURCE: Bureau of Justice Statistics, 1980 National Crime Survey.

everyone. Neither fear nor victimization are limited to the poorest populations. Yet if crime touches everyone, it is also true that it touches some more than others. The poor, who because of their poverty are least able to purchase protection against crime, to insure themselves against losses, or to avoid the areas where crime strikes most often, are without question touched most seriously. For the poor, the crime problem is really three problems: the problem of victimization, the problem of fear, and the problem of offending. Disproportionately the poor are both the victims and the offenders in crimes of violence. As a group, they are among the most afraid in our society, and they are the most dependent upon state and local government for protection.

The Problem of Victimization

The relationship between poverty and victimization for crimes of violence is strikingly strong within Boston, within the state as a whole, and indeed, nationwide. The Massachusetts data from the 1980 National Crime Survey (NCS is based on interviews with sample households rather than official crime reports) is summarized in Tables 8–1 and 8–2. It was found that the rate of victimization for the poorest groups was two to three times as high as that of the middle- and upper-income population. Nearly one in ten poor Massachusetts residents over 12 years old (family income under $3,000) was the victim of a crime of violence in 1980. Virtually the same pattern held for burglary, where close to 15 of every 100 poor households were burglarized, and for personal crimes of theft, where nearly 17 of every 100 poor people were victimized. Only with respect to household larceny and motor vehicle theft were the poor relatively better off.

The same pattern was found in an earlier NCS survey of the City of Boston, which accounts for 10 percent of the state's population and (officially) 20 percent of its serious crime. The poor in Boston— like the poor statewide—are disproportionately the victims of violent crimes, burglaries, and personal crimes of theft.[1]

National data, which portray the same pattern, further amplify the picture of victimization of our poorest population.[2] Not only are the poor victimized more often but the consequences of their victimizations tend to be more severe: The lower the family income, the greater the chance of physical injury. And, contrary to common assumptions, stranger-on-stranger violent crime (the focus of the political debate) is as much a problem for the poor as for the well-to-do. In the lowest-income group, 61.9 percent of crimes of violence involve strangers; the equivalent figure in the highest-income group is 65.7 percent.

Losses from property crimes are more difficult to compare. In household larcenies, wealthier households tend to lose more in absolute dollar terms, but relative losses for the poor may be greater. And while·the NCS does not ask the question, there would seem to be little doubt that the wealthier the household, the more likely that it is insured against the loss.[3]

Income is not, of course, the only significant variable in assessing the risk of victimization. Race, sex, age, and place of residence also affect substantially one's vulnerability to victimization. Black victimization for crimes of violence (40.6 per 1,000) is over 20 percent higher than white victimization; white females over 65 have the lowest rate of any race/age/sex group (5.7), while black males aged 12–15 have the highest (115.1).

Residence is perhaps the critical factor. The rate of violent crime for center city residents (45.9 per 1,000) is more than twice that for residents of nonmetropolitan areas (21.6). The larger the metropolitan area, the higher the crime rate, although the center city factor rather than the size of the metropolitan area is clearly most critical. In the center city of metropolitan areas of 1 million or more the rate is 49.5; in center cities of smaller metropolitan areas (50,000 to 249,999) the rate is 42.3.

The overall picture is clear: For the poor who live in central cities, the risk of violent crime is substantial; and it is greater for the men there than the women, for the young than the old, for blacks than for whites. Why? At least a large part of the answer lies in recognition of the fact that crime is primarily a "local" phenomenon; the picture of the most likely victim is, demographically, very close to the picture of the most likely offender.

The Problem of Fear

There is no question that fear of crime among every group is high and increasing. An eight-city victimization survey, for example, found that 45 percent of all respondents limited their personal activity because of fear of crime.[4] In Michigan a statewide study found that 66 percent of all respondents identified some places they would not go because of crime;[5] 67 percent of those surveyed in Kansas City avoided some parts of the city because of fear of victimization.[6]

But while fear, like victimization, touches all, it is not evenly distributed across the population. For the poor, especially women and the elderly poor and those who live in center cities, fear of crime is a substantial problem independent of actual risk of victimization. Fear takes its own toll and imposes its own costs, both economic and social. It imposes limits on individual freedom—on one's willingness to travel to jobs and stores, to take advantage of parks and playgrounds—and it contributes to the breakdown of social cohesion and community spirit. And fear may even contribute to victimization: When fear limits traffic on the streets at night, those streets may well become even more dangerous for the few who dare to travel on them or who have no choice in the matter.

National Crime Surveys in selected cities have found definite correlations between income, fear, and limits on individual activity. When asked whether they thought their neighborhood was safe at night, for example, 60 percent of those with incomes under $3,000 responded that they felt either somewhat or very unsafe, compared with 31 percent whose incomes were over $25,000. Over half of those in the lowest-income group reported that they limited their activity because of crime, while well over 60 percent in the upper-income groups did not. Far more than the rich, the poor viewed their own neighborhoods as more dangerous than other parts of the metropolitan area. And, as income increased, so did one's approval of the performance of the police.

Individual studies of behavior also report patterns of fear and avoidance among low-income individuals living in high-crime areas. In a 1967 study of residents of high-crime areas in Boston and Chicago, Albert Reiss found that 43 percent of those questioned stayed off the streets at night and 39 percent avoided going out alone at night.[7] In a later study, 42 percent of the elderly residents of selected central city low-rent public housing projects told researchers that they avoided certain locations in their own neighborhoods.[8] And in a study of black families with teenage children in Philadelphia, many of whom were low-income, 80 percent of the adults reported staying home more at night and 77 percent reported making more efforts to avoid subways than they had in the past.[9]

Income is not the only demographic factor that correlates with fear and avoidance. Sex and age are even stronger predictors: elderly women are the most afraid, followed by young women, elderly men, and young men in that order.

Why are the poor so afraid? Certainly, an important part of the answer lies in the fact that they live disproportionately in high-crime central cities where the risks of victimization are, in fact, greater. Yet victimization rates provide only part of the answer; they do not explain why women are more afraid than men and why the elderly are more afraid than the young, even though victimization rates are exactly the opposite.[10]

Another part of the answer surely lies in the individual's sense of vulnerability. Researchers have repeatedly suggested that high fear rates among women and the aged may be as much a product of the sense of these groups that they are defenseless in the face of an attack by a stronger, younger man as of the objective risks of victimization. The same may be true of the poor as a group: Unlike better-off individuals, they simply cannot afford to take the protective actions, individually or collectively, that make an individual or a neighborhood at least seem safer. They cannot afford expensive burglar alarms and computerized systems to light lamps and turn on stereos. They cannot afford to join their neighbors to install better lighting or to hire private security guards to patrol the street or the apartment building. Nor are the avoidance tactics common among the better-off equally available to the poor. For recreation, their only choice may be public parks; for transportation, their only choice public transit; and, most important of all, for housing, their only choice the center city.

Another factor that must be examined in understanding fear, particularly among urban populations, is the role of public disorder and incivilities. When residents of an urban housing project were asked what they considered the most dangerous spot in the vicinity of the project, their answer was an area where youths tended to congregate and to drink beer and play music. In fact, according to a victimization survey conducted at the same time, not a single crime had taken place in that area.[11]

While some low-income urban residents may have little first-hand experience with violent crime, they are frequently exposed to disorder in their surroundings and in the behavior of others—unruly youngsters, dilapidated buildings, loud music, and conspicuous alcohol and drug use. Conditions and disturbances of this nature were termed "incivilities" by a research group that studied fear and crime in Boston housing projects. The results of the study were striking. The researchers found that the level of fear in most of the housing projects was more a function of the level of incivilities present than of the level of crime. In 10 of the 15 projects the level of fear (low, medium, or high) matched the level of incivility (for example, medium fear coexisted with medium-level incivility). When a similar comparison was done for levels of fear and crime, no pattern emerged. Only six of the projects showed a match between levels of fear and crime, and four of the projects showed an inverse type of relationship (low fear coexisted with high crime, and high fear coexisted with low crime), something not found when comparing fear with incivilities. Given these relationships and the fact that the tenants considered vandalism, teen gangs, and harassment as among the biggest crime problems in the project, the report concluded that minor offenses were the most significant factor in resident fear levels.[12] Such offenses may not be serious in themselves, but the fear they generate is. The project resident is constantly reminded of a world of disorder behind which she pictures violence.

The Problem of Offending

The distribution of offending, like patterns of victimization and fear, is not spread evenly across socio-economic groups. In some respects, however, the information here is even less complete than in the prior two categories. Nationally less than 10 percent of all robberies are even cleared by an arrest; the chance of arrest *and* conviction is close to 3 percent, and the corresponding probabilities for a burglary are lower still.[13] In other words, we simply do not know—at least officially—who commits most offenses.

We do, of course, know a good deal about those who are arrested and convicted, particularly if they are sentenced to prison or jail. And the picture derived from those surveys is a fairly clear one. The majority of young men who grow up in the center cities, drop out of high school, and have trouble holding jobs do not end up in Massachusetts correctional institutions. But of the people who are in prison, a majority clearly fits this description.[14]

Over a third of those in Massachusetts prisons are from the city of Boston; over half are from the Boston metropolitan area. Ninety-five percent of them are male; 31 percent are black. They tend to be poorly educated: 58 percent have an education of tenth grade or less, and for 26 percent the last year completed in school was eighth grade. And they tend to have troubled employment histories: 30 percent have never held any job for more than 4 months, and for over half the longest job held was for one year. Most have been in and out of the criminal justice system many times before: 27 percent of the prison population were committed to the Department of Youth Services while a juvenile; 60 percent had nine or more prior court appearances; and 58 percent had served time in a local, state, or federal facility while an adult.

The Massachusetts data are fairly consistent with national surveys, which provide more detailed information as to income. Nationally 60 percent of those incarcerated in state correctional facilities had earned less than $6,000 the preceding year according to their arrests. As for the nation's jails, 46 percent earned income under $3,000 in the preceding year, and 63 percent qualified under local standards as indigent for purposes of appointed counsel.[15]

It is far easier to recite than to explain the data. Certainly it is true that some who grow up in middle-class suburban neighborhoods and are well educated and consistently employed do commit crimes, including crimes of violence. And it is equally true that most of those who grow up poor do not become serious criminals, despite the disadvantages they encounter. Yet the correlation between poverty, poor education, and poor employment prospects remains. How one explains it depends, at least in part, on one's perspective. Economists often focus on the opportunity costs—or lack thereof—noting that the poor have less to lose by crime and few other avenues to satisfy widely shared desires for affluence and material possessions. That perspective may explain economic crime (burglary and robbery), but it does not help very much in explaining other pure crimes of violence (although such crimes are much rarer). Sociologists tend to focus on culture, emphasizing the "culture of poverty" which renders unlawful behavior and even violence more acceptable among the poor than in middle-class communities. And city planners often point to the more tempting opportunities for crime in poorly designed inner city housing projects than in suburban developments. Whatever theory one emphasizes, however, it is clear that if we are concerned with crime and the poor, then we must be concerned with the problem of offending among the poor.

Responding to the Problem: The Criminal Justice System

The most immediate response of government to the problem of crime—and, for some, the only appropriate response—is the criminal justice system: police, courts, and corrections. It is, of course, not really one system, and this fact complicates analysis of how the state actually responds or should respond to crime. Police are primarily funded locally, and police commissioners or chiefs chosen by the mayor or an executive. District attorneys' offices in Massachusetts are funded by the state, but policy is set and administered by the winners of county-wide elections. The same is true, at least to a substantial extent, for county jails. While courts are funded and administered statewide, indigent representation is often provided by county rather than statewide organizations.

How does this system serve its poorest clients? Certainly not as well as it could. But before looking at the components of this

system separately, two general points should be raised. The first
is a question of priorities. There seems to be a consensus, in
Massachusetts and in the nation as a whole, that the criminal
justice system should place first priority on violent crime, particularly violent crimes committed by strangers on strangers. It is
such crime, certainly, that people fear most and that generates the
greatest public and media attention. Does such a priority serve
the poor? On the one hand, the poor are disproportionately the
victims of violent crime and are victimized by strangers almost as
often (as a percentage) as are the rich. The poor, like the rich, fear
violent crime but possess fewer resources to avoid the risks or to
protect themselves. Yet placing a first priority on violent crime,
particularly when defined, as it usually is, to include burglaries
(which could, of course, be robberies had the victim been at
home) means placing first priority for stricter enforcement and
tougher punishment on the "poor man's" crime. The poor man
burgles, the rich man embezzles; the poor man steals on the
street, the rich man steals in the boardroom. Is "pro-poor" policy
one that focuses resources and sanctions on the crimes that victimize the poor most directly or one that focuses equally on the
crimes committed by the rich? In a state of limited resources,
which ours surely is today, the priorities question is critical.

The second general point relates to realities. There is no question that the operation of the criminal justice system is a vitally
important aspect of government's response to crime. At the least it
can and should be fair and just; at the most we can strive to make
it efficient and effective. But under no circumstances should we
delude ourselves into believing that anything the criminal justice
system does or does not do will eliminate crime completely—or
even almost completely. Moreover, efforts to achieve greater
crime control through the criminal justice system may well run
counter to the ends of justice that should be primary in that
system. While it is almost as unfashionable today to talk of the
roots of crime as it is to speak of rehabilitation as a feasible and
important goal, the fact is that if we are really intent upon
seriously reducing violent crime in the first instance (and that is
without question a pro-poor policy) then we will have to look
beyond the criminal justice system to do it.

The Police

Of the three components of the criminal justice system, policing
is both the most expensive and the most local: Well over 85
percent of police expenditures are made at the local level. On

average Massachusetts cities and towns spend about 20 percent of their budgets on police. And while most communities have not been expanding their police forces in the wake of Proposition 2½ (the recently enacted tax-limiting legislation), police have, with a few exceptions, been spared in the budget-cutting process—itself a reflection of the priority attached to controlling crime in Massachusetts.

Logically—perhaps one should say, ideally—police should be distributed to reflect the risks and fear in individual communities and neighborhoods. Poor, high-crime neighborhoods should come first because the risks there are greater, the fear greater, and the options for private protection most limited. But police protection, like public education, is dependent on revenues from the property tax; thus, poorer communities that need protection most may well have relatively fewer officers or have to pay relatively much more to have as much protection.

The budget figures for Massachusetts cities and towns bear out this disparity. Higher-crime (and relatively poorer) cities do tend to spend more per capita and to have more police officers per capita than safer suburban and rural communities, but the differences do not even approach the differences in the crime rates. Figures made available by local police departments show that Boston, for example, spends almost $93.00 per capita for police protection, or $30 more than Concord; it has 3.4 police officers per 1,000 population, compared with Concord's 2.6. But Boston's police expenditure per index crime ($689.11) is less than a third of Concord's ($2167.07). Lynn, with an index crime rate nearly four times as high as Wellesley's, has only .5 police officers more per 1,000 population than does Wellesley. With regard to police employees per index crime, Wellesley has four times as many as Lynn, Sudbury nearly three times as many, and Newton nearly twice as many.[16] Moreover, not only are police resources unevenly distributed in various communities, but it has long been suggested that within a single community police may be allocated more on the basis of the political power of neighborhoods than on their need for protection.

Thus, one key policing issue for the poor in Massachusetts is that, given the risks they face, the poor pay relatively more (since police are financed primarily by the regressive property tax) for relatively less protection. Equally important, however, is a second problem: the ineffectiveness of current policing strategies in addressing the acute problems of victimization and fear faced by the poor.

Today, the norm in Massachusetts is vehicle patrol, with two officers in a patrol car responding to calls on the radio. Police effectiveness is measured, at least in large part, by response time. And response time is quite short in many communities.

But does it matter?

Police in cars do not, surveys have repeatedly found, make people feel less afraid. Increasing the number of patrol cars in selected areas of Kansas City was found to have no impact on citizen fear of crime.[17] Nor does general response time seem to have a substantial impact on crime prevention or crime solving: in the overwhelming majority of cases, the crime is well over before even quickly responding police arrive. And in a vehicle patrol strategy, priorities are largely determined not by police, not even by communities, but by the individual callers who, in a very real sense, make the allocation decision.

The problems of policing, both of distribution and effectiveness, are problems that have largely been ignored by state government. The major source of state assistance is through general local aid. The state role is otherwise limited to support of the MDC and the state police (which have relatively little to do with protecting poor people), to a police training program (which is most important for the smaller town departments, which cannot train on their own), to an inadequate crime lab and medical examiner system, and to a largely inoperative system of computerized criminal histories to aid local police and prosecutors. There is little question, of course, that policing is and will remain an essentially local function. But the state should do more. Given the budgetary constraints of many police departments, given the real and the political recognition of the importance of policing, given the forces of inertia within many departments, and given the complexities of implementing and evaluating potentially more effective strategies even in police departments willing to experiment, an enhanced and more directed state role in improving local police effectiveness is both critical and possible. With the elimination of the major federal grant program (LEAA), and with Proposition 2½ in effect locally, Massachusetts state government can and should assume a more aggressive role in sponsoring experiments that have worked elsewhere and in aiding local departments in developing, implementing, and evaluating new strategies. Financial and technical assistance is needed not only to convince localities to try new strategies but also to ensure that experimentation by a community is accompanied by the kind of evaluation that allows policymakers to learn whether the program has worked, why it has worked, and how it might work elsewhere. And the state effort to improve police effectiveness should be targeted on the communities and neighborhoods where crime is greatest and where police distribution problems are most serious—that is, on the communities and neighborhoods where the poor live.

There are no easy or certain answers. New strategies bring new problems. But there at least are three areas with the potential to produce results, particularly for the poor.

The first is improving systems of police deployment within communities. There seems to be little question that police resources should be deployed on the basis of crime rates and risks. That they are not is partly a function of politics but also partly a function of the relatively rudimentary systems used by most police departments to make deployment decisions. Even where politics is not an issue, deployment decisions tend to be made on the basis of rather rough assessments of crime risks and rates in different areas and at different times. And because the system is as rough as it is makes it easier—and more defensible—for political considerations to enter into the process. Given the state of computer technology in Massachusetts, computerized systems of crime analysis that incorporate the significant variance in crime rates (between neighborhoods, between blocks, at different times of day and night and on different days of the week) should be in place at least for the largest departments. Police resources could then be deployed with greater flexibility and greater responsiveness to crime and, therefore, to the needs of the poor. The input for such systems already exists in the form of thousands of police reports; what is needed are the resources to refine software, to pay the initial costs for hardware, and to evaluate the systems once in place.

A second area with the potential to produce results is in the development of foot patrol strategies that emphasize the police order maintenance function.[18] In this view, the job of the police is to get out of their cars, get into the community, and enforce order according to the community rules. It may mean disbanding gangs of teenagers on street corners, limiting public drinking, or stopping "strangers" from harassing those who live in the neighborhood. The strategy has a number of advantages. As implemented in Newark, New Jersey, it made residents of the center city neighborhood feel safer. If it is true that the poor are among the most afraid in our state and that "incivilities" are a major cause of fear, then the maintenance of order in poor neighborhoods could bring important benefits to our state's poor citizens. The strategy also brought demonstrable improvements in police-community relations; by definition, the function of the foot patrol officer seeking to maintain order is to enforce the norms set by the community. And while the strategy did not result in any immediately measurable reductions in the crime rate, James Q. Wilson and George Kelling have argued with some force that an orderly neighborhood is in fact a safer one and that "serious street crime flourishes in areas in which disorderly behavior goes unchecked." In short, the arguments in favor of a foot patrol/order maintenance strategy, particularly in poor neighborhoods, where disorderly behavior currently goes unchecked, are powerful ones.

But even if it is accepted, as it appears to have been only recently in Boston, that foot patrol deserves greater emphasis, important questions and uncertainties remain. For better or for worse, we cannot simply return to the "good old days" of the cop on the beat. The crime control benefits of foot patrol in the 1980s have yet to be established by any study. And the Newark experiment raises at least as many questions as it answers as to how and where foot patrol officers can most effectively be deployed, what powers they should be given, and what standards should guide their exercise of discretion. Serious civil liberties problems remain. A police officer enforcing public order often will impose at least limited sanctions (to move along, to answer questions) on people violating no criminal law. To be effective, he must have the power to back up his orders with the threat of arrest (generally for such "crimes" as public disorder, vagrancy, and the like) at his own discretion. It would be quite easy—indeed, almost natural—for the police officer to use the weapons at his disposal in a way that reflects whatever prejudice and bigotry dominates the community. And Wilson and Kelling, while recognizing the problem, admit that they can offer no wholly satisfactory solution, nor are they certain that one exists. What all of this suggests is not that we should eschew foot patrol because of its problems and uncertainties but rather that carefully planned efforts and scrupulously objective evaluations are essential if the very real potential here is to be realized. In that process, state assistance is critical.

A third area for potential improvement is in the investigation phase. Techniques that increase what is now known to be a very small risk of either apprehension or felony conviction deserve serious attention. And here again, there are signs of progress. In New York City, programs are working to increase apprehension rates and conviction rates for burglary and robbery (two of the crimes which prey most heavily on the poor), and burglaries and robberies are declining.[19] In the 90th precinct in Brooklyn, robbery dropped 40 percent (with no signs of displacement) after police compiled new, separate mug books of all "likely" robbers (those with previous records of robbery and larceny with contact) living in the precinct, made it a standard practice to visit the homes of all robbery victims on the same day of the complaint, secured nearly twice as many identifications, and then provided immediate information and incentives for the uniformed police officers to make arrests. Not only did the percentages of cases resulting in arrest increase substantially, but the absolute number of robberies declined—presumably because robbery is a "local" offense and word quickly got out to would-be-robbers in the community that their pictures were in circulation, thus increasing their risk of being identified, apprehended, and punished.

In the 43rd precinct in the Bronx between 1979 and 1981, the indictment rate for robbery arrests rose from 39 to 66 percent, the conviction rate rose from 51 to 74 percent, and the incarceration rate rose from 30 to 44 percent as direct results of an experimental program of enhanced "felony case preparation," a program involving immediate post-arrest police investigation and presentation of written reports to prosecutors in cases of burglary and robbery arrests. Punishment was also enhanced, and sentences of five years or more for robbery tripled. Among burglary arrests the indictment rate more than doubled and the conviction rate rose from 56 to 68 percent. The experiments, since expanded citywide, worked; the immediate investigation and the written reports of results alleviated common problems of stale and disappearing witnesses, allowed prosecutors to make informed decisions as to charging, and strengthened their hands in plea negotiations.

What works in New York may or may not work as well in Massachusetts. But, at the very least, law enforcement officials in one state need to know about what is working successfully elsewhere, and they need financial and technical assistance if they are to try such programs, to evaluate accurately their effectiveness, and to adapt them to local problems and conditions.

The Courts

The poor come into the criminal courts of Massachusetts in two positions: as defendants and as victims/witnesses. In both instances they are almost entirely dependent on the state. As defendants they must depend on the state's appointment of counsel to represent them, a matter in which they have virtually no choice. And as victims they are wholly dependent on the district attorney's office and on court officials to take their claims and concerns seriously. In both contexts, there is reason to believe that Massachusetts could do a better job than it does now.

1. *Poor Defendants in the Courts.*   Massachusetts spends over
$13 million per year providing legal representation to indigent
defendants in criminal courts as required by the state Constitution.[20] There are three components of the system: (1) the Massachusetts Defenders Committee (MDC), which handles most
representation in the superior courts, where more serious crimes
are tried; (2) county bar advocate programs, in which private
firms or corporations provide coverage on a contractual basis
with the county in district court cases; and (3) appointments of
private counsel on a fee-per hour basis in superior court where
MDC (usually because of conflicts of interest) will not handle the
case and in district courts (notably including Suffolk County
including Boston) which do not have a county bar advocate
program. All of these programs are funded by the state as a result
of the court reorganization legislation signed in 1978.

The Massachusetts Defenders Committee has received generally positive reviews from those who have evaluated its operations. That is not to say that the program is without problems;
even the strongest supporters of MDC recognize the need for
improvements in training and supervision of young attorneys and
in salaries for more experienced lawyers. Contrary to common
perceptions, however, the MDC is not the major source of representation for indigents, at least as judged in terms of dollars. In FY
1982 MDC operated on a budget of $4,194,887; private bar
appointments totalled $4,067,645 and county bar advocate pro-
grams cost the state $4,471,283. In other words, the latter two
sources of counsel accounted for appropriations more than twice
as large as MDC's, even though it is MDC that handles nearly all
of the most serious cases against indigents in the state.

Both private appointments and county bar programs carry
with them real incentives for attorneys to dispose of cases
assigned to them with dispatch. Under the county bar advocate
program, the private attorneys retained by the corporation are
paid $125 per day for their first day's work on a case or a group of
cases, and $50 per day for each additional day. Clearly, the
incentive is to dispose of the case in a day and start a new one. It
may be that most misdemeanors require little more than that.
Even so, what is involved for the poor defendant is his liberty;
misdemeanors may be punished by up to a year in jail. In some
cases, effective assistance of counsel will require more than a
day's work. The county bar advocate program seems designed to
insure that the work will not be done.

Nor is the defendent likely to fare much better if private
counsel is appointed by the court to represent him. In district
court, appointed attorneys are paid $35 per hour for time spent in

court and $25 per hour for preparation, and advance permission from the court is required if more than one hour's work in court or more than five hours out of court is to be compensated. Given that every defendant must at least be arraigned, enter a plea, and receive a sentence (which may take up the hour), the systemic incentive is to keep out of court and to dispose of the case with a plea bargain in less than five hours. The Superior Court system, where defendants accused of the most serious crimes can find themselves facing as much as life imprisonment, works almost the same way. The rate schedule is the same; without special action by the court, attorneys representing defendants charged with felonies are limited to $1000 compensation.

Once in a while a qualified, competent, and dedicated private attorney is appointed to represent an indigent defendant. The attorney soon finds the fees paid by the state nowhere near adequate—let alone competitive—but provides effective representation nonetheless. That defendant is one of the lucky few. For the vast majority, county bar and private appointments spell inadequate representation. According to a Boston Bar Association study,[21] the county bar programs were found to provide representation of an "unacceptable quality." Patronage plays a major role in both systems. Attorneys who depend for their livelihood on appointments tend to develop closer and stronger relationships with the judges who appoint them than with the clients they represent; the result, not surprisingly, is a reduced vigor in representing their clients and in challenging judicial rulings. The hourly fees are just too low to attract anyone who can attract paying clients; indeed the only way that any attorney can profit from the system is by disposing of a maximum number of cases in a minimum amount of time, and many lawyers do just that.

There is no real dispute that the MDC provides better representation to the poor and does so at a lower cost to the taxpayer then either county bar or private appointment programs. Nonetheless the latter two programs continue to cost the state more than twice what MDC does. Financially, at least, the prime beneficiaries of Massachusetts indigent counsel programs appear to be the least successful, politically best-connected, members of the private bar. The indigent counsel program is, to a substantial extent, just that—a program for the least wealthy attorneys, whose costs are borne by the taxpayer and by the poor.

2. *Poor Victims.* The problem of uncooperative victims was "discovered" in the criminal justice community in the late 1960s.[22] Surveys across the country revealed not only that much crime goes unreported but that, even where crimes were reported and

arrests made, a substantial percentage of cases were dismissed because the victims refused to cooperate in their prosecution. By 1974, with the evidence of a problem mounting, LEAA initiated a program to fund 19 victim/witness projects, many within prosecutors' offices. The programs, in general, sought to improve victim/witness cooperation by reducing the costs to the witness: Victims were told exactly when they were expected and where; transportation and child care were provided; efforts were made to improve coordination and reduce the number of required appearances. Every district attorney's office in the state now has some such program, funded by the state but designed and controlled locally. Such programs, however, are proven failures at improving court attendance by victims and witnesses and reducing dismissals occasioned by victim non-cooperation. Study after study has demonstrated that even the best-designed and best-run victim/witness programs have virtually no impact on convictions.

Complainants, researchers have found, expect to incur certain costs in pursuing their cases through the criminal justice system. But these costs have very little to do with the decision whether to attend court and cooperate. Those who refuse to cooperate most often do so not because of the costs of cooperation but because the criminal justice system does not appear to offer them what they need or want. On the one hand, the criminal courts may represent the only legal avenue to pursue restitution or retribution; on the other hand, the choices actually afforded within the system (probation or incarceration) are often wholly unresponsive to the victim's wants and needs. A woman who has been beaten by her husband or "boyfriend" may understandably view both a suspended sentence with probation (effectively no punishment) and incarceration as unacceptable alternatives. What she wants is help and protection for both herself and her assailant. The criminal justice system is not structured to offer that and the woman, knowing this, does not cooperate. So too, for many cases of personal and property crime within families, apartment buildings, and neighborhoods. The resulting noncooperation is unresponsive to programs that simply reduce the personal costs of participating in the existing system.

That is not to say that these programs, including the vast majority in Massachusetts, ought to be abandoned. Reducing the costs of cooperation to victims is itself a value, regardless of the impact on convictions. Moreover, in practice such programs may improve resource allocation efficiency within prosecutors' offices by allowing trained social workers to assume functions relating to victims (from handholding to scheduling) which would otherwise consume the time of prosecutors themselves. But until and unless these programs are coupled with more basic changes in the system—changes including alternative means of resolving disputes outside the criminal justice system and real alternatives to the current incarceration/no punishment choice—the needs of a large percentage of poor victims will continue to go unmet, and they will continue to respond by not cooperating with prosecutors.

As difficult as the plight of this group is, however, another group of victims suffer even more: the victims whose perpetrators are never caught. They never even face the decision of whether to cooperate with prosecutors; for them, the victim-witness programs within prosecutors' offices are entirely irrelevant because their cases never get that far. In Massachusetts this group of victims is the overwhelming majority, and they are almost completely ignored. In a few of the major cities, rape crisis programs operate out of local hospitals to provide aid to the victims of rapes, whether or not their perpetrators are caught. In addition, there is a 1967 state law establishing a victim of violent crime compensation program, but almost no one knows about it—which may be just as well, considering both its limited appropriations and the many limits on eligibility.[23] For the majority of victims and their families, and particularly for the poor victims who are most in need, neither the state nor anyone else provides any help in coping with the emotional and financial costs of crime. If we are serious about crime and the poor, then victimization programs cannot be limited to district attorneys' and thus to the victims whose alleged perpetrators are apprehended. Victims' units within high-crime police precincts themselves, formed to provide emergency aid and referrals as well as counseling and information to all victims, may have far more impact on victim perception of the criminal justice system and will almost surely provide more help to more people than the programs we now find in the district attorneys' offices.

In the last analysis, if the criminal justice system is to serve the poor, it must do so by ensuring adequate assistance not only for those who commit crimes but also for those who are victimized by them. Otherwise, both groups (and both groups are disproportionately comprised of poor people) will be unnecessarily disaffected from the system. And that situation will have costs not only for the individual but for the long-run effectiveness of the system as a whole.

Corrections

Massachusetts today suffers the distinction of having one of the most overcrowded prison systems in the nation.[24] The facilities operated by the state Department of Corrections have a capacity of 3,002—and a population of 4,112. Health care in the prisons is administered under the terms of a consent decree resulting from a 1978 lawsuit. Vocational programs are closing in the prisons more quickly than they are opening; the computer training programs at three facilities, which accounted for roughly 30 percent of vocational training in the system as a whole, closed completely in 1982. And it is in the area of employment that the Senate Ways and Means Committee has found the Department of Corrections "most lacking in its responsibility to its inmate population." The cornerstone of the employment program, an industries program in which inmates are employed to manufacture goods, employs less than 10 percent of the prison population. Last year at Walpole State Prison, 400 of 665 inmates had no jobs at all.

Nor are the state's jails, where those awaiting trial and those sentenced to shorter terms are incarcerated, in any better shape. The county system is as much as 30 percent over capacity itself, and unconstitutional conditions have generated several successful lawsuits. Even so, rudimentary facilities such as plumbing within cells are still lacking in a number of counties, which continue to double- and triple-cell inmates with plastic buckets instead of toilets.

A correctional system as overcrowded as Massachusetts' cannot hope to do more than maintain order within the walls. Education and employment training, which the average young, poor, and poorly skilled prisoner needs if he is to have any chance in the future, are luxuries in the current system. And the prospects for improvement in the situation in the foreseeable future are not very promising. To be sure, the legislature in 1982 approved a $114 million capital outlay budget to finance 878 additional prison beds and 460 additional jail beds in the next 30 months. But that will barely address the current overcrowding problems. And even as this legislation passed, other bills have been proposed, and in some cases passed, to extend the period before parole eligibility, to establish mandatory sentences for drug offenses and drunken driving, and to extend required sentences for both violent and property crimes. Such bills will, of course, increase the pressures on the system.

Perhaps *because* of their limited capacity, Massachusetts prisons are also among the most selective in the nation.[25] Approximately 82 percent of the inmates of state prison facilities are serving sentences for violent crimes, compared with a national average of 49 percent. Only 12 percent are serving sentences for property offenses and only 4 percent are incarcerated for drug offenses. And the overwhelming majority of the prisoners are in the first year of their sentences.

The selectivity of the current prison system raises an important question as to the other "half" of corrections: our treatment of the low-level or property offender who is not currently being incarcerated in a state's prison. In fact, this is more than half the problem: the population of the DOC facilities represents only a small fraction of those who come through the system in any given year. In the state as a whole, as many as 35,000 criminal cases are disposed of every year; less than 5 percent result in prison sentences. Instead, where cases are pursued to conviction, short jail terms, fines, or probation are imposed, until the offender reaches the point where, with as many as nine previous charges (the average for Massachusetts prisoners), a prison term is imposed.

The fact is that we have not developed means to deliver punishment (let alone rehabilitation) outside of prison, that the costs just to incarcerate (let alone educate, employ, or train) our current population are substantial, and that the pressures are growing faster than our ability to meet them. The situation raises at least two important questions.

First, what can we hope to accomplish by the enactment of legislation that will expand our prison population further by extending prison terms? Surely such measures will bring some incapacitative effects, but at extremely high costs—particularly in light of the general tendency of offenders to "age out" of criminal activity in their middle and later twenties. As for deterrence, when fewer than 10 percent or less of all offenses even result in arrests, and when the bulk of offenders in any event appear to have little to lose by offending, the efficacy of deterrence is at least open to question.

Second, we should ask whether it is possible—indeed, the most fiscally responsible course—to develop means which would punish, and perhaps even rehabilitate, less violent and less serious offenders short of incarceration. The need to develop alternatives is perhaps the most pressing corrections issue we face. It takes two forms.

The most pressing need is to develop alternatives to incarceration for those offenders whose records and offenses demand that they be punished. A major part of the jail-crowding problem in Massachusetts is caused by repeat petty offenders serving short terms (30, 60, or 90 days) of incarceration. Faced with defendants who have committed five and six previous offenses, judges understandably believe that some real punishment is deserved. In Massachusetts today, that means a short jail term—the form of punishment most costly to the taxpayer and, with this population at least, proven to deliver little in the way of crime reduction or deterrence. For this group, the development of alternatives such as community service sentencing (unpaid work) backed up by a real threat of jail for noncompliance deserves greater attention.

We also need alternatives to the practice of giving no punishment at all to first-, second-, or third-time offenders, as now occurs even in some cases of serious crime. The system now tends to do absolutely nothing to the offender until and unless he has committed a third, fourth, or fifth offense. First-and second-time assaults and thefts are ignored, both because the system lacks the facilities to incarcerate these offenders and because most of them will "drop out" of crime on their own in any event. Probation is no punishment at all, as everyone in the system knows; probation officers lack the resources to deliver on the threat of jail for noncompliance. The answer for this group, which includes most youthful offenders, is surely not jail or prison, given both the costs of incarceration and the real likelihood that it might result in a greater, not a lesser, proportion pursuing criminal careers. But neither is it at all clear that the best answer is the one the system currently gives—that is, nothing. Alternatives such as supported work and restitution have been used successfully for this group, and they, too, deserve greater attention.

Beyond the Criminal Justice System: The Community and Crime Control

It is perfectly appropriate for the citizens of a state to demand a criminal justice system that is fair and effective and just; it is wholly unfair of them to expect—and of politicians to suggest— that changing sentencing laws or expanding prison capacity or adding prosecutors will eliminate the problem of crime. Whether such steps will have any impact on crime rates is much debated; but no one who has studied the problem has ever seriously suggested that they are *the* only answers. The poor in Massachusetts need better police protection and more skilled counsel and improved corrections facilities. But if we are serious about their crime problems, we must also look beyond the criminal justice system for answers.

Nearly everyone agrees that a strong community is critical in limiting criminal opportunities and preventing crime. The problem is that nearly everyone has a different notion of what the term "strong community" means or how to create it.[26]

Over the past ten years, with help in the early days from LEAA, private citizens and community organizations have sought to get together to "do something" about crime.[27] The "something" ranges from citizen patrol and "crime watch" programs to engraving valuables. There is evidence that these types of collective responses tend to reduce fear in the community and to increase pride among the participants. They may improve relationships between the community and the police and increase citizen input to the operation of the criminal justice system. But whether they actually reduce crime is far from clear. Very few such programs have been the subject of substantial investigations; for the few that have, almost all conclusions are ambiguous, inconsistent, or negative. Moreover, any reports of changes in the crime rate as a result of community programs must be examined with caution. On the one hand, to the extent that such programs encourage citizen reporting to the police and foster better community relations with the criminal justice system, they may increase the proportion of crimes that are officially reported. As a result, the crime rate may appear to be increasing or stabilizing even though it is actually decreasing.[29] But, on the other hand, decreasing crime rates may simply reflect displacement: Crime prevention programs on one block may reduce victimization there while increasing it in another area.

The notion of "community" involves more than merely citizen organization. Others have argued that emphasis should be placed on literally building a stronger and more cohesive community. The theory, based initially on work by Oscar Newman analyzing crime rates in public housing projects,[29] is that the built environment (project size, building type, placement of parks and recreation areas) plays a critical role in creating, or destroying, a sense of community within projects and thus in increasing or reducing criminal victimizations there.

Certainly, there are links between crime and the built environment. Simple elements of "target hardening"—the installation of better doors, locks, and alarms—have proved effective in reducing victimizations and increasing apprehension of offenders, particularly in the case of burglary. In Seattle, for example, three out of four public housing developments showed a significant decrease in burglaries after target-hardening efforts were completed.[30] In that case, the efforts involved installation of deadbolt locks and solid case doors, construction of short walls to prevent exterior access, and restriction of window openings. Similarly, a study in the Cabrini-Green housing project in Chicago found that installation of locks on doors and stairways, along with other elements of an architectural security program, contributed to reduction in interior crimes in the experimental buildings.[31] These successful projects suggest simple steps (generally taken by the middle class on its own) that might be undertaken with government assistance in poor neighborhood and housing projects.

Whether we can go further in building community in poor neighborhoods, however, is far from clear. Victimization surveys and individual studies have consistently found that poorly lighted areas, with opportunities for concealment and accessibility to outside traffic, make certain locations more dangerous than others. But a 1977 report reviewing 41 street lighting projects and evaluating the leading 15 studies in the area concluded that, while there was strong evidence that improved lighting decreased the fear of crime, there was no statistically significant evidence that it had any impact on the actual level of crime.[32] As for more dramatic changes, two studies did find that programs altering street and traffic patterns and providing better definition of space for residents (such as new entranceways, and sitting areas) resulted in reductions of both fear and victimization.[33] It is not clear why this is true. It may be that the changes simply make certain opportunities less attractive to the offender himself; or it may be, as the theorists argue, that the critical factor is the social cohesion within the community encouraged by these changes. Empirical evidence is largely lacking.

Nonetheless, there are important lessons here. The first, and the clearest, is that community participation can make people feel safer, and that at least some changes in the built environment—from door locks to better street design—may actually allow them to live more safely. That is surely important, particularly in poor communities more dependent on government to structure their built environment. But there is a second lesson as well. If, as everyone seems to agree, community is important with respect to the problems of fear and victimization, then it should be clear that an entire range of government policies not commonly thought to have much to do with crime—policies which may strengthen families or contribute to the disintegration, as well as those designed to strengthen neighborhoods, improve housing, and the like—may in the long run be more important in dealing with crime than anything we do or don't do in the criminal justice system itself. And perhaps most important of all are the policies and practices that determine whether and when the would-be offender is himself integrated into the community.

The crimes that most often victimize, and are most feared by, the poor are the robberies, burglaries, and assaults which tend to be committed by young men who are themselves poor, poorly educated, and unemployed. Yet even this group of youngsters are not permanent criminals. By their mid-twenties or so, most violent youngsters "age out" of violent crime. While the phenomenon of "age out" is widely known and accepted, the reasons underlying it are not. But the most compelling explanation seems to be that as these young people grow up, even the least trained tend finally to find some types of jobs; as they do, the influence of teen gangs decreases; a reasonably steady source of income allows them to settle down and make family commitments which, in turn, serve as a powerful deterrent to criminal activity. The process of growing up, of joining the community and developing a stake in it, may in the last analysis be the most powerful force preventing crime in our society.[39] The increasing problems for the young and the poor in Massachusetts and elsewhere—problems of mounting unemployment, poor education and training, and lack of opportunity for young people and young families—demand attention as a matter of human dignity. And to the extent that these problems threaten the very process by which poor young men "age out" of crime, we ignore them at our peril.

Endnotes

1. See *Criminal Victimization Surveys in Thirteen American Cities* (Washington, D.C.: U.S. Department of Justice, June 1975).
2. The national victimization data presented in this chapter are from *Criminal Victimization in the United States, 1978* (Washington, D.C.: U.S. Department of Justice, 1980).
3. Insurance may also be at least one of the reasons that wealthier households are more likely to report property crimes to police than poorer households.
4. J. Garofalo, *Public Opinion About Crime* (Washington, D.C.: U.S. Department of Justice, 1977).
5. *The Michigan Public Speaks Out on Crime* (Market Opinion Research, 1977).
6. G. Kelling, *et al., The Kansas City Preventive Patrol Experiment: A Technical Report* (Washington, D.C.: The Police Foundation, 1974). *See* generally F.

DuBow, E. McCabe & G. Kaplan, *Reactions to Crime: A Critical Review of the Literature* (Washington, D.C.: U.S. Department of Justice, 1979).

7. A. Reiss, Jr., *Studies in Crime and Law Enforcement in Major Metropolitan Areas* (Washington, D.C.: U.S. Government Printing Office, 1967).

8. M. Lawton *et al.*, "Psychological Aspects of Crime and Fear of Crime," in *Crime and the Elderly* (J. & S. Goldsmith, eds.) (1976).

9. L. Savitz *et al.*, *City Life and Delinquency: Victimization, Fear of Crime and Gang Membership* (Washington, D.C.: U.S. Department of Justice, 1977).

10. Of course, to some extent the lower victimization rates for women and the elderly may themselves be related to the higher rates of fear and to the self-imposed limitations on exposure to public places which fear produces. It may also be that young men are at some level more fearful then they admit, or that their lack of fear is more a product of social conditioning than anything else.

11. S.E. Merry, "The Management of Danger in a High Crime Urban Neighborhood" (Wellesley College, 1976).

12. Wasserman *et al.*, Security in Public Housing: A Report for the Boston Housing Authority; J.Q. Wilson, "The Urban Unease: Community vs. City," *The Public Interest* 25–39 (Summer 1968).

13. *See* A. Blumstein and J. Cohen, "Estimation of Individual Crime Rates from Arrest Records," *J. Criminal Law & Criminology* 561 (1979).

14. The information on Massachusetts prisoners in this section was made available by the Massachusetts Department of Corrections.

15. Abt Associates, *American Prisons and Jails* (U.S. Department of Justice, 1980); "Prisoners in 1980," *Bureau of Justice Statistics Bulletin*, (May 1981). There is no standard definition of "indigency" counsel. In Massachusetts, the appointment decision is within the discretion of the local judge, and cases challenging such decisions are rare. Constitutionally, the right to appointed counsel extends to any defendant who is actually punished by incarceration and "who is too poor to hire a lawyer." See *Gideon v. Wainwright*, 372 U.S. 335 (1963); *Scott v. Illinois*, 440 U.S. 367 (1979).

16. These figures, as well as city crime rates, are drawn from the official Uniform Crime Reports, *Crime in the United States, 1980* (U.S. Department of Justice, 1981).

17. *See* G. Kelling, *et al.*, *supra* note 5. *See also* T. Pate *et al.*, *Three Approaches to Criminal Apprehension in Kansas City* (Washington, D.C.: Police Foundation , 1976).

18. *See* J.Q. Wilson and G. Kelling, "Broken Windows: The Police and Neighborhood Safety,"*The Atlantic* (March 1982).

19. *See* J. McElroy *et al.*, *Felony Case Preparation: Quality Counts* (New York: Vera Institute of Justice, 1981).

20. *See* generally Senate Committee on Ways and Means, Report on S. No. 1900, Policy Report #10 (June, 1982).

21. W. Rose & R. Spangenberg, *Action Plan for Legal Services to the Poor: Part 2* (Boston, Mass.: Boston Bar Association, 1978).

22. *See generally* R. Davis, V. Russell, and F. Kunreuther, *The Role of the Complaining Witness in an Urban Criminal Court* (New York: Vera Institute of Justice, 1980); A.D. Biderman *et al.*, *Report on a Pilot Study in the District*

of Columbia on Victimization and Attitudes Toward Law Enforcement (Washington, D.C.: U.S. Department of Justice, 1967).

23. In fact, the victim who actually seeks to recover from the fund may feel twice victimized when he discovers that, for reasons which can only appear "technical" (i.e. a prior relationship with the perpetrator), he is ineligible. Moreover, the fact that the program specifically excludes compensation for property damage and losses from theft (even if uninsured) and includes a $100.00 "deductible" for medical expenses, makes it even less well-targeted to the needs of poor victims.

24. *See generally* Senate Report, *supra* note 20, Policy Report #16.

25. *See* Abt Associates, *supra* note 15.

26. E. Currie, "Fighting Crime," *Working Papers* (July–August 1982).

27. *See generally* F. DuBow *et al.*, *supra* note 6.

28. They may also improve the accuracy of public perceptions of crime rates, something which may or may not reduce fear. Indeed, in order to promote participation in the first instance, program sponsors may well take steps— i.e., publicizing crime in the community which people were not aware of—which in the first instance increase fear.

29. O. Newman, *Defensible Space* (1972). *See generally*, H. Rubinstein, *et al.*, *The Link Between Crime and the Built Environment*, Volume I (Washington, D.C.: U.S. Dept. of Justice, 1980).

30. Seattle Law and Justice Planning Office, *Burglary Reduction Program: Final Report* (Washington, D.C.: U.S. Department of Justice, 1975).

31. Arthur Young & Company, *Evaluation of the Cabrini-Green High Impact Program* (Chicago Department of Development and Planning, 1979).

32. J.M. Tien, *et. al.*, *Street Lighting Projects: National Evaluation Program, Phase I* (Cambridge, Mass.: Public Systems Evaluation, Inc., 1977).

33. F. Fowler, *Reducing Residential Crime and Fear: The Hartford Neighborhood Prevention Program* (Boston, Mass: Joint Center for Urban Studies, 1979); L. Hand, "Cincinnati Housing Authority Builds Safety into Project," *HUD Challenge* (March 1977).

34. *See* M.E. Smith and J.W. Thompson, "Employment, Youth and Violent Crime," *Journal of Ideas and Politics* (Spring 1983).

Part Three

IMPLEMENTING AND FINANCING PROGRAMS FOR THE POOR

The three chapters in this part consider the financial and institutional problems encountered in adopting the policies to prevent and amerliorate poverty discussed in previous chapters. Chapter 9 looks at taxation and the basic problem of how programs for the poor (as well as other state programs) ought to be financed. It discusses the current tax burden on the poor and suggests ways to make the tax system more progressive. It then discusses the effect of the recently enacted property tax limitation measure (Proposition 2½) on both the taxes paid by and the benefits received by the poor.

Chapter 10 raises the issue of how programs for the poor ought to be planned and coordinated within state government. It describes the reasons why planning is important and why planning for the poor ought to be part of an overall state planning function rather than a separate activity. The author then suggests ways in which the planning and budgeting functions could be effectively coordinated.

Our final chapter takes up the general question of governance as it relates to programs for the poor. It raises the issues of political power, of the role of the state in the federalist system, and of the importance of establishing a moral consensus on the legitimacy of programs for the poor. It thus defines the political and managerial context in which any progress against poverty

233

must take place and makes suggestions for improving performance in both areas.

The basic issue taken up in these chapters, as in the previous
chapters, is how to organize and use money, people, and energy
most effectively. The problems that Massachusetts faces in these
areas, like those discussed in our previous chapters, are not unique to this state. All states face serious financing problems and all
are squeezed by the recession, by cutbacks of federal funds, and
by public resistence to (if not legal prohibitions against) raising
state and local taxes. The role of the state in financing services,
including some historically seen as local responsibilities, is being
examined everywhere. Though the mechanisms by which states
collect taxes, finance education, and distribute general aid to
local government obviously differ, the general issues and approaches are common across states.

Also common across the states are the issues around management and governance that are taken up in Chapters 10 and 11.
There are two basic problems, the first having to do with the
mobilization of political support for action against poverty. In no
state are the poor a majority of voters; in all states political
support must come from the moral commitment of the population. The second problem has to do with the organization and
management of government: What is the role of the state? What is
the best way to coordinate state actions that must be carried out
by different agencies of government? Our chapters propose a
model of a planning process and an approach to organizational
issues that can be applied in many states.

Chapter 9

TAXATION AND THE POOR

by Helen F. Ladd and Herman B. Leonard

State taxes are the primary means of financing the public programs described in other chapters of this book. Assuring adequate revenues for these and other public programs requires a
fair and efficient tax structure. Maintaining a strong state tax
structure is particularly important in Massachusetts because of
the pressures on the state tax system from voter-imposed tax
limitations at the local level and from cutbacks in federal programs and intergovernmental aid. A thorough evaluation of the
Massachusetts tax structure, however, would raise a number of
issues beyond the scope of this book and, hence, is not attempted
here. Like other chapters, this one will focus on poor people. We
shall examine the impact of the current tax structure and recent
trends on poor people and recommend changes to reduce the
burden of taxes on this group.

In the aftermath of Proposition 2½ (the initiative law limiting the
property tax), the fiction of separation between state and local
fiscal policies is, perhaps forever, laid to rest. One cannot effectively consider issues of state tax policy without being attentive to
the overall fiscal context of state and local financial issues within
which these policies and the public debate that surrounds them
are played out. An understanding of the interrelation between the
issues of state and local finance that is manifest in the political
aftermath of Proposition 2½ is particularly crucial for developing
a full appreciation for the stake of the poor in the overall fiscal
system of the state.

We begin, therefore, with a discussion of the structure, trends,
and incidence of the state and local tax system in Massachusetts,
with particular attention to identifying the issues of importance

for the poor. Having discussed these general issues, we then turn to a detailed treatment of the effects of Proposition 2½ on the fiscal system of Massachusetts as it affects the poor. The final section will provide a set of broad recommendations with a brief discussion.

The Massachusetts Tax Structure

Massachusetts has long been known for its relatively high taxes. Overall, however, the total tax burden in Massachusetts is not so different as it is sometimes made to seem from that in other states. From 1960 until 1971, Massachusetts' total tax burden as a fraction of income, which rose steadily from about 10 percent to almost 16 percent, was lower than the national average. Since 1971 the total state and local tax burden has continued to grow slowly, and Massachusetts' level has been about one percent higher than the national average.[1]

Tax burdens for certain visible taxes, however, far exceed the national average. In fiscal year 1980 Massachusetts ranked fifth in the nation in 1978 in property tax collections per capita ($522) and sonal income, taking an average of 3.6 cents of each dollar. If we exclude Alaska, which is unique because of its reliance on property taxes paid by oil companies, Massachusetts ranked first in the nation in 1978 in property tax collection per capita ($522) and per dollar of personal income (7.9 cents). In 1980 the state ranked second (to New Hampshire) in property tax collections as a fraction of total state and local own source revenues, with a total of 45 percent of own revenues raised through the property tax vehicle.[2]

The state's reliance on other traditionally important tax sources is correspondingly relatively low. In 1977, for example, Massachusetts ranked 44th in the nation in general sales tax collections as a fraction of retail sales; its reliance on indirect business taxes is also relatively slight.[3]

The composition of Massachusetts taxation before the advent of Proposition 2½ thus clearly differed substantially from that of the typical state. Table 9–1 compares Massachusetts tax burdens as a fraction of personal income with the average burden across all states for a variety of revenue sources in 1979–1980. Three features of the table are particularly noteworthy. First, Massachusetts had a very high level of local property taxes and a correspondingly very low level of non-property taxes at the local level. Thus, the composition of local own-source revenues in Massachusetts was dramatically shifted toward property taxes from the

Table 9-1 Comparison of the State and Local Revenues per $1000 of Personal Income Between Massachusetts and All States, 1979–1980

Revenue Source	Revenues Per $1000 of Personal Income		Percentage Difference
	Mass.	*All States*	
Local non-property taxes	$4.5	$10.8	–58%
Local fees and charges	12.2	22.6	–46
State general sales	14.5	22.4	–35
State fees and charges	14.1	16.7	–14
State selective sales taxes	11.8	12.8	– 8
State taxes on business	10.4	6.9	+50
Local property tax	62.0	33.9	+82
State income tax	36.3	19.2	+89

SOURCE: U.S. Bureau of the Census: Governmental Finances in 1979–1980, Table 12 (p. 41), Table 27 (p. 95); State Government Finances in 1980, Table 7 (p. 29).

national average. Second, personal income tax burdens were almost 90 percent higher on average in Massachusetts than in other states. Third, while the reliance on the general sales tax was about 35 percent less than in the average state (as a fraction of total personal income), reliance on selective sales taxes was relatively higher, only about 8 percent lower than the national average.

Tax Incidence

The implications of the composition of the state's tax system for the poor of the state are not easy to discern. The relatively heavy reliance on income taxes, generally regarded as falling more heavily on the rich than on the poor, and correspondingly low reliance on sales taxes, which usually constitute a greater fraction of the incomes of the poor than of the rich, tends to make the Massachusetts tax system relatively progressive. The very high levels of property taxation, however, make the overall pattern of impact quite uncertain.

In examining the fairness of a tax system, experts usually consider the fraction of a taxpayer's income that a given tax payment represents. A tax is said to be progressive if it constitutes a larger fraction of the income of wealthier taxpayers. If poor taxpayers pay a larger fraction of their incomes than wealthier taxpayers, it is said to be regressive. A tax is said to be proportional if all taxpayers pay a similar fraction of their incomes for it. Generally speaking, a shift toward more progressive taxation will increase the burden borne by the rich, both in absolute terms and as a fraction of their income. A shift toward more regressive taxation involves a relative decrease in the tax burden of the rich, considered as a fraction of their income.

Tax experts do not always agree about the "incidence"—that is, the pattern of burdens as a fraction of income across different income groups of taxpayers—of various taxes. The incidence of a tax is supposed to represent the actual burden of the tax, which is not necessarily borne by the person who makes the tax payment to the state. For example, retail shopkeepers forward retail sales taxes to the state, but they are presumably not the ultimate "taxpayers"; retail sales taxes are usually assumed to be paid by those who buy the items taxes, rather than by those who sell them. Regarding some taxes there is little disagreement. Income taxes, for example, are typically assumed to be paid by the person or household that submits the income tax return. Similarly, taxes on alcoholic beverages are assumed to be paid by those who consume them. But for some taxes, there is substantial and important disagreement about who the ultimate taxpayer is. Property tax incidence, for example, is among the most controversial. For our purposes here, we need to have as good a sense as possible of the pattern of burdens for the major taxes. Fortunately, there is some very good recent evidence for two of the most important taxes, income and sales taxes. Unfortunately, there is no reliable quantitative information about the incidence of property taxes, though we can get some sense of the pattern by examining the pattern of property tax rates among Massachusetts communities.

Incidence of the Income Tax.   An excellent recent study by Andrew Reschovsky and others has provided a careful and detailed examination of the incidence of the Massachusetts income tax.[4] Using data from a large sample of Massachusetts households, Reschovsky constructed a simulation model of the income tax from which he computed the tax payment of every taxpayer in the sample. These payments were then related to income and the pattern of effective rates observed.

The results are presented in Figure 9-1, which shows tax payments as a fraction of money income received by the household for a variety of income classes. Since state income tax payments are deductible from income before federal income taxes are computed, the net payment of state income taxes is less than the direct payment made, especially for higher-income taxpayers who face higher federal tax rates. This net impact, after allowing for the federal offset, seems to us the more appropriate view of the actual impact of the state tax on the disposable income of its citizens, and we will concentrate on it in discussing the impacts of

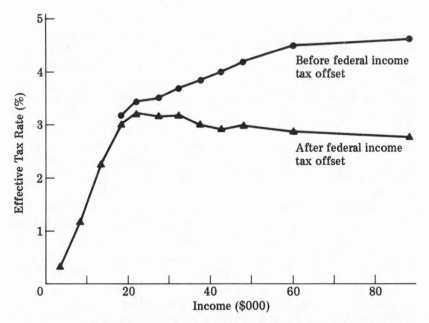

Figure 9-1   Income Tax Payments as a Fraction of Money Income in
            Massachusetts, 1982. *Source*: Andrew Reschovsky *et al.*, *State
            Tax Policy: Evaluating the Issues* (Cambridge, Mass.: Joint
            Center for Urban Studies of MIT and Harvard University,
            1983), Table 3.4, p. 78.

the state income tax. As the figure indicates, the income tax is
progressive even after the federal offset at least up to $20,000 of
money income, and it is approximately proportional from
$20,000 to $70,000. Above $70,000 the tax burden net of the
federal offset decreases as a fraction of income. Over the range
relevant for most Massachusetts taxpayers, the income tax is at
least proportional, and it appears to be progressive over the
lowest income ranges. At the lower end, this pattern reflects the
existence of deductions and exemptions; above $20,000 it reflects
the counterbalancing effects of a larger federal income tax offset
and the higher rate of tax on unearned income, which constitutes
a higher share of the income of wealthier households.

Incidence of Sales Taxes.   Sales taxes, which are generally
directed at consumption spending of one form or another, are
generally thought to be regressive since the poor spend a greater
fraction of their income than the rich on basic consumption items.
Sales taxes in Massachusetts, however, are less regressive than
they are in oither states, since the tax base excludes a variety of
items that make up a considerable fraction of the consumption

budgets of poor taxpayers. The "general" sales tax (including the meals tax), through which almost two thirds of total sales taxes are raised, is in fact defined over a relatively narrow base that excludes housing, food consumed at home, nearly all clothing, and most services. Indeed, only about 20 cents of each dollar spent by Massachusetts residents is subject to the "general" sales tax. Table 9–2 shows the number of states that include each of thirteen categories of expenditures in their sales tax bases. Of these thirteen categories, only clothing items costing over $175 are taxed in Massachusetts. As the table indicates, the "general" sales tax base in Massachusetts is among the most narrowly defined in the nation.

The relative narrowness of the tax base makes the Massachusetts general sales tax system less regressive than it would otherwise be, and indeed the tax is almost proportional as a consequence. Reschovsky and others, using a methodology similar to that of the income tax study referred to above, found that the current general sales tax is essentially proportional up to about $60,000 of income. Figure 9–2 shows the effective rates for the general sales tax as a function of income, as reported in the Reschovsky study. The most notable features are that the burdens are uniformly low, with tax payments hovering around one per-

Table 9–2 Number of States Applying Sales Taxes to Selected Categories of Expenditures

Expenditure Category	Number of States Imposing Taxes*
Clothing	43
Food consumed at home	9
Admissions	38
Repair services	25
Dry cleaning	21
Utilities	21
Computer services	12
Janitorial services	13
Consulting, research, and public relations	8
Hotels	34
Intrastate telephone calls	21
Printing	14
Parking	8

SOURCE: Reprinted from Andrew Reschovsky *et al.*, "State Tax Policy: Evaluating the Issues" (Cambridge, Mass.: Joint Center for Urban Studies of MIT and Harvard University, 1983), Table 2.4, p. 27.
*Including the District of Columbia.

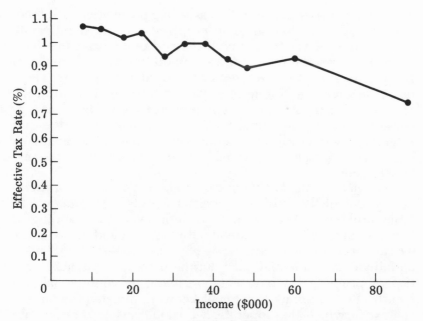

Figure 9-2   General Sales Tax (Including Meals Tax) Payments as a Fraction of Income in Massachusetts, 1982. *Source*: Andrew
Reschovsky *et al., State Tax Policy: Evaluating the Issues*
(Cambridge, Mass.: Joint Center for Urban Studies of MIT
and Harvard University, 1983), Table 2.9, p. 43.

cent of income, and that the rates decline almost not at all below
$25,000 of income.

We have not reported the Reschovsky *et al.* estimate of the
effective rate of taxation in the lowest income bracket (the category below $5000) because it is difficult to interpret. The income
figures available for this income class include cash transfers but
do not include food stamps, so they understate the purchasing
power of "income" more broadly defined. Moreover, income is,
for this income category, a poor measure of command over
resources. Many households in this income group have a total
consumption considerably in excess of their measured income; in
part, this results from their "non-income" receipts like food
stamps, but it also stems in part from dissaving, particularly by
the elderly. All of these factors serve to make a reported "incidence" of sales tax as a fraction of income highly unreliable
within this income group.

Massachusetts has a variety of sales taxes other than its "general" retail levy. These "selective" taxes include levies on alcoholic beverages, tobacco, and motor vehicle fuel. While there are

no recent comprehensive studies assessing the incidence of these selective excises, they are generally regarded as significantly more regressive than the narrowly defined general sales tax.[5] This is because expenditures on these commodities generally make up a larger fraction of the budgets of less wealthy taxpayers. These taxes, then, constitute one important regressive element in the Massachusetts tax structure. Moreover, as we saw above, Massachusetts' lower than average reliance on sales taxes does not extend to selective sales taxes; the composition of Massachusetts sales taxes is shifted toward selective taxes from the national average.

Incidence of the Property Tax. The incidence of property taxes is one of the most controversial aspects of tax policy. The basic problem is that, without a definitive understanding of how housing markets operate in both the short and the long run, we cannot be sure who ultimately pays the property taxes levied on individual residential units. Furthermore, a substantial fraction of property tax payments are made by commercial and industrial establishments; without knowing in detail the market context in which they operate, we cannot assess the ultimate distribution of these tax payments either. Theories of tax incidence with widely differing implications are strongly advocated, and no one theory has been widely validated empirically or accepted by tax experts.

In the absence of a strong working foundation for assessing the incidence of property taxes, what can be said about whether they constitute a regressive or progressive feature of the Massachusetts tax system? The most persuasive reasoning about property tax incidence holds that local differentials in property tax rates are likely to be borne as an excise tax on the service provided by the taxed property. For the residential part of the property tax levy, this would imply that taxpayers in relatively high tax rate jurisdictions would effectively pay property taxes in a form similar to a sales tax on housing. Since communities with high property tax rates in Massachusetts tend to be those with high concentrations of poor households, the statewide impact of having a fiscal system heavily financed by the property tax is almost certainly regressive. We will return to this issue in more detail below when we consider the impacts of Proposition 2½ on the poor. In addition, since the consumption of housing services increases relatively slowly with income, the residential property tax levy is probably a somewhat regressive tax within a particular jurisdiction. This tendency has been exacerbated historically by assessment practices; high-market-value properties tended to be undervalued by assessors relative to low-value properties, so assessed property taxes tended to rise even less than actual property values as one moves up the income scale. Whether this historical trend will continue in the face of court-ordered "full valuation" remains to be seen.

The Overall Incidence of Taxation in Massachusetts: Massachusetts has a relatively strong and progessive tax system. Although its income tax is not among the most progressive of state income taxes, heavy reliance on income taxation more than makes up for what the income tax itself lacks. Heavy reliance on property taxation, however, has in all likelihood been a regressive feature; this has been mitigated to some extent by the reductions associated with Proposition 2½, as we shall discuss later on. Morever, while it relies less heavily than other states on sales taxation, Massachusetts' sales taxes are differentially weighted toward selective taxes, which probably fall most heavily on the poor. Thus, while the tax system avoids the regressivity associated with sales taxation of basic necessities like food and clothing, it loses some of these gains by correspondingly heavier reliance on selective sales taxes like those on alcoholic beverages and tobacco. The state's tax system retains a number of regressive features, but its heavy reliance on income taxation keeps it from being a substantially regressive system overall.

There are still, however, substantial absolute tax burdens levied on the poor. This means that significant improvements in the net fiscal impact of the state and local government on the poor can still be achieved through modifications of the tax system. Indeed, the strength and broad proportionality of the state tax system across all but the very highest income classes implies that the burden of reducing taxes for the poor could be equitably spread across all other income groups. Moreover, while the absolute burdens of taxation on the poor are significant to them, the total taxes raised from the poor are a small fraction of total tax revenues. Thus, relatively minor alterations of the tax system could result in substantial improvements of the net fiscal impact on the poor while spreading this fairly small additional burden relatively equitably among other income categories. We will return to these observations when we discuss tax reform in the final section.

Trends in Taxation

The composition of state government tax revenues in Massachusetts has shifted continuously over the past decade. The state government tax system is probably more progressive than it used

Table 9–3   Massachusetts State Government Tax Revenues, FY 1975 and FY 1982

Tax	1975 Revenue (millions)	1975 Share	1983 Revenue (millions)	1983 Share	Real Change
Alcoholic beverages	$ 65	3%	$ 87	2%	−24%
Tobacco	114	5	147	3	−26
Corporations	223	11	520	10	33
Income	985	47	2510	50	45
Motor fuel	180	9	280	6	−11
General sales	315	15	1023	20	85
Other	236	11	429	9	4

SOURCE: Senate Ways and Means Committee, "Senate Number 1900," Budget for Fiscal Year 1983, Volume I, pp. 3–5.

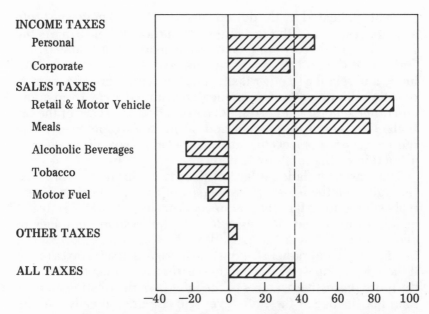

INCOME TAXES
  Personal
  Corporate
SALES TAXES
  Retail & Motor Vehicle
  Meals
  Alcoholic Beverages
  Tobacco
  Motor Fuel

OTHER TAXES

ALL TAXES

−40 −20 0 20 40 60 80 100

Figure 9-3   Percentage Change in Taxes (in Real Dollars) in Massachusetts, 1975-1983. The dashed line indicates the real growth of all taxes taken together. Taxes that grew faster than this increased as a *share* of total taxes; those that grew slower decreased as a share. *Source*: 1983 Senate Ways and Means Budget, Vol. 1, pages 3-5. Figures adjusted to constant dollars using CPI for all urban consumers.

to be, since its reliance on its relatively progressive features is increasing at the expense of some of its less progressive aspects, as shown in Table 9–3. The striking trend is that the most regressive features of the state government's tax structure have been decreasing as a share of the total taxes raised and, for the most part, have also been shrinking absolutely when measured in constant dollars. Thus, the state tax system appears to have shifted toward greater progressivity. Taxes on alcoholic beverages and tobacco declined as share of total tax revenues and actually shrank absolutely when measured in constant dollars (each by over 20 percent). The excise on motor fuel has also decreased as a share of the tax budget and in real terms. Income and general sales taxes, two of the features of the tax system that are progressive or least regressive, expanded considerably both absolutely and as a fraction of the tax system.

Figure 9–3 shows graphically the changes, measured in real terms, in the tax revenues collected from each tax source from 1975 to 1983. All taxes taken together increased in real terms by about 35 percent; only those that increased by more than this amount (indicated by the dotted line in the figure) now constitute a larger fraction of the tax system than they did in 1975. As the figure indicates, corporate taxes are essentially unchanged as a fraction of the budget, while income taxes have increased absolutely and relative to other taxes. The two least regressive aspects of state sales taxes, excises on meals consumed away from home and other general sales taxes, have expanded as a share of the tax budget by about 30 percent and 40 percent respectively. The most regressive aspects of state sales taxation have diminished as a fraction of the total tax structure.

The rapid inflation-adjusted increases in taxes collected through even the least regressive part of the sales tax has potentially serious long-term consequences for the poor of the state if it continues unabated. If Massachusetts' tax system continues to evolve as it did over this period, with modest real increases in income taxes and rather striking real increases in sales taxes (even if these are mitigated by reductions in the taxes collected through the more regressive features of the sales tax), the relative share of sales tax finance at the state level will rise dramatically and the relative progressivity the system derives from its heavy reliance on income taxation will be reduced.

With this caveat, however, it appears that the composition of taxes collected at the state level has shifted toward greater progressivity. Whether the increased real tax burden is compensated for by the shift toward progressive finance and by changes in expenditures is an open question.

State and Local Tax Expenditures

Most state and local expenditures are represented directly within budgets passed by the appropriate legal authority. In some cases, however, benefits are granted to particular taxpayers through tax relief rather than through spending. If, for example, particular taxpayers are not required to pay taxes on what would usually be a taxable activity, they benefit just as if the taxes had been collected and then returned. This concept of benefits given through the tax system (labeled "tax expenditures" by Harvard Law School Professor Stanley Surrey) is now embodied by law in the federal budget documents considered by the Congress. Tax expenditures have not, however, been studied extensively for states, though they may be just as important at the state as at the federal level.

The basic concept of tax expenditures is that these benefits are a mixture of tax and expenditure policy. They are granted in the form of relief from taxes—that is, in the form of failure to collect taxes. Thus, they constitute a portion of tax policy. On the other hand, they can easily be thought of as expenditures, since they are negative taxes. Thus, one might argue that they should be considered by the appropriations committees rather than by the finance committees, since it is the appropriations committees that are charged with the obligation of disbursing funds.

Whatever one resolves about the appropriate authority to grant tax expenditures if they are to be granted, making the concept operational requires the specification of a comprehensive tax base so that the tax expenditures (the failure to define the tax base appropriately broadly) can be recognized. Agreement on the definition of the appropriate comprehensive tax base to use as a point of departure is far from universal, even with regard to relatively simple tax bases such as personal income. When one considers sales and property as additional tax bases for which a comprehensively defined base must be specified, the task of devising a tax expenditure budget becomes quite difficult.

The tax expenditure budget is, however, important for assessing the impact of the state's fiscal system on the poor. First, there are more than a few tax expenditures specifically directed at the poor; in particular, we may understate the breadth of anti-poverty program impacts if the tax expenditures are not considered. Second, there are a number of tax expenditures directed at the rich, and they make the tax system less progressive than it would otherwise be. More accurate estimation of tax expenditures will enable the state to better assess the full impact of its programs, both on the rich and on the poor. Third, some tax expenditures are best viewed simply as revenue losses associated with no clear expenditure or distributive purpose. By reducing such tax expenditures, tax rates can be reduced or additional services provided. Thus, general discussions of expanding the base of taxation can be fitted nicely into the tax expenditure budget and discussion.

The state should move as quickly as is practical to devise and present annually a comprehensive tax expenditure budget. The tax expenditure document prepared for the Congress appears to have become a useful point of departure for discussions of tax policy at the federal level, and it provides a helpful digest of information on the current configuration (and the cost) of tax policies. We cannot here pretend to develop a comprehensive tax expenditure budget for the state; in the remainder of this section, we shall merely consider briefly a number of the more obvious features of state tax policy that should be considered tax expenditures and provide very crude estimates of their size and impact.

Tax Expenditures in the Income Tax. The income tax as defined in Massachusetts constitutes a relatively broad-based tax, with few exemptions and deductions once the general concept of income has been defined. The main exemption—or, more accurately, the first major structural feature of the tax—is the "personal exemption" of the first $2000 of income ($3000 for a married couple). Above the exemption, earnings are taxed at the flat proportional rate of 5.375 percent; "unearned income" (dividends, most interest, and other returns to capital) are taxed at 10.75 percent. The progressivity of the tax comes from its exclusion of the first portion of earnings, which reduces the income subject to tax substantially more for lower income than for higher income taxpayers. Exemptions of $700 are provided for dependents and for being over 65; since both large families and the elderly are differentially poor, these constitute relatively pro-poor tax expenditures, but they also benefit wealthier taxpayers who happen to qualify.

It is worth noting that the exemptions that constitute part of the structure of the Massachusetts income tax system are stated in nominal terms—that is, there is no automatic yearly adjustment for inflation. They tend to be changed at irregular intervals, and they have declined substantially in real terms in the past half decade. They may once have been a significant fraction of "poverty-level" income, so that those living with incomes below the poverty line were essentially excluded from paying state income tax. That is certainly no longer the case; for many poverty-level families, the exemptions shield less than half of their income. The fact that the income tax structure has been legislated in fixed nominal terms means that an increasing real burden has been levied on those living below the poverty line over time. We suspect that this is an unintentional consequence of the way the structure is established, and we believe it should be altered. This could easily be done by indexing the exemptions or by tying the exemptions to the definition of poverty income, which is adjusted each year.

The major deductions allowed from income tax before computation of the tax are payments of Social Security taxes and the rental deduction permitted pursuant to Proposition 2½. It is arguable whether the comprehensively defined tax base should permit exclusion of Social Security tax payments. If the Social Security deduction is treated as a tax expenditure, it probably constitutes a benefit to low-and middle-income taxpayers; its effect on the taxes paid by the lowest-income taxpayers is likely to be negligible because the very poor pay little income tax anyway.

Deductions are also permitted for child care, disabled dependent or spouse expenses, excess medical expenses, and dependents under 12 years of age. To the extent that these are relatively more frequent in poorer families or constitute a larger fraction of low-income household expenses, they represent pro-poor tax expenditures, but there is little evidence to suggest that they are particularly helpful to low-income households—especially to the very poor.

The total bill for tax expenditures made through the income tax is substantial. Table 9-4, from Reschovsky's study of the Massachusetts income tax, shows the total amount of the exemptions or deductions taken, together with their impact on tax revenues collected, for fiscal 1982. The exemptions for dependents and the elderly, together with the payroll tax deductions, constitute the bulk of the tax expenditures. Of these, only the tax expenditure on the elderly is particularly pro-poor. The total income tax expenditure budget amounts to about $460 million, or almost 20 percent of the total income tax revenue that would be raised if these tax expenditures were not made. This amounts to a substantial "expenditure" package, and the state would do well to consider more systematically and in more detail whether it serves a well-formulated set of policy objectives or whether there are other less expensive ways of meeting the same ends.

The rental deduction, by contrast with the other large components of the income tax expenditure package, is relatively pro-poor. Reschovsky and his collaborators find that over 60 percent of renter households have incomes under $15,000 in 1982.[6] According to their simulations, the total tax expenditure associated with the rent deduction (the amount of tax revenue that is

Table 9-4   Revenue Cost of Income Tax Expenditures in Massachusetts, 1982
(millions of dollars)

Tax Expenditure Item	Total Exemption	Tax Expenditure (Revenue Loss)
Child care expenses	$ 978	$ 53
Social security taxes*	2928	157
Dependent under 12 years of age	385	21
Medical deduction	1811	97
Exemptions for dependents	1456	78
Exemptions for the elderly	498	27
Rent deduction	1256	48

SOURCE: Excerpted from Andrew Reschovsky, *et al.*, "State Tax Policy: Evaluating the Issues," (Cambridge, Mass.: Joint Center for Urban Studies of MIT and Harvard University, 1983), Table 3.2, p. 73.
* Payroll taxes.

not collected as a consequence of the rental deduction) was approximately $48 million in 1982. The latest arrival on the income tax expenditure scene and in many respects the most capricious of the income tax expenditures, this is by any measure a substantial "expenditure" program focused mainly on some relatively low income households. Figure 9–4 shows the average percentage reduction in income tax liability as a function of household income found by Reschovsky. One notable feature of the pattern of percentage rate reductions is that low-income taxpayers generally receive a substantially larger percentage reduction in tax liability as a consequence of the deduction than do higher-income taxpayers. This implies that the rent deduction adds to the progressivity of the income tax.

We do not believe, however, that the rental deduction adds to tax fairness. First of all, many low-income households are not renters. Second, many in the lowest income bracket are not required to pay any tax and therefore receive no benefits from the deduction. Finally, deductions are based on contract rent, which for some renters includes utilities and for others does not.

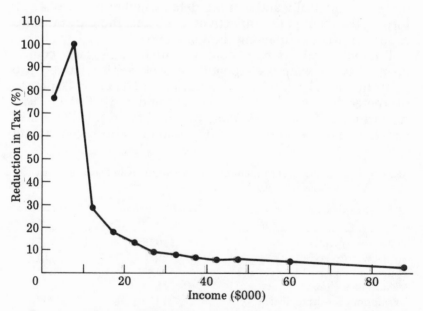

Figure 9-4   Percentage Reductions in Income Tax Liabilities as a Consequence of the Rental Deduction Tax Expenditure in Massachusetts, 1982. *Source*: Andrew Reschovsky *et al.*, *State Tax
Policy: Evaluating the Issues* (Cambridge, Mass.: Joint Center
for Urban Studies of MIT and Harvard University, 1983),
Table 3.5, p. 81.

Thus, the "horizontal equity" of this deduction (the extent to which it treats taxpayers in similar financial positions alike) is anything but exemplary. Thus, while the rent deduction does help many low-income households, it is by no means a sound model for equitable tax reform. Unfortunately, it is politically secure, since it was voted in as part of Proposition 2½.

Tax Expenditures in the Sales Tax.   Repeated mention has been made of the narrowness of the sales tax base in Massachusetts, particularly that of the "general" sales tax. While a fully comprehensive general sales tax base is difficult to define precisely, any acceptably broad definition would include a number of categories of sales excluded from the Massachusetts base. The exclusion of these items thus constitutes "tax expenditures" in the same way that granting deductions or exemptions from the income tax base does.

There appears to be little likelihood of an extension of the sales tax to food consumed at home, and since all but nine states exclude it from their tax base it may not be appropriate to consider it a tax expenditure. Among the items currently excluded from the sales tax that might conceivably be added to the base are clothing and a variety of retail commodities and services such as admissions, repairs, utilities, hotel bills, and telephone calls. For purposes of this discussion, these will be considered tax expenditures. We will not treat the exclusion of various business transactions as tax expenditures, first because there is less than universal agreement about whether they constitute an appropriate part of the tax base and second because their incidence is hard to assess.

The revenue loss associated with sales tax expenditures is quite substantial. Table 9–5 presents estimates of the revenues lost when a variety of retail services are excluded from the sales tax base; these were developed by Reschovsky and others in their evaluation of sales tax reform in Massachusetts. These estimates assume that there is no change in the tax rate. Unfortunately, we have no way to construct comparable estimates of the revenue loss from the exclusion of clothing purchases under $175. The largest single item that can be adequately estimated comes from the extension of the sales tax to cover wholesale and retail alcoholic beverage purchases. There are, however, already special excises in place on alcoholic beverages, so it may not be fair to view this entire amount as a tax expenditure. But even with this caveat, the magnitude of sales tax expenditures is quite substantial, amounting to between $300 and $400 million in 1983, or about 20 percent of the revenues that could be raised through a broader sales tax.

Table 9-5   Revenue Cost of Sales Tax Expenditures in Massachusetts, 1983
            through 1985 (Estimated*) (millions of dollars)

Tax Expenditure Item	Estimated Revenue Loss		
	1983	1984	1985
Personal services	$ 69	$ 76	$ 84
Automotive services	43	48	53
Entertainment services	46	53	59
Alcoholic beverages			
(wholesale and retail)	135	149	165
Cigarettes	45	50	50
Miscellaneous	53	58	65
Total of all retail services	391	434	480

SOURCE: Excerpted from Andrew Reschovsky, *et al.,* "State Tax Policy: Evaluating
the Issues" (Cambridge, Mass.: Joint Center for Urban Studies of MIT and Harvard University, 1983), Table 2.5, p. 29.
*These estimates assume that the tax rate is unchanged as the base is expanded. Comparable figures for extension of the base to include clothing purchases for items under $175 are not available.

Whether, on balance, the poor are better off as a consequence of these tax expenditures depends on whether they spend a higher fraction of their income on the excluded commodities than do households generally. The conventional wisdom is that taxation of personal services would add a progressive element to a sales tax system that currently excludes them. This contention is based on the general feeling that many service purchases are of a luxury nature and therefore probably constitute a higher fraction of the income of more wealthy taxpayers.

This conventional view turns out to be wrong, at least for Massachusetts. By any measure, the inclusion of retail services and clothing within the taxable sales base would increase the regressivity of the Massachusetts general sales tax, as demonstrated in Figure 9-5.[7] Since the base is expanded for all taxpayers, the tax burden would be increased by the reduction in sales tax expenditures, as indicated in Figure 9-5 by the higher level of taxation at every income level. But it is also clear from Figure 9-5 that the effective rates rise more for the poor than for the rich. In the income categories below $10,000 the effective tax rate rises from about 1.06 percent of income to about 2.31 percent, or by about 1.25 percentage points, whereas for taxpayers with incomes above $70,000 it rises by only about .62 percentage points.

While the pattern of these tax expenditures is pro-poor, most of the tax reductions are still received by the rich. Thus, a relatively

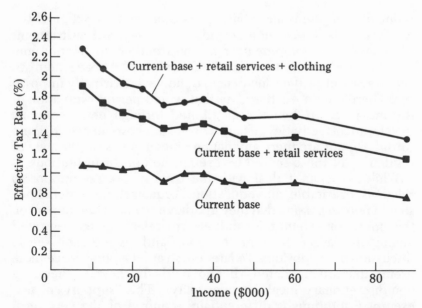

Figure 9-5   Incidence of General Sales Tax Current Base Compared to Incidences with Base Expanded to Include Retail Personal Services in Massachusetts, 1982. *Source*: Andrew Reschovsky *et al.*, *State Tax Policy: Evaluating the Issues* (Cambridge, Mass.: Joint Center for Urban Studies of MIT and Harvard University, 1983), Table 2.11, p. 46.

slight improvement in the progressivity of the general sales tax is being obtained through a revenue loss of more than $400 million, only a small fraction of which is received by the poor. If the sales tax base were expanded, the regressive impact could be mitigated relatively easily by instituting a refundable sales tax credit for the poor. With this modification, the state could achieve a substantial revenue gain without incurring an additional regressive element in its tax system. We will return to this issue when we discuss tax reform later.

Tax Expenditures in the Property Tax. Massachusetts has three separate types of tax expenditures given through its property tax system. First, a wide variety of educational and charitable organizations are completely exempt from local property taxes as a matter of state law. Second, the state legislature has authorized communities to use property tax abatements, known as "Chapter 121 A Agreements," as a means of attracting new economic development activities into their jurisdictions. Finally, a variety of personal abatements are granted to individual taxpayers. A comprehensive treatment of the incidence of the institutional exemptions and abatements is beyond the scope of this work. The claim that these subsidies are effective as instruments of economic development or as contributions to worthy non-profit causes is almost universally discounted by tax economists. An assessment of their incidence, is, however, virtually impossible. There are no existing data that would permit estimation of the incidence of benefits distributed through new economic development activities (if any arise as a consequence of these subsidies), nor are there any data on the incomes (or the state of residence) of those served by exempt non-profit institutions.

While we cannot deal with the issue of tax exemptions to religious, charitable, and educational organizations in detail, we should note in passing that they may have an important impact on the poor. Tax-exempt institutions are relatively concentrated among the larger cities of the state, and, as we shall see in discussion of Proposition 2½ later on, so are the poor. Since these exemptions are mandated—but not paid—by the state, they are a non-discretionary local "responsibility." This "support" of tax-exempt institutions is differentially required of the very local jurisdictions that have higher than average responsibilities for providing public services to the poor. In this sense, the existing system of state mandated and locally financed tax exemptions forces a competition for local resources between tax-exempt institutions and the poor. The obvious solution is to move responsibility for paying state-mandated tax exemptions to the state level.

We can provide at least some sense of the impact of personal property tax exemptions, though even here the data are sketchy. Massachusetts has a considerable number of personal tax expenditures made through the property tax system. Some are mandatory abatements of local property taxes; these are generally refunded to the local jurisdiction by the state. Others are discretionary "hardship" abatements, granted by the local assessors and not generally refunded by the state. There is little information about the income of the recipients of either form of abatement, but it is generally believed that most recipients are poor. Property tax expenditures are concentrated on the elderly and veterans, particulary those who are disabled. Abatements of property taxes of course benefit only those who own property. Because they treat households who own property differently from those with otherwise similar financial needs who rent, these property tax abatements may be deemed horizontally inequitable, despite the fact that the beneficiaries are typically poor.

The magnitude of property tax expenditures is substantial, with nearly $75 million of tax liabilities forgiven in 1977. Table 9–6 shows estimated revenue losses (and corresponding state refunds to local jurisdictions) for a variety of property tax abatements for 1977. Although these programs are not generally conditioned directly on the financial need of the recipients, there is good reason to believe that few of the recipients are wealthy by any reasonable standard.

Little is known about the discretionary abatements given by local jurisdictions. Their magnitude statewide has been estimated at $2 million for 1977, as indicated in Table 9–6. In most communities, they constitute a relatively small fraction of the property tax levy and there is a strong presumption that they involve real financial hardship in most cases. Thus, they probably constitute a tax expenditure program directly focused on the needy. It is worth noting again, however, that abatements are based on the financial hardship of the property taxpayer, which is not necessarily that of the property resident. Thus, the program benefits only financially pressed homeowners.

Table 9–6　Revenue Losses from Property Tax Expenditures in Massachusetts, 1977

Tax Expenditure Item	Approximate Number Aided (thousands)	Estimated Revenue Loss (millions of $)
Exemption for senior citizens	68	39.4
Exemption for elderly, infirm, and poor (discretionary hardship abatements)	5	2.0
Exemption for surviving spouses and children, and persons 70 years old and older	20	9.9
Exemption for widows and/or children of firemen and policemen	.2	.1
Exemption for blind persons	3	2.8
Tax relief for veterans:		
General veterans exemption	70	18.7
Additional special relief for disabled veterans	4	2.5
Total of all property tax expenditures	165	75.4

SOURCE: William J. Lawrence, and Stephen Leeds, An Inventory of State and Local Income Transfer Programs, Fiscal Year 1977 (White Plains, New York: The Institute for Socioeconomic Studies, 1979), pp. 135–143.

There is one additional "tax expenditure" feature of the property tax system worth noting. Elderly homeowners with incomes of less than $20,000 are permitted to defer payment of their local property taxes through a program under which the state loans them the amount of their tax payments. These loans bear interest at 8 percent, considerably below current interest rates; the principal and interest of these loans is recovered by the state from the estate of the taxpayer. This program constitutes a subsidy because of the below-market interest rate charged; it is not a "tax expenditure" of the traditional sort inasmuch as the subsidy does not come in the form of an actual reduction in tax payments but, rather, in their deferral. Since the taxpayer does eventually repay them, the net "tax expenditure" is the present value of the interest subsidy granted. For a homeowner who enters this program at age 65 and who lives for 15 years, this could easily amount to a 50 percent reduction in the actual tax burden borne. Of course, the size of the subsidy depends crucially on the prevailing market interest rates, so it is important to scrutinize this program carefully as interest rates fluctuate. The program is not very extensively used; only 350 households were aided through it in 1977. It could, however, become a sizable program if a larger fraction of the nearly 70,000 households aided through general property tax relief to the elderly join it in the future. The program is focused on a relatively needy group and it is limited to those with relatively low incomes, so that its benefits are reasonably well concentrated on poor recipients. Like other property tax expenditures, however, it does not provide any relief to renters, and it cannot therefore be viewed as a "horizontally" equitable tax expenditure.

Summary

Massachusetts has a relatively strong and roughly proportional tax system, largely due to its heavy reliance on income taxation. The general tendency over time has been toward increasing reliance at the state level on income and general sales taxes, and on balance this has probably reduced the regressivity of the state government's tax system.

Still, the system retains many regressive features. Selective sales taxes which fall heavily on the poor are relatively high as a fraction of sales taxes generally. A great many tax expenditures, many of them sizable, are of greater benefit to the middle class and to the rich than to the poor. Given the general strength of its revenue system, the state government could fairly substantially reduce the absolute burden of its tax system on the poor while spreading what would be the relatively small additional burden of doing so equitably across the remaining income classes.

None of these changes at the state level can be seriously contemplated, however, without a thorough review of the powerful interlock between state and local fiscal policies constituted by Proposition 2½. It is to this that we now turn.

The Impact of Property Tax Limitation on the Poor

The single most important factor influencing the current fiscal situation in Massachusetts is Proposition 2½, the property tax limitation measure supported by 59 percent of those who voted in November 1980. Because Proposition 2½ imposes such severe limitations on local governments' only source of tax revenues and has such different impacts across communities, state policymakers are now faced with major decisions about the amount and distribution of state aid in the post-Proposition 2½ era and about whether local governments should be allowed to use new broad-based revenue sources. This section adds to this broader policy debate a focus on the effects of Proposition 2½ on the regressivity of Massachusetts taxes and its overall effects on poor people. While these are clearly not the only considerations that should influence the policy outcome, any attempt to resolve the broader issues of Proposition 2½ without reference to its effects on the poor will have failed to deal with some of its most powerful and important impacts.

The central fact about Proposition 2½ is that it has a larger effect in some communities than in others. This has important consequences for the poor, who are overrepresented in the cities facing the largest required tax reduction. Proposition 2½ requires high-tax-rate communities to reduce property taxes by 15 percent per year until the tax rate reaches the maximum allowable rate of 2½ percent of full and fair property value. Of the state's 351 cities and towns, 182 communities encompassing about 80 percent of the state's population were required to reduce property tax levies in the first year under this provision, and 40 face reductions in subsequent years as well. Once communities reach the 2½ percent rate limit, their tax levies are limited to an annual growth rate of 2½ percent. This growth limit also applies to all communities with rates below the 2½ percent tax rate ceiling.[8]

In addition, the measure lowers the motor vehicle excise tax from 6.6 percent of valuation to 2.5 percent; this tax is levied at a statewide uniform rate but accrues to local treasuries. Together, these provisions reduced the tax revenues of local governments by about 14 percent in fiscal year 1982, with larger cities generally facing reductions well above this statewide average. The only provision affecting state revenues provides for renters to deduct half their rent from state taxable income. The Proposition also gives local voters more control over public spending by reducing the power of school committees; it shifts control over the total school appropriation, but not its constituent parts, away from the school committee to the local legislative body.

Impact on Incidence of Taxes

As pointed out above, pre-Proposition 2½ property tax burdens were extremely high in Massachusetts relative to the national average. Moreover, the state's heavy reliance on property taxes probably contributed a significant regressive element to the state's tax structure, particularly because of the pattern of tax rates across jurisdictions. Despite our incomplete understanding of the incidence of the existing property tax, we can still draw some conclusions about the income distributional effects of the specific pattern of changes required by Proposition 2½. By reducing property taxes, Proposition 2½ makes the state's tax system less regressive. This occurs in large part because property taxes are reduced the most in the communities where the poor are overrepresented.

Table 9–7 shows the estimated average percentage reductions in property taxes required in communities of different sizes during the first year under Proposition 2½. The communities are grouped by the size of their population in 1980. Average property tax reductions ranged from 1.5 percent in the small communities to 14.9 percent in the largest communities. This variation across groups reflects the higher pre-Proposition 2½ tax rates in the larger communities. It should be noted, however, that, with the exception of one group, there is substantial variation from the average across communities within each group. The exception is the group of largest cities and towns, virtually all of which were required to reduce property taxes by 15 percent in fiscal year 1982. Columns 2–4 indicate how poor and non-poor people are distributed among the five groups of communities. Poor people are more heavily concentrated in the large communities than are either total residents or non-poor residents. Fifty-six percent of the poor, but only 36 percent of the non-poor, live in the largest communities—the ones that, on average, were required to reduce property taxes the most during Proposition 2½'s first year. Thus,

Table 9–7 Average Reduction in Property Taxes Required by Proposition 2½ in FY 1982

Population in 1980	Number of Cities and Towns[a]	% Change in Property Tax Levy[b]	% of Population (1980)	% of Poor (1980)	% of Non-Poor Population (1980)
5,000 or less	110	−1.5%	4.3%	3.5%	4.9%
5,000 to 10,000	75	−2.5	9.1	5.8	9.5
10,000 to 25,000	91	−5.9	25.5	15.0	26.7
25,000 to 50,000	39	−9.0	22.9	19.3	23.2
50,000 or more	21	−14.9	38.2	56.4	35.7

SOURCE: Katharine L. Bradbury and Helen F. Ladd, with Claire Christopherson, "Proposition 2½: Initial Impacts, Part II," *New England Economic Review* (March/April, 1982), and U.S. Census 1980.
a The 15 towns with population under 500 were excluded.
b As estimated by the Massachusetts Department of Revenue in July 1981.

compared with a typical non-poor person, the typical poor person lives in a community with a larger required reduction in FY 1982 taxes.

In sum, during the first year of Proposition 2½, required property tax reductions were larger in communities where the poor were over-represented than in other communities. The poor are also over-represented in the communities that will face required reductions in future years. Eighteen communities were required to reduce their property tax levies by the full 15 percent in FY 1983.[9] As shown by Table 9–8, poor people are disproportionately represented in these communities; the communities include 50 percent of the state's poor people but only 31 percent of the state's population. Twenty-two other communities were also required to reduce property taxes in FY 1983, but not by the full 15 percent. Within this second group of communities, poor people are approximately proportionately represented. Many of the eighteen communities with 15 percent cutbacks in FY 1983 will require additional reductions in future years as well. Precise statements about the total reductions required are not possible because many of these communities have not yet completed revaluing their taxable property.

What does this imply for poor people? Poor homeowners in these communities benefit directly through lower property tax

Table 9-8   Cities and Towns Requiring 15 Percent Reductions in Property
Taxes in FY 1983

City or Town	Poor People (1980)	% Poor (1980)	1980 Population	1982 Tax Rate*
Boston	106,770	20.2%	562,118	$7.47
Brockton	15,883	9.7	94,990	4.28
Brookline	5,125	9.6	54,675	N/A
Cambridge	12,593	15.1	95,351	4.66
Chelsea	5,352	21.4	25,420	6.90
Fall River	13,485	14.8	92,240	3.82
Fitchburg	4,866	12.9	39,332	3.96
Greenfield	2,139	11.9	18,415	3.77
Hull	964	9.9	9,735	4.49
Lynn	10,642	13.8	78,299	5.29
Malden	4,959	9.4	53,431	3.98
New Bedford	15,671	16.2	98,397	3.52
Pittsfield	5,295	10.3	51,942	3.45
Quincy	6,831	8.2	83,904	N/A
Revere	4,464	10.6	42,256	4.39
Somerville	9,345	12.4	77,393	N/A
Springfield	26,306	17.8	152,212	3.57
Worcester	21,818	14.4	161,384	N/A
Percentage of State total	51%		31%	
Average		13.3%		

SOURCES: Massachusetts Department of Revenue; U.S. Census, 1980; and Massachusetts Taxpayers' Foundation.

*Full-value tax rates as reported by the Massachusetts Taxpayers' Foundation. These figures provide some indication of the additional reductions required. The fact that all the estimated 1982 tax rates are more than 15 percent above the limit implies that additional cuts would be required in all of these communities were it not for the possibility that revaluation may raise valuations and thereby lower effective tax rates in some communities.

payments.[10] Renters, on the other hand, benefit only to the extent that landlords pass their tax savings on to renters in the form of lower rents. Even if renters received only limited benefits, however, figures on the relative probabilities of homeownership among the poor and the non-poor, along with average spending and income data, suggest that a mythical "average" poor person would receive greater benefits in relation to income than an average non-poor person.[11] Some poor people (namely the renters) would receive small benefits and others (the homeowners) would receive large benefits in relation to income. As discussed further below, however, this differential treatment of renters and homeowners is offset somewhat by the income tax deductibility of rent payments included as another part of Proposition 2½.

To summarize, the property tax reductions required by Proposition 2½ make the Massachusetts tax system less regressive than it was before the tax limitation measure passed. Specifically, it provides larger tax savings as a share of income for the poor than for the rich. Because other taxes have not been raised to offset property tax losses, however, the Proposition accomplishes this reduction in regressivity by reducing total state and local taxes, rather then by substituting a more progressive tax for a regressive one. Moreover, the absolute tax savings of the poor were small relative to those of the rich because the poor typically pay less than the rich in taxes. In addition the change in tax structure associated with Proposition 2½ imposes potentially high costs on local communities in the form of less local autonomy, heavier dependence on unpredictable state aid, and the possibility that some communities will end up with insufficient revenues to meet basic service needs. Thus, the reduced regressivity of the tax structure is not the whole story, especially insofar as poor people are concerned.

The analysis is expanded in the next section to include both direct and indirect effects of the Proposition. In addition, we shall focus on absolute impacts rather than impacts expressed as a percentage of income. This approach will provide a more direct answer to the question of how poor people have fared under the tax limitation measure.

First-Year Impact on the Poor

Despite the fact that Proposition 2½ has produced a less regressive tax structure, its net impact on poor people appears to be harmful. During the Proposition's first year, the average poor household probably was hurt more by service cutbacks than it was helped by tax reductions, and poor people will probably continue to be adversely affected in the future. Poor people apparently anticipated this outcome; more than half opposed the tax limitation measure. Based on a large statewide survey of Massachusetts household heads interviewed by telephone during the two weeks following the November 1980 vote, Table 9–9 shows that 44 percent of the household heads with income less than $10,000 and 45 percent of those on welfare supported the tax limitation measure. In contrast, support among other income groups ranged from 56 to 68 percent and support among voters in households not dependent on welfare was 59 percent. Support of non-whites (38 percent) is among the lowest of any of the many subgroups examined. Only renters who never planned to own (many of whom are poor) and local public sector employees exhibit equally limited support for the tax limitation measure

Table 9-9   Support for Proposition 2½ Among Subgroups of Voters

Subgroup	% Who Voted "Yes" on Proposition 2½	Number of Voters in Sample
Total	58.0%	1243
Household Income:		
Less than $10,000	46.7	107
$10,001 to $20,000	60.3	368
$20,001 to $30,000	56.0	375
$30,001 to $50,000	61.7	313
More than $50,000	60.3	60
Welfare Usage:		
Use	44.6	65
Do not use	58.7	1178
Race:		
Non-white	38.0	50
White	58.8	1193

SOURCE: Helen F. Ladd and Julie Boatright Wilson, "Who Supports Tax Limitation: Evidence from Proposition 2½," *Journal of Policy Analysis and Management,* Volume 2, No. 2 (Winter 1983).

(data not shown). Thus, the survey results suggest that expected net benefits from Proposition 2½ varied by income class and by race and imply that the Proposition was passed against the wishes of a majority of poor people.[12]

The net benefits to any household from Proposition 2½ can be expressed as the sum of the benefits from tax reductions minus the disbenefits from service reductions. The Proposition directly reduced local property taxes in many communities, motor vehicle excise taxes in all communities, and state income taxes for renters. On the service side, the most obvious impacts were on local public services. One must consider as well the cutbacks that occurred at the state level, however, since the state government provided new state aid for local governments without raising state taxes. For an individual household, we can write net benefits as follows:

Net benefits = reduction in local taxes + reduction in state taxes – reduction in local public services – reduction in state provided public services.

Ideally, the change in taxes and services experienced by any household would be measured relative to what they would have been in the absence of Proposition 2½. Because this approach would require arbitrary assumptions about what would otherwise have occurred, we simply focus instead on the differences between tax and service level changes before and after the introduction of the tax-limitation measure. This methodology tends to understate the absolute effects of the Propostion but does not invalidate the comparison of major interest here—namely, that between the net benefits accruing to a typical poor household and those accruing to a typical non-poor household.

Reductions in Local Taxes. We concluded above that the benefits from property tax reductions were greater as a fraction of income for households with low income than for those with high income. This reflects the low income of poor people, however, rather than their large tax benefits. Indeed, despite the fact that low-income people were more likely than high-income people to live in communities experiencing above-average tax reductions, the actual tax savings of low-income households during the Proposition's first year were small. Among homeowners the benefits are smaller for the poor than the non-poor because poor people live in less expensive houses and consequently paid less in property taxes before Proposition 2½. Hence, a given percentage reduction in the local tax rate means fewer dollars saved for the poor household than for the non-poor household. We estimate that poor homeowners in the Boston metropolitan area received tax benefits that were less than 80 percent those of the average non-poor homeowner.[13]

Many of the poor are renters who received no direct benefits from the reductions in local property taxes. Even if they received indirect benefits in the form of lower rents, their savings were small relative to those of the non-poor, once again because of the less expensive units in which the poor live. Using the assumption most favorable to renters—that is, that they benefited through lower rents—we can estimate that the rent reductions received by poor renters in the Boston area were 30 percent less than those received by non-poor renters and more than 50 percent less than the direct property tax savings received by non-poor homeowners.

The conclusion is clear and unambiguous. Under various sets of assumptions, the magnitude of the direct or indirect savings from property tax reductions is smaller for the poor than for the non-poor, and this is especially true for poor renters who constitute the bulk of the poor households.

Households with cars also benefit from the 62 percent reduction in the motor vehicle excise tax. Because the rate reduction was uniform across the state, the benefit to a particular household does not vary by the household's location but instead depends only on whether the household owns a car and on the value of the car. As shown in Table 6–1 of Chapter 6, households with income less than $6000 are 20 percentage points less likely than all households to have a car, and the average age of their cars exceeds the overall average by 2 years. Thus, the reduction in auto excise taxes also provides larger benefits for the average non-poor than for the average poor household.

Reductions in State Taxes.   Recognizing that renters might not benefit directly from the reduction in local property taxes, the sponsors of Proposition 2½ included a provision allowing renters to deduct half their rent from their state taxable income. (A legislative amendment has subsequently limited the annual deduction to $2500.) Because poor people are more likely than non-poor people to be renters, one might suspect that this deduction helps the poor relative to the non-poor. But while 47 percent of the renter households have income below $10,000, only 16 percent of the tax benefits from the rental deduction accrue to this group.[14] Even more striking is the finding that renter households with income under $5000 represent 37 percent of all rental households and 30 percent of all potential rental deductions, but account for only 3.5 percent of the total tax benefits from the rent-deduction provision. This low share of tax benefits reflects the fact that many of the state's poorest families paid no income tax even before the rent deduction and that, for many, the size of the rent deduction exceeds their taxable income. Only with a refundable payment would these low-income renters benefit fully from this provision. The effect of the current provision is to provide an average benefit of $6 to renter households with income less than $5000 and about $100 for non-poor renter households. Hence, even taking account of the higher probability that a poor household is a renter, we conclude that, on average, non-poor households benefit more in terms of absolute dollars from the rent deduction than do poor households.

Reductions in Taxes: A Summary.   During its first year, Proposition 2½ provided smaller direct or indirect tax savings to the average poor household than to the average non-poor household. In large part this occurred because poor homeowners typically had lower tax burdens than their richer counterparts before Proposition 2½ and because poor households are more likely than non-poor households to be renters. It also reflects poor households' lower savings in motor vehicle excise taxes and their limited ability to benefit from the rent deduction. At the same time that the poor received smaller tax benefits, however, they seem to have been disproportionately hurt by service cutbacks, as we show in the next section.

Reductions in Local Public Services. The evidence suggests that, during its first year, Proposition 2½ reduced services for poor households more than for non-poor households. First, poor households are disproportionately concentrated in the communities facing the largest cutbacks and, second, a disproportionate share of the cuts within individual jurisdictions were in programs benefiting the poor, particularly poor children. Table 9–10 provides estimates of the average revenue reductions required by the tax-limitation measure expressed as a fraction of each community's nonfixed or discretionary expenditures in 1981. Had the state not provided additional aid, expenditure reductions would have averaged 13.4 percent of expenditures in the largest communities and 5.4 percent in the smallest communities. The new state aid lowered the average expenditure impacts to 7.8 percent in the large and 1.7 percent in the small communities. Within each category, however, the expenditure impacts varied greatly; this is especially true for the impacts net of the new state aid since the amount of aid distributed to each community under the so-called lottery formula bore no systematic relationship to a community's first-year revenue loss.

Because poor people are more heavily concentrated in the large communities, 56 percent of the poor (in contrast to 36 percent of the nonpoor) live in communities that faced average required reductions of 7.8 percent. To the extent that expenditure reductions were offset by efficiency gains, cuts in expenditures would not translate directly into service reductions. Although some efficiency gains were undoubtedly achieved, it is reasonable to assume that such gains accounted for only a small part of the expenditure reduction, especially in those communities facing large reductions. Moreover, we have no reason to suspect that efficiency gains were greater in communities facing larger cutbacks than in those facing small cutbacks. This situation suggests that the larger expenditure reductions in the communities where the poor are over-represented translate into larger service reductions. Moreover, the expenditure reductions cited here are expressed in nominal terms. Adjusting them for inflation would better indicate the magnitude of the potential impacts on service levels.

A closer look at the types of services actually cut reinforces the conclusion that poor people, especially those with children, were hurt more by service reductions than were the non-poor. We base this conclusion on the fragmentary evidence in Table 9–11, which provides information on budget cutbacks in 75 communities responding to a survey of its membership by the Massachusetts Municipal Association and in 44 communities for which the

Table 9-10 Required Reductions in FY 1982 Revenues as a Percentage of 1981 Non-fixed Expenditures

Population Group	Change in Revenue as % of 1981 Non-Fixed Expenditures*		% of Population (1980)	% of Poor (1980)	% of Non-Poor (1980)
	Before New Aid	After New Aid			
5,000 or less	− 5.3%	−1.7%	4.3%	3.5%	4.9%
5,001 to 10,000	− 5.9	−1.7	9.1	5.8	9.5
10,001 to 25,000	− 8.1	−4.0	25.5	15.0	26.7
25,001 to 50,000	−10.5	−6.3	22.9	19.3	23.2
50,000 or more	−13.4	−7.8	38.2	56.4	35.7

SOURCE: Katharine L. Bradbury and Helen F. Ladd, with Claire Christopherson, "Proposition 2½: Initial Impacts, Part II, *New England Economic Review*, (March/April 1982); and U.S. Census, 1980.
*Required change in revenue includes both the reduction in motor vehicle excise revenues and the change in property taxes as estimated by the Massachusetts Department of Revenue in July 1981. Non-fixed expenditures are defined as total expenditures minus debt service and pensions.

Table 9-11 Budget Impacts by Service Category: Percentage Change in Appropriations FY 1981-FY 1982

| Category | Mass. Municipal Association Survey[a] | | Impact 2½ Project Survey[b] |
	Severely Impacted (33)	Moderately Impacted (42)	(44)
Police	− 3.5%	+ 0.9%	− 0.5%
Fire	− 4.8	− 3.6	− 4.2
Public works	−10.8	− 2.8	−10.6
Schools	− 9.9	− 4.8	− 6.5
Recreation	−25.8	−11.1	−22.9
Libraries	−14.6	− 1.5	−10.5

[a] Based on a survey of 75 communities conducted by the Massachusetts Municipal Association during the fall of 1981 and reported in *Report on the Impact of Proposition 2½* (January 1982). "Severely impacted" communities typically had to roll back their property taxes by 10 percent or more.
[b] Based on actual appropriations in FY 1981 and FY 1982 (as verified by town accountants) for a nonrandom sample of 44 communities gathered by the Impact 2½ project at MIT under the direction of Lawrence Susskind. The communities were purposely chosen to over-represent severely affected communities.

Impact 2½ Project at MIT has collected and verified appropriations data. These data show that school and recreation budgets were relatively hard hit in many communities.

If all local services provided equal benefits to all local residents, the distribution of cutbacks within each community would be neither pro-poor nor pro-rich in absolute terms. Services such as police, fire, and street repair probably fell into this category. Cutbacks in such services are likely to have a community-wide impact, although in some cases, of course, services might be cut back more in some sections of the city than others. As shown in Table 9-11, cutbacks in police and fire services were limited; indeed, in many communities expenditures on such services were increased in nominal terms, though not in real terms. Among the group of services that provide benefits to all local residents, only public works faced severe reductions, presumably because such cuts required few personnel cuts and had little immediate impact on service levels.

At the other extreme, cutbacks in social services oriented specifically toward the poor, such as provision of free health care for the destitute in community hospitals or services for the elderly, would have a strong anti-poor distributional impact. Unfortunately, information on the extent to which such services were cut is unavailable. Because local governments have limited financial responsibility for such services in Massachusetts, cutbacks in

social service programs were unlikely to account for a large
portion of the local budget reductions. Only in cities with municipal hospitals do social service expenditures account for more than
10 percent of local budgets. On the other hand, because locally
financed social service programs tend to be more extensive in the
cities facing large revenue losses, it is reasonable to assume that
some cuts were made in these programs and that, as a result, the
poor were adversely affected.

Among the services included in Table 9–11, the relatively large
cutbacks in appropriations for local public schools are likely to
hurt poor people the most. This follows first because local schools
primarily serve children and because children are disproportionately represented among the state's poor. Second, children from
poor households have fewer alternatives to public education than
do children from wealthier households. Hence, the relatively
large percentage cutbacks in local school budgets, especially
those in communities severely affected by the tax-limitation measure, probably imposed a disproportionate burden on children
from poor households. Although the percentage reductions in
recreation and library budgets exceeded those of school budgets
in many communities, expenditures on these activities are small
compared with those on schools.

Table 9–12 provides additional information on the magnitude
of the reductions in local elementary and secondary school systems that most affected poor children. The table lists the 23
school districts in the state that serve more than one thousand
pupils from low-income households and indicates the percentages by which the professional staff and all other personnel were
reduced in fiscal year 1982 in each district for which information
is available. Serving 64 percent of the state's low-income pupils,
these districts experienced cutbacks in professional staff ranging
from 2 percent in Revere to 30 percent in Quincy. Boston, with
21.5 percent of the state's low-income pupils, reduced the size of
its professional staff by 17 percent. The average poor pupil in the
20 school districts for which information is available lived in a
district that reduced its professional staff by almost 12 percent.
Reductions in other personnel (including teacher aids and administrative, custodial, clerical and other staff) were even larger.
Weighted by the low-income children in each district, the reductions averaged 23 percent.

While declining enrollments may partially justify some of the
individual reductions, the fact remains that staff reductions of the
size reported here are disruptive when accomplished in a single
year. Moreover, preliminary evidence suggests that, overall, the

Proposition widened the disparities in educational service levels across school districts. This occurred because wealthy, high-spending jurisdictions were less constrained by the limitation measure than were the communities included in Table 9–12.[15]

Changes in State-Provided Services. Public services provided by local governments in Massachusetts would have been reduced even more during the Proposition's first year had the state not provided $265 million in new state aid for local governments. As shown above in Table 9–10, this new aid reduced the expenditure reductions required by Proposition 2½ by approximately half. Because this new aid was not financed by higher state taxes, one must ask about the extent to which it was financed by reducing services for poor households. To the extent that this was the case, one might argue that the state bail-out of local communities was harmful rather than helpful to the poor; the new aid would have reduced state services for the poor at the same time that it allowed local communities to maintain services such as police and fire that provide benefits to all local residents.

The determination of which specific state services were reduced to finance the new state aid is tricky. One can never know for sure what would have happened in the absence of the new state aid. Because then Governor Edward King initially proposed a FY 1982 budget that included almost no new state aid for local communities, one approach is to compare the components of the final budget with the Governor's initial budget. Based on this approach, we find little evidence that poor people bore the brunt of the financing, although they undoubtedly bore some of it. For each of the expenditure items included in the Senate Ways and Means Committee anti-poverty budget, we compared the final appropriations with the Governor's requests. In seven of ten program areas, we find that the legislature increased the Governor's proposed spending. Only in three areas were appropriations decreased: human services by $1.7 million, public health by $3.5 million, and transportation subsidies by $25 million. Moreover, some of the reduction in these budgets was in the administrative rather than the service accounts. Overall we find that FY 1982 appropriations for the anti-poverty programs were about $50 million more than those requested by the Governor, despite the additional state aid, and $125 million more than they were in 1982. This small overall year-to-year increase suggests that the anti-tax sentiment within the state has taken its toll on anti-poverty programs. At the same time, the evidence suggests that the legislative decision to provide substantial new aid to local governments in FY 1982 did not contribute substantially to the

Table 9-12   School Cutbacks and Low-Income Pupils, FY 1982 (For Districts with More than 1000 Low-Income Pupils)

City or Town	Number of Low-Income Pupils	% Reduction in Professional Staff [a]	% Reduction in Other Staff [a]
Boston	32,828	17%	33%
Brockton	4,295	8	15
Cambridge	2,155	16	21
Chelsea	1,770	N/A	N/A
Chicopee	1,525	12	21
Everett	1,266	N/A	N/A
Fall River	3,823	5	3
Fitchburg	1,242	14	N/A
Haverhill	1,438	13	12
Holyoke	3,182	7	28
Lawrence	3,464	10	31
Lowell	3,402	2	16
Lynn	3,891	6	13
Malden	1,530	N/A	N/A
New Bedford	4,603	7	N/A
Pittsfield	1,598	18	28
Quincy	1,782	30	31
Revere	1,397	4[b]	6
Somerville	2,281	9	19
Springfield	10,660	3	8
Taunton	1,350	12	17
Weymouth	1,151	20	18
Worcester	6,637	13	29
Percentage of all low-income pupils	64%		
Average reduction		11.3%	19.4%
Average reduction (weighted by low-income pupils)		11.7%	23.3%

SOURCES: Massachusetts Association of School Committees, "The Impact of Proposition 2½ on the Public Schools"; and Massachusetts Department of Education.
[a] Incorporates changes made in response to the new state aid.
[b] Before the adjustment to new state aid.

failure of anti-poverty programs to expand in real terms. It is, of course, possible that the legislature would have altered the budget from the governor's request in any case, so we cannot be sure that some of the increased state aid did not come out of funds that would otherwise have been used in state government expenditures focussed on the poor.

Summary of First Year Impacts. During the first year under Proposition 2½ the average poor household received substantially smaller benefits in terms of tax savings than did the average non-poor household. This fact represents cause for concern inasmuch as the poor were simultaneously hurt disproportionately by the service cutbacks. Not only do the poor tend to live in communities that were most seriously affected by the limitation measure but they also were disproportionately affected by the large education reductions. We conclude, however, that the state acted responsibly by providing additional aid that forestalled even more drastic cuts in local services and by not financing the aid by disproportionate reductions in state-provided services for the poor.

Long-Term Outlook and Policy Options

Proposition 2½ has brought a fundamental change in the operation of local governments in Massachusetts. Not only is the growth of local revenues constrained but also total property tax revenues are much more closely tied to the size of a community's tax base than in the past. Wide variation in property tax bases across jurisdictions means that from now on there will be dramatic differences in the per capita amounts of local taxes that communities are permitted to raise. Communities can no longer compensate for below-average tax bases by choosing to tax themselves at above-average tax rates; despite the new override provisions passed by the legislature in late 1981, no community can raise its tax rate above 2½ percent of the total market value of property in the community.

This presents a potentially serious problem for poor people who tend to be concentrated in communities with the largest expenditure demands in relation to their tax bases—that is, those with the highest pre-Proposition 2½ tax rates. Without explicit state action these jurisdictions, unlike those with lower tax rates, have to reduce spending substantially to meet the requirements of Proposition 2½. In the likely event that spending reductions translate into reductions in local public services, these reductions would adversely affect all residents of such communities, but especially the poor. Compared with wealthier residents, the poor are less able to adjust to lower public service levels; typically they cannot flee to a wealthier community nor do they have sufficient income to substitute private goods and services, such as alarm systems or private schools, for publicly provided services. Moreover, public schools, the one locally provided service that disproportionately serves the poor in large cities, are likely to face the greatest political obstacles to continued public support.

The state legislature has recognized the need for state action and, three years in a row, has responded to the requests of local governments for more state aid to help offset the effects of the tax-limitation measure. A more permanent solution is now required. The state could either establish a state revenue sharing program that guarantees state aid for local governments or could pass legislation enabling local jurisdictions to use local income, sales, or other broad-based taxes. Under a third alternative, the state could increase state aid for education and permit limited use of new local taxes for non-school purposes. A full evaluation of these three options is beyond the scope of this chapter; instead we focus here on the issues that are pertinent to poor people.

First, consider a guaranteed state revenue sharing program. Ideally under such a program state aid to local governments would be distributed inversely with the local property tax base (or some other measure of local fiscal capacity) and directly with local public service costs, objectively defined. In addition, such aid should be removed from the annual state budgetary process to prevent the common past practice in Massachusetts of varying the size of the local aid package to balance the state budget. One reasonable approach would link the amount of state aid to the growth of state revenues. In this way, local governments would have a relatively predictable revenue source and would share in the growth and decline of the state economy. A general revenue sharing program of this type is attractive in many ways and has been advocated as an appropriate policy response to Proposition 2½.[16]

Viewed solely from the perspective of poor people, however, it has some potential imperfections. First, unless aid is directed toward the communities where the poor live, the poor may be differentially hurt by such a solution. This would not be a problem if an adequate measure of service costs were incorporated into the formula by which funds were distributed among communities; the poor clearly tend to live in communities with high service costs where such costs are related to objective measures such as the age and density of the city's housing stock and the number of people working (but not living) in the city. The difficulty arises both in developing an objective measure of service costs and in convincing the legislature that high public spending in certain cities is a legitimate response to public service costs and is not exclusively the result of waste and mismanagement.

Second, local officials may not allocate the general purpose aid they receive to the services such as education that disproportionately serve the poor. From a more general perspective, this aspect of a revenue sharing program is advantageous in that it leaves recipient jurisdictions free to set their own priorities. It is less advantageous, however, if the state goal is to help poor people. Third, and perhaps most important, a large guaranteed state revenue sharing program leaves less money for direct state programs unless new revenue sources are tapped or rates on existing taxes raised. Because many state expenditure programs directly assist poor people, even a partial transfer of funds from existing state programs to local aid might hurt poor people on balance.

Permitting local governments to use new local taxes to supplement property taxes would restore to local voters the power to determine their own tax and spending levels. In addition, new taxing authority would allow local governments to tap new taxpayers such as tourists, commuters (provided revenue from a local income tax accrues to place of work rather than place of residence), and employees of non-profit institutions which do not pay property taxes. Some people might argue as well that this policy response would provide more incentive for local officials to minimize waste and inefficiency by making local governments more dependent on their own revenue sources than they would be with the revenue sharing option. The magnitude of this alleged benefit is hard to quantify, however, and is probably small.

On the other hand, the distortions and inequities created by local income taxes and sales taxes, especially when such taxes are used in jurisdictions that are as small and as varied as they are in Massachusetts, are well known. With small jurisdictions imposing differential tax rates, both consumers and firms can easily avoid the taxes by changing their behavior. In addition, particularly with a local sales tax, some communities (namely, those with shopping malls) can raise substantially more revenue with a given tax rate than can others. Absolute disparities among jurisdictions would be somewhat less with a local income tax than with a local sales tax, but because many communities that are rich in terms of property wealth are also rich in terms of income, a local-option income tax would similarly increase the variation in taxable capacity among jurisdictions. These disparities in revenue-raising potential pose a particular problem for the financing of elementary and secondary education. In light of successful court cases challenging systems of education finance in other states and the pending Webbe v. Dukakis case in Massachusetts, the goal should be to narrow, not widen, the fiscal disparities among jurisdictions.

An alternative solution should also be considered if the focus is on poor people. The state government could both increase aid to education in a highly equalizing manner, reaching and perhaps exceeding the 50 percent state share that education reformers in the state have long sought, and, at the same time, give local governments the option of using alternative broad-based local taxes for non-school expenditures. The aid to education should be equalizing across jurisdictions and should include sufficient controls to assure that state goals with respect to the poor and other disadvantaged groups are met. (See Chapter 4 for more details.) In contrast to education expenditures where inter-jurisdictional equity is a major concern, local non-school expenditures are more appropriately financed in part by non-property tax revenue sources. As noted above, local sales or income taxes would allow local jurisdictions to tax certain groups who impose costs on the community or who benefit from local services while paying no direct property taxes. Moreover, if restricted to non-education services and used strictly as a supplement to local property taxes, tax rates would presumably be low in those communities that chose to introduce new taxes, thereby minimizing their distorting effects.

Fiscal Reform and the Poor

A vast array of "reforms" of the Massachusetts fiscal structure have been proposed in recent years—too many to analyze in detail here. In the preceding sections, we have considered the basic characteristics of various potential reforms, particularly as they might affect the poor. In this section, we outline a series of proposals which, in our view, would make the Massachusetts fiscal structure more equitable and less burdensome on the poor.

State Taxes

Income Tax:

- Expand the refundable low-income credit to offset the regressive effects of broader-based sales taxation.
- Increase the amounts of personal and household exemptions.
- Eliminate the rent deduction.
- Raise the tax rate, if necessary, to recover revenues lost through the preceding alternatives.

Sales Taxes:

- Expand the existing general sales tax base to include retail personal services.

- Provide a vanishing refundable income tax credit of at least one percent of income for households below the poverty level.
- Reduce reliance on selective sales taxes by increasing revenues from the general sales tax.

Local Government Revenue:

- Develop a new package of state aid and possibly alternative local revenue sources to assure adequate local revenues in the context of Proposition 2½.
- Finance additional aid to local governments out of increased tax revenues, not out of budget cuts in anti-poverty programs.

Tax Expenditures:

- Report a comprehensive tax expenditure budget annually as part of the normal budgetary process.

As a general matter, the income tax is the best of the broad-based taxes Massachusetts has available for funding public programs. Therefore, strengthening this tax base and utilizing it more effectively are important objectives of tax reform. Though it is currently progressive, it should be made more so; this goal can be achieved by higher exemptions and a larger refundable low-income credit. The rent deduction is an ineffectively targeted and horizontally inequitable tax expenditure and should be eliminated.

Our views about sales taxation are somewhat more ambiguous. Massachusetts' very narrow sales tax base makes the general sales tax less regressive than it would otherwise be, but it is still not a progressive tax. It is, however, relatively easy to administer and its incidence across income groups is approximately proportional. Accordingly it is a necessary—if imperfect—source of considerable state revenue. In keeping with this pragmatic view, the negative aspects of sales taxes can be mitigated by providing a reasonably large—perhaps $50 or $100—vanishing refundable income tax credit to offset sales tax collections. With this alteration to reduce the impact on the very poor, the state could expand its reliance on this revenue source without adversely affecting the progressivity of its fiscal system. This could be done either by expanding the tax base or by increasing the tax rate. Expanding the tax base is desirable because of the extreme narrowness of the base currently used in Massachusetts compared with that in other states.

Proposition 2½ is in Massachusetts to stay. By forcing communities with high tax rates to roll back local property tax rates, Proposition 2½ has reduced the regressivity of the overall state tax structure. At the same time, it has weakened the ability of local governements to finance public services out of their own resources, a result that may have particularly serious consequences for the adequacy of the local public services available to poor people. This situation calls for a package of new revenues for local governments.

Given our focus here on poor people, the preferred solution is to increase the amount of state aid, with such aid financed out of increases in state tax revenues rather than by cuts in anti-poverty programs. To minimize the adverse effects of Proposition 2½ on poor people, particular attention must be paid to the formula by which such aid is distributed and to the restrictions and requirements needed to assure the achievement of state goals such as assuring adequate provision of elementary and secondary education to low-income children.

If political resistance to increases in state taxes means that new state aid would be financed in part by cuts in state anti-poverty programs, new local-option sales or income taxes may be appropriate. Such taxes should not be used for financing elementary and secondary education, however, and any package of local-option taxes should include a substantial increase in equalizing state aid for education.

The current fiscal environment requires that all expenditure budgets be examined annually to ensure that each expenditure program is meeting its goals in a cost-effective way. "Tax expenditures" are similar to regular expenditures, and the state should therefore prepare annually a tax expenditure budget. This would provide the information necessary for the state to consider its tax expenditures more systematically and thoroughly than it has in the past.

Endnotes

1. See, for example, Massachusetts Taxpayers Foundation, "A Massachusetts Primer" (undated), page 24.
2. Advisory Commission on Intergovernmental Relations, "Significant Facts of Fiscal Federalism, 1980-81" (Washington, D.C.: U.S. Government Printing Office, 1982); Massachusetts Taxpayers Foundation, "The Numbers Book" (mimeo, August 1980), pages 17–23.
3. Massachusetts Taxpayers Foundation, "The Numbers Book" (mimeo, August 1980).

4. Andrew Reschovsky *et al.*, "State Tax Policy: Evaluating the Issues." (Cambridge, Mass.: Joint Center for Urban Studies of MIT and Harvard University, 1983).

5. Reschovsky and his collaborators do report results for alcohol and tobacco, which indicate quite regressive patterns. See their Table 2.9, page 43.

6. Andrew Reschovsky *et al.*, "State Tax Policy: Evaluating the Issues" (Cambridge, Mass.: Joint Center for Urban Studies of MIT and Harvard University, 1983), page 80.

7. "Retail services" include (1) personal services (repairs, laundry, haircuts), (2) automobile services, (3) entertainment, and (4) a miscellaneous category including alcohol, cigarettes, hotel lodging, and newsstand purchases.

8. A statutory amendment to Proposition 2½ now permits two-thirds of the board of selectmen or city council to set up a referendum override vote at any time. A majority vote in such a referendum can slow revenue cuts from 15 percent to 7½ percent or can increase the levy growth limit from 2½ percent to 5 percent. A two-thirds vote can completely eliminate the revenue reduction or can remove the limit on levy increases for the year. In no case, however, may a community vote to increase its tax rate above 2½ percent.

9. In the spring of 1982 Cambridge residents voted to delay their required 15 percent reduction for one year.

10. Community-wide revaluation of property complicates the analysis, especially in those communities where revaluation redistributed the tax burden away from business property onto residential property. Within the class of residential property, revaluation generally reduced the relative tax burdens of poor people since low-valued property typically was overassessed relative to high-valued property before revaluation.

11. This statement is based on data from the 1977 Annual Housing Survey for the Boston SMSA, Table A-1.

12. Helen F. Ladd and Julie Boatwight Wilson, "Who Supports Tax Limitations: Evidence from Massachusetts' Proposition 2½" *Journal of Policy Analysis and Management* Vol. 2, No. 2 (Winter 1983).

13. Based on data from the 1977 Annual Housing Survey for the Boston SMSA, Table A-1.

14. This statement and the following ones are based on Andrew Reschovsky, *et al.*, "State Tax Policy: Evaluating the Issues," (Cambridge, Mass.: Joint Center for Urban Studies of MIT and Harvard University, 1983).

15. See Katharine L. Bradbury and Helen F. Ladd, with Claire Christopherson, "Proposition 2½: Initial Impacts, Part II," *New England Economic Review* (March–April 1982), pp. 48–62.

16. See Katherine L. Bradbury and Helen F. Ladd, with Claire Christopherson, "Proposition 2½: Initial Impacts, Part II," *New England Economic Review* (March–April 1982), pp. 48–62.

Chapter 10

POLICY PLANNING
AND THE POOR

by Walter D. Broadnax

In recent years there has been a revival of the notion that state governments are the most appropriate focal points for the planning, design, and implementation of many domestic social programs. Following the tremendous outpouring of dollars and programs that were a part of the Great Society (which, unlike the New Deal, bypassed the states), the Nixon Administration introduced the concept of a "new federalism." A fundamental aspect of the new federalism was a greater sharing of responsibility between the federal and state governments, with fewer rules, guidelines, and planning requirements for states. By reducing the number of strings and the complexity of the relationship between the states and the federal government, proponents then believed that the states could better plan their destinies because of their closer perception of need and citizen concern. Similarly, the Reagan Administration from the beginning believed that more recent policies had forced the states to pursue goals and objectives established in Washington by officials who were removed generally from the concerns and interests of the people within the individual states. As in the Nixon era, many policymakers currently believe that a return of policy and program authority to the states is in order.

Increased state responsibility with fewer interventions by the federal government presumes that states are prepared politically, institutionally, and financially to pursue actively a state-based process of goal- and agenda-setting. Furthermore, a shift of power presumes that governors, legislators, and key officials are able and inclined to create the necessary vehicles and procure the necessary talent requisite to the systematic development of a statewide policy agenda.

The problems and issues related to the overall capability of the state to respond to the needs of the poor are discussed in this chapter. Such a discussion of policy planning will be facilitated by an initial—although cursory—treatment of certain germane contextual issues.

State Planning Capacity

In order to address successfully the needs of the poor, governors, legislators, and other key officials must position themselves to plan, design, implement, and manage domestic social programs in a manner that will serve the needs of the poor. This may be done best within the context of an overall state planning process that serves other beneficiaries as well as the poor. As states acquire greater responsibility and autonomy in the selection, design, and implementation of policies and programs, state-level decisionmakers will increasingly need a process and a methodology for deciding who gets what and why.

The context within which governors, legislators, and other state-level public policymakers must operate is extremely complex. State governments have become so large and complex that they have often outgrown the ability of their officials to perform responsibly. There has been tremendous growth in state government. This growth has produced a welter of agencies, many of which are virtually autonomous and most of which change slowly because of organizational barriers and rigidity, as well as political inertia.[1]

Elected officials confronted with the realities of trying to make rational decisions within a very complex and often resistant environment face enormous difficulties. These officials are finding it increasingly difficult to decide how best to serve public needs because they have inadequate knowledge of the nature of the problems involved (which are becoming increasingly complex) and the potential as well as current impact of programs on these problems. Elected officials' problems are further exacerbated by the fact that they are heavily dependent upon state agencies or interest groups for information. For example, it is reported that the Anti-Poverty Budget produced by the Massachusetts Committee on Ways and Means contains 150 line items found in seven secretariats of the executive branch and the judicial branch of state government.[2]

Agency heads and their staffs, in turn, are not exempt from the problems of complexity and knowledge shortage confronted by elected officials. They often have little knowledge of how their agencies' resources are being utilized or of the effectiveness of their programs. Agency heads, particularly, often find themselves bogged down in day-to-day operations, to the extent that they lack the time necessary for developing adequate information systems or for evaluating programs, not to mention time for looking ahead and developing more effective programs for future implementation. Indeed, shortly after appointment, an agency head is expected to begin resolving a plethora of accumulated issues from the past.

Given this situation in which elected officials, agency heads, and their staffs find themselves, it is hard to imagine how state governments can weed out inertia and avoid ill-conceived responses to crises without the capability of systemativ planning. If the state is to develop an effective planning function, policymakers and managers must address four basic questions. First, do the services the state performs respond to current needs? Clearly, the state cannot afford, either financially or politically, to performs services that lack relevance. Planners must know whether and how beneficiary needs change over time in order to ensure that government policy and programs are responsive. Second, what is the degree to which the present or anticipated level of effort is causing, or will cause, the desired response or reduce the perceived level of the needs the programs address? Third, what is the level of efficiency within the state's various domestic social programs? Moreover, are the resources targeted in such a way as to achieve the greatest output for the least input? Fourthly, can the needs of the poor be addressed more constructively within a coherent policy planning process?

To address these questions, state governments need to develop comprehensive policy planning processes for all their activities. While some programs are designated specifically as anti-poverty in nature, there are many other functions in state government that may impact upon the poor. For example, civil rights activities are often concerned with women, handicapped people, or minorities who are poor. Therefore, state civil rights policies and programs should be planned and developed with an eye to the needs of the poor. Each program and policy should be carefully examined for its anti-poverty potential as well as other more broadly defined policy objectives.

Policy planning for the poor is a necessary step within the framework of developing an effective overall state policy planning process. Without conscious planning and program strategies that seek to spotlight and grapple with the needs of the poor across various beneficiary groups, the poor will either receive in the aggregate far less than the state is able and willing to provide or they will receive assistance not directly related to their needs— that is, they may receive far more than is necessary in some areas and nothing at all where their need is greatest. At the same time, it must be recognized that the most elegant of processes and the most powerful of policy tools cannot be effective without compassion and the political will necessary to focus attention and resources on the problems of the poor. Also, given the size of state budgets today, clandestine approaches to the problems of the poor may well result in disaster when such hidden policy choices eventually come to light. To serve the poor effectively, policy choices must be made openly and within the framework of overall state policy development and implementation processes.

The balance of this chapter will be devoted to national planning developments, the evolution of planning in Massachusetts, policy planning for the poor and its benefits, and a suggested approach to policy planning for the poor in Massachusetts (and other states). We shall address the foregoing questions about how the state should respond to the need for policy planning in general and for the poor specifically.

National and State Planning Developments

The roots of state planning as a conscious activity may be traced to the New Deal and, before that, to municipal master planning activities. Clearly, state planning bloomed as a result of federal interest and funding during the national effort to address problems that sprang from the Great Depression. The Public Works Administration stimulated the development of state planning agencies to undergird and parallel the formation of the National Planning Board in 1933. As a part of the overall national effort to overcome the Great Depression, these state planning bodies focused their attention on the conservation of human and natural resources and on the development of physical facilities and infrastructure. Largely because these early planning agencies were dependent primarily upon federal support, however, they did not develop strong roots within the states. As a result, state planning efforts declined in the late 1930s and early 1940s. When the public works type of program began to taper off and when federal priorities shifted in preparation for World War II, state planning became an early casualty. Concommitantly, these early planning vehicles tended to become and remain isolated from the flow of politics and from the influence of elected and key appointed state officials, a situation that further contributed to their decline.

During the 1960s state planning enjoyed a renaissance. Planning as a permanently organized function, rather than as a requirement under various federal formula grants, began once again to occupy a place of significance in the overall national strategy for addressing various social and domestic needs. Again, the initiative for this rebirth was federally sponsored and played a critical role in the development and character of state planning as a meaningful endeavor.

Specifically, the National Housing Act was amended to provide federal matching funds for state planning.[4] The potential and opportunity for state planning was gaining momentum, but rapid growth in the various federal grants-in-aid programs to the states during the 1960s created coordination and management problems at the state level. Difficulties in program integration and in development of coherent coordination strategies were legion. Moreover, the fragmentation of most state governments, which were characterized by a potpourri of separate boards, commissions, bureaus, agencies, and departments (many operating under varying degrees of autonomy and relatively weak central authority), caused increasing concern regarding the capacity of states to respond to current needs. These conditions resulted in renewed national interest in state planning, for national officials saw state planning as a means of enhancing the effectiveness of federal grants-in-aid.

Throughout the 1960s planning enjoyed a renewed emphasis and respect, primarily at the national level but increasingly also at the state level. Program Planning and Budgeting Systems (PPBS), initially employed at the Department of Defense and later tailored for and employed by domestically oriented agencies, helped shape national opinion regarding the strengths and weaknesses of planning as a means of achieving national objectives. Interestingly, PPBS developed a relatively strong position in certain domestic agencies (HEW, HUD, Interior), while it suffered setbacks within the environment (Defense) which spawned it. Many felt that planning was oversold in the defense community; as the Viet-Nam War began to go badly, the highly sophisticated planning apparatus developed under Robert McNamara came increasingly under attack. With the demise of PPBS in the late

1960s and the introduction of the new federalism of the 1970s, the status of planning began once again to suffer a gradual but steady decline.

As mentioned earlier, the 1960s set the tone for the 1970s. Leaders at the time suggested that the best approach to our social and domestic problems was to give states greater responsibility and autonomy because state-level policymakers could best address specific social and domestic issues. The trend toward decentralization became clearer, emphasizing state control over the poverty programs created during the zenith of the Great Society.

The Reagan Administration has continued to advocate expanding the responsibility of the states for social and domestic programs in general and for poverty-oriented programs in particular.[5] Given this emphasis, states may well expect less general financial and capacity-building support from the federal level. Increased autonomy for the states will bring greatly increased responsibility for development of rational systems for addressing and meeting the needs of all residents—including the poor. This need must be met, despite the fact that planning in Massachusetts, as in many states, has waxed and waned over the past several decades but has never been utilized as a tool for specifically addressing the needs of the poor.

Planning in Massachusetts

Although several Massachusetts agencies have had planning units for some time, and although several recent governors have appointed planners to their staffs, planning as a conscious effort was reborn in Massachusetts as a result of gubernatorial politics and not simply a desire to develop a policy planning mechanism.[6] During the administrations of Governor John Volpe and his successor, Francis Sargent, a means was sought to maintain the momentum of the administration's leadership and to avoid partisan conflict with the legislature. Governor Volpe and his aides settled upon reorganization of state government (later called "modernization" because of its broader appeal) because this issue was less susceptible to partisan treatment and because federal funds were available for state planning, including reorganization of the executive branch.[7]

Having agreed on the course to follow, officials began the process of securing federal funds to develop a central planning unit. Although Governor Volpe's interest was primarily in the area of reorganization, all concerned were interested in improving the overall effectiveness of state government. In August 1967 the U.S. Department of Housing and Urban Development (HUD) awarded Massachusetts half a million dollars; in response, a quarter of a million dollars in staff time was solicited from several state agencies.[8]

The successful negotiations with HUD led to the creation of the Office of Program Planning and Coordination (OPPC). Rather than pursue its creation by legislation or executive order, state officials took the administrative route, designating as its primary mission the establishment of a cabinet form of government and a computer-based system of management controls. Having completed the reorganization, but forgoing establishment of a computer-based system of management controls, OPPC was reconstituted administratively in 1969 as the Office of Planning and Management (OPM) with the primary mission of managing the state bureaucracy. From 1969 to 1975, OPM functioned as the management and planning unit within the Executive Office, reporting directly to Governor Sargent. Some insight as to how OPM functioned during the Sargent administration is provided by Weinberg:[9]

> In the Sargent administration, except for instances that involved a highly visible issue or an issue that directly affected the governor's position with the electorate, initiation or change of policy on the part of the governor's office was largely dependent on the talent, personal inclination, and assignment of the functional policy specialists who worked for (OPM) Robert Kramer.

OPM was rather broad-based in its approach in that its focus was on policy matters generally rather than on a particular program such as economic development or state modernization.

In 1975, following his election, Governor Michael Dukakis created the Office of State Planning (OSP) and appointed Frank Keefe as its director. Again, neither enabling legislation nor an executive order facilitated the creation of this state planning operation, and funding was federally provided. In this instance, funding was secured by combining grant monies from the Economic Development Administration (EDA) of the U.S. Department of Commerce and from HUD.

With the creation of OSP there came another change in the focus of state planning activity. Located within the Department of Administration and Finance, OSP concentrated its energies on economic development and physical planning issues. The approach was that of a project-by-project or regional-needs basis. The office concentrated a goodly portion of its energies on the acquisition of federal grant monies, with an emphasis on urban development and physical planning—for example, shopping center location, downtown revitalization, and transportation routing.

Under the leadership of Keefe, who held cabinet rank as the Director of OSP, the Dukakis Administration was very active in economic development and physical planning across the state. Access to the Governor was excellent, and the staff of approximately 15 planners were respected throughout state government, primarily because of their perceived ability to influence economic development policy. As a mechanism for further strengthening the development thrust within his administration, Governor Dukakis created the "Development Cabinet," which was chaired by the Director of OSP. The Development Cabinet was composed of secretariat-level departments such as the Executive Office of Economic Affairs, the Executive Office of Community Development, and the Executive Office of Environmental Affairs. Under the leadership of Keefe, planning developed a prominent role within the Dukakis Administration. Although the focus of OSP was consciously narrow and its role was considered initially a nuisance by some, OSP's ability to provide the governor with information and guidance regarding development issues and policies was strong.[10]

Upon assuming office in 1979, Governor Edward King abolished the Office of State Planning, transferring certain vestiges to the Executive Office of Economic Affairs. The motives for this action were unclear, but the King Administration did create the Office of Policy Development (OPD). Originally, OPD's function was to develop policy position papers, but it was soon discovered that this approach did not have much influence on the policymaking process. In 1982, approximately one year before the end of his administration, the Governor created the position of Special Assistant to the Governor for Policy Development.[11] This official's role was that of "ramrod," including responsibility for coordination and follow-through on various policy issues of particular interest to the Governor.

In 1983 the situation in Massachusetts reflected once again a decline in the role and significance of state planning as a conscious endeavor. There now existed a smattering of various forms and types of planning units within several departments and agencies across state government. For example, the Massachusetts Commission Against Discrimination had no internal planning unit, the contention being that planning was done by the chairman and the two commissioners. Nevertheless, the Department of Education had an Office of Executive Planning, and another type and form of planning organization, called the Policy and Development Group, existed within the Department of Welfare. As of the present, therefore, the planning terrain in Massachusetts is quite uneven and there exists no formal mechanism within the Office of the Governor to perform a comprehensive state policy planning function.[12] The need for policy planning in Massachusetts has not vanished, but a mechanism to address that need specifically still does not exist. This lack of policy planning is central to the matter of responding to the needs of the poor.

Conscientious policy planning can have a significant positive effect upon the poor. However, past policy planning attempts in Massachusetts have been limited and the results have been mixed. Indeed, policy planning efforts focused on the needs of the poor have had an uneven and rather uneventful existence within state government.[13] Nonetheless, there has been some appreciation of the contribution such planning could make. Planning for the poor is quite obviously just as important as planning for any state activity, program, or operation.

Benefits of State Planning

There are four major benefits for the poor which may be derived from the development of a comprehensive state policy planning apparatus:

1. the ability to target resources effectively and efficiently.
2. the creation of incentives for developing an agenda of state governmental policies and programs.
3. the development of levers to assist managers in their efforts to improve, change, or fine-tune service delivery systems.
4. the creation of an environment in which the governor, legislators, and appointed officials can firmly take the managerial reins of state government, particularly as related to poverty issues.

The policy planning approach is to build an agenda from program data, assessment of need, demographic data, and the policy preferences, value orientations, and predilections of elected officials and their chief lieutenants. Such an approach will per force help officials decide where they wish to concentrate their energies. For example, if education is a key policy agenda item, with the improvement of reading skills for poor children as a significant need, the bureaucracy can be signalled, challenged, and monitored in terms of its responses. Agenda-setting in its simplest terms provides a road map for the administration and priorities for the bureaucracy. It enables elected officials to pursue their identified objectives rather than those of the bureaucracy or of single-focus interest groups.

One of the important elements of being able to develop a policy plan is targeting. Targeting and agenda setting are closely related within the context of developing a comprehensive policy plan. Once a broad agenda has been set, decisionmakers can focus resources (target) on selected areas of their choice.

Agenda-Setting

Governors, legislators, and key officials have several ways in which they may go about setting an agenda for state government. The most traditional approach is to ascertain what problems most concern the citizens and to promise improvement of conditions in these areas. In this process, politics sets the most basic agenda: If an official who campaigned against a particular condition wins, then at least one agenda item is likely to be ways to bring about the desired changes. Another approach to agenda setting—the approach that still dominates most state governments—is to let the bureaucracy set the basic agenda, while the governor selects those issues and policies with which he would most like to be identified. Martha Weinberg confirms for Massachusetts what others have observed nationally:

> . . . Contrary to what democratic theory would lead us to believe, it is clear that the preference of specialized bureaucrats often dominate the choice of policies and the outcome of issues with or without the consent of the elected or appointed generalist to whom in theory they are accountable.

If the bureaucracy has an agenda, it is typically much more policy specific than the agenda broadly outlined by elected officials. It then becomes the responsibility of the policy planning process to infuse compatible elements from the pre-existing bureaucratic agenda into the broad agenda developed by elected officials and their agency executives.

Building on the previous example of improving reading skills, elected officials and their chief lieutenants will have a broad outline of their objective. The bureaucracy will most probably have several policy-specific proposals it has previously developed or ongoing programs related generally to the development of reading skills. The policy planning process would then provide a mechanism whereby structured interactions between the bureaucracy and policy officials could take place in the development of a comprehensive agenda for improving reading skills. These structured interactions, based on existing information the bureaucracy may already have or has been directed to develop and the general outline of what the leaders may wish to achieve, can then produce a rational agenda. Once developed, such an agenda would have the advantage of committing the bureaucracy and the political leadership generally to the same course of action.

Once a course of action has been determined, choices regarding the utilization of fiscal and human resources can be made. Clearly, the objective is to concentrate resources on the problems identified within the policy agenda. It is at this point that targeting becomes extremely important in the policy planning process.

Targeting

The term "targeting" implies focusing resources on a relatively well-defined problem. Usually, it also implies dedicating resources for a specific population—for example, the handicapped and school drop-outs. Funding for various groups and programs often flows through different streams. It is also not unusual for several agencies or parts of agencies to be concerned with overlapping populations and problems. Therefore, a mechanism is needed to draw information and resources together from these disparate sources in order to attack the problem in a concerted fashion.

As a second step in the agenda-setting activity, the policy planning process becomes a means of identifying the various funding streams, discrete ongoing programmatic activities, personnel, and target population. The process of rationally and methodically researching the source of funds, ascertaining the availability of staff, and assessing the present level of state commitment to the problem adds coherence to the proposed actions.

In some instances staff and funds existing within several organizational units across state government may already have been dedicated to solving the same or a similar problem. In such cases, the approaches used by various organizations may be quite similar, or they may be very different. A central policy planning mechanism, through its ability to consciously structure a state-oriented approach to solving the problem, should be able to utilize resources from across state government and avoid duplication of effort.

Each bureaucracy tends to feel ownership of its programs. It therefore is often necessary for leadership from above to bring about a concerted and coordinated use of resources from across various structures. The policy planning process consciously forces each agency into a posture of thinking *state* programs rather than simply thinking *department* or *agency* programs. The central policy planning mechanism makes it possible to identify resources and information throughout the bureaucracy and bring them together. With information concerning the nature of the problem, affected groups, program overlap, and fiscal and human resources, decisionmakers can consciously choose where they wish to focus their resources.

Having identified targets for change and decided how to proceed rationally to solve those problems, the bureaucracy and decisionmakers can competently focus their attention on the delivery of the desired services.

Service Delivery

Policy planning is predicated on bringing rationality to decision processes and service delivery systems. Creating a structure for setting an agenda and targeting resources makes it much easier to monitor the delivery of services. One of the recurring complaints about government is that it often does things no one wanted it to do or that is doing something poorly. If a consciously developed plan exists for the delivery of services, successes can be monitored and weaknesses identified. Moreover, the process of targeting may have identified areas of potential concern to decisionmakers.

Feedback systems are critical to improving or adjusting service delivery systems. However, the large number of state government programs with differing funding streams, accounting systems, rules and regulations, and overlapping populations makes it extremely difficult to ascertain the effectiveness of the state's overall impact on selected problem areas. Agenda setting and targeting are often therefore prerequisites to effective service delivery.

A comprehensive policy planning operation is able to provide feedback on how well programs are operating. It has the ability to find out whether the desired outcomes are being achieved and whether unintended outcomes are being experienced. For example, programs designed for one group may have unintended effects on other groups. Targeting day care services for persons in the AFDC program may cause strains on the existing day care system which provides services to non-AFDC children. If the state has a comprehensive day care policy plan and wishes to target a designated number of places within the day care system for use by AFDC children, a service delivery feedback system will pinpoint the optimum mix of AFDC and non-AFDC children who can be accommodated by the existing system.

Once sound information (feedback) has been received concerning outcomes, decisionmakers can make rational decisions regarding appropriate system adjustments. In the case of the day care example, it could be decided that the state may wish to contribute to the expansion of the overall day care system (number of providers and/or available slots) or adjust the number of AFDC children receiving services. When the choice is to provide more day care slots for AFDC children and fewer for non-AFDC children or to expand the system in order to accommodate greater numbers of both, feedback systems developed from a well-structured, comprehensive policy plan for the delivery of day care services will afford policymakers an opportunity to consciously and rationally choose a course of action.

A common concern of both elected officials and agency heads is how well are programs being managed. A complaint often heard is that a program is out of control. While *management* is the act of taking control of programs, *policy planning* is an essential aid to this end.

Manageability

Simply defined, management is the art and science of utilizing human and fiscal resources for the achievement of organizational goals and objectives. The governor, as the chief executive of the state, is expected to manage the state's affairs. Legislators who make broad policy through the passage of legislation and the appropriation of funds are to some extent looking to the governor to exercise leadership and management skills necessary to the achievement of desired policy goals and objectives.

If the chief executive and his lieutenants have developed a course for his administration with a set of relatively well-articulated goals and objectives, then state government becomes a more manageable enterprise. Utilizing the processes, tools and mechanism of policy planning, the governor can clearly transmit his policy choices and receive orderly and meaningful feedback concerning problems, crises, and programmatic outcomes. This feedback will enable the governor and legislature to respond with appropriate changes in the various policies and programs.

Moreover, the planning process will increase the chief executive's ability to direct the human and fiscal resources of state government toward certain objectives and goals.

Policy planning processes can provide several tools and mechanisms to aid the chief executive and his lieutenants in their efforts to improve management: (1) structured decision processes, (2) programmatic feedback, (3) rationally developed sets of alternatives, and (4) increased interaction between and among agencies around various policy initiatives. By carefully structuring the path for reaching decisions regarding the development of a policy and by relying to some extent on data received concerning the prior performance of programs, the policy planning organization can provide rational alternatives for action. The planning process, because it seeks information across various bureaucratic structures, will create greater interaction among those agencies to be affected. These mechanisms then improve the executive's ability to make conscious choices about the direction and desired outcomes for state actions.

The poor, probably more than other beneficiaries, can least afford for state government to proceed haphazardly in its approach to addressing their needs. Given the current limitations on available resources and the ever-present demands on the chief executive's and legislators' time, a more rational policymaking process will enable key officials efficiently and effectively to focus attention and resources on the needs of the poor. Moreover, the entire state enterprise will have an enhanced ability to shift its focus, change delivery systems, and follow overall management guidance.

Cross-Cutting Strategies and Poverty

We have discussed the benefits to be derived from a state policy planning organization. Embedded in the overall discussion is the conceptual notion of how various programs and policies across state governments flow to various beneficiary groups. For example, health services usually flow from the health department, nutritional services may flow from the welfare department, and educational guidance may flow from the educational department. The hope is that these services, flowing through different streams, will reach the desired beneficiary population. From the executive office, these streams are often seen as independent flows of cash and services. During policy and program deliberations, each policy and/or program is typically examined and discussed separately, often to the total exclusion of other policies and programs which may also impact upon the beneficiary group being considered. This situation is further exacerbated when we consider the fact that governors and legislators—but particularly governors—tend to deal with various agency heads serially. This approach affords governors little opportunity to discuss the inter- active quality and nature of various policies and programs. It also limits the executive's ability to make synergistic proposals across the state governmental structure. Such limitations and barriers to programmatic synergy can have a negative impact on the poor.

Cross-cutting strategies can assist decisionmakers in their efforts to pull various programmatic flows and funding streams together for a particular group. Policy planning from the vantage point of the executive office is an appropriate methodology for designing and implementing cross-cutting initiatives. A good example of what cross-cutting initiatives can achieve may be found in the field of children's services. Here we have several independent streams of funds and programs intended for certain groups of children. However, each stream flows separately, and opportunities for increased power in the various programmatic inputs are limited because they flow independently. Early Periodic Screening Diagnostic and Testing (EPSDT), day care services, dental services, nutritional services, bonding pro- grams, protective services, and child-rearing programs all flow separately. But, the development of a cross-cutting program called "home visitor" pulls these various services together so that they may be concentrated on the target population.[15] This con- centration provides an increase in the power of potentially posi- tive programs.

The central policy planning operation should be designed to provide a focal point where various programs and initiatives may be examined for possible cross-cutting opportunities. Unlike dis- crete departmentally initiated activities, the policy planning apparatus would receive its rewards from streamlining and coor- dinating various programs. A policy planning office located within the office of the chief executive would exist solely on the basis of its ability to develop means and methods for combining various activities across bureaucratic structures; it thus would have motivations different from the departments and agencies.

Good examples of an effective central policy planning opera- tion are the Office of Domestic Policy in the Executive Office of the President and the President's National Security Staff. both of these operations develop initiatives and programs that draw re- sources together across various bureaucratic structures within the domestic and defense portions of the federal bureaucracy. For example, the Office of Domestic Policy has led in the initiation of housing programs designed to draw resources from the departments of Health and Human Services, Housing and Urban Development, Agriculture, and Commerce. The target population in this case was Aid to Families with Dependent Children living in public housing; the services were nutrition, housing, economic development, and social services—all deliverable on the housing site.

As the states gain increasing responsibility and autonomy in the conduct of social and domestic programs, governors will have increasingly greater opportunities to develop cross-cutting initiatives. Indeed, this is one of the major arguments for the block grant strategy. Governors' ability through good analysis and planning to pull various funding streams together for beneficiary groups can increase the effectiveness and efficiency of state government. Governors and legislators need tools and methods for developing such strategies, particularly in times when states are being called upon to do more with less.

As states gain increased responsibility for conceptual design and financing of various social and domestic programs, they will also acquire the responsibility and the potential ability to reconfigure what were formerly categorical programs. Heretofore, child health programs, mental health programs, protective services for children, day care services, correctional services, and head start programs have existed apart from each other. Although these programs were conceived for the purpose of meeting children's needs, they often have proceeded as though there were different beneficiary populations, when in reality they overlap significantly. These specific objectives all tend to relate to the improved welfare of poor children. Rather than continue growth in the number of discrete children's programs, various strategies for folding various of these programs and their funding streams together could produce enhanced benefits for children, decreased administrative complexity, increased effectiveness in meeting program objectives, and more efficient utilization of available human and fiscal resources.

Cross-cutting strategies are fundamental to policy planning. This is particularly true in case of the poor, where we see tremendous overlap between various programs attempting to serve numerous categories of beneficiaries receiving services on a discrete (categorical) rather than a beneficiary-oriented (cross-cutting) basis.

The last topic to be considered relative to various aspects of policy planning and its potential benefits for the poor is evaluation. The ability to determine whether programs and policies are producing a desired result or any results at all is very important to the decisionmaker and manager.

Evaluation

Each time governors, legislators, and departmental executives make decisions regarding a particular policy or program, they must make some subjective or objective evaluation. Questions such as the following are often raised but rarely answered to the satisfaction of most state policymakers and managers: How well is the program meeting the needs of the client population? Have the needs of the target population changed? Are we serving the most needy segment of the population? What differences would a 10 percent increase in funding make? What is the goal of the program?

Questions such as these haunt governors, legislators, and managers every day, yet many states have not yet developed adequately the capacity to address them—particularly across state government. As was noted earlier, planning capability is quite uneven across Massachusetts state government, and there presently exists no executive-level central planning apparatus. However, evaluation performed at the level of the chief executive can help answer many of the questions posed here.

Evaluation can take two forms: summative and formative. *Summative* evaluation of end results shows how effectively programs have produced the results desired at the time of implementation. *Formative* evaluation is designed to inform the policy process prior to the development and implementation of a policy or to aid in find-tuning program design and operations. Formative evaluation often is described as "policy analysis." Two of the most popular approaches found among evaluators today are pre-treatment versus post-treatment and cost-benefit studies.[16]

The benefits to be derived from applying evaluation methods and techniques to various programs are many, if one wishes to develop an effective policy planning process. These benefits can accrue especially to the poor. For example, if a formative evaluation indicates that the benefits derived from a particular programmatic effort are minimal when compared with the costs, decisionmakers may then pursue other policy options that possess greater benefits and that may be had for lower or equal cost. Using formative techniques to analyze the various impacts of disparate programs across government on specific beneficiary groups may also be helpful to the poor, particularly where cross-cutting initiatives including several separate departments are employed. Last, but by no means least, evaluation enhances the capacity of state government to terminate ineffective programs. This ability frees resources for other beneficiary groups possessing greater needs. Depending on the value orientation and policy predilection of the chief executive and the legislators, such methods can increase the overall benefit package for the poor and secondarily for society as a whole.

Specifically related to the role and import of evaluation is the need for a strong connection between the statewide policy planning operation and the various programs and operations throughout the many departments within state government. Each agency head or cabinet officer can benefit greatly from the existence of a planning and evaluation unit within his or her domain. As programs are conceived and implemented, critical information related to the continued effective operation of these programs can be made available to agency decisionmakers and also shared with the central policy planning staff for their consideration.

The relationship between agency planning and evaluation units and the central policy planning operation can be critical to the overall policy planning process. Therefore, questions related to the effectiveness and efficiency of programs within the various agencies are also critical to that relationship. Evaluation can form the adhesive necessary for building a strong bond between agency planning units and the central policy planning staff. The central issue always facing a decisionmaker is how well the program worked, or how well it will work. Without answers to these evaluation-oriented questions, it is virtually impossible to rationally expend public funds for the poor or any other beneficiary group. Clearly, evaluation is one of the important tools to be applied within the framework of the policy planning mechanisms discussed earlier in this chapter.

Having discussed the general benefits that might accrue to the poor from a policy planning apparatus in the state of Massachusetts, it is important to consider a model for policy planning within state government.

A Policy Planning Model

The foregoing sections have addressed in some depth the several elements of policy planning. Now let us consider the elements of a successful policy planning organization for Massachusetts. The need for such a body has been articulated by the Chairman of the

Massachusetts Senate Committee on Ways and Means, Senator Chester Atkins:[17]

> *The state is becoming the center for policy development in antipoverty matters, and one other thing is clear: the state has no rational overall policy for how and where it spends money to best serve those in the commonwealth most in need.*

Development of a policy planning body specifically for anti-poverty matters would be a step in the right direction. There are, however, many potential benefits that could accrue to the poor from programs existing outside the traditional complex of anti-poverty programs. Consider, for example, decisions related to automobile insurance. Insurance rates and requirements for operating an automobile can greatly affect poor people's access to an automobile. Decisions that increase the number of restrictions on automobile ownership tend to deprive the poor of an important employment, health, and recreational mode of transportation. Thus, a unit focusing its attention only on anti-poverty matters as such might overlook certain issues important to the poor.

To insure that the poor consistently receive attention in the policy planning process, the governor could require that each initiative clearly articulate possible benefits and costs to the poor. Such a planning process would be inclusionary, rather than exclusionary. Through such an approach, the poor's interests would be considered in relevant decisions and policies being generated across state government.

Linking Planning and Budgeting

Although Massachusetts has had several offices for planning during the past two decades, none has been structured or empowered to pursue policy planning on a conscious level. Furthermore, even though the planning operations of the past have been located periodically within what is now called the Executive Office of Finance and Administration, budgeting and planning have traditionally proceeded on tracks quite independent of each other. Reportedly during one administration very little attention was paid to the state budget at all.[18] This situation is revealing when one considers that the state was actively engaged in a reorganization effort predicated partially on the development of information systems designed to better inform policymakers and managers.

Key to the development of a viable policy planning apparatus in Massachusetts is the development of a method for linking policy planning and budgeting—a difficult assignment. Most budget officers contend that they already do planning and that there is no need to develop a separate entity for that specific and separate purpose. However, the link should be made. The budget office is already the repository of a great deal of information germane to the policy planning process. Moreover, every agency is deeply concerned about its funding for each fiscal year. As a result, agencies pay close attention to the needs and concerns of the budget office.

There are two basic organizational approaches that Massachusetts could follow in order to link planning and budgeting: (1) locate planning within the Executive Office of Administration and Finance and direct that they be linked for policy planning purposes, or (2) create an Office of Policy Planning within the Office of the Governor and take steps to insure that the Secretary of Administration and Finance and the Director of the Office of Policy Planning link the two activities so that the linkage facilitates a policy planning process.

The second approach affords the governor a greater opportunity to control the process and establish his own agenda. A creative tension between the heads of the Office of Policy Planning and Administration and Finance would place the governor in a mediating role. Through his mediating role he would remain a critical and ongoing part of the process in terms of setting the agenda and signalling his choices regarding the various options the process procedures. The weakness of the first approach is that day-to-day activities may overwhelm the Secretary of Administration and Finance. Furthermore, there is a greater opportunity for budgeting requirements to dominate the policy planning process.

Linking planning and budgeting increases opportunities for including the interest of the poor in a broad array of policy issues. Clearly, as has been described elsewhere in this chapter, fiscal concerns are omnipresent in the policy planning process. But, how better could one enhance fiscal consciousness within the policy planning process than by linking it with the overall budget process?

Strategically, the initial activity for the policy planning process should be to develop an executive poverty budget. The executive Anti-Poverty Budget could be a refined version of the Anti-Poverty Budget developed by the Senate Ways and Means Committee in 1982.[19] This innovative step taken by the legislative branch should become an activity driven by the executive branch. Certainly the legislative branch should be involved and may even wish to develop a counter budget; however, the chief executive's responsibility is to present a budget to the legislative body for its review and disposition.

Through such a process, the strengths, weaknesses, and soft spots in the various poor people's programs can be highlighted. Moreover, it will become apparent how much of the state's resources are being dedicated specifically to meeting the needs of poor people. However, it is important that such an activity take place within an overall policy planning process. It should be highlighted and given as much visibility as the governor and legislature may choose to give it. Policy planning in those areas which fall outside of the Anti-Poverty Budget should, of course, be occurring simultaneously. Certainly, the governor will identify certain issue areas for concentration of his energies and political capital. This approach will determine the major foci of the policy planning operation. Moreover, it will result in the governor and legislature being able to set budget priorities for the state, generally, and for the poor, specifically.

The results of such an approach would be improved ability to target the state's resources on those people in greatest need, to set an agenda for the state and for poor people within various beneficiary categories, to improve service delivery (especially with the improved capacity to develop fairly well-articulated goals and objectives), and to enhance the governor's and his lieutenants' ability to manage state government in Massachusetts. Also, with planning and budgeting closely linked, opportunities for developing meaningful cross-cutting strategies for policy development will be enhanced. Linking health, welfare, education, and economic development, for example, in an effort to improve certain aspects of the lives of the poor may be a reasonable approach. Even better, the development of cross-cutting strategies that pull together services in a manner such that individuals can move out of poverty may be developed not simply by focusing on the welfare budget and its programs but by looking more broadly at the capacity of state government to respond to the poor and other beneficiaries simultaneously and equitably.

By providing increased flexibility in funding and greater discretion in program design, a rational policy plannig process will give decisionmakers at least one additional mechanism for responding to the needs of people and the plethora of beneficiaries and beneficiary categories. Informed decisionmaking is what policy planning is designed to produce; it is not intended as a substitute for political will or social values. The process could, however, provide at least several perspectives on issues and do so from a statewide viewpoint as opposed to a balkanized program-by-program approach.

Conclusions

Policy planning is a means by which decisionmakers can bring a form of rationality to the overall process of governing. It is not a panacea, but it can provide critical information and sometimes solid answers to many questions faced by managers as well as elected officials. Citizens look to governors to propose policies and manage state government; they look to the legislature to pass laws codifying certain policy choices and to raise the necessary revenue to finance them. In these times, where citizens press for greater efficiency and effectiveness in government and greater responsiveness on the part of elected and appointed officials, while simultaneously wishing to reduce the cost of government, it will be necessary for states to become more creative and less irrational in terms of how programs are developed, implemented, and managed. A sound policy planning process and a strong executive planning apparatus can help Massachusetts and other states respond successfully to the needs of all of its beneficiaries, including the poor.

Endnotes

1. See Policy Report #1 of the *Report of the Senate Committee on Ways and Means* (June 1982) for the Commonwealth of Massachusetts, which highlights these weaknesses as they relate specifically to anti-poverty efforts.
2. *Ibid.*
3. See National Industrial Recovery Act of 1933 and the Council of State Governments, *Planning Services for State Government* (Chicago, 1956).
4. Public Law 86–372, *Housing Act of 1959* 73 STAT. 654. In 1954, under Section 701 of the Act, federal funds were first made available to the states in order that they might carry out regional (intra-state) planning efforts.
5. President Ronald Reagan has articulated an interest in the federal government's role becoming that of an internationally oriented bureaucracy which would focus its energies on international issues and transfer the responsibility for the majority of domestic programs to the states.
6. Basil F. Mott, "State Planning" in Samuel H. Beer, *The State and the Poor* (Cambridge, Mass.: Winthrop Publishers, 1970), p. 254.
7. B.F. Mott, *loc. cit.*
8. B.F. Mott, *loc. cit.*

9. Martha Wagner Weinberg, *Managing the State* (Cambridge, Mass.: MIT Press, 1977), p. 26.
10. Diane Doherty, *Interview* (March 1982).
11. Edward Reily, *Interview* (November 1982).
12. These findings are the results of interviews, state documents, and reports provided by state officials, in particular by staff within the Office of Administration and Finance.
13. B.F. Mott, *op. cit.*, p. 264.
14. M.W. Weinberg, *op. cit.*, p. 4.
15. Home visitor was a program designed by the Office of Planning and Evaluation at the U.S. Department of Health and Human Services. It provided the delivery of various children services through visiting nurses. It would have reduced transportation, personnel, and other program costs as well as shaped the delivery and follow-up for beneficiaries.
16. Thomas V. Greer and Joanne G. Greer, "Problems in Evaluating Costs and Benefits of Social Programs," *Public Administration Review*, 42 (March/April 1982), p. 151.
7. Kirk Scharfenberg, "State Lacks Policy on Poverty Funds," *The Boston Globe* (May 15, 1982), p. 11.
8. M.W. Weinberg, *op. cit.*, p. 38.
19. See *Report of the Senate Committee on Ways and Means*, Commonwealth of Massachusetts (June, 1982).

Chapter 11

GOVERNANCE

by Manuel Carballo

As long as poverty is limited to a small portion of the population, it is evident that the poor will never be a dominant concern of the state or the nation for an extended time. One lesson of the past two decades is clear: Although concerned leaders such as Presidents Kennedy and Johnson may place poverty high on the national agenda, over time other issues such as war, the environment, and energy will overshadow it. During the 1980s, unless current economic policies once again give us a nation that is one-third ill-housed, ill-fed, and ill-clothed, there is every reason to believe that poverty will be in the background. Given that the concerns of the majority should prevail in a democracy and given our good fortune in having a non-poor majority, this is in part as it should be.

But only in part. The price of poverty in a democracy is high. More than any other form of governance, democracy turns on a sense of community—a sense which led the founders of Massachusetts to label it a "commonwealth." That the sense of shared interests cannot be measured or clearly defined has led us often to ignore it. We do so at our peril and expense. When a significant portion of a society begins to feel excluded from some control over its own destiny, it withdraws from the larger society. The more it withdraws, the more "different" it becomes. The more "different" it becomes, the less the larger community feels obliged to deal with it, to compromise and adjust. It was just such a pattern that led mainly poor Catholic immigrants in Massachusetts out of "Protestant"-controlled public schools to their own parochial ones. This withdrawal served as proof of the "Romish" minority plot to subvert the majority community. In turn, it contributed to the sweep of state executive and legislative offices by the bigoted and nativist "Order of the Star Spangled Banner" (Know-Nothings). Massachusetts took time to recover. It paid the price of excluding a minority from having a sense of a fair and responsible political process.

What we see today in the Massachusetts communities of Charlestown, Roxbury, and Hyde Park is only partly a racial tragedy. It is also a loss of faith in recourse to government for a remedy by both poor blacks *and* poor whites. There is a sense of injustice and impotence at the root of the malaise. Some of it comes from the limited weight of the poor in the political process. Some of it comes from abdication by the political process to the courts on tough issues, making the limited weight of the poor in the process even less relevant. Some of it may come from the astute perception that the political dialogue has once again muted the language of commonwealth and justice and made the sole end of government not to govern well but to govern least.

These undercurrents run much deeper than the problem of poverty. Most Americans speak of "the government" as if it were something other than us. This attitude is reflected in generally low voter participation, but it is acute among the poor. Those concerned about poverty must ask two questions: How can poverty be made part of the public agenda, and how can the poor join in shaping that agenda? But first one must answer the question of whose agenda: federal, state, or local?

Ex Pluribus Unum—or Why the State?

Perhaps the two most dramatic changes in the past two decades have been the national government's shift from initiator to decimator of public anti-poverty programs, and the state's takeover of municipal relief obligations in 1967. While the attitude of Massachusetts at the initiation of the anti-poverty programs of the 1960s was generally receptive, the initiative came from Washington. The opposite may be true today. Despite the liberal conventional wisdom, this is not an unusual situation for many states, especially Massachusetts. "Mother's aid," the precurser to AFDC, was established in 1913, and statewide old-age assistance in 1930. Indeed, the laws of the Bay Colony since 1639 commanded, "Every town shall relieve and support all poor and indigent persons...," until 1967, when the state directly assumed the full cost and administration of the charge.[1]

The depression changed all that by showing that there were limits to what a state and its municipal agents could do alone— even though willing. We are led for the first time to a serious question of federalism: Who should tend to the poor?

Much can be learned from the decision of Massachusetts to take over local welfare, best chronicled by Martha Derthick's *The Influence of Federal Grants* (1970).[2] The arguments for state action are not too different from the arguments for federal action. In summary, there are four principal arguments:

1. Municipal relief led to inequities in how the poor were treated between one municipality and another. People with equal needs were treated unequally. The same concern appears in state to state differences in benefits.

2. Some municipalities were less able than others to carry the fiscal burdens that resulted from the historical accidents of an imbalance in the distribution of the poor relative to the local tax base. Indeed, municipalities that were "open" to the poor arguably reduced their tax base by thereby reducing the "quality of life" in their community relative to others who zoned out the poor. Similarly the distribution of the poor among the states bears no relation to the strength of state tax bases.

3. Some savings in administration could result from "economies of scale" in state administration, and less energy would be wasted on "settlement" questions, such as finding out which municipality would bear the costs of benefits). Unfortunately, the comparison of administrative costs for SSI, which "nationalized" previously state-administered programs for the elderly and disabled, is not conclusive, but similar arguments could be made for AFDC.

4. Greater professionalism was sought at the state level. Local determinations of benefits were seen as insufficiently objective and subject to the whims of local cronyism, patronage, or animosities. Whether more is gained by a further shift to the national level is an open question, but what is lost by "objectivity" at either the state or federal level is precisely the flexibility of local knowledge of local circumstances. Just as political wardheelers have lately been partially rehabilitated by recent scholarly literature, there is something to be said for limiting the rigidity of machine bureaucracies in human judgements. States may provide a reasonable middle ground between national homogeniety and municipal subjectivity.

These arguments—fairly traditional "good government" points—can be complemented by a larger framework from political economy.

Putting aside for the moment the question of political will, what are the strengths and weaknesses of state government in addressing poverty? Among the limits on state action are, first, the fact that the national government determines, through its macroeconomic policies, the economic environment in which the state operates. These policies have both direct and indirect effects on state budgets and operations. On the one hand, state revenue sources can be affected (for example, sales and income taxes), as can the costs of state operations be increased by inflation or the costs of borrowing. On the expenditure side, the portion of poverty in Massachusetts attributable to unemployment and national tariff and industrial policy is largely beyond the state's control. This is not to gainsay the influence of the Massachusetts congressional delegation—especially given the national prominence of some of its members—but it will always be one of 50 delegations.

Second, national revenue and expenditure patterns will shape, if not determine, many local decisions. Massachusetts unemployment insurance is still grounded on a federal tax. Most significantly for poverty, the level of federal social security payments and Medicare are major determinants of how much Massachusetts needs to do about poverty through supplementing SSI, Medicaid, or general relief.

Third, ultimately federal policies may be less significant than the structure of the federal union itself. Massachusetts is in the world's first common market. Every state is an "open economy," competing with other states for people and jobs. While this competitive effect has been greatly overstated (neither people nor capital move for purely "economic" reasons), it is there. More importantly, people believe it is there. States and cities may choose to compete on low taxes or high services, but in either case there is an implicit limit on local action. Beyond some point of low services or high taxes, some people will move out, taking their revenues with them. At some point of high services and low taxes people will move in, overloading the system and reducing quality or raising costs. Where that "tipping point" is can be much debated, but the belief that there is one limits local actions.

Finally, there is the historical accident of national pre-emption of income-based taxes. Generally these have been more responsive to economic growth and revenue gains have been possible without the political cost of tax increases. State and local taxes have tended to require more local political valor, calling for legislative or executive action more often. Moreover, a more progressive national tax structure provides a fairer base for helping the poor and is less easily escaped than local efforts at progressivity.

Most of these factors favor a national fiscal base for income transfers to the poor, but there are actions states can take that are their strengths. They are, in effect, the limits on federal action. First, to the degree poverty results from social (non-economic) factors, it is the states that hold formal constitutional authority. It is only the states that can shape a true family policy and indeed which make and dissolve marriages, succor abused children, and decide whether adult children shall support elderly parents. It is the municipal agents of states that police crime. It is state-delegated decisions on zoning and housing policy that allow or may require the poor to be concentrated in numbers beyond the capacity of one municipal tax base to absorb. It is the states that shape, or allow school districts to shape, the education that is intended to prepare children for an adult life of work, family, and community responsibilities. National programs influence these choices, but generally at the margin.

Second, it is also the state that has the primary (although not exclusive) role in defining institutions, jurisdictions, and authority within its boundaries. States set the rules of the political game. The access the poor have to the electoral system turns on districting, registration requirements, and information which come from the state. Their access to a jurisdiction which can provide an adequate level of municipal services may depend on the tax bases the state allows. Local income taxes, annexation, and regionalization are all possibilities states can and have used to expand the reach and adequacy of the local tax base.

Third, even in the economic domain the state can be a significant, albeit secondary, actor. State licensing and regulation can be barriers to employment of the poor. Regulation of utilities, banking, and insurance can have a major impact on the budgets of the poor—as, for example, in the case of auto insurance rates.

While this list is not exhaustive, it does broadly suggest which items should be on whose agenda, with one major conclusion: If the income poverty aspect of a program is the major or sole component of a costly program, the primary program cost should be born nationally. How the program is administered is another question, to which we shall come.

There remains a more fundamental question: Whichever the correct level of government, how can the poor gain access to it?

There are essentially two ways for a minority to prevail: by
alliances leading to a majority or by the willingness of the majority to help (or at least not oppose) the minority. What are the
chances of the former?

Vote Early and Often

The central means available to the poor and others for shaping
the state agenda is the electoral process. How many votes do the
poor have? Unfortunately we do not know. The issue is of course
complicated by the fact that the poor are not a block of votes in
any case; they are the elderly, the unemployed, welfare mothers,
and many other groups. Those whose votes will be driven by a
candidate's position on social security are more likely to vote as
the elderly than as the poor, despite the fact that it is social
security that lifts the majority of the poor elderly out of poverty.

Using the OMB definition of poverty, there were in 1979
345,000 poor persons in Massachusetts over 18 years old. Put
another way, 202,000 (37 percent) of the poor are children and
thus unable to vote. They are thus about 9.4 percent of all Massachusetts eligible voters—slightly less than their share of the population, but not significantly. To set the number in context it may
be noted that veterans constitute about 17 percent of the adult
population, while the elderly (over 65) constitute about 13 percent of the total.

These numbers both overstate and understate the political
potential of the poor. They overstate it because of the enormous
difference between eligibility to vote and voting. Voter participation is notoriously lower among lower-income groups. Conversely, because voter participation is generally low, a few votes
can make a major difference. The Boston mayoralty has been
won by 13 percent of eligible voters, and state legislative districts
(many of which have unopposed candidates) have been won
by less.

On balance, though, the numbers overstate significantly the
potential of the poor at the state level. This is because the poor are
primarily younger, are blacks and Hispanics, and do not see
themselves as a block of votes. The poor are very divided by age,
race, and sex.

These divisions are exacerbated by the federal system, which
ironically serves to fragment the political interests of the poor.
For the elderly poor it is the federal government that is of vital
interest—through social security, SSI, and Medicare. The states

are merely a drain on limited resources, relying as they do on consumption and property taxes, and so are local governments and especially local schools. Only Medicaid long-term care remains a major state electoral interest for the elderly as state voters which may make them identify with the non-elderly poor on the state level. The same is true of poor veterans. Both political realities are reflected by the emphasis placed by both veterans and the elderly in separate departments of veterans' and elder affairs at state and national levels.

Similarly, Massachusetts blacks and Hispanics must look to the national government, although for different reasons. Hispanics, for instance, are such a small percentage of the Massachusetts population that they can expect little here, whereas their numbers in the Southwest can give them influence in Congress (although to conceive of Hispanics as a voting block is about as useful as using the term "British" in describing the voting behavior of the Irish, Scots, Welsh, and English). Blacks, in turn, have an especial historical relationship with the national government going back to the Civil War, which has fitfully served as the primary engine of civil rights. Consequently, a political coalition of the poor, which is difficult enough to build, is made more difficult by the roles played by different political fora in federalism.

When to these difficulties is added the role of campaign finance in shaping the issues and the candidates, there is little cause for optimism. By definition, the poor are not the best source of campaign contributions. Even as campaign workers they can be limited in effectiveness to their own ethnic group. It has not been below the "dirty tricks" department of some campaigns to use organized crime innuendo against Italians or to send black campaign workers into hostile white neighborhods "on behalf" of the opposition. More importantly, however, the rise of political action committees (PAC's) as a principal source of campaign and lobbying funds has compounded the disadvantage of the poor. While the PAC's may not "buy" election success, in under-financed state and local campaigns they can be quite important.

Despite these difficulties increased participation by the poor is desirable both as an end in itself and as a means of improving the responsiveness of the state to the poor. Possible measures include:

- •Efforts to increase voter registration generally, but especially among the poor. Door-to-door canvassing in poor neighborhoods is probably both effective and least liable to abuse. It can be left to the parties to "pull" votes once they are registered.

•Greater use of bilingual election information (93,000 Massachusetts adults told the Census they did not speak English at
   all or "not well.")
•Simplify registration and re-registration on change of residence within the state.
•Take the poverty into account as a factor in redistricting.

None of these measures will work wonders, but they move in the
right direction, especially where the poor are more concentrated
in local and legislative district elections.

The Morality of Poverty

Since electoral politics offer only limited hope, one may well ask,
"How have the poor survived?" Part of the answer lies in the fact
that people do not vote their narrow self-interest exclusively, and
neither do elected leaders. They frequently act with generosity
and compassion. While altruism is easier when times are flush,
even in hard times it requires very mean spirits to totally abandon
a "safety net."

The moral obligation that people feel to help the poor is therefore an important political force. To the degree political leaders
feel such an obligation, they influence public opinion in that
direction. To the degree public opinion reflects that moral obligation, it will influence leaders accordingly. The problem is that
underlying moral values are generally complex, sometimes contradictory, and often unarticulated premises. They are not often
the grist of journalism, campaigns, or even scholarly articles. Yet
laws and social institutions tend to reflect these values, so one
may boldly draw some inferences from them. They tell us a great
deal about ourselves and our willingness to help the poor.

Behind many of our laws and institutions lurks the Aquinan
concept of free will, imported to the state in its later Calvinist
guise and its attendant concept, guilt. One must work for both
sustenance and salvation. It is joined, however, by the Judeo-
Christian-Muslim *caritas*, especially for the aged, children, and
the infirm. The result is a public policy that has two common
themes.

•Those unable to work through no choice of their own (children, the aged, the ill, and the disabled) did not *choose* their
   condition and should be supported. At the turn of the century,
   widows were also seen in this light, a perception resulting in
   "widow's aid."

•Those able to work but unemployed due to economic forces (the modern *deus ex machina*) should be supported, but only temporarily, lest they dally. If one must *choose* to move to find work, so be it. Also, those able to work but who must care for those who cannot work (mainly mothers with children) may also be supported while there are children. Until recently, of course, one was presumed not to *choose* to have children. They just happened.

In short, those who can work, should, and those that cannot work by reason of forces beyond their control should be helped.

This approach raises two problems, one "technical" in nature, the other more overtly moral. The technical problem is how to calibrate eligibility and levels of support so as to provide "adequate" support without creating a deterrent to work where choice may be exercised. At two extremes of this question are two strategies. One is to make payments less than adequate so as to drive people to meet their needs—that is, to make the "choice" of dependence uncomfortable. The other is to encourage work by reducing benefits at a ratio of less than 1:1 up to some ceiling amounts. Both strategies obviously temper, or reject, the notion of inability to work. They imply that some choice is possible. The technical issue is described elsewhere in this book, but two political/moral issues should be discussed here.

First, the notion of "adequate" support is based on a standard of need. The dilemma of incentives to work is that since they build on that standard they necessarily create inequities with those whose income is determined not by need but by economic circumstance. Thus, a person's minimum wage is not adjusted for number of children (as is AFDC) or whether she has a spouse (as under the "extra" payment to the over 62 for the non-working spouse of the retired wage-earner). There are two ways to deal with this problem: cut back on the standard of need or provide benefits to the "needy" but not poor. Costs are obviously a factor. Whatever the solution, the issue of horizontal equity must be addressed.

Second, the issue of welfare mothers highlights the price of values in conflict. Perhaps this is made clearer by stating some implicit reasoning behind this conflict, which may be inferred from our "poor laws" and programs.

•The only reason we help able-bodied women is because they have children. Their benefits are really ancillary to the children. On balance we think it is best for the children (and certainly cheaper) to be kept in the family.

- •On the other hand, mothers can work, although they may need supports like day care. Taking care of home and child is not "work" in this line of reasoning.
- •Especially nettlesome is the fact that in this age of family planning and contraception, illegitimate births abound. Is this a "choice" not to work, adding the sin of sloth to that of lust? (AFDC was unavailable to "unfit" mothers until 1937.) In any event, what to do with the child, who is innocent of this "choice."
- •Finally, public policy may now accept divorce, but if the marriage was a mistake—if someone chose the wrong spouse—why should the public pay for it?

It is this conflict of values that results in AFDC grants well below those of SSI recipients—and "unworthy" poor. We are sure about helping the elderly and disabled but uncertain about able-bodied mothers. When this uncertainty is added to perceptions of fraud and mismanagement, it is easy to see why AFDC *is* the "welfare problem," despite declining caseloads and costs in real dollars.

Public policy generally reflects values rather than leads them. In the face of conflicting values it is therefore not surprising to see confused policy. Still, there are short-run steps that can be taken to minimize the political friction created by those factors.

- •Family planning programs should be aggressively pursued, especially to prevent teenage pregnancies.
- •Custody arrangements after divorce should not be predicated on the presumption of maternal custody.
- •Child support payments should be aggressively pursued.
- •A careful review should be made of unemployment insurance, AFDC, the minimum wage, and fringe benefits to low-income wage earners to determine what parity is warranted.
- •Work requirements for AFDC mothers should be assessed in a broader review of family policy. The issue is not solely one of economic incentives to work but of social and personal judgement as to whether child-rearing is not only "work" but more important than work in the marketplace.

In the long run, while it is easy to get lost in the vagueness and vagaries of the benefits and values that shape majority attitudes toward the poor, it is important not to lose sight of them. Poll after poll reflects a willingness to help the needy and antipathy to "welfare." As long as that generous sentiment is there (and distinguished from flawed *means* of helping the needy such as AFDC), the poor as a minority can count on majority support.

That support must be nurtured by public leaders. It is the foundation upon which specific budgets, laws, and regulations rest.

The Rules of the Game

The politics of poverty are played out in many different arenas, and generally the state establishes the rules of the game. How it does so helps to determine what allies the poor can muster in their political sorties. It can create an "enlightened self-interest" in the non-poor to join with the poor. On occasion, the national government provides or is an ally. The coalitions that result are episodic, unstable, and very much turn on the issue at hand. In this regard, it is important to distinguish three types of programs or policies affecting the poor:

1. Cash transfers exclusively to the poor (for example, AFDC).
2. Policies or services primarily but not exclusively for the poor (for example, Medicaid or day care) and provided by the non-poor.
3. Policies or services essential to the poor but of general public interest (for example, public health, schools, consumer protection).

The dynamics of each are different.

There are few allies for direct cash transfers. The benefits to the non-poor are diffuse. Food stamps briefly had some national support as a way of diminishing farm surplus, but that passed. In fact, as pointed out earlier, the "nationalization" of aid to the elderly and disabled poor, by creating SSI, served to further limit the size of the state-level coalition around cash transfers to those who worry about AFDC. For instance, while AFDC is the state's second largest children's program (after education), it remains a bit of a stepchild for the "children's lobby."

Services to the poor, rather than cash transfers, are another story. With the decline of the community action agencies—with some exceptions—into simply alternative service bureaucracies, increasingly it has been the non-poor who provide goods or services for the poor and become indirect allies of the poor. The best example of a program securing politically powerful (if not numerically large) allies is Medicaid. Enlisting as it does physicians, hospitals, and nursing home operators, it perceptibly changes the dynamics of funding or cutting Medicaid as opposed to, say, AFDC.

The political gain comes with a cost as well. There is, first, the essential loss of control to the third-party provider. Potentially more significant today is the fact that in times of limited resources this type of ally may extract a high price literally and figuratively. At one level, the added clout of the third-party provider may distort priorities in terms of the needs of the poor. It is doubtful, for instance, whether the poor in Massachusetts would elect to have about $2 of health care costs for every $1 of AFDC and SSI state supplement.

Which suggests the other price—reflected in an 11 percent increase in the price of health. There is no intention to pick on health care. Salaries of other third-party providers both public and private *may* grow at a faster rate than the quality and quantity of services delivered to the poor. When this occurs, costs tallied as benefiting the poor are actually benefiting the non-poor. In this respect the poor are no different than taxpayers and consumers in general, except that the impact on the poor may be proportionately heavier. Nonetheless, the political value of such allies may increase the net benefits to the poor overall.

Public services essential to the poor but not primarily for them are the third category. As other parts of this book make clear, the poor are also beneficiaries of general public services from schools to transit. Indeed, some of these services rival "targeted" programs in cost ($3000/child in the Boston school system), number of poor served (most poor school-age children are in public schools), and in potential for reducing poverty (which bears an inverse relation to school years completed). Unfortunately we often do not know how many of the poor are benefited by general purpose programs or how many, for example, by flouridation of the water supply (the poor typically underutilize dentists). If we did, we might be able to identify some general purpose programs that can be more cost-effective in serving the poor. In such programs, however, the political weight of the concerns of the poor tends to be submerged in larger issues. The potential for the broadest alliances exists here, though, difficult as they may be to forge.

The different political dynamics of these different policies and programs make it very difficult to establish some helpful rules of the game. Narrowly targeted programs and policies, while more "cost-effective," tend to isolate further an already politically isolated group. Purchase of service programs build a broader political base but cost more and may distort priorities. Programs potentially available to all—like universal day care or two years of kindergarten—become very expensive and tied to a totally different array of policy questions than simply serving the poor.

Consequently, the best strategy may be a mixed one which simply seeks to give the poor something with which to bargain— something they can bring to the table. Herein resides the importance, in cities in which the poor are concentrated in certain residential areas, of selecting city councilors on a ward rather than at-large basis. It may favor proportional representation (although Cambridge's combination of PR with the city manager form would seem to limit the value of PR). In both cases, legislative deliberations—that seamless web of explicit and implicit exchanges—could have a vote and a voice to shape the outcome to favor the poor.

What should have been learned in the past two decades, however, is that federally sponsored altenative structures intended to serve *in lieu* of state and local government will eventually be captured by them or atrophy. (Head Start is a notable exception.) Model Cities and Community Action Agencies can, and did, serve as catalysts to change local policies by developing a generation of new political leaders, putting the interests of the poor on the political agenda, and sometimes "leveraging" local expenditures with their own limited funds. Similar catalysts may be useful in the future.

In the end, however, the long-haul war against poverty is fought in the school, welfare, employment, and health bureaucracies of general purpose state and local governments. State employment services, for instance, are notorious for their unwillingness to work hard at placing welfare recipients in jobs. In fact, they are not totally to blame, since federal policies measure success by the number of job placements, not the difficulty of the placement. Unless the state legislature or top management creates incentives against "creaming" and offers rewards for doing the tough job, the outcome is predictable.

What is equally apparent is that, at least for the first half of the 1980s if not longer, the elaborate alternative structures built to serve the poor with federal funds will atrophy substantially. This will put pressure on traditional state and local finance systems to serve the poor better. The task that the "War on Poverty" avoided—reforming existing sevices—by its "blitzkreig" creation of non-profit directly funded federal alternatives must now be undertaken by the state and its municipalities. Given such tax-limiting measures as Proposition 2½ in Massachusetts, at least the financial, if not the administrative, burden will fall on the state.

A short list is illustrative of the questions ahead for state managers and policymakers.

- •Head Start and Title I seemed to work. How can their concepts be "fit" into the regular public schools curriculum?
- •Community Health and Mental Health Clinics seemed to work. How can they best mesh with state and municipal hospitals and public and mental health departments?
- •Parts of CETA seemed to work. How do they fit into vocational education?
- •Section 8 leased public housing held promise. Should a state housing authority like MHFA administer it statewide rather than municipal authorities?
- •Home care for the elderly seems to work. Will it receive continued support?

By no means should the state simply absorb federal programs or solutions; it could not afford to in any case. The question is one of picking and choosing and then mustering the political allies to give the poor a fair share. It is not apparent that this can be done without the inducement of federal funds. It was those funds that created an "un-holy" alliance of the poor and those that would "maximize federal return of our tax dollars." The result may be that the fortunes of the poor within these programs will turn on accidents of local influence or variations of the "trickle-down" theory.

See You in Court

Some services, however, are the poor's as a matter of legal right, independent of political alliances. The traditional recourse of minorities in America has been to the courts. The poor are only catching up. Two questions of governance arise, however. The first is that diminished funding of the financed Legal Services Corporation and other advocacy programs will have two undesireable effects. Private litigation is a means of enforcing public policy—for example, on building code compliance. Policies that may help the poor can be undercut by poor enforcement. Also, as often as not, the state will share the plaintiffs' interest when the federal government is a defendant, as in food stamp eligibility. On both counts there is a state interest in supporting legal and advocacy services. This interest was recently demonstrated by state funding of appeals for denial of federal disability benefits. It is surely more generic.

Second, and even more direct, is the state interest in providing an alternative to judicial administration of public programs through receiverships or court-appointed masters. While no ready altenative exists for state agencies, the state can serve as receiver for local government. Certainly in those cases in which a responsibility is vested with the state but delegated to local execution (as in education) a more direct state role is appropriate. Not only is it more responsive to an electorate, albeit a statewide rather than local one, but it puts local administration into the hands of the executive branch rather than the judicial one. The former is presumed to know how to run things better. Use of state receivership has apparently been tried with some success in the housing area by the state, and should it be tried in other areas.

Getting There

Even if the policy were to decide to deal with poverty, it would still have to manage well to do it. Unfortunately, the track record of anti-poverty efforts has not been inspiring.

IDEA

The first necessary ingredient and manifestation of good management is a state strategy for dealing with poverty. By a "strategy" I most decidedly do not mean a master plan in five volumes but a set of concerted actions over a period of two to three years. The FY 1983 Massachusetts Senate Ways and Means Poverty Budget serves as an initial inventory of resources and problems. Of necessity it is limited to budgetary concerns, and a parallel list of statutory and regulatory issues is needed. A survey of municipal concerns would help.

GET THIS.

Based on this inventory some priorities for state agencies could be established. Each department and secretariat could be responsible for implementation and developing the means to accomplish a given objective. For example, to reduce the rate of teen-age pregnancies by 15 percent by 1985, possible action by the Departments of Public Health, Education, Social Services might be proposed and monitored by a sub-cabinet committee or taskforce. Such a strategy could be developed in a number of ways. What is essential is that it be limited to perhaps a half-dozen major initiatives and that it not be another cumbersome or complex overlay on the budget or other processes.

MGMT

Deciding what to do and doing it, however, are two different things. The first question is the efficiency and effectiveness of state agencies. One can assume that state agencies dealing with the poor share many of the strengths and weaknesses of other state agencies. There are some special problems, however, especially with agencies that deal with personal services such as health, education, or social work. Such agencies deal in inherently hard to measure and judgmental areas. They frequently are dominated by professionals both inside and outside the agencies, whether a professional formally runs the organization or not.

Such organizations tend to suspect that good management and good professional care are mutually exclusive. It is therefore important not only that management be part of the agenda but that a governor and legislature stress a course of "compassionate efficiency." Within that context a number of areas need to be reviewed:

- The adequacy of management training supervisors, especially professionals up from "clinical" work.
- The use of management accounting concepts such as cost accounting and responsibility centers.
- The development of improved work methods, standards, and productivity goals.
- With civil service and union participation, improved job design and compensation schedules.
- Management information systems and data processing.

While organizational structure is secondary, accountability is not, and the final establishment of the secretariats as line supervisors of the various departments should be brought to fruition.

A second area of concern is the entire purchase-of-service system. As a first step, a fair procedure for state "make-or-buy" decisions should be developed. There should be no presumption that either public or private provision of services is inherently better. Once the decision to "buy" is reached, several procurement questions need to be raised and resolved.

- Is the contract management function adequately staffed and organized?
- Does an independent rate-setting commission weaken contract administration more than it controls costs?
- Where should vouchers be substituted for contracts?
- Should uniform accounting procedures be required?

Reliance on the non-profit corporate form for many state contracts is probably desirable; however, they share many of the managerial weaknesses of the agencies they serve. In those cases in which state contractors do not also do a substantial portion of non-public work (where the state is a "monopsonist"), the state should consider extending its management improvement efforts to its contractors.

Governance without good management is an illusion the poor cannot afford.

Conclusion

A chapter ranging from federalism to contract terms can only be suggestive. It is intended to more than suggest that in thinking about poverty we are thinking about how decisions are made and implemented in Massachusetts—about governance. A major flaw in past skirmishes with poverty has been the failure to think through the weight and power of constitutional and political traditions, the underlying role of values in the policy, and the need to manage it all with a sense of strategy and detail. It may be too ambitious an agenda, but it is a necessary one.

Endnotes

1. Derthick, Martha, *The Influence of Federal Grants; Public Assistance in Massachusetts* (Cambridge, Massachusetts: Harvard University Press, 1970).
2. *Ibid.*

INDEX

child support payments and, 139–140

elderly and disabled in, 125–126

male-headed households and, 127

policy questions in, 137–140

poverty rates in, 123, 124

spending on, 120–123

work requirements and benefits in, 138–139

Massachusetts policy planning, 284–287

age composition and, 17

agenda-setting in, 288–289

benefits of, 287–296

cross-cutting strategies and poverty and, 292–295

distinctive demographic features of, 17–18

evaluation in, 295–296

geographical distribution and, 18

linking planning and budgeting in, 297–300

manageability in, 291–292

racial composition and, 17–18

service delivery in, 290–291

targeting in, 289–290

Massachusetts poor, 1–12

age of, 2

changes over time for, 5–9

duration of poverty spell in, 9

dynamics of poverty in, 9–11

family status of, 2

groups included in, 1–4

income sources and work data on, 9–10

race and, 2–4

underclass status for, 11–12

U.S. data comparisons with, 4–5, 6, 10

Massachusetts Rehabilitation Commission, 158, 160, 162

Massachusetts taxation, 235–276

in comparison with other states, 236–237

discretionary property abatements from local jurisdictions in, 255

fiscal reform in, 274–276

income tax expenditures in, 248–251

income tax incidence in, 238–239

long-term outlook and policy options in, 271–274

property tax incidence in, 242–243

Proposition 2½ and (*see* Proposition 2½)

public services reduction and, 265–269

rental deduction in, 248, 249–251

revenue sharing programs and, 272–273

sales tax expenditures in, 251–256

sales tax incidence in, 239–242

state aid programs and, 269–270

structure of, 236–257

tax-exempt institutions in, 254

tax expenditures in, 246–256

tax incidence in, 237–242

trends in, 243–246

Massachusetts transportation programs, 143

current programs in, 153–160

mass transit programs in, 153–157

special elderly and handicapped programs, 157–160

subsidies in, 153–156

travel patterns of poor and, 145–147

van services in, 159–160

Mass transit programs

current programs, 153–157

handicapped and elderly in, 147–150, 157–160

lifts for handicapped in, 159

riding patterns in, 156

subsidies in, 153–156, 162–164

travel patterns of poor and, 144, 146

van services in, 158, 159–160

Maternal and Child Health Program, 67–68

Medicaid, 49, 55–63

characteristics of, 55–56

community health centers (CHCs) and, 63, 65–66

cost containment programs in, 59–60, 61–62

costs of, 56–57, 137

electoral process and, 308, 309

eligibility policy in, 55

health status and, 58

hospital utilization in, 56–57

impact of, 57–58

long-term care and, 62–63

physician reimbursement under, 56, 61